D1601550

Basque Violence Metaphor and Sacrament

BOOKS IN THE BASQUE SERIES

A Book of the Basques
by Rodney Gallop

In A Hundred Graves: A Basque Portrait
by Robert Laxalt

Basque Nationalism
by Stanley G. Payne

Amerikanuak: Basques in the New World
by William A. Douglass and Jon Bilbao

Beltran: Basque Sheepman of the American West
by Beltran Paris, as told to William A. Douglass

The Basques: The Franco Years and Beyond
by Robert P. Clark

The Witches' Advocate: Basque Witchcraft and the Spanish Inquisition (1609–1614)
by Gustav Henningsen

Navarra: The Durable Kingdom
by Rachel Bard

The Guernica Generation: Basque Refugee Children of the Spanish Civil War
by Dorothy Legarreta

Basque Sheepherders of the American West
Photographs by Richard H. Lane
Text by William A. Douglass

A Cup of Tea in Pamplona
by Robert Laxalt

Sweet Promised Land
by Robert Laxalt

Traditional Basque Cooking: History and Preparation
by José María Busca Isusi

Basque Violence: Metaphor and Sacrament
by Joseba Zulaika

The Basque Series

Joseba Zulaika

University of Nevada Press

Reno & Las Vegas

Basque Violence

Metaphor and Sacrament

Basque Series Editor: William A. Douglass

The paper used in this book meets the requirements of American National Standard for Information Sciences—Permanence of Paper for Printed Library Materials. ANSI Z39.48-1984. Binding materials were chosen for strength and durability. ∞

Library of Congress Cataloging-in-Publication Data
Zulaika, Joseba.
Basque violence : metaphor and sacrament / Joseba Zulaika.
p. cm.—(Basque series)
Based on the author's thesis (Ph. D.)—Princeton University, 1982.
Bibliography: p.
Includes index.
ISBN 0-87417-132-6 (alk. Paper)
1. Violence—Spain. 2. Basques—Social conditions. I. Title.
II. Series.
HN590.Z9V59 1988
303.6′2′0946—dc 19 87-35432
CIP

University of Nevada Press
Reno, Nevada 89557 USA

Printed in the United States of America
Designed by Richard Hendel

Contents

Acknowledgments

The people presently living in Itziar are my *argumenti personae*. With their consent I have not tried to hide their biographies nor have I changed their proper names. Unless otherwise noted, all conversations quoted in the text took place during my fieldwork (1979–1981) and all translations are my own. At moments I have imagined this ethnography of Itziar as a Homeric tragedy of which I am the narrator but which is acted out in real life by the community of villagers, myself included. In a substantive sense this work is a collective creation by Itziar's villagers, the live protagonists of this book, which is dedicated to them.

During the years I devoted to writing this book I contracted debts with many people. The book is based on a doctoral dissertation submitted in 1982 at Princeton University, where faculty and graduate students of the anthropology department made my years of study most stimulating and enjoyable. Lisa Harrison shared with me the initial stage of the writing. Professors David Crabb, Teófilo Ruiz, Gananath Obeyesekere, and Rena Lederman read the first drafts of some chapters and made important suggestions. The assistance I received at the Basque Studies Program at the University of Nevada, Reno, from anthropologist William Douglass, linguist William Jacobsen, bibliographer Jon Bilbao, and folklorist Sven Liljeblad was invaluable. Professor Hildred Geertz provided a detailed and perceptive commentary on the strengths and weaknesses of my dissertation. I owe the greatest debt to my mentor, Professor James Fernandez, who during my graduate years took attentive intellectual care of my work. They all have my lasting gratitude and affection.

In the final writing I was aided immensely by William Douglass, who extensively edited the whole of the book at various stages and provided substantial suggestions regarding form and content. I am indeed fortunate to have been assisted by someone who combines an in-depth knowledge of Basque society with long-tested editorial skills and who is also a dear friend. He has rewritten entire paragraphs with the same care he would give to a book of his own, and at times I felt he was more faithful than I was to the way Basques experience political violence, even if that meant wrestling with and cutting down passages that had become almost sacred to me. Robert Clark read the completed manuscript and made pertinent observations, which I have incorporated. Critical remarks by Peter Loizos and an anonymous reviewer were helpful. I have also profited from Don Julio Caro Baroja's comments on this work and from comments by my colleagues Jesús Azcona, Teresa del Valle, Joxe Azurmendi, and the students of symbolic anthropology at the Basque University. Koldo Larrañaga, William Christian, Sandra Ott, María Cátedra, Carmelo Urza, Mateo Osa, and Mikel Azurmendi read parts of the manuscript and suggested corrections. I am grateful to them all. None of them shares responsibility for any inadequacy in this book. I owe special thanks to Kate Harrie for her careful editing.

The fieldwork on which this study is based was made possible by the financial support of the Department of Anthropology of Princeton University, a grant from the National Science Foundation, and three summer grants from the Comité Hispano-Americano. A postdoctoral grant from the Basque Studies Program at the University of Nevada, Reno, was decisive in converting the dissertation into a book. The chapter on ritual action is the initial result of a longer project on ritual models of causation underlying Basque violence, which was financed by the H. F. Guggenheim Foundation. I am indebted to them for their generous support.

During my fieldwork I was helped by many people. I am particularly indebted to the families of Menpe and Mantxuene, who housed me for a summer, when I was in the Viscayan town of Mendata. In Itziar not only was I assisted by everyone in one way or another but also frequently confronted in my views and queried as to what should be done to resolve a given problem. I owe much to my own family, who had to put up with my presence and my questions for long periods: my late mother provided much sociological information on the older generations of Lastur and Itziar, and during the writing phase my father wrote me several letters in response to my queries.

Through this work I came to better know and appreciate many of my fellow villagers, who shared with me their friendship and life experiences. The protagonism I have conferred on some people over others reflects only my own subjective selection for the purposes of the plot of the book. The only person who, of necessity, acquires an unduly prominent role is the writer himself. Just as the events narrated here, including heroic action and ritual killing, are constructed collectively by the community of Itziar, so is this book a collective creation aesthetically reflecting the living experience in which all we villagers are participants.

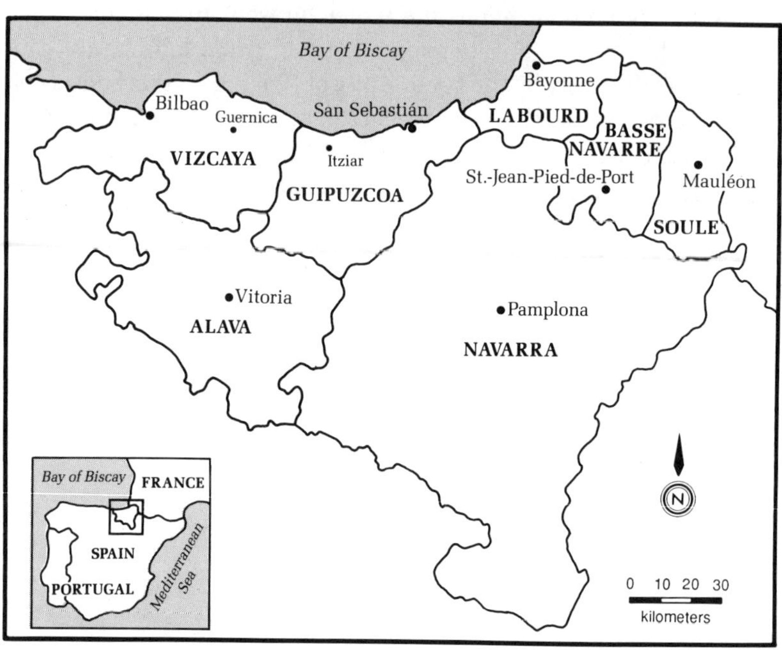

Euzkadi: The seven Basque provinces.

Prologue

Return to Itziar

In the summer of 1979 I returned to Itziar to do fieldwork on Basque political violence. Itziar is a small village of peasants and factory workers on the Cantabrian coast in the province of Guipúzcoa (Spain).[1] I was born in Itziar-Lastur in 1948 and spent my childhood there. Since I was twelve years old I have lived away from the community, attending seminaries and colleges. When I went back in 1979 I was a philosophy licentiate and had studied anthropology for four years at Memorial University (Canada) and Princeton University, where I was a doctoral candidate. Now I was again living in my natal village, where I hoped to immerse myself in local affairs. This was my anthropological jungle; I had returned to Itziar as both native and observer.

Between 1975 and 1980, Itziar, a village of about one thousand people, was shaken by six political murders. The armed group ETA (Euskadi Ta Askatasuna [Euskadi and Freedom]) was responsible for killing two police informers from Itziar and a civil guard married to an Itziar woman and resident in the village. An industrialist kidnapped by four ETA youths from Itziar was murdered in the village after the negotiations for his ransom between ETA and his family failed. A politically uninvolved worker married to a woman from Itziar and popular there, though residing and working in the next village, was killed mistakenly by ETA, which confused him with an alleged police informer. The civil guards killed an ETA operative from Itziar in the nearby town of Orio.

These political murders have been viewed as heinous crimes by outsiders and as revolutionary actions by Basques involved in the radical movement for independence. However, an ethnographer analyzing political violence should seek to recreate the contexts of meaning and acting in which these violent activities are performed and understood by the wider society. The violent events themselves mark only the background against which the ethnographer attempts to reconstruct, as if in a Homeric tragedy, the conditions under which the actors and their audience create each other and ultimately become each other's dilemma.

Violence and Ethnographic Distance

This is not the place for indignation. The purpose of this essay is once more to accept the reality of to-day, which is logical crime, and to examine meticulously the arguments by which it is sustained; it is an attempt to understand the time I live in.
Camus, The Rebel

Given the nature of my study, I owe the reader an explanation of how I chose political violence as my topic of field research, even at the risk of appearing confessional. My mentor, James Fernandez, helped me overcome much personal resistance to studying my native culture and wisely encouraged me to return to my own society. Thus, I was asked to replace "the tale of the fieldworker as lone heroic victim" (R. Rosaldo 1986:93) in some exotic culture with that of the fieldworker returning to his natal village with newly acquired perceptive powers and academic detachment. The events I had witnessed in Itziar had produced such a profound sense of shock and dilemma that I agreed only on condition that I be allowed to study political violence. Several of my friends had become local heroes in their struggle as members of ETA. Some had killed and some had been killed. To the Spanish media they were terrorists. Like Diana's King of the Wood each was at once "a priest and a murderer" (Frazer 1963:1). It was obvious that in the patriotic motivation of these youths, symbolic and self-transcending elements were decisive. The return to Itziar was thus a return to the classic Frazerian question of murder that is also a ritual sacrifice. This was the major collective performance in which we Basques had been involved since the late 1950s. To write about Basque violence seemed to me a difficult test both of myself and of anthropology. For years I had resisted the appeal of the extreme personal surrender of the political activist. In a sense, the topic of study was forced upon me by my own biography and by the events I witnessed in my village. The real challenge for me then and now has been how to react, which in my case is tantamount to how to be able to write meaningfully at all. This work was to be my way of participating in the perplexing violence that is deeply affecting all Basques.

Since anthropology is fundamentally the doing of ethnography in a field situation, my own participation as anthropologist and native has become an essential component of this study. Writing about one's own culture more effectively precludes the anthropologist from imposing on his informants sets of values that are deemed radically incompatible with his own. A comparison with a recent study of a headhunting society illustrates this point well. Headhunting in a Philippine culture and political murder among Basques, despite their widely different ideological justifications and social meanings, are nevertheless comparable in that in both places the killing itself is experienced as a ritual necessity. That is, in both cases killing becomes a ritual of manhood, a recourse to a culturally idealized situation. M. Rosaldo rightly concentrated her study not on headhunting per se but on its relation to a particular social and cultural system. The disturbing fact is, however, that she did actually want to know "why" the Ilongot were killers. After a native's otiose explanation, which remained in her notes as a mockery, she gave up any attempt to understand it:

> We resigned ourselves to the sense in which we never would be able fully to accept or understand a world whose values seemed as arbitrary as they were abhorrent to our own. Tukbaw's "customs" were not ours, nor could we hope to grasp them. I still do not know why Ilongots find deep psychological satisfaction in killing, in slashing victims, and in severing and tossing to the ground a human head. (1980: 137–38)

Some analytical and ethical implications are obvious. The anthropologist writes on how "meaningful" headhunting is to Ilongot notions of self and social life. The crucial irony is that while savagery per se was tolerated by the writer and made the subject of a fascinating study, this tolerance ultimately was permissible because it is the product of a society whose fundamental values were "abhorrent to our own." It is arbitrary barbarism but it is "theirs." The social context and cultural meanings can be grasped and valued by the anthropologist only at the expense of the thing itself being considered incomprehensible and abominable. What made Ilongot killing seem so barbaric was the presence of an anthropologist who claimed a different set of values for her own society. Yet, while she was conducting fieldwork among the headhunters, her country's military was involved in the Vietnam War. How might she have answered had an Ilongot asked "why" her fellow Americans were killing Vietnamese. The imposed dichotomy of values prevents the anthropologist from drawing for his or her own society the lesson learned from such ritualized acts of killing.

In stark and painful contrast, I cannot posit a savagery in my informants against which I can raise the pretense of different values for my society and myself. The political killings of Itziar pertain to me in the profound sense that my village has produced them and that close friends and relatives of mine have directly participated in or supported them. Moreover, as the chapter on the recent history of Itziar makes plain, participation in Basque radical protest became an ideological necessity during the late sixties for the youth, and active membership in ETA was the undisputed model of heroic activity for the political and cultural survival of the country. Like many other adolescents in Itziar and elsewhere, for years I experienced the anxiety provoked by such heroic demands imposed on me by my society and the guilt generated by resisting such cultural appeals. The violence has been, therefore, a fact of daily experience and a value in itself shared by a substantial segment of Basque society and at the same time considered horrible by them. The monstrosity of arbitrary killing shows itself to me not only as an analytical issue but also as the reality of the cultural models and values of my own society.

To look at killing as "their" abhorrent custom (they being savages or military men distanced from oneself) is significantly different from accepting killing as a fact of one's own society for which the writer, too, is responsible. Wittgenstein's critique of Frazer's treatment of magical and religious notions, in which they "appear as *mistakes*," is a good theoretical parallel. Wittgenstein contended that such religious beliefs and practices are not mistakes except when they are set forth as a theory. Truth being only the hypothesis that is found to work best, he pointed out that the "errors" of primitive peoples were "simply hypotheses, justifiable as such at the time when they were propounded" (1967:20). Wittgenstein held that error belongs with opinion and added that "a religious symbol does not rest on any opinion." He noted:

> What makes human sacrifice something deep and sinister anyway? Is it only the suffering of the victim that impresses us in this way? All manner of diseases bring just as much suffering and do *not* make this impression. No, this deep and sinister aspect is not obvious just from learning the history of the external action, but *we* impute it from an experience in ourselves. (Ibid.:40; his emphasis)

Wittgenstein argued that we are impressed with "the *environment* of a way of acting." He raised the question, "When I see someone being killed—is it simply what I see that makes an impression on me or does this come with the hypothesis that someone is being killed here?" (ibid.:41). It is the anthropologist's implicit hypothesis that makes Ilongot headhunting "arbitrary" and "abhorrent." No matter how primitive and crude it seems, I must look at political killing among Basques as embedded in a cultural hypothesis. Durkheim's words are significant here: "At any given moment the moral constitution of society establishes the contingent of voluntary deaths. There is, therefore, for each people a collective force of a definite amount of energy, impelling men to self-destruction" (1951:299). Yet I will not be aiming at a mere representation of the culture of violence, even less will I be doing "salvage ethnography." At times I will be compelled to speak against the culture, challenged by the need to create a new one for my society's sake.

The reader of this ethnography is likely to be searching for the author's position regarding political crime. This is an important question, but all I can reply is that the ethnography has to speak for itself. The ethnographer as author has no objective reality to impose on his informants, co-villagers in my case. If a novelist such as Dostoevsky can discover "the man in man" by letting his fictional heroes be themselves without finalizing them from an external viewpoint (Bakhtin 1984), can the ethnographer aspire to less?

After all, his subjects are actual human beings rather than fictional creations, who in many respects exercise life choices that they themselves are capable of interpreting. As a writer I am basically concerned with the "truth," but it is the truth of the actors' own self-consciousness, much as Dostoevsky was concerned, say, with Raskolnikov in *Crime and Punishment*. This by no means implies that the writer renounces his own consciousness and implicitly agrees with murder committed for personal or political reasons. My analytical position consists in studying the history to discover the genesis of the violence and its cultural patterns and metaphors. My personal position in the village is best reflected in the talk I was asked to give in Itziar, which concludes the Epilogue.

Despite whatever personal disagreement I might have with the ongoing violence, for which I have been accused of ambiguity in the pro-ETA media and of opportunism in Itziar, as author I must portray accurately and respectfully the consciousness of people involved in political killing and their supporters. I am aware, however, that a very different position can be taken regarding the violence of small insurgent groups. That of Peter Loizos is a case in point when he states of the EOKA B men, the Greek Cypriot activists who are in many ways similar to ETA operatives, "Once, they had been a puzzle to me, and as such had forced me into some of my best intellectual work, an attempt to explain how they saw the world, the reasons for their resentments and militancy. But the practical harm they had done us all now extinguished any residue of curiosity, and this meant that as an observer I was rarely capable of the restraint needed to learn anything of value from them" (1981 : 191). I have great respect for Loizos's reaction and had I been in his situation I might have felt similarly. Still, by having grown up in Itziar and by observing my own relationship to the genesis and evolution of Basque violence, my attitude toward ETA and its supporters is bound to be starkly different. As ethnographer I find myself learning the most from such extremes of action.

For most Basques, ETA members have provided the images that embody the central contradictions of their society during the last twenty-five years. The young fighters have operated as markers of what the notions of ideal person, society, and politics should be for Basques by themselves assuming the antithetical properties of such categories. As in former times witches adopted animal images and enacted rituals that apparently were aimed at preserving cultural systems fatally threatened by historical change, in these years it has been the fate of ETA members to live out, as if in a state of possession, the central cultural and political contradictions of Basque society. Thus, I cannot posit one set of values for the culture of the natives and another for my own culture in relation to political murder. As a consequence it is easier to view the Basque case as a microcosm of violent processes that immediately speak to larger contexts of political and military antagonism. Simpler forms of action are revelatory in that they allow for more controlled perception of the basic logic and legitimations of such violent processes.

Development of the Argument

In this ethnography I have isolated five dimensions—historical representations, social institutions and ideology, cultural models, primordial metaphors, and ritual performances—that in the overall organization of the work can be contemplated as reflections or translations of each other at various levels of meaning. Each of the five points of view is an autonomous descriptive frame of understanding as well as an avenue to the other four dimensions. The relevance of major themes—such as polarization, negation, self-transcendence, preverbal experience, condensation of action—emerges from their presence in the various frames. In part 1, dealing with history, the relevant issues concerning political violence are organized as historical representations that concentrate or distort time processes by rendering them mythically nonprogressive, militarily antagonistic, heroically consummate, or tragically deadlocked. Some of these characteristics are translated sociologically into perceptions of communal territory, transcendent motherland, or totalistic institutional traits. Polarization, improvisation, the dissolving of categories between human and beast—features essential to Itziar's history and society—are, on the other hand, some of the basic cultural traits taught by the traditional Basque models of performance, such as games, hunting, and the singing of verses. At the level of imagery, these performances are imbued in the culture with the metaphoric use of the bestiary present in a peasant society and with the religious use of transcendent figures. A major aspect of the overall argument is the decisive role of primordial factors of experience. Finally, all these models and metaphors require acting out in ritualized performances. In accordance with these expository schemata, the understanding of violent behavior implies considering its signification in each of these various dimensions and in its relationship to the overall picture. Itziar serves as the stage upon which the dynamics of the ongoing violence are played out, but it should be obvious that this is not a little community study or the classic ethnography of a Basque village. Nor is this a study of social change in a rural area besieged by industry and modernization, although cultural patterns and ideas provide a main source of information. In short, locale, time, and change are descriptive priorities only to the extent that they provide us with adequate ethnographic frames in which to situate the phenomenon of political violence. Ethnographically "the thing" itself is the pattern of interrelated equivalences.

The Metaphor and the Sacrament

D: Well then, what sort of a relationship?

F: I don't know. A metaphoric relationship?

& & &

F: And then there is that other relationship which is emphatically *not* "sort of." Many men have gone to the stake for the proposition that the bread and wine are *not* "sort of" the body and blood.

D: But is that the same thing? I mean—is the swan ballet a sacrament?

F: Yes—I think so—at least for some people. In Protestant language we might say that the swanlike costume and movements of the dancer are "outward and visible signs of some inward and spiritual grace" of woman. But in Catholic language that would make the ballet into a mere metaphor and not a sacrament.

D: But you said that for some people it is a sacrament. You mean for Protestants?

F: No, no. I mean that if for some people the bread and wine are only a metaphor, while for others—Catholics—the bread and

> wine are a sacrament; then, if there be some for whom the ballet is a metaphor, there may be others for whom it is emphatically more than a metaphor—but rather a sacrament.
>
> D: In the Catholic sense?
>
> F: Yes. (Bateson 1972 : 35–36)

The complex interaction between actors, audience, and the writer himself in the constitution or dissolution of political violence has led me into resorting to explanatory devices such as constructing cultural models of performance (part 3), insisting on ritual kinds of causation (part 5), or distinguishing the subjective experience of sacramental matters from metaphoric "sort of" relationships. The last distinction is reminiscent of religious controversies between Catholics and Protestants: for some, the bread and wine are a sacrament; for others, they are only a metaphor. First and foremost, the notion of sacrament is called for by the ethnographic materials themselves, for Itziar is a Catholic village whose religious experience hinges fundamentally on sacramental symbolism. Apart from religion, the tension between metaphor and sacrament can be observed as well in other activities that combine primary and secondary processes, such as art or certain kinds of politics in which "we can recognize an attempt to deny the difference between map and territory, and to get back to the absolute innocence of communication by means of pure mood-signs" (Bateson 1972 : 183). As Fanon remarked, certain political identifications "take on during the colonial epoch a sacramental signification" (1963 : 68). Ultimately, it is the concern with certain limiting concepts having to do with life as a whole, the notion of death included, that takes the form of a sacrament (Winch 1977 : 110).

In this book I examine ethnographically the myth and the metaphor in the ongoing Basque political violence; in doing so I attempt to unmask the illusion of liberty behind patriotic causes. Still, the ethnographer has to capture the contexts of action in which the violence takes place, and for this the mere perception of the myth and the metaphor may not be sufficient. The anthropologist seeks to enter a particular microcosm of cultural representations; this requires that he grasp the kinds of symbolism present in that culture. The true return to Itziar has implied for me revisiting the Catholic symbolism in which I was raised and observing its iconic imagery and sacramental aspects as constitutive elements of nationalist violence. This symbolism evokes Vico's "imaginative universals," in which metaphors and fables have "univocal, not analogical meaning." Therefore, the imaginative character is the reality that anchors particular perception and individual self, in which the power to assert identities surpasses the search for conceptual similarities. Writers who miss the cultural basis in which Basque violence is grounded fail to understand the actual experience of the actors and the spectators of the violence. Thus, I do not approach Basque violence as a kind of cognitive aberration; in fact, the more that institutions such as ritual killing or police torture are regarded as normal in a society that practices them the more instructive they become. The characterizing mark of anthropology is its capacity to take into account the totality of a social phenomenon by placing the actors' idioms and actions in their local context. While this analysis seeks to examine the social facts from an external perspective, it does so without violating their internal logic—"the (conscious and unconscious) subjective comprehension that we would adopt if, men after all, ourselves would live the fact as a native instead of observing it as an ethnographer" (Lévi-Strauss 1950: xxvii).

The act of writing this book has led me to see Itziar in a different light. I have been struck by the revelatory depth of what at first blush seemed most familiar and obvious in the recent history of its living generations. Although Itziar is an ordinary Basque village, I could not fail to perceive its singular beauty when contemplating its setting on a hill overlooking the Cantabrian Sea under Mount Andutz, its landscape dotted with the small hamlets and dispersed *baserri* farmsteads, its territory sheltering prehistoric caves containing the Magdalenian paintings of horses and skulls of ancient men, its graceful icon of the Amabirjina (Mother Virgin) and her centuries-old shrine beckoning and protecting the pilgrims of the surrounding area. In viewing Basque political violence as generated by and patterned after traditional cultural models, I realized that Itziar is only one small setting in which such processes can be recorded. However, through its condensation of primordial imagery and ritualized kinds of action, Itziar increasingly became for me a vivid metaphor of the larger ongoing political confrontation.

Nevertheless, confronted with the sacramental-like surrender of those engaged in the patriotic struggle and its tragic results, at critical moments Itziar has ceased to be for me a mere metaphor. I am still puzzled by something I did during my first months of field research. It is something I consciously knew was foolish, yet I seemed to have no control over the matter. Contrary to common sense and knowing that my professors would have been outraged, I asked for membership in the politico-military branch of ETA through a village friend who was a militant in the organization. I stated clearly that my only motive was to learn about the actual conditions of ETA activists' life-style in order to write an ethnography about it. I had no willingness to give my life for the Basque cause, yet I was ready to assume all the consequences deriving from membership in ETA. Initially they seemed willing to accept me. After a few months I was summoned to their hideout in southern France for an interview. In the discussion between myself and the four ETA members who had to decide my unusual case, I was repeatedly asked about the overall purpose of my research—"What do you want to prove?" I replied that for an ethnographic study it is essential that the anthropologist enter the field without preconceptions of what he is going to find, that I was not particularly interested in their ideology but if they were true revolutionaries in their everyday lives that should not escape my notice. Expectably they insisted that anything written by me on their life-style could be used by the police against them and that they wished someone would write a study of the Spanish police so they could read of their adversaries' weaknesses as well. To this I replied that ETA's interests were likely to be hurt if Basques were to read a sensitive ethnography that would put a human face on policemen killed by ETA. In the end, taking me into the organization presented uncontrollable risks for them and I was denied entry. As understandable as their decision was, still the refusal was deeply disappointing to me. I found the four young men educated and sensitive, yet they could not think in terms other than of military polarity. My desire to join ETA as a fieldwork requirement, fortunately thwarted, has since puzzled me. I found that I could not consciously control when Basque political violence is mere metaphor and when sacrament for myself as well. I had truly returned to Itziar.

"But How Can That Be?"

"Crime? What crime?" he suddenly shouted. . . . "I understand my crime less than ever! I have never, never felt stronger and more convinced than now!" Dostoevsky, Crime and Punishment

This ethnography began on a summer day in 1975 (reported in chapter 4) when several Itziar women, who had just witnessed the killing of a villager, assailed me with wide-open eyes and the question "But how can that be?" It was not properly a question but the expression of an unanswerable puzzlement, as when spectators are compelled to witness an epic drama in which men become gods and beasts and are capable of heroic deeds and tragic errors.

Yet, unlike the representation of tragedy, which is mere imitation of life, the events of Itziar are those of real life. The description of these events makes this book an ethnography and thus recreates an adequate context for the literal understanding of that question. Still, to the extent that the question points to the inexpressible puzzlement produced by witnessing tragedy, this ethnography resembles the script of an epic poem in which the literalness of the plot is a literary convention for the poet's song on men's honors and shames. In this respect it is not the work of an "expert" searching for a "solution" to the Basque problem; its goals are closer to the poet's attempts to turn into a song what is self-generating and incomprehensible in human experience.

If ethnography, as a work of art, does not aim at conveying anything but itself, a policy-minded reader may wonder what are the consequences of this sort of explanation in pragmatic terms, for it appears to deprive of meaning any attempt at imposing instrumental remedies on the violence. Indeed, this book has been written with no such practical goals. Yet I am well aware that political terrorism raises particularly acute demands at the policy level. Furthermore, it happens that in 1985 the local government did hire a committee of "international experts on terrorism" in order to find out the "causes" of the problem and offer the appropriate suggestions to handle it. A situation that for Basques is grounded in political and historical logics and is investigated in this ethnography in cultural terms (that is, conceptual and aesthetic) was thus reduced to a technical issue that could be diagnosed and correctly resolved thanks to supposed experts whose findings were allegedly kept partly secret from the public. I can scarcely conceive of grosser intellectual perversion than focusing "scientific" expertise on a people's collective agony, and I need not insist here that such research goals are the polar opposite of my own (see Zulaika 1987b). Nor could I reduce the lives of my subjects into some objectified field of knowledge such as the study of *homo criminalis*. Rather than being concerned with "a truth which . . . has turned the assertion of guilt into a strange scientifico-juridical complex," we ask, "What *is* this act, what *is* this act of violence or this murder? To what level or to what field of reality does it belong? Is it a phantasy, a psychotic reaction, a delusional episode, a perverse action?" (Foucalt 1977: 19).

Hart Crane wrote, "It seems to me that a poet will accidentally define his time well enough simply by reacting honestly and to the full extent of his sensibilities to the states of passion, experience and rumination that fate forces on him first hand" (1966: 218). This book is an attempt by a native villager at such an approximation of the paradoxical experience of Basque political violence in Itziar. It is a reconstruction of the basic cultural structure in which that violence is situated and the ideational and emotional attitudes of Itziar villagers to the phenomenon. At times I have thought I was describing a Homeric society in which fighting for the community's rights was an inalienable human duty. Contexts in which the logic of military antagonism still provide the basic thinking, even in a nuclear era, are illuminated, I think, by this ethnographic microcosm. The historical, sociological, and cultural locus of the events narrated here—insignificant within the larger framework of Basque violence, which in turn is insignificant on the wider stage of the world's contemporary violence—constitutes the substantive part of this ethnographic analysis. I am not propounding, however, as a sociologist or political scientist might, an overall explanation of Basque violence that aims at having general validity for wherever the phenomenon occurs. Rather than writing a journalistic report or sociological treatise, which surrender to the moment in which they are produced, this ethnography of Itziar seeks to capture the essence of a story that preserves in a condensed manner "the epic side of truth" (Benjamin 1955: 87). The ultimate goal is to picture a pattern of experiential totality. Side by side with a detailed attention to diachronic and synchronic structures, the requirements of this holistic approach have led me to resort as well to the logics of metaphor, sacrament, and ritual.

Ethnographic writing has been compared to "reading a poem" rather than "achieving communion" (Geertz 1976:237). Yet at times Itziar has compelled me to experience the writing of ethnography not only as a textual commentary but also as displaying an aesthetic whole resembling a Homeric poem in which the ethnographic text itself becomes, to again use Crane's words, "self-evident as an active principle in the reader's consciousness" (1966:221). Itziar has turned for me into such a principle, substantially transforming my perception of the dynamics of military violence; and through this book I try to provoke a similar reaction in the reader's sensibility. A poem, a dance, a sacrament—all affect what they signify. In similar fashion, an anthropologist's work can also be aesthetically what it means.

At times the reader may think that I have gone too far in my disinterest in the search for cause-and-effect relations; yet, since I am investigating the culturally communicative and ritually efficient contexts of violence, it is imperative that I stress the shallowness of the current instrumentally causal explanations of violence, for its comprehension "is more like interpreting a constellation of symptoms than tracing a chain of causes" (Geertz 1973:316). It is the mark of an anthropological explanation that it embraces as well the unconscious foundations of a custom, belief, or institution; thus, I am not primarily interested in recording the native moral justifications or in reconstructing with rational arguments the positively linear explanations given to the violence.

An ultimate lesson Basques are taught by their political violence is that they must face the compelling presence of its paradoxical results, which call for new solutions. In ethnography as in art, the paralysis brought by the tragic drama or the paradoxical question can be enlightening and lead in praxis to new acts of creation. And were this prospect accused of being the play of an aesthete rather than the work of a social scientist, I would reply with Lévi-Strauss that "I accept the characterization of aesthete in so far as I believe the ultimate goal of the human sciences to be not to constitute, but to dissolve man" (1966:247). This work has taught me that I should aim at dissolving nationalist militarism by recomposing it on a different plane.

From the above it should be clear that this ethnography is both a criticism and an affirmation of culture. The description itself may reveal that a community cultivates kinds of action that are self-defeating and glorifies actors who are characteristic of its culture. At the same time this ethnography is also an unmistakable appraisal of the heroic consciousness within the boundaries of culture. As a poet of Itziar's drama, I have taken no less pleasure in witnessing the true greatness of its ordinary men confronted with their political contradictions than I have been pained by the tragic results of our course of action. At times I felt I was being true to Picasso's dictum that "one must only paint what one loves." At the same time, I can say with Montaigne, "I have no more made my book than my book has made me."

Part 1

Historical Representations

Introduction

Myth, war, heroism, and tragedy may seem pretentious themes for small-scale settings such as Itziar, yet it is the purpose of the narratives that follow to show the full force of such collective representations in the village. The major events in the history of the living generations of Itziar are recorded in the chapters in part 1. These chapters are indispensable in that, while providing an explanatory framework on their own terms, they also serve as an introduction to the central issues to be dealt with in the subsequent ethnographic descriptions.

The individual subject of this narrative condenses these various dimensions of historical mythification—from the imagination of the prehistoric past to the anticipation of the unconquered future, from the memory of recent wars to the participation in the present fight, and from heroic consciousness to its tragic results. This is a history made by and for the ongoing violence; as such, it affords an essential form of intelligibility to that violence. Yet, from the perspective of an integrated cultural understanding, the quest for intelligibility does not conclude in history per se. These concrete historical representations are themselves something to be explained; toward this end the remaining four parts of the book are directed.

CHAPTER ONE

History as Myth, Legend, and Devotion

Itziar is the home of important prehistoric sites. Seven miles from the village center is the cave of Ekain.[1] Here prehistoric man painted his awesomely beautiful horses millennia ago. In the cave of Urtiaga, a mile from Itziar's center, skulls dating to as far back as the Azilian and the Upper Paleolithic were found.[2] In their prehistoric imagination, Basques intimately associate their non-Indo-European language with such archaeological evidences; Itziar villagers speak only Euskera. The first historical account of Itziar is based on the legendary apparition of the Amabirjina (Mother Virgin) in the early Middle Ages. A sanctuary built for the image has made Itziar a center of pilgrimage and Marian devotion for the past seven centuries.

Such mythical and legendary narratives are relevant in that they form part of the thought and social life directly observable in Itziar. As Evans-Pritchard observed, "Myth and history are in important respects different in character" (1961:8). We are not concerned with the historicity of the stories but with their mythical quality, for "a story may be true yet mythical in character" (ibid.). This chapter describes those events of the ancient past that are remembered in present thought and the historical implications to which they are related. This kind of prehistoric and legendary coding of history is a significant aspect of Basque identity and it becomes part of political attitudes.

Ekain, Urtiaga, and Maria

Less and less frequently do we encounter people with the ability to tell a tale properly. . . . One reason for this phenomenon is obvious: experience has fallen in value. W. Benjamin, Illuminations

Maria, from the house Errementeri, was the children's favorite storyteller in the Itziar of the fifties when I grew up. Her incredible stories about the flying lady Mari, witchcraft metamorphoses, and legendary figures had a strong impact on our imaginations and became frequent topics of wonder in our conversations. As fantastic as they were, her stories were most credible to us, for she would narrate them as concrete events that happened to her or to actual people that she would name. She was a delightful woman, much loved and respected in the neighborhood, and there was nothing in her that would raise a doubt as to the veracity of her fantastic yet factual stories. On one occasion, she used to say, she became so seriously ill after one such frightening witchcraft encounter that she was forced to stay in bed for three months.

The fascination exerted by Maria upon us children was not accidental, for she was skillfully articulating for us in the form of *kontuak* (stories) the mythical imagination of former generations. She was lovable in recreating for us a bizarre and dreadful world without losing any of her ordinary composure and kindness. Her candid confession as to her unwanted participation in such a reality added credibility to her stories; they were not mere fancy but events that she was confiding to us as a secret knowledge authenticated by her having witnessed them. Maria's stories about the flying Mari and witchcraft metamorphoses had a decisive impact on my imagination as a child. Even before I began to study anthropology, my first fieldwork experience was taping her stories. A significant factor pushing me to anthropology was the strong presence of this magical mentality in the world of my parents. Maria was also the first to speak to us about an exceptional ethnographer, José Miguel de Barandiaran, who decades earlier had repeatedly visited Itziar, conducting archaeological digs in Urtiaga and gathering folkloric material.[3]

By the fifties Maria's esoteric world was already obsolete. Each household harbored in secrecy any disgraceful complicity with such an outmoded worldview. Yet, although by then discredited and repressed, Maria was only voicing events that were indisputably part of the behavioral reality of her generation. As I grew older and inquired into my own family's history, it was easy to discover significant contacts with such beliefs and practices. My own grandfather rather frequently used to hear Mateo Txistu whistling and his dogs barking at night. Mateo Txistu was the priest-hunter of legend whose excessive inclination toward hunting earned him the punishment of having to wander with his dogs around the world for all eternity. It is obviously not incidental that my grandfather was an inveterate hunter. My grandmother and other members of her family had seen Mari fly in the air in the form of a ball of fire. This was an event repeatedly commented on at my mother's farm during her childhood and youth. At the *baserria* (farmstead) where my father served in his youth, the master of the household frequently used to watch Mari flying. One night she would go in a given direction, the next in the opposite one, but always traveling the same route between the two highest mountains of the area. My father was himself in his early twenties the subject of frightening witchcraft tricks.[4]

In the course of my fieldwork I found these events confirmed in similar family stories in other houses. Maria's kontuak were for us the equivalent of fairy tales. Yet they were "true" in that she told them as autobiographical events and our parents would not deny the actual reality of such happenings. It can be said of these stories that they transcend the distinction between the real and the imaginary. As I recall from my own experience, for a child there was nothing more puzzling than being told that witchcraft was genuinely "real" only a few decades earlier but that it did not exist anymore. The saying became popular that all witches disappeared with the shotguns of Eibar, the nearby town that manufactured the guns. Although no longer "real" for adult generations, Maria's storytelling offered us a significant access to their mental configuration.

Although Itziar is a separate parish, it pertains municipally to Deba, and there are over fifty caves in this municipality. In some of these caves—Urtiaga, Ermitia, Ekain, Arbil, Aitz-Beltz—important prehistoric materials have been found in the form of remains and fossils of humans, mammals, birds, shellfish, and fish as well as ceramics, drawings, and rupestrian paintings. In 1969 the paintings of Ekain were discovered. The estimated dating of the paintings is in 14,000 B.C. There are depicted thirty-three horses, ten bison, two bears, two deer, four goats, two fish, and many other nonfigurative marks. A rock at the center of the cave shaped in obvious resemblance to a horse's head made archaeologists hypothesize that Paleolithic man used the cave as a chapel to the horse. There is an intimate relationship between these cave paintings and the images of Maria's stories, as Barandiaran has pointed out.[5]

Ekain is presently closed to the public. During my fieldwork I proposed arranging a visit to show the cave to the youth. They were enthusiastic and grew impatient when the visit had to be postponed several times. Finally one Sunday morning, we entered Ekain in the company of an archaeologist. We were entranced by the arresting beauty of the prehistoric horses painted millennia ago right in our neighborhood. They were images of the past filled with a magical presence that affected us powerfully. Nor was this interest in archaeology a momentary affair, for in 1980 a group of Itziar adolescents formed an amateur team that found no greater weekend entertainment than archaeological outings and digs.

Maria's stories were of course told in Euskera, the only language she knew. The formation of their language is also a prehistoric matter for Basques, who imagine their cave ancestors speaking the same Euskera they still preserve. Their language is the outstanding feature that, more than anything else, makes Basques the subject of curiosity. Being the only non-Indo-European language in Western Europe, it has attracted the attention of eminent linguists and men and women of letters.[6] Basques are intensely conscious of the linguistic heritage they preserve. The reconstruction of proto-Euskera has been the main goal of Basque linguists (Michelena 1976). Language is again a fundamental factor through which Basques look at their prehistoric past in search of their identity. The linguistic link with the timeless past, with no elements of connection with other languages that might relativize its singularity, functions as a mythical operator that turns all other prehistoric remains into similarly exclusive facts of Basque origin. If in all historical reconstruction an element of myth can be postulated, there is an added dimension when there is no initial limit to the time frame. Various farfetched scholarly theories about Euskera contribute to this mythmaking process (Tovar 1980). However, no theory about the language, regardless of its scientific merit, can touch the core of the matter, which is the complete identification most Basques make between Euskera and their own cultural identity. Many Basques equate its potential loss with the total demise of Basque identity. This unconditional attitude toward the preservation of their endangered language forces Basque patriots to experience "the *Euskera* as agony and sacrament" (Oteiza 1983:317).

Not only in Itziar do Basques have a close relationship with their mythical past. In connection with their linguistic insularity, Basque identity is founded on an acute awareness of their enigmatic past. Their being a "mystery people" is also what seems to be of most interest about Basques to outsiders. No founding myth or political revolution substitutes for such an archaic definition of their group origin. Identity runs in an unbroken line from the ancestors who came from nowhere else but Urtiaga and Ekain, who achieved their human condition right there in those nearby underground dwellings. These caves provide for Basques the tangible context in which their imagination of the past finds its home. From a perspective of mythical timeless past anything historic belongs to a radically different classification of time; in conversations with Basques it is not unusual to hear expressions such as "that happened *only* 5,000 B.C." When a situation obtains that experiences the past in prehistoric coding, history is simply valueless, spurious time.

In the early 1970s a nuclear power plant was proposed for a site about two miles away from Urtiaga and ten from Ekain. The new myth of boundless nuclear energy might perhaps dismiss once and for all the old mythology. An antinuclear protest was soon ignited at the provincial level, which prevented the plant's construction and thus "the loss of Itziar."

There is historical evidence concerning the existence of Itziar from the early Middle Ages. Documents of the Episcopal See of Pamplona (Kingdom of Navarre) show that Itziar existed at least as far back as the beginning of the tenth century.[7] Sancho IV, king of Castile, on June 24, 1294, granted to Itziar the rights and privileges of a villa.[8]

A Sanctuary for the Amabirjina

If Itziar's antiquity can be kept guarded in underground shelters and prehistoric fossils, the history of Itziar can be captured with the naked eye in its sanctuary, which architecturally towers over the surrounding houses. When approaching the village from any direction, the medieval church stands out as an imposing fortress. Since the early Middle Ages this sanctuary has been a prominent center of pilgrimage as the shrine of the Amabirjina, the popular name for the icon of the Virgin Mary. The emplacement of Itziar on the northern route of Saint James of Compostela caused it to flourish. The icon is one of the oldest Basque icons (considered to be earlier than the thirteenth century) and, in the words of the Franciscan monk Lizarralde (1926:39), "the most beautiful" of them all.

The legend of how the Amabirjina appeared is common knowledge to the people of Itziar. A young girl from the baserria of Erreten Zar, close to the sanctuary, had the privilege of one day seeing "among the brushwoods, and blackthorns of that uncultivated place a most beautiful Lady full of light with a lovely Child at her breast" (Esnaola 1927:29). The girl asked her who she was and what she wanted, to which she replied: "I am the Queen of Angels, Mary, and it is my will, that you build me a church in this place, in which I wish to stay, and be worshiped with my Son" (ibid.). The spot where the Amabirjina appeared is called Lizarbe.[9] This is a place known in the area for the quality of water in its copious spring. Housewives from Itziar did their washing in Lizarbe's waters until the recent arrival of washing machines.

Esnaola believes that two earlier churches preceded the one now standing. Itziar possessed a pre-Romanesque or Romanesque temple when its founding charter was granted. The temple seems to have been replaced by a new one at the beginning of the fourteenth century. Sometime in the sixteenth century the present church was built over the second Romanesque church and as an extension of it.[10]

In the history of the sanctuary we find that there is a special relationship between fishermen and the cult of the Virgin.[11] As far back as the thirteenth century a Cofradia de Navegantes (Brotherhood of Seamen) existed in Itziar. A royal document dated 1448 gives approval for new chapters to be added to the statutes of such brotherhoods. Esnaola notes: "Although this Brotherhood was eminently religious, nevertheless its articles included themes related to the good government and administration of the society in its purely civil aspects" (1927:113). These statutes were concerned mainly with the organization of the brotherhood for the collection and distribution of alms among its membership, which was restricted to men only.[12]

A further historical note concerns the Amabirjina's church serving as the center of geographical and social space in Itziar. The centrality of the village church in the social space of traditional Basque society has been investigated by Arpal.[13] The ecclesiastical autonomy of the church was not challenged by the town council until the second decade of the nineteenth century.

The outstanding manifestation of the tie between the village church and each household in Basque society is each baserria's *sepulturia*, or symbolic grave site, on the church's floor, which is owned by that house.[14] The church's religious space is therefore a synthesis of the village's social space. The massive sanctuary of the shrine, built and rebuilt in a communal effort by Itziar and surrounding villages over the centuries, is a majestic statement of the village church's domination over its parishioners' households. The geography of Itziar is spotted with points from which one can see the Virgin's sanctuary. These are called *Amabirjina bistak* (the view of the Amabirjina). Traditionally, prayers were said when passing by them. These spots mark a Marian orientation for the entire area and show that the Amabirjina in her shrine has provided the undisputed geographical, social, and religious center of Itziar.[15]

"What Are We Going to See?"

Itziar's Amabirjina is only one among the many Basque icons of the Virgin. Lizarralde (1926) recorded over seventy such sculptures in Guipúzcoa alone. In the early 1930s, during the lifetime of Itziar's older generations, the apparitions of the Virgin in the Guipuzcoan town of Ezkioga made the town a center of regional and international attraction (Christian 1984). Multitudes went to Ezkioga to see the Virgin. People from Itziar were no exception. The apparitions were finally dismissed as being false by the Catholic church.

Among the devout visitors was Tene Mujika, a well-known playwright born in Deba and baptized in Itziar. When in the course of my work I visited her in 1980, she was ninety-two years old and her sight was much deteriorated. Yet talking about those trips to Ezkioga she would stare at me squarely and remark with intensity, as if summing up everything, "We wanted to see. We wanted to believe." Despite repeated visits, Tene never saw the Amabirjina. On one of the days that I visited her, Tene was seeing strange things. As I sat in the kitchen in front of her, she began to hallucinate and see a lady by my side. Since the previous year when I had visited her, Tene's sight had deteriorated to the point that she could scarcely recognize my features. In the meantime she had started having frequent hallucinations that she knew were "nothing" but deeply bothered her. I took the opportunity of her hallucination of a figure at my side to ask about apparitions and the role of vision in religious experience.

Because she was almost blind, I first asked her about her sight. Tene explained in detail that she did have problems with her sight when she was five, but she had been cured by an herbalist who "cleaned up" her eyes with his tongue and applied walnut extract. Tene said, "He opened up my eyes when I was five and up to now I have seen fine."

Tene stressed the annoyance that the hallucination provoked in her. She described for me what she saw: a well-dressed woman who was looking at her. She asked me once and then again, "Do you see her?" She commented, "I am tired of this." It seemed as if her mind could not focus on anything else while that vision remained. She addressed the fictional young lady behind me forcefully: "Who are you?" She poked her cane at the image invisible to me. "I touch her and she disappears," she commented. And again, desolate, "It is nothing. And yet it is a woman for me."

Tene was an extraordinary woman who in the prewar period had become a leading Basque playwright. During the war she had displayed unusual courage in organizing the evacuation of children to England and France from occupied Bilbao. I became aware that I could hardly find a more qualified Basque informant to explain the role of vision in traditional religious experience. What follow are parts of a conversation taped in 1980. She died shortly thereafter.

J. Z.: What is the difference between seeing the apparition of the Amabirjina of Itziar, seeing Mari of Anboto [the mythical flying witch], or seeing the woman you have now in front of you?

Tene: I think they don't have anything in common. The Amabirjina is a heavenly thing, you understand? She has enjoyed a great devotion from the seamen. . . .

J. Z.: Let us suppose that you see here now the Amabirjina instead of that woman. Wouldn't that be an apparition? Would there be a difference between that one and the one seen by the girl of Erreten?

Tene: A tremendous one.

J. Z.: Why?

Tene: Because one is divine. And the other is from below. We still say that something is a *sorginkeria* [witchy thing].

J. Z.: And what you are seeing now here, what is that then?

Tene: That must be something like witches. For you know that when something is from heaven, it must have something else. I think that our spirit would rise up, that it would become divine; so it seems to me that we would increase in faith. . . .

J. Z.: Why should they be different, the one Amabirjina that appeared in Itziar and the one that might appear here to you?

Tene: They would always be different. I think that the Amabirjina is natural, she came down with clothes and everything, walking and everything, much greater, much more sublime.

J. Z.: Why?

Tene: Because she comes from God. . . .

J. Z.: And what about the Amabirjina of Ezkioga?

Tene: About Ezkioga, yes and no. I also went there. All the mountain was full of people. The last day, when a miracle was expected, what a multitude of people! Many did not believe it and we, too, didn't believe too much. But we wanted to see, we wanted to believe. And to believe we wanted to actually see. A friend of mine and myself stayed apart from the multitude. And near us there was a woman with a small child of about eight months in her hands. And further back there was also a priest holding a tree as if in ecstacy. That child impressed me. When the Amabirjina appeared everybody was shouting: "Oh Mother!" And that child became as if out of himself; he was not a year old yet, he could not talk yet. And, "Look! What is happening to this child?" The woman: "I don't know, he becomes like this every day!" I told her: "He cannot be simulating false things." "That is what I think too, but everybody says that it is a lie." The child was so out of himself that I did believe in something. Everybody would laugh at me at home, but I still believe that that child saw. He would slowly place himself, looking at the spot where everybody had fixed their eyes, and the mother would touch the child and the child would not pay attention to her. And the mother would talk to him and he would ignore her; he was in ecstacy. There was no lie there. The mother told us that at home he was like the rest. If you had seen him you, too, would believe. The mother was crying. . . .

J. Z.: And this female you are seeing here behind me, is she from this world or from the other?

Tene: That one is from nowhere. . . .

J. Z.: Are images from this world or from the other?

Tene: Images are from this world, they are made by artists. They help us on the way to heaven but they belong to this world.

J. Z.: Couldn't the image of that woman you are seeing here now belong to the other world? Why not?

Tene: Because there everything will be beauty. I believe that God has to be something that brings us to himself, a love that unites us with himself. And so must be the Amabirjina.

"But we wanted to see, we wanted to believe. And to believe we wanted to actually see." Vision becomes a condition of belief and religious experience. As Tene repeatedly affirmed, the visions of the Amabirjina, Mari of Anboto, or her own hallucinations are entirely different because of the different spiritual effects they provoke. A divine vision comes from God and provokes a godly state in the soul. A mythical apparition "is not certainly an ordinary thing," yet it belongs to this world. The human figures of her hallucinations simply bother or scare her. It is interesting that Tene would trust a child's perception as more innocent and authentic than hers. Contrary to the "unreality" of her hallucinations, in a genuine apparition there is a naturalness by which the miraculous vision behaves entirely as an actual person, "walking and everything."

What validates the cult of the Amabirjina is that she actually "appeared" in Itziar in a legendary past. Her only deed in relation to Itziar was having been seen by a young girl. Sight is the primary sense for perceiving the apparition; hearing follows sight. In a religious worldview the "apparition" becomes a miracle and a church and a cult are offered to her effigy.

Truly dramatic changes in the conceptions of the self-validating power of mythical-religious images can be confirmed for the short span of the living generations of Itziar. Even a superficial discussion with members of the older generation easily turns into an absorbed consideration of incomprehensible changes in religious imagery and belief. The ongoing political violence, with its demands to abandon traditional ethical codes and religious practices, is but one more step. Using the metaphor of sight, there is a constantly heard expression that best sums up this state of drastic cultural transformation: "Zer ikusi bear degu?" (What are we going to see?). As Tene's generation well understands, the puzzlement provoked by mentality changes is best reflected in what one is forced to see.

The changes that the older generations of Itziar have been compelled to observe during their lifetimes are remarkable. The twenties and thirties posed the problem for the older generation of a belief system centered upon the traditional cosmology of mythical images and witchcraft practices becoming obsolete. Although not fully credible at that time, witchcraft was at least still tolerated as a worldview in its own terms, one to which everybody had access as a cultural articulation of otherwise unexplained phenomena. Suddenly, however, belief in the flying Mari of Anboto and all the universe of witches became merely fantastic ignorance to be laughed at and pushed into oblivion. My generation grew up hearing accounts of witchcraft as factual events. At the same time, they belonged to a world that made them our equivalent of fairy tales. For a child there was nothing more puzzling than being told that witchcraft had been "real" only a few decades earlier but that it no longer existed. The

Christian worldview also ran into problems; its reliance on visual perception as proof of supernatural realities became questionable. The apparitions of Ezkioga commented on above by Tene and declared false by the Catholic church are a case in point. The church had to handle other kinds of apparitions as well.[16]

It is since the early 1970s that Christian images and devotional practices have been abandoned in Itziar by people under thirty. This is the new "crisis of faith," which has wounded many families when older and younger generations irreconcilably disagree over the meaning of religious ceremonies and question the value of believing. Mythical images and witchcraft practices of the traditional cosmology failed to gain validation a few decades ago from the generation now over fifty. A crisis of similar magnitude is now affecting traditional forms of religion, the cult of the Amabirjina included. As expressive as was the saying that the shotguns of Eibar frightened away the witches, it is just as accurate to say that the guns of ETA have taken Basque youth away from the churches and seminaries.

Pilgrims and Soldiers

The Amabirjina—her wooden carving, her sanctuary, her devotional appeal—has granted to Itziar a distinctly spiritual personality as a center of pilgrimage and sacramental life. As mentioned by Esnaola and documented by the archives of the parish, pilgrims used to come to this shrine during the Middle Ages, not only from Guipúzcoa and Vizcaya but also from both sides of the Pyrenees and from Castilian lands.

In the long tradition of pilgrimage, some events stand out. During the first week of September 1884, for instance, pilgrims from twenty-five surrounding towns gathered in Itziar in a grandiose demonstration of Marian faith; during the eight days of the gathering "more than six thousand people received the Sacred Communion, and all the surroundings of the Sanctuary made with it a single temple, in which Masses were celebrated without interruption" (Aldazabal as quoted in Esnaola 1927:138). A literary-artistic contest accompanied the religious activities. In 1904 another of these massive pilgrimages took place with sixteen thousand worshippers.

Nowadays most of the pilgrimages are concentrated in the month of May, each Sunday of which is assigned to either one or several towns of the nearby area. Since the crowning of the Amabirjina in 1952 there has been an annual pilgrimage from the provincial capital, San Sebastián, in which an estimated two to three thousand people walk overnight the fifty kilometers to Itziar. It is customary during these pilgrimages to go to confession and to take Communion during the Mass. Marian songs play an important role in expressing devotional sentiment in the Mass.

Fervently singing these Marian songs and renewing themselves in sacramental life, one group of pilgrims in late August of 1931 deserves attention. This was the time of the First Spanish Republic. The Basque Nationalist party (PNV) founded by Sabino Arana at the turn of the century, had become the major Basque political force. Its youth was formed into an organization called Mendigoizaleak (Mountaineers), an activist group radically opposed to any compromise with the Spanish government.[17] The organization needed a protector saint and decided to come to Itziar as pilgrims to proclaim the Amabirjina as its patron.

This mingling of religious and nationalist fervor under the protection of Amabirjina's white-clad icon was soon to be baptized in blood in the impending civil war. While singing to her "Agur Itziarko Birjina Ederra" (Hail Beautiful Virgin of Itziar), the young soldier-pilgrims were getting ready to give their lives for *Ama* (Mother)—country, land, language, Euzkadi, Amabirjina.[18] The farewell song "Agur Jesusen Ama" (Hail Mother of Jesus), with *agur* meaning both "good-bye" and "hail"), sung with the vibrant rhythm of a *zortziko*,[19] was both a good-bye to the image and a salute to her inner everlasting presence in the clamors of battle:

Baina zugandik alde	But apart from you
biotzak ezin du;	the heart cannot endure;
zuregana dijoa,	it returns to you,
zugan bizi nai du.	it wants to live in you.
Birjin paregabea,	Virgin unique,
onetsi nazazu.	bless me.
Agur, Ama nerea,	Good-bye, Mother of mine,
agur, agur, agur.	good-bye, good-bye, good-bye.

CHAPTER TWO

History as War

No generational account of political violence can be even begun in Itziar without reference to the 1936 to 1939 Spanish civil war. Over thirty villagers died during the war; most of them were farmers in their early twenties who as soldiers were killed on the battlefield. The tragedy of that war left unforgettable images and experiences in the memory of those who lived it. These were vividly described to us youths during our upbringing. After five decades and despite the pervasiveness of the recent political violence, still the great divide in the history of Itziar's living generations is "before the war" and "after the war." "Gerra aurreko kontuak" (stories from before the war) is an expression indicating a period whose historical reality appears to be of a different order than the postwar history. For those who experienced it, that war presents a clear paradigm of what war actually is; and, inevitably, all recent exercises in political violence are seen through that example and measured by their proximity to the pure case. To better appreciate the significance of the nationalist cause in Itziar, a brief historical sketch of Basque nationalism is in order.

Basque Nationalism

Basques have made strong claims to ethnic uniqueness on the basis of their language, their blood-type frequencies (which differ from those of surrounding European populations), and the archaeological evidence suggesting that Basque evolution took place in situ well before the subsequent invasions of the European continent by people speaking Indo-European languages. The nationalist ideology fostered this sense of ethnic awareness and found historical antecedents of obstinate resistance to foreign powers in the annals of Strabo, which provide accounts of Basque opposition to Roman rule, as well as in later resistance to Visigothic, Frankish, and Arab invaders.

The rise of the Kingdom of Navarre in A.D. 905, encompassing all of the present-day Basque area as well as parts of southern France and northern Spain, gave political coherence to the Basques. By the twelfth century the kingdom had been reduced to an area that approximated present-day Navarre. The provinces of Alava, Guipúzcoa, and Vizcaya came under the aegis of the king of Castile. In 1512 the Kingdom of Navarre fell to the Catholic Kings and in 1590 Basse Navarre was annexed by the French monarchy.

These developments did not mean, however, a total loss of political autonomy, for local affairs were conducted through a set of charters, or *fueros,* wherein each province, governed by local councils, was granted substantial powers of self-government.[1] These charters were in effect in France until the revolution at the end of the eighteenth century and in Spain until 1876. Under the fueros the Basques were free from direct Spanish taxation, customs duties, and conscription into the army for the purpose of fighting outside of the Basque area.

With the ascendance of the Bourbon dynasty to the Spanish throne in the eighteenth century and the advent of a liberal regime in Madrid in the early nineteenth century, state centralism became the overriding national goal. Since the promulgation of a liberal centralizing constitution in 1812, there has been a struggle between centralism and regionalism in Spain, which continues to this day. Fearing the end of their regional autonomy, the traditionalist Basques aligned with the Catholic church and the followers of Don Carlos, a pretender to the Spanish throne, in a civil war against the liberal government. The defeat of the Carlist coalition in 1839 marked the end of the First Carlist War. A similar fate awaited the regionalists in the Second Carlist War, 1873 to 1876, a defeat that was particularly devastating for the Basque provinces, which constituted the backbone of the Carlist movement.[2] These wars had no separatist goals but were aimed at changing Spanish political life from within. In the Basque Country itself there was a split between the traditionalists of the interior and the liberal Basques of Bilbao and San Sebastián. As a consequence of the Carlist defeats, Spanish Basques lost their fueros and their leadership. Their culture and language (outlawed in the printed media) were under attack in their homeland.

The modern Basque nationalist movement, founded by a young journalist named Sabino Arana, was born out of this climate in the last decade of the nineteenth century. The PNV, or Partido Nacionalista Vasco (Basque Nationalist Party), was the product of urbanites from Bilbao and San Sebastián, the capitals of the two Basque provinces undergoing rapid industrialization with a large influx of Spanish workers. More than just a political party, the PNV "has been a social movement which has attempted to make itself into a nationalist community encompassing a multitude of aspects of social life, with the final objective that their progressive development would result in the identification of nationalist community with Basque community and the Nationalist Party with Euskadi" (Granja 1985: 157). Arana called for Basque independence and coined the term Euzkadi to refer to the Basque nation. He set out to purge the language (which he learned as an adult) of foreign influences. The racist view that Basques are the purest race remaining in Europe is evident in his writings. Urban middle classes, students, and the Basque clergy were most responsive to Arana, who, in 1898, was elected as a representative to the provincial government of Vizcaya. Broken by his numerous terms in prison, he died in 1903 in his late thirties, a martyr to the nationalist cause. From 1903 until the dictatorship of Primo de Rivera in 1921 the nationalist movement gained strength, particularly in Vizcaya, where the PNV took control of the Diputación, or provincial government, in 1918.[3]

The degree to which Basque separatism was an attainable goal was a major controversy within the ranks of the nationalists. There was also the notion, which continues to this day among nationalists, that the solution to the "Basque problem" might lie in the wider scenario of Europe unified along ethnic rather than national lines. During the first decades of the twentieth entury a cultural revival stimulated interest in Basque folklore, dancing, prehistory, and ethnography. Basque scholarly journals were founded[4] and in 1919 the First Congress of Basque Studies was organized.

Curiously, the urban nativistic political movement opted for rural symbolism, and "the message began to lean heavily upon the use of rural symbols as a means of invoking traditional values" (Douglass and da Silva 1971 : 160). The baserri farmstead was praised as the bastion of Basque culture. The nationalists were in part simply reacting against too-rapid urbanization, a feature that still can be considered an important factor in fostering political violence.

Itziar was not immune to the new nationalist fervor. A remarkable expression of the nationalist impact can be observed in the chronicles that during the 1920s and 1930s several local amateur writers produced in a weekly periodical of regional circulation called *Argia*. At one point as many as seven chroniclers participated in reporting on social events and the ideological ambient of the moment. In 1931 a *batzoki* (PNV's meeting place, which combines cultural activities with the services of an eating club) was opened in Itziar. Among the new activities promoted by the nationalist movement were staging theater plays, learning folk dances and songs, reading the nationalist literature, and chronicling.

The advent of the Republic in 1931 signaled a new climate of political freedom in Spain. Under the leadership of a young lawyer, José Antonio Aguirre, a new dynamism emerged in the nationalist party. The second generation of nationalist leaders, having gained control of the electorate of Vizcaya and Guipúzcoa from the traditional Carlist party, successfully campaigned for election to the Cortes, or parliament, in Madrid and converted the movement into a respectable factor in Spain's political life.

In 1932 a statute of autonomy was approved by a plebiscite in the three provinces of Alava, Guipúzcoa, and Vizcaya; Basque nationalists did not carry Navarra, which remained Carlist. The Republican government in Madrid failed to act on the plebiscite, but at the outbreak of the Spanish civil war in 1936 the beleaguered Republican government granted the Basques their autonomy. In October of that year, Aguirre was named president of the Basque government, which, besides the nationalists, included Spanish Republicans, socialists, and communists. The Basque government fielded an army against Franco's troops, issued passports and a currency, and sent out diplomatic missions to foreign countries.

Within nine months the Basque resistance collapsed and its government went into exile in France. Several thousand Basque nationalists were executed or jailed. An estimated 100,000 to 150,000 Basques accompanied the leaders into exile in 1937. The loss of the war was followed by suppression of civil liberties and a fierce repression of the Basque language and culture. With the German invasion of France during the Second World War, most of the Basque nationalist leadership was forced to flee to South America, where nuclei of Basque resistance were formed in several capitals.

War Stories

I record here fragments and shortened versions of much longer taped narratives. They can be taken as vignettes of war events as experienced in Itziar and speak for themselves.

CASE I. ABENE

When the civil war broke out Abene was sixteen. Her family was Itziar's stronghold of Basque nationalism. She is now in her sixties, living alone in her home after the rest of the family moved to a Basque provincial capital. "Just think what you would do if war would catch you up so young and then everything is finished," she comments. At times while recounting war events she will pull together all her energies, and simply say, "No war, no war." She repeats over and over again, "The worst thing that can happen is war."

I dare to suggest to her that many young people nowadays see war as the only means to overcome oppression, and she reacts viscerally: "No war, no war; if they want war let them fight, but let them not involve the rest of us; let them make it with the extreme Right." And when I further continue by raising the point that the older generations, too, during the Republic thought the war was justified, she replies rapidly: "An error, a mistake; after the two Carlist wars it was the third mistake."

Abene also described her father's arrest. One day, footsteps were heard coming up the stairs, and her mother commented: "Look, it must be Antonio with the new table" (they had ordered a table from the carpenter), and three civil guards showed up to arrest Abene's father. He was given permission to eat dinner before leaving. The mother anxiously sent her children to look for the road they were taking; later the family was told the father was in the prison of Ondarreta (San Sebastián). Abene showed me letters written home from prison; the basic tone of the letters is one of religious forbearance. When her father returned home his first words were: "Well, we are all alive at least, thank God." He had been in prison for three years. Likewise, Abene's seventeen-year-old brother, Luzio, was imprisoned for three years for his nationalist allegiances, made evident by his having volunteered to become an *ertzaina*, or Basque policeman.

We began to discuss the changes in normal people's behavior during the war. "You cannot even say how much people change. It wasn't Franco who harmed us, but people from here—the village." In fact, what emerges from her conversation as responsible for her family's suffering is mainly "the hatred of the villagers." This hatred was expressed in concrete actions. She recalls with a frightened face an occasion when her mother was coming home from church. A young boy stood in front of her, walking backwards while saying of the husband and son who were both imprisoned, "When they come, . . ." adding a gesture of cutting their heads off. Those words were directed to Abene herself as well while she was serving people in her family's store.

Abene has memories of people killed in Itziar during the war. Looking at her face while she recalls them it would seem she is visualizing utter darkness, a kind of disembodied evil that transcends even the "they" and "us" pronouns. If anything, these killings appear in her conversation as beyond comprehension. She starts by remembering a killing committed by "the Reds" in Deba. The soldiers came asking for rooms at a hotel, and the doorman said there were none available. They went upstairs to find that the entire hotel was empty, and in revenge for his lying they killed him on the spot. The only thing Abene can say is, "Isn't that horrifying, eh? It was the war." And she continues without distinguishing between "their" and "our" crimes of war, for the crimes seem to be even beyond antagonism. She tells of a Republican soldier caught in Lizarbe and later killed. Lizarbe is the spot just one hundred meters from the church where tradition has it that the Virgin Mary appeared. She adds: "Later on I found at home his personal records. I am pretty sure that they are his because the photograph looks like him." A militiaman was caught signaling an airplane; he was denounced and executed in Deba. Another militiaman was captured wounded; "I saw him going down the street with his face covered with shame."

He was also executed in Deba. And finally she tells of the soldiers from Itziar on the battlefront. "Gerria zan" (it was the war)—this is Abene's only frame to situate somewhere what seems to be in itself beyond categorization.

The church's fate is best disclosed by the personal fate of Itziar's clergy. When Franco's troops entered Itziar, Abene witnessed this scene. The military chief approached the priests and assailed the pastor: "You are a nationalist!" He replied, "I am a religious man." Three times the same exchange was repeated, and each time the chief moved closer to him. A coadjutor priest intervened by saying, "We are four priests, two gave their vote to the Nationalists and two to the Carlists." Of the four priests, Abene recalls, "The parish priest died soon afterward out of fear" and "the other Nationalist priest later on became a Carthusian; one of the Carlists was killed by the Republican leftists; the other Carlist priest hid out in a cave until Franco's troops entered Itziar at the end of September."[5]

There is a point in the conversation when Abene, intending to sum it all up, says, "You suddenly realize that *that* is not reality, that your world is not reality. It is what is happening to *them* [the Francoists] now." The schizophrenic aspect reveals the intrusion of the war frame into everyday society as making "another world" to the point that the traditional cultural institutions and values on which one's own worldview is based appear entirely displaced by it. The social and emotional milieu of the loser becomes so impotent that he or she comes to accept its unreality. Putting it another way, the two antagonistic worlds become so total in their mutual exclusion that the imposition of one implies the complete negation of the other's social and emotional reality.

The two irreconcilable worlds appear inextricably yet incompatibly intertwined in Abene's narration. Someone is walking up the stairs; the sound of the footsteps becomes associated with the expected carpenter; a comment is made about his coming; and the mind creates the image of the new table; but in reality there are three civil guards coming to arrest the father for no justifiable reason, taking him to an unknown place during an utterly uncertain period, maybe never to return home. Peasants witness against her father, knowing that it might mean his arrest and subsequent execution. They accuse him of carrying arms and participating in the

Carlist priest's killing. Later on, face-to-face with the accused and in front of a judge, in a "personal" relationship with him (outside the war frame), they are simply unable to lie because "he himself was there present." The mother and the man from Deba who has the power to release her son meet each other; an awkward exchange of words is produced: "Most likely you want your son back home," he says; "Of course," she replies.

Abene's mother is at the same time the wife of an exile and the mother of a prisoner supporting the Republic as well as the aunt of a Carlist fighting against the Republic. On the battlefront, her son and nephew are deadly enemies, but when the nephew is in the hospital, wounded, the kinship frame applies—she goes to visit and comfort him and he beseeches her, "I want to live!"

Abene's recall is couched in traumatized terms. From time to time she says, "Even to think of it makes me hurt. I don't even want to think of it." At times she will emphasize the vividness of the memories by going into a detailed description of how she remembers them. "I still have it in my mind as if it was happening now. I am still seeing it here. The day they entered was beautiful but sad; the colors were different that day, at three o'clock in the afternoon, at the hour Christ was killed. I have it all taped here [pointing to her forehead], as if it was present here, all those moments." This traumatized memory may break into emotional outbursts, as when she heard the nationalist politician Ajuriagerra being interviewed on television. In response to a question about when he cried for the last time, he answered, "When Bilbao fell." Abene herself then "started crying for a long time, but how I cried!"

Faced with the injustice in the reciprocity between the two worlds, hers is felt as completely excluded even from that most communitarian institution—the church. There is a statement Abene asserted several times as particularly significant: "We have never hated." It appears as if, following the political-military polarization, the entire psyche was also pulled into a love/hate dichotomy, hate being constantly read into "they" and love becoming an indispensable means of keeping the identity and moral superiority of "we." Hatred is associated with the war frame and the "they" who are implementing it locally. In Abene's view, "we" do not want to debase ourselves into that dehumanized frame in which "they" are the masters and winners, but prefer to retain the moral identity that never legitimizes hatred. Being losers, the only means for "us" to win is through a higher morality, personally vindicated.

CASE 2. MARTIN

Martin, from the Andutzene farm, joined the Basque Nationalist party and fought on the Republican side during the civil war. He described in detail how he fell into the hands of Franco's Italian allies and became a prisoner of war in Castro in August 1937. After forty days in Castro and Santoña, where he was one of the more than thirty-five hundred prisoners of war, he was taken to Extremadura in southern Spain to a concentration camp. He mentioned the disappointment in Seville of the crowd that gathered to receive them because "the beastly Reds" actually had no tails, as the crowd had been promised.

After two years of forced work, Martin was released by the military on August 31, 1939. Then, in June 1940, after he had found a job, he was taken back to a concentration camp in Miranda "because we had been of the Red Zone." He was released from the "battalion of workers" in May 1942. He had been in the war or imprisoned since the summer of 1936, nearly seven years. Here is his description of what it is to be a prisoner:

M.: To be a prisoner is the last thing.

J. Z.: Isn't it better than being on the battlefield constantly risking your own life?

M.: No, no, no. When you are in the battlefield you are defending what is yours, and you have the weapon with you, you have the bullets for the gun, you will have the pistol, hand grenade, and friends, too. You are there defending your side. The others will be attacking you from above with aircraft, or from below, but you, too, you defend yourself with what is yours. But when you are a prisoner you have nothing. They tell you everything, they scorn you, you have to put up with everything, always under someone else—that is what is worthless. To be a prisoner is the worst thing.

CASE 3. SIMON

Simon belonged to a Carlist family when the war broke out. Like most local boys eligible for military service, he fought with the insurrectionist army led by Franco and Mola. I quote his final comments on the war, narrated after the battlefront incidents.

J. Z.: Back at the farm when the war was over, was life again the same?

S.: Just the same. Among my friends some had been with the Reds, such as Luzio and Isasi, but I was friends with them as before. That's it. I never denounced anybody. I have a clean conscience about that at least.

J. Z.: You must have changed somewhat after the war.

S.: What would you change? Look what might have changed. A lot of discipline, not enough bread, no money, and, yes, a terrible hunger. At least that's what I saw, and others, too.

J. Z.: When the war was over, did you know who had been the winners in the war?

S.: The military. That everything was in the hands of the military. That was it.

J. Z.: Don't you get angry knowing that you fought for Franco?

S.: It was something compulsory. You had to go with either one or the other side. I have thought many times that many unnecessary, foolish things took place. Now we have extensive experience in case it comes to it again. Those things will happen again if the war comes, if you start it up with young people, those foolish things.

J. Z.: You told me earlier also that to go to war was a kind of game for you.

S.: That was so for me. You don't even think of what is war. Je! Dress up with the cartridge belt and you feel as if you were something.

J. Z.: And like you, everybody else.

S.: Just the same.

J. Z.: When you [the veterans] get together now, what do you think or say about war?

S.: War is a bad thing. Yes, boy. If there is any possible way to avoid it, no war. I would say that.

J. Z.: Are you afraid that war may come back?

S.: Yes, I am. The war against another country is a beautiful one. But that war against one another . . . that is a hard thing. Nobody who hasn't experienced it knows what it's like.

CASE 4. JOSÉ MARI

José Mari was from the Isasi farm. Five brothers from Isasi participated in the civil war. Two fought with the socialists, two with the nationalists. The fifth was a priest who was caught up with "the movement" while serving in a town from the province of Alava; he remained with the anti-Republican side. The older of the two socialist brothers died on the battlefront. The narration that follows is by the younger socialist brother, who recalls also his socialist brother's record, which inspired him. It should be borne in mind that these brothers, with the exception of the priest, are all *baserritarrak* (peasants) without any formal education and that their decisions reflect the ideological background of Basque rural society during the thirties. The narrator joined the socialist battalion Saseta in Eibar. The following are some excerpts from interviews with him; they begin with battlefield stories and conclude with the ideological beliefs that have oriented his life since.[6]

J. Z.: What armaments did you have in your battalion?

J. M.: Up to that moment we had either three or four armored cars in Malzaga because that was a crossroad. But at the end, on the slope of Bolívar, there were two. There they started saying that we had to get out, we had to get out [from Bolívar]. I will never forget what happened then: going up the slope of Bolívar there is a small village to the left, Zenarruza, and they were pealing the bells; we had to pass through there to get to Munitibar. We came out to the open field on the left, looked back, and six tanks [of the enemy] were behind us, right there! They themselves didn't dare [to shoot], we were maybe two or three thousand all formed up [marching] row by row. In any event, because maybe the enemy might try for a mass slaughter, the two armored cars of our battalion were left there as roadblocks for the tanks.

So we passed, and when we arrived in Munitibar everything was on fire. From there [we went] walking to Guernica. We arrived in Guernica at about six in the morning, and everything was burned out, everything on fire.[7] From there, to Amorebieta and Bilbao.

Here is an interesting event, just to see how things are. Beside me was Intxaurraga, the boy who had a death sentence that I told you about yesterday. And it happened that he was recognized by someone from the other side:

"Good heavens! You are Intxaurraga!"

"Yes, and who are you?"

"I'm not going to tell you who I am."

"Why not, why shouldn't you say?"

"I won't tell you who I am."

And he asked again who he was, and:

"I am someone who has drunk many *chiquitos* [small glasses of wine] offered by you."

That sure is pulling one's leg, isn't it? Many times that night we were talking to each other across the battle line, although they were on the other side. But by then we were aware that there was much movement around, sounds of armored cars at night and so on.

J. Z.: You used to talk with people from the opposite front?

J. M.: Yes! All those words that I told you, they were spoken with people from the other side.

J. Z.: And how would you come together?

J. M.: Talking, talking from one front to the other; for instance, we were five hundred meters or two hundred meters apart.

J. Z.: Wasn't there any more distance than that?

J. M.: No, no. No more, not over there at least. Even less since they were close hills. And talking like this. I can remember it:

"I am someone who has drunk many *chiquitos* given by you. Pass to this side. Don't be foolish. Tomorrow it will be too late."

"What is the news from Eibar?"

"From Eibar? That the girl from Txaltxas [the name of a private house], Juli, remains beautiful. I saw her just the other day before coming to the front and she is beautiful." . . .

J. Z.: Tell me, how did you find your brother dead?

J. M.: It was in Peña Lemona. We were going forward, and when we were nearly on the top, at the right side there was an official on the ground, and ours [his brother] was a bit further down, and a third one a bit further down. They were like that, the three of them dead like that, but they were killed two or three days earlier. There I saw him, and I kicked him once and again. And what a thing a person's inability to recognize is, to recognize my own brother, yes, but I couldn't believe it. How could I? I had been the previous day with him, and, besides, I did not know they had left from there. I was unaware. His lips were blackened and swollen, all deformed, you know. His face had his presence, I soon realized that, but maybe it was somebody else, maybe he was all right. And I would kick him with my foot and keep on doing it. And I didn't start inspecting him or anything. I would like to have his identity card now. . . .

J. Z.: We were in Bilbao.

J. M.: Yes. Well, and that youth [whom he had suspected was a spy] was brought back again eight days later, caught by a guard on the street. And look what becomes of a person. I asked the guard, "Are you incapable of shooting him?" I was angry. "Well, if you don't shoot him I am capable myself of doing it." They wouldn't shoot him. But I don't know whether I wouldn't have done something silly if I had been allowed to at that moment. My brother had just been killed and I was angry. My other brother had left no trace, and the other two were also missing. And I was angry, angry, angry. I don't regret today that nothing happened, but at that moment I do not know what I might have done, for I thought that many lives were there in danger, depending on the guy; in Bilbao many lives were endangered by those spies. . . .

As I said earlier, I don't regret what I was; I mean that I am satisfied with the path I have taken. Isn't that a beautiful thing? As I see it today, I told you this, too, I think that it needs to be from the political Left, not from the Right or the Center.

CASE 5. JOSEFA

Josefa was married to a man who fought on Franco's side. When the war broke out her nationalist boyfriend at the time was in Bilbao and fought with the nationalist forces. She preferred to stay home.

Later on she married in Itziar center, where she manages a bar and restaurant.

One day I was having a casual conversation with Josefa. Suddenly, she intently fixed her eyes on me as if to dismiss our conversation and capture my mind at another level. In a different tone she said, "Well, now I have to put a question to you—is a world war coming?"

From then on our conversation turned around war. War was the most terrible thing that had happened in her life, she said, but the war now approaching, compared to the previous one, would be much more horrible. I asked her to tell me concrete war events, and she recalled this one:

> We were going to church to give thanks to the Amabirjina because Itziar had been "liberated" [that is, taken by the insurgent soldiers]. And going up Lizarbe we met with a wounded *miliciano*. The two of us looked into each other's eyes—he had had breakfast at my home the previous day and we recognized each other. The chief of the Franco forces, who saw that we were looking at each other, asked me whether we were acquaintances. I said, "No." They took him to the cemetery and there they gave him the last shot. I will never forget that.

I find this incident almost beyond any comment. From a local viewpoint a stronger statement of what war is can hardly be made. On the one hand, she was going to visit the Amabirjina to thank her for "liberating" Itziar. On the other hand, on her way she was forced to stare at a soldier whose death was required by the "liberation," a person who the day before had eaten in the kitchen at her home, a person who could look into her eyes and communicate unmistakably the message "I am a human being." In order to look at the "liberated" Amabirjina, she would have to close her eyes to the prisoner soon to be killed. In order to achieve the blessing of the smiling Amabirjina's graceful look, the soldier "on the other side" had to be shot. Such was the paradox faced by Josefa in Lizarbe, which has never left her mind.

Of course, had the "liberators" been the nationalists and the captive a Francoist, the same exclusive disjunction between the graceful look of the liberated Amabirjina and the prisoner's inimical look was likely to have obtained. That is, essential to the war frame is the statement that "our" ultimate image of ourselves (patriotic and religious) is based on the exclusion of the enemy's image. The ultimate icon (Amabirjina or nation) tends to be similar for both contending parties. What is specific to the war frame is that this ultimate image is based on both exclusion and totality.

CASE 6. SORASU

Sorasu was a village personality who, even while taking the first glass of wine of the day right after Sunday's High Mass, would become a center of deviant fun. Despite his badly broken health, Sorasu never lost the knack for a truly satirical sparkle and flamboyant manners in constantly reaffirming his bottomless physical force against those who from all sides would be picking a quarrel with him, pointing at his short stature and lack of *indarra* (strength). He was partly a verse singer, partly a version of *baserritar* hobo, all his life a bachelor, a *morroe* (peasant laborer), and a *burrukalari* (fighter), and the youth used to greatly enjoy his enigmatic intelligence and his renowned personal stories.

On the several occasions that I found him in the tavern in his usual boozy state, war stories would spontaneously creep into his conversation or verses. In a series of wartime verses that I heard him sing one day, he finished with this barely audible strophe:

Fusil bat anparu baino	Nothing but a gun
besterik ez nuan.	had I for shelter.
Aura dek munduan	What in the world
aditu nun duan?	was my ordeal?
Zer trantze nituan.	Pay good attention.
Iltzeko esperantzak	The hopes to die
an jun ituan.	there they went away.

Sorasu's wartime comrades have hilarious stories about him. Purportedly, on several occasions he was lost on the battlefield and inadvertently passed over to the enemy's side. Once, completely drunk, he fell from a second floor onto his captain's lodgings. On another occasion the troops lost him for three days; he had remained somewhere sleeping due to his drunkenness. Sorasu's job was to carry ammunition on his shoulders, and when he showed up on the third day, he made for himself a triumphal reentry: he held the box of ammunition in his arms, playing it as if it were an accordion while whistling and dancing. Reportedly, on another occasion, on which his captain had ordered the execution of a captured woman soldier, Sorasu interfered, arguing that she was very brave and that they would have to kill him, too, if they would not spare her life; she was not executed. He was also credited with having shot down a chief commander on his own side for giving reckless orders to the soldiers. Another time he got lost and ended up on the side of the enemy; when I inquired of him what he was doing there, he explained: "Shit on God. The captain asked me: 'Where have you been?' 'Well, I was over there. There were walnuts and figs over on the other side and I went to steal them.' The captain said: 'You have balls, you.'"

But it was on a Monday night that Sorasu seemed to me to be revealing even more than usual of his real self. He was left alone in a corner of the tavern, drunk as usual, when I approached him. Without any introduction he went straight into telling me the following war event that apparently was haunting his mind at the moment. The underlying message to me was: You should understand this if you want to know the truth of things.

The story was situated on the battlefront during an evening when he was ordered to unload three trucks with a singular cargo: dead soldiers. While giving details of the stink of the dead bodies, a deep-seated nausea could be observed on his face. "After that, I couldn't eat at dinnertime. The captain said to me: 'What, aren't you eating?' I said, 'No.' I drank a glass of wine, that was beautiful. I got completely drunk that night." He himself remained in silence as if facing the immensity of his memory. Later on he commented: "How can a man have to be three years as I did shooting?" He accompanied his words with gestures of his hand holding a gun and the finger heavily pulling the trigger. The story and the gestures were a confession beyond words. So he kept drinking silently.

Sorasu had fought with the victorious party. That same cold November night, when he was walking home drunk, he did not see the police roadblock and got into an argument with them; the police hit him in the chest and sent him back to Itziar center. When José Ignacio and I found him late at night, sitting on a bench near the closed tavern, he was mumbling: "I didn't see them. I told them I had defended Spain during three years. I would kill them all." He was back again in the war.

The War Frame in the Local Experience

"Franco hasn't been my enemy. My enemies have all been from here." Atxurra repeated this statement several times while recounting for me his war trials as a Basque nationalist in Itziar. In the local experience these are, ideal-typically, the basic characteristics of a war situation:

1. A polarized structure: there are only two sides and two pronouns—"their side" and "our side," "they" and "us."
2. The two polar sides are in a disjunctive relationship of either/or. Anybody who belongs to one side or faction cannot belong to the other; membership in both factions is utterly precluded.
3. There is an injunction by which no individual can escape this antagonistic structure: you must belong to either one or the other faction.
4. Exclusion is sufficient condition for being made part of the basic bipolar structure: someone who is not of "ours" is assigned automatically, by exclusion, to "theirs."
5. When the polarized frame is established, the decision of who belongs to which side is based on an inference from his or her behavior prior to the existence of the bipolar frame itself. When the war starts you are *fichado* (on record). An either/or side is inferred and ascribed to everybody.
6. No ambiguity or double meaning is permitted. All double dealings are reduced to the "they/us" alternative.
7. In cases in which the previous record does not show a clear election for one or the other side, ascription is made rather mechanically. A distinction should be made here between those who go to fight as soldiers and those who stay behind. In theory, people in the age group to fight have an option of two parties. In practice, with the exception of a few politi-

cally sophisticated ones, in rural areas such as Itziar they simply obeyed the official army's orders.

8. Associated with this mechanical ascription to the faction is the lack of personal responsibility for choice.
9. The principle of totality is applied to the either/or dichotomy. Any performance of any kind by the adversary's side becomes a threat to one's own side. A separation of domains, by which in certain "warlike" respects they are enemies but in others they are friends, is precluded by the war frame.
10. Totality applies as well to the potential nature of the threats and actions—they rapidly become matters of life or death.
11. The relationship between the two sides is one of direct confrontation, that is, there is no rule for mediation.
12. The frame places the two sides in total confrontation. Each side has to seek the complete subordination of the other for the conflict to end.
13. The defense of "our" side is equivalent to the defense of its individual lives and the survival of the group identity. Therefore, there is no possible doubt as to the excellence of the cause, which entails not only the defense of a country but even biological survival during the struggle.
14. The "right" and "wrong" positions on the war frame's structure cannot be determined by a positive or negative outcome. The "cause" for the war is not removed after a defeat. You may be defeated, but the "rightness" of the cause will not be eradicated; you may die, but the heroism of your death will never be "wrong"; winning does not add anything essentially new to the truth of the cause.
15. The postwar society will be dominated exclusively by one of the disjunctive either/or parties—the winning faction. The losers will disappear either physically (death, imprisonment, hiding) or politically. The distribution of power is restricted to the winning faction.
16. In the total either/or factional disjunction, the only means of changing factions implies a complete desertion and betrayal of the opposing one.
17. Once the war frame has been triggered, from the local perspective the initial and global military aims subside into the

background; that is, the war frame becomes operative at the local level independent of the overall military goals that will decide the victorious side. Subsequently, military victory will not signal the end of the war experience.

18. At the local level the war frame does not deal primarily with military actions; the war frame will be used locally to gain institutional advantages. The enemy becomes completely odious and there should not be any qualms about depriving him or her of any social and economic status.
19. The war frame therefore implies a radical disruption of the ordinary social rules by which a community was governed prior to the war situation. The entire normative system based on law and custom is displaced so as not to intrude on the now more fundamental rules of the war frame.
20. The imposition of the new normative system and ideology is arbitrated exclusively by the winning side. When the war is over, a major concern of the winning party is the redefinition of what will constitute war in the future.

The Postwar Period

In a perspective that lacks a sense of historical continuity, *gerria* (the war) is perceived as a sudden outburst erupting like a volcano, as if it were a phenomenon belonging more to nature than to society. The civil war was an event that originated and was decided outside local boundaries. It belongs to village life as a reflection and indicator of larger processes that transcend local society. As such, this transcendent single event is fit to become the backbone of the past. In the phenomenology of "what we have gone through," "what we have seen," "what we have lived," gerria becomes the climactic center that is beyond the normal course of events. Although its logic differs from the mythical past of Ekain and Urtiaga, gerria becomes also a center of experience that is outside the normal circle of history. In relation to this "original" event, what followed was a mere aftermath and what preceded was only a preparation, nothing but the initial attraction precipitated by the inexorable magnet behind it—war.

Gosia (hunger) is vivid in the villagers' memory of the postwar situation. Economically, "red misery"; socially, "the hate of the other's sight"; familially, division within the same house; politically, fear; religiously, guilt—these are some most noticeably chaotic effects of war, which seemed to have defied all mechanisms of cultural control. For the villagers, who were startled by this runaway situation, *gerra ondorena* (the postwar) was a time of economic and psychological atonement for the preceding chaos and a period of slow return to normal cultural models of behavior.

The meaning of gerria is, however, substantially different for the older and younger generations. For the people who actually experienced it, war was the source of dreadful memories to be turned into "stories" that are meant to embody the essence of the antisociety's complete lack of ordinary rules and values. For them, from the present perspective, the meaning of war is the projection of a past history replete with tragedy and defeat. In crucial contrast, one could generalize that for the most active generations in Itziar, now between twenty and forty, war is the likely outcome of contemporary reality in Euskadi—the ideal battleground in which the enemy's past victories can be disputed.

CHAPTER THREE

History as Heroism

At the conclusion of the Second World War, Franco's Spain was identified with Hitler and Mussolini and an international boycott of the country fostered hopes that the dictator's days were numbered. Basque resistance succeeded in organizing general strikes in 1947 and 1951. However, Spain's isolation was broken by a pact signed with the United States in 1951; this was a serious blow for Basque nationalists. In the ensuing decade the leaders of the PNV, increasingly moderate in their actions, tried to revitalize its youth group, known as EGI, the acronym for Eusko Gaztedi del Interior (Basque Youth of the Interior).[1] An EGI cell was formed in Itziar in the late fifties. In the early 1950s, a group of students had founded in Bilbao the organization Ekin (Action), engaged initially in study sessions and consciousness-raising; they were co-opted by EGI in 1957. Discontented with the PNV's moderation, the group of students opted for a hard-line approach, meeting Franco's repressive regime with an armed struggle. This group broke with the PNV and in 1959 founded ETA.[2]

Viewed variously as the problem, the symptom, or the solution, during the seventies political violence acquired overriding importance in Basque society. Itziar was no exception. This chapter briefly sketches the escalation of political violence in Itziar since the late fifties. It is intended as a narrative that constitutes the historical-cultural context in which the ensuing chapter "History as Tragedy" has to be situated. It also introduces substantive themes to be discussed in subsequent parts of the book.

A Religious Conversion

When the four brothers of the Isasi farm left for the battlefront in the summer of 1936, the one married at home left his firstborn baby son Martin in his mother's care. While José Mari's uncle Martin from Andutzene was a prisoner of war in the concentration camps of southern Spain, José Mari himself was being cared for by his aunt as well. Martin and José Mari both went to Itziar's public school. Martin recalls that he had a male teacher named Jesús Llanos:

> He was a very good teacher; you could tell his pupils by their learning. He was a staunch Francoist and would castigate harshly anyone speaking Basque, either in school or in the street. He had *chivatos* [informers] to tell him who had been speaking in Basque and then would hit them in school.

José Mari attended Itziar's school until he was twelve. He was then taken to Deba to the Colegio of San Viator during the 1949–50 course in an effort to round off the teachings of the elementary school. Later he acquired an education in mechanics. José Mari became aware of repression on the part of the friars of Deba—he was not allowed to speak Basque even during the breaks. Outside the school situation, both José Mari and Martin recall the readiness of Itziar's parish priest in the late 1940s and early 1950s to speak Spanish during the sermons as soon as a "foreigner" appeared in the church.

After speaking with Martin and José Mari, two of the most representative men of their generation, three distinct stages can easily be observed in their life stories. First, there was the youthful period of fun and revelry (*juerguista*); second, in their early twenties a real conversion of a social-religious nature took place followed by intense activism; and third, after six to eight years of activism, their interests became dominated by family life and the practice of their earlier social ideals in their work environment.

The main activities during the juerguista period of fun consisted of drinking, quarreling, being the last to retire, and bothering girls. The *burrukak* (fights) were an important element.[3] The older generations' burrukak are remembered as having surpassed anything the postwar generation did. Although never up to the older standards, the postwar generation, too, made *kristonak* (those of Christ; that is, unbelievable things). They fought burrukak with sticks; groups of youths who had come to the village to *neska-laguntza* (accompany the girls)[4] were attacked by the youth of Itziar with sticks and left "right completely on the ground." Outsiders were attacked with dirt clods on their way home after a fiesta, and so on.

However, a drastic change in their mores was under way for a substantial group of Itziar's youth. A preparatory event was the crowning of the Amabirjina of Itziar, a huge demonstration of Marian devotion that required the youth's organized participation; its success resulted in local pride. A yearly night pilgrimage from San Sebastián was held after the coronation. But perhaps the most important single influence was added in 1955, when a new coadjutor priest, Don José María, was assigned to the village (until the middle seventies Itziar had one parish priest and three coadjutors). Don José María had attended the seminary after the war, where his education combined a total apoliticism and the suppression of Basque cultural interests in favor of strong emphasis upon a pious religious life. He himself was an accomplished model of this devotional doctrine—impeccable in his church services, very kind and with a constant smile on his face, ardently eloquent in his sermons, fond of youth and children, sincerely devout in his personal life.

Don José María soon was adored by everybody and was in charge of the Luistarrak (the Louises, or male youth). The other two religious groups were the Mariaren Alabak (the Daughters of Mary) and Irugarrendarrak (Those of the Third Order), the latter under the patron Saint Francis and composed of married people. In the absence of other social networks such as the groups of peers known as *cuadrilla* (Heiberg 1982:255–62) and eating clubs, which in Basque town life provide the basic structure for social relations, these religious sodalities were the principal associations in small rural villages such as Itziar.

Don José María took good care of the Luistarrak. But he did something of far greater significance, which no sermon or attendance at Mass could replace: he created a small, compact, motivated group of eight boys who held regular weekly meetings. In Don José María's view, "The main purpose of the group was religious. We dealt also with social issues based on the baserri peasant life and aimed at the formation of the youth's own personality."

The initial event that had a profound effect in creating the group's solidarity and deciding the future course of action was a week's retreat in San Sebastián for spiritual exercises. As one of the members of the group, José Mari from Andutzene, puts it now, "That was a brainwashing," or, using the vocabulary of the times, "a total conversion." "Conversion" is indeed the word generally used by the next generation of youth when describing what happened to this fervent group. The change was soon reflected in actual behavior: no neska-laguntza, no social (as opposed to folk) dancing, no drinking, no cursing. The following year the dynamic group of converts succeeded in persuading thirty-six youth from Itziar to spend a week in seclusion in San Sebastián doing spiritual exercises. The youth of Itziar was undergoing a radical change toward religious practices as reflected in an exemplary life-style. Don José María agrees, "Yes, it was a kind of conversion, but it was also the most normal thing at the time." Similar cases of group conversions occurred in other rural towns as well.

What was the method and what were the issues discussed in these meetings? A concrete theme was chosen, such as the *agarrado,* or social dance, why girls preferred outsider boys, the problems of authority in a baserri family, how to sanctify the Lenten period, and so on. A solution through concrete action was sought. How things ideally should be was known in advance. The issue was to realize them in practice. As Martin put it to me, "This was the major thing: that a youth had to be *ekintzaile* [activist]." The notion of *ekintza* (action) was the central one. As an attitude it meant the readiness to make the commitment as far as possible to implement in secular life what the religious belief dictated to be true. After discussing the disparities between the ideal and the factual a decision was made that had to be carried out through the performance of a concrete ekintza. The example of Don José María, himself a model practitioner of his doctrines, was a forceful example of the conversion of good words and intentions into reality. Hence, the group acquired a sense of mission—members had to convert themselves and convert Itziar.

Baserri Gaztedi

After the civil war, official ideology was termed in Spain "the National Movement." A parallel use of the movement metaphor was applied to church activities as well. The best channel for this ecclesiastical movement was Acción Católica (Catholic Action), in which the central attitude and method was summed up by the all-pervasive notion of "militancy"—to be a militant was fundamentally the central vocation of any Christian. The Basque rural branch of the national Acción Católica was named Baserri Gaztedi (Baserri Youth).

At the forefront of the church movements were priests who acted as counselors. They bore direct ideological and administrative responsibility for their organizations. The leaders of Baserri Gaztedi describe their organization mostly in contrast to the more urban and working-class-oriented JOC, Juventudes Obreras Católicas (Catholic Workers' Youths), the competing Catholic organization at the regional level. The provincial counselor at the time, the priest Zamora, explains: "Baserri Gaztedi was not centered in a single class, as was the JOC with the workers, but it embraced the entirety of social life." The distinction mirrors a basic difference between work in a factory occupation and work in the baserri institution, as will be examined in part 2. Language was another key difference in the two organizations: Baserri Gaztedi used Euskera at all levels. Politically, Baserri Gaztedi used to accuse JOC of "centralism"; that is, direct dependency upon Madrid. The main strategy for the JOC was class action. Baserri Gaztedi thought that *herria* (the people or the country) was a more fundamental and inclusive concept.

The populist ideology of Baserri Gaztedi differed as well from JOC's tendency to focus on a small select group of militants. There was a problem with reduced groups: they were liable to be accused of engaging in some conspiratorial action—of "doing politics." Both the state and the church strongly condemned any thoughtless "getting into politics," and the Basque priests of Baserri Gaztedi did not want to shoulder the drastic consequences of such accusations. Along with herria, a key concept was *herrigintza* (the making of a people-country). As the priest Zamora put it, "Ultimately we were doing anti-Francoist work by awakening the youth." But no political notion of *aberri* (nation), and even less Euskadi, was present at all in Baserri Gaztedi's ideology.

Baserri Gaztedi borrowed from Acción Católica the central concept of militancy as well as the action orientation. There were two categories of people: the *ekintzaile* (activist) and the *eragile* (instigator) of actions (the second group was composed mostly of the priests themselves and the local and regional lay leaders). The reunions were intent upon "analyzing the milieu with a Christian eye," for which the famous method of the Christian movements was adopted: "ver, juzgar, actuar" (see, judge, act). This was in stark contrast to the traditional peasant maxim "ver, oir, callar" (see, listen, be silent).

In Itziar the select group of eight fervent youths received their ideas about Baserri Gaztedi from Don José María. He learned about these Catholic movements during his seminary years and swiftly put their doctrine into practice. Despite its all-too-exemplary purpose of "turning the Gospel into action," the Baserri Gaztedi group of Itziar soon provoked rumors. What were they actually doing in their private weekly meetings? The Francoist mayor of Itziar apparently had been questioning Carlos, one of the eight, as to what was going on.

In the meantime a major break with the church-imposed sex roles and leisure habits was taking place. From time to time chestnut-gathering picnics were organized in which boys and girls participated jointly; these became major events that signaled a rupture with past customs. Reacting against the initial ascetic tendency to withdraw from the world, a new attitude of entering into any place, even dances, was favored by Baserri Gaztedi. The Baserri Gaztedi reunions themselves were soon attended jointly by boys and girls, which provoked comment.

Two major turnovers of priests occurred in Itziar in 1957: Don José María was transferred, and the old parish priest died. The new parish priest, Don Juan, was a man highly respected by priests and laypeople alike. In his political leanings he was *abertzale* (Basque nationalist) and had contacts with the PNV. He made major changes in the village church. A man of rich personality, he became an invaluable source of support for the younger priests serving in Itziar.

Don José María was replaced by a recently ordained priest whose first post was Itziar—Don Antonio. He was from a strongly abertzale family. One of his uncles, a priest, had been executed by Franco's troops during the civil war. His seminary education in San Sebastián during the fifties had been strictly in Spanish. One of his friends requested that there be courses to learn the Basque language and was ordered to beg pardon in public—this was 1954, and such was the affront inherent in the request.

Upon his arrival in Itziar, Don Antonio encountered the dynamic Baserri Gaztedi group composed of elements such as Martin from Isasi and José Mari from Andutzene. Fully supported by the parish priest, Don Antonio led the group until he left Itziar in 1960. By the time Don Antonio assumed direction of Baserri Gaztedi, Carlos, one of the original members questioned by the mayor, had stopped attending the weekly meetings. The group decided that it would be safer if Carlos actually attended the meetings; this would be a sign to the authorities that nothing strange or "political" was going on. They succeeded in bringing Carlos back to the meetings, and "he did get integrated very well in the group," as Don Antonio recalls. (Next chapter we will describe the lives of Carlos and Martin as two archetypal figures that reflect Itziar's recent history.)

The new leader's style was not as intensely devout as Don José María's. Besides his family tradition of intense Basque nationalism, his seminary education had made him already conscious of the cultural repression in which the Catholic church collaborated. Don Antonio had joined a group of six teachers and twenty seminarians learning the Basque language in his final seminary years. Baserri Gaztedi itself was evolving toward more social issues. The insistence upon spiritual exercises and not dancing the agarrado was being replaced by theater and other more educational "actions." Don Juan was an excellent drama director, and he is credited with staging about ten plays during the years 1957 to 1960. Some of them had considerable success both in Itziar and outside the village. Moreover, another great novelty for Itziar, they began to show movies nearly every Sunday.

EGI

The Baserri Gaztedi group became more politicized under the guidance of Don Antonio. Carlos's friend José Mari puts it this way, "What Don Antonio did was to say that politics was not a sin, that getting into politics was nothing more than any person's right." Don Antonio underscored the case of French Basques, who participated in democratic elections and therefore in politics. Under the new definition, politics simply meant assuming responsibility for the problems of a people and, moreover, "not getting into politics was in itself politics"; that is, being uncritical of the status quo imposed by Franco was in itself an act of political compliance.

To José Mari and the rest of Itziar's postwar generation, politics had previously always been depicted as a most dangerous thing, the "source of all evil," war being its perfect offspring. José Mari recalls: "At home, mother would always say that politics should be forgotten, that we had suffered enough already because of politics. But then the next day my family would again be telling stories of the war; they couldn't keep silent about them." Traumatized memory had to recall past experiences compulsively, but only as "stories," as narrative models, as clichés of past horror. Actual reflection on the stories, an emotional response to their implied meanings, or holding onto any ideological resistance to the military establishment was to be carefully avoided. It was useless pain, dangerous politics.

Don Antonio brought a Basque priest from France to speak to Itziar's militant youth on French Basque political organizations and on cooperativism.[5] The French priest brought firsthand experience and the message that Christians could engage in politics. That had a profound impact.

Soon after, a contact came from Zarautz to Itziar and talked with Martin about the advisability of joining EGI. EGI was the youth organization of the historical Basque Nationalist party (PNV). The contact, who was a convincing abertzale affiliated with the PNV, argued that Itziar was the only village in the area without a connection with the nationalist movement. Martin talked to José Mari and both decided to join. Martin explains, "that was a more genuine ekintza and we got into it." José Mari asked Don Antonio's opinion. The priest told him that it was their decision to make.

Why was EGI *benetakoagoa* (more genuine) than, say, a theater play? Martin felt it was more difficult and more risky, and it involved consciousness-raising as one rejected the repression of the people. The basic mission of EGI at the time was to disseminate propaganda. What really distinguished EGI activities from Baserri Gaztedi was its clandestine nature. Martin and José Mari had to attend meetings in Zarautz at 3:00 and 4:00 A.M. The propaganda itself was top secret—illegal. However, the mentality with which Martin and José Mari were operating in both Baserri Gaztedi and EGI was pretty much the same. In both organizations their motivations were summarized in the term *herrigintza* and what really mattered was concrete ekintza. They were already engaged in social and cultural promotion through the religious sodality Luistarrak and Baserri Gaztedi. The requirement of underground secrecy for the more political type of ekintza was a proof of its importance. The high risk involved in following the dictates of one's conscience exposed the intrinsically evil nature of the existing political establishment and gave a moral, almost sacred imperative to the ekintza.

The acronyms themselves were indicators of political insurgency. Besides EGI another acronym was heard for the first time by Martin and José Mari in one of the Zarautz secret meetings—ETA, which stands for Euskadi Ta Askatasuna (Euskadi and Freedom). The acronyms rivaled each other at the time; but for José Mari and Martin they did not present alternatives, they were basically the same thing—the clandestine, politically fateful challenge one had to face in order to assume responsibility for the Basque Country's prostration.

The year 1960 marked a turning point in Itziar. That spring, José Antonio Aguirre, the respected president of the Basque government-in-exile, died in Paris. In a time sequence that cannot be ignored, by the summer of 1960 a collective letter was written by 339 Basque priests to their bishops. It constituted the major Basque ethnopolitical statement drafted since the war. The letter had three parts: "Reaffirmation of Principles." "Analysis of the Reality," and "Defense of the Rights of the Basque Country." The priests vigorously denounced the political persecution "of the ethnic, linguistic, and social characteristics that God gave to the Basques." In their letter the 339 priests deemed this cultural genocide and found it "an imperative of our consciences" to denounce it. They underscored that the Basque language is "a necessary instrument for the evangelization and culture of the Basque Country," which "has a right to life and of being cultivated."

This was 1960. More than twenty years of Franco's dictatorship had gone by since the civil war. Not only had the normal democratic rights such as free association in political parties, a free press, and working unions been banned, but the native language itself, Euskera, was systematically abolished from the school system, the media, and even from the official church of which they, the priests, were custodians. As a result of this cultural repression, Basque people after the war became illiterate in their own language. Itziar was no exception, of course; none of my primary schoolteachers during the late fifties ever knew Basque or permitted us to speak it in the school. At home many parents, my own mother included, did not speak anything but Basque.

The letter caused a great stir. The newly awakening political forces welcomed it warmly; not so the bishop of the province. In Itziar he punished Don Antonio for having collected signatures on the letter, banishing him to a new destination, a very isolated small parish in a rural area. The first Sunday in his new parish, Don Antonio approached the altar to celebrate Mass and found that the pews were filled with Itziar's youth. He was so moved that he could scarcely proceed.

The First Fall

Despite the impact of the letter on the ecclesiastical and political establishment, the state-controlled media never made it public. EGI decided to circulate the letter during the nighttime pilgrimage to the sanctuary of the Virgin of Aranzazu, which used to take place annually on the last Sunday of August. As many as ten to fifteen thousand Basque youths regularly attended the event. It seemed like an excellent opportunity for the type of ultrasecret propaganda operation for which groups such as EGI and ETA were formed.

The mission failed, however. Having passed the propaganda package from France through the customs in Irun, the contact was arrested in San Sebastián's Amara train station. Among the names in his address book was José Mari from Itziar. On August 16, San Roque's Day, José Mari arrived in Deba from Bilbao to attend that town's fiesta. As he reached Deba he was told in a bar that a friend of his had been arrested. A few minutes later, Benito, a civil guard from Castile later married to an Itziar woman, and another civil guard arrested him. That San Roque's evening witnessed the first fall in Itziar, the first link in the chain of "terrorism" that still grips the village.

José Mari was taken to the civil guards' quarters, handcuffed, and conducted to a vehicle where the other three arrested members of his EGI cell were waiting for him. On the way to San Sebastián he succeeded in throwing away his address book. He spent the night in the basement of the guards' quarters in San Sebastián and next morning was called to the interrogation room. At first he denied all charges against him. He resisted torture until the next midday. But it became clear that someone else had spoken out, so he had to admit his involvement in EGI and the plan to spread the priests' letter. José Mari's chest was badly injured as the guards kicked him while he was rolling on the floor. Martin, meanwhile, was at home fearing the arrest that never came.

After the questioning, the guards pushed José Mari down a flight of stairs, dislocating his arm. They then took him to the prison of Martutene, where he stayed in solitary confinement for twenty-nine days in a humid cell. He lost his sense of time and became completely obsessed with trivial ideas such as figuring out which day it might be. After the twenty-nine days of isolation he was taken to the infirmary, where a German doctor cared for his arm. José Mari still wonders: "Could he have been a Nazi, from among those who helped Franco win the war?"

José Mari was detained in Martutene for another month before release. There he met other EGI people as well as founders of ETA such as Txillardegi and Etxabe. The fundamental issue José Mari remembers being discussed was the futility of activism limited to propagandizing. ETA people stressed that an armed struggle was imperative.

After torture and a month of solitary confinement José Mari was never again the same man. His health had been badly impaired. This he kept secret from everybody except his wife. During my fieldwork, twenty years after, he was still frequently ill and often had to be hospitalized. "The doctor tells me that I have an old tuberculosis; he asks me whether I have stayed in humid places." All he could think of were the boots striking his chest during the torture and the month of solitary confinment in the humid dungeon. During the autumn of 1981 he survived critical surgery on his lungs and has felt well since.

The Critique of Sacraments

The priest Don Antonio had taken a very important new step regarding sacramental practice: he instituted private talks between himself and each of the active Catholic youth outside the confessional. On a monthly basis, during these meetings between the priest and the youth, any personal or political issue could be discussed. Thus, conversations that previously could take place only within the sacramental context of confession were suddenly treated as nonsacramental. The priest could be seen as another man or even as a friend, rather than as a representative of God. Classically, Catholic confession includes five steps, which must be strictly observed if the sacrament is to be valid: examination of conscience, oral confession, repentance, firm purpose of amendment, and reparation.

When the youth of Itziar began to meet in open face-to-face conversation with Don Antonio the magnitude of the change went mostly unnoticed by them. Confessions were still confessions and private talks were private talks, but the programmed and methodical nature of the personal meetings had an impact on desacralizing the role of the priest and the issues discussed. The tension inherent in the new accommodation must have been two-directional. On the one hand, the words of the priest were no longer strictly sacramental given the new context; on the other, the priest could extend his influence to other domains, and his social or political opinions were likely to be perceived almost sacramentally. In any case, members of Itziar's first generation of youth actively involved in social and political matters have stressed to me the singular significance of these private talks in their personal participation in the nationalist movement.

When Don Antonio was punished by the bishop with removal from Itziar, he was replaced by another exceptionally reflective priest, Don Miguel. This is Don Miguel's own synthesis of his undertaking during the 1960 to 1962 years of service in Itziar:

> My main contribution to the group of activist Christians in Itziar was a critique of sacramental life. One's entire life has to be a sacrament. To confess and to receive Communion is not sufficient. You have to show you are a Christian in your daily life.

This was indeed unusual preaching for a Catholic priest in the early sixties. Consistent with his theories, Don Miguel ended up abandoning his own sacrament of sacred vows and writing a book called *Sekularrak Apaiztu* (Laymen to the Priesthood). He argues in it that the priesthood as a sacrament resides in the community of believers and does not necessarily have to be tied to the historical forms imposed by the church, such as celibacy or male exclusiveness. He tried, in his own terms, to purge the religion of Itziar, anchored in sacramental practice, of its "magical" elements. From the very beginning one of the most painful priestly duties for him was hearing confessions; the judgment of what constituted sin was highly problematic when people would confess as delicts what in his opinion should not be taken as sin. He ended up listening to whatever was divulged and simply giving absolution without comment.

Not all the four priests of Itziar shared these innovative attitudes. Don Bitor, for example, who stayed in Itziar from the middle forties to the middle seventies, continued preaching the classical religious scheme in which sacraments were the only channels of grace mediated through the Amabirjina. But by the middle sixties people were disagreeing with him and publicly questioning his views on the necessity of sacraments.

Don Miguel's desacramentalization should not be misunderstood, however. What he called into question was the dichotomy between sacramental religiosity reserved to church practices and everyday practicality left for worldly affairs. The change he suggested pointed to a different experiencing of the sacramental life, but concurrently it demanded a more religious experience of worldly life—the entirety of life became a sacrament. The desacramentalization of church symbols is thus complemented by the resacramentalization of daily experience.

The great lesson that Itziar villagers received about sacraments from Don Miguel, however, derived not only from his preaching but even more from his personal example. In 1967 he secularized himself and, loyal to his pedagogical method, came to Itziar to explain to his former parishioners his decision to abandon the priesthood in its present form so that they would not be scandalized. He was surprised that, contrary to his fears, Itziar parishioners actually understood and accepted his change quite positively. It was the first known case in Itziar's history in which a priest presented his decision to desert the priesthood in public as a layman while employing theological and sociological arguments. On the local level the magnitude of his lesson reminds one of Luther's reform. At the provincial level his book was decisive in emptying the seminary. In successive years other priests who had served in Itziar were to teach again the same lesson of laicization. The obvious statements were: sacraments need not be eternal; Christianity can relativize sacramental experience; one can be saved by following what his or her conscience dictates; personal faith and personal experience take precedence over any institutional vow or form; the magical act of sacramental performance can be dispensed with.

Yet, unlike Luther, Don Miguel did not give up the sacrament of the priesthood as such; his argument was that the priesthood resides in the community of believers. This critique of the sacramental experience and traditional forms of religiosity became a key element in the teaching of Herri Gaztedi.

Herri Gaztedi and Gaztetxoak

José Mari's imprisonment and Don Antonio's removal from the village in 1960 marked a political watershed for Itziar. Parents became alarmed and tightened control of their sons. The church definitely seemed to be "doing politics" after all. Under the new priest, Itziar was experiencing some interesting revisions in the sacramental doctrine, but the more strictly social or political dimensions were in retreat.

A new name was substituted for priest Zamora's Baserri Gaztedi. After Zamora left for Madrid in 1964 to be the national director, the new provincial *conciliario* (counselor) and undisputed leader until 1970 was the priest Xipri. The new name for the organization was Herri Gaztedi (People's Youth). *Herri* means "town, country, people" and is indicative of a significant change of orientation from the *baserri*, which is the name for the traditional farmstead.

Promulgated by Don Juan, the parish priest, a new wave of militancy in Itziar was under way by 1965. A Herri Gaztedi group was formed in which Gregorio (younger brother of José Mari) and concerned young women such as Marisol and Miren took part. Xipri would personally attend the meetings in Zumaia, where another priest, Juanito, who had just left Itziar, was in charge. Itziar's group started to interact with other district groups in Zumaia. This had an important effect. Acquaintance among the activist representatives of the small towns around Zumaia such as Ukia, Aizarna, Aizarnazabal, Arrua, and Itziar led to expanded cooperation among those communities in organizing their village events and in spending the weekends together. The already established mentality of doing ekintzak prevailed. The method in use was still "see, judge, act."

Any ekintza was held to be fine; what was more difficult was the development of a critical attitude. What really bothered these militants at times was that in their meetings they had problems finding actual cases to which to apply their seeing-judging-acting method. Family problems and the difficult relationships between boys and girls provided most of the opportunities. This was a very telling situation, and Itziar's youth would find itself in the same situation in other periods as well: there was a compelling urge to do things without the ability to know for sure what should be done.

During these same years, Herri Gaztedi never took into consideration that something could be done from inside the town council as well. Representative of the official polity, it belonged to the adversary and was simply ignored. This nearly complete lack of institutional concern was symptomatic of the action mentality typical of the times. It was rooted in the peasant mentality of the baserria by which society's image is one of individual households rather than institutional networks. It was sustained by the cultural perception that efficacy resides in sudden dramatic actions rather than in a steady routine. The town council, the school system, adult education, sanitation, industrial labor relations, and recreation were larger issues beyond ekintza requiring a policy and continuity. The search for cases was implicitly the search for new social and cultural orientations.

The new director of Herri Gaztedi, Xipri, was not particularly fond of ekintza. Known for his intensity, occasionally a source of dismay for the Itziar group, Xipri put priority into something else—ideology. Reading, studying, lecturing were more conducive to that. Marxism became the fashionable topic. The real ekintza was to spread new revolutionary ideas and obtain the commitment of the most dedicated youth to them. The organization's leaders gave lectures on the hot topics of capitalism and communism.

From the very beginnings of Baserri Gaztedi the key pedagogical idea had been one of individual growth for the realization of one's own personality. In the baserri mentality this was summed up in being *jatorra* (authentic) and having the personal fortitude to be able to say no to what did not meet certain standards. With Herri Gaztedi this same notion evolved into the organization becoming a platform from which each individual received the necessary social and political instruction so that he or she was prepared to make personal decisions. Still under the direct supervision of the ecclesiastical hierarchy, the declared apoliticism of the organization was combined with this preparatory work in raising ideological awareness. Officially it was apolitical; in practice, dozens of the youths prepared by Herri Gaztedi were getting into the real stuff—ETA.

Loyal to the powerful tradition of Itziar's activist organizing, from 1967 on a new youth organization flourished with remarkable impetus. For a young male, after taking at twelve the "Big Communion"[6] and leaving school, it was still too soon to get into the Luistarrak. The idea that there should be an organization for the youth between ages twelve and sixteen materialized, and the organization took the name Gaztetxoak, which means simply "adolescents."

A group of about sixty youths became affiliated. They were distributed in *bailarak* (neighborhoods): Itxaspe, Mardari, Egia, Anduzpe. Each community section had its own cashier. Xili was the general cashier and José Antonio the president. An organization without the church's protection was still unthinkable, and they chose as their priest-in-charge Don Juan José, with whom they got along very well. The basic organizational structure hinged upon the collection of monthly dues of a duro (five pesetas). Following the Luistarrak churchly model, Gaztetxoak members had as their major event a meeting on the second Sunday of each month during the morning Mass. They collected the cash in the sacristy. Since the organization was patronized by the church it was normal that this relationship should be expressed by some churchgoing practice. But, as Xili made clear, unlike the Luistarrak, who emphasized sacramental practice, the new youth organization was primarily based on the collection of cash. With the collected money, Gaztetxoak bought decks of cards, board games, and other recreational items. From time to time they held chocolate-eating parties or organized excursions.

In 1969 Don Juan José left Itziar. By 1965 the parish priest Don Juan had left as well and had been replaced by a new priest, who took charge of the Gaztetxoak. During the 1969 to 1971 years the youth organization and the new parish priest became intensely inimical to each other. There was, for instance, constant feuding over the keys to the *salon*, a church locale prepared for village meetings. The parish priest was reluctant to hand the keys over each time the Gaztetxoak wanted them for a meeting. They found it infuriating that he would go to play *mus* cards when he should be attending a meeting. What finally snapped the youths' patience was the incident of the excursion. When the parish priest heard that the group was thinking of a bus trip, he arranged the itinerary on his own without consulting them. This ended the relationship between the Gaztetxoak and the parish priest. The break amounted to an end of the relationship between the youth and the church.

The youths started accusing the parish priest of falseness, an accusation they brought to the Guraso Elkartea (Association of Parents) of Itziar. This was an association recently created by parents such as Martin from Isasi under the church's patronage. A representative from the youth group was permitted to attend the meetings. Through Martin, chairman of the Guraso Elkartea, the Gaztetxoak succeeded in getting a key to the salon. However, by then the youths were thinking of having a locale of their own. They asked to build it under the church, where there was a basement space that could accommodate the meetings. The parish priest denied them permission.

Unprotected by the church, Gaztetxoak as an organization soon disappeared. They had started as a junior organization modeled after the Luistarrak, whose demise was also provoked by the parish priest's antagonism to the opinion of the youth. He regarded the youths' adversarial attitude as a sudden change and rejection of any priestly presence at their meetings. The youths, who had enjoyed Don Juan José's leadership, blamed the dissolution of their organization and their subsequent distancing from the church on what they perceived as deceitful behavior on the part of the parish priest.

The Seminarians' Leadership

During the fifties and sixties in a rural area such as Itziar, the only practical possibility for a peasant youth to get secondary education was in the seminary. By the middle sixties some technical schools were attended by a few youths, nearly exclusively boys. Still well into the seventies, with some rare exceptions, the people who had formally attended secondary school were seminarians. In the late fifties four youths from Itziar attended the diocesan seminary of San Sebastián. In veiled rivalry with the diocesan priests, religious orders sent as well their "vocation-collectors" to primary schools to recruit schoolboys for the seminary. Blending exotic missionizing ideals with pictures of a new *pelota* court or playground, they tried to rouse the dormant interior by calling in impressionable young boys.

In the late sixties, Manolo, one of Itziar's youths, had just left the seminary. He was in his late teens. In addition to the increasingly politicized climate, recent critiques of the traditional forms of priesthood, such as the one by Don Miguel described above, had emptied the seminary of San Sebastián. Under the leadership of Manolo, in 1969 Herri Gaztedi was again organized in Itziar with a vigor only comparable to that of Baserri Gaztedi during the late fifties.

Another key figure was Mari Tere, who lived in Itziar from early 1970 to 1975. Previously she had lived in southern Spain, working as a lay missionary. As Manolo was in charge of the male Herri Gaztedi group, Mari Tere took responsibility for the female group of twelve to fourteen girls. Upon the dissolution of Gaztetxoak, its most active members joined Herri Gaztedi; under the care of an older youth they formed the youngest branch of the organization with meetings and activities of their own.

Herri Gaztedi had four levels of organization: town- or village-based groups such as Itziar; zonal ones such as Zumaia, to which Itziar belonged; provinces, Guipúzcoa and Vizcaya mostly; and the Basque Country. At the zonal level, the *responsable,* or person in charge, in Zumaia with a direct influence in Itziar was José Mari, another seminarian. The priest Xipri was the provincial leader; in 1970 another priest, Sakone, replaced him. By then Herri Gaztedi had in Guipúzcoa alone, besides the priest counselors, two male and two female youth *liberados* (liberated). These liberados were dedicated full time to organizational tasks, and their election was a major statement of the direction in which Herri Gaztedi was being led. The social base of the liberados was still the baserria.

The revival of Herri Gaztedi in Itziar was "quite easy," in the words of José Mari. There was the "old people's" example to begin with (the Baserri Gaztedi cohort), and there were meeting places, another key factor for the organization. One priest who had recently served in Itziar was at the time in Zumaia. There were the ties already established between Itziar and Zumaia from 1965 to 1967. Most of all, and this is emphasized by José Mari, "there was an ambience" as a consequence of the previous history of Itziar.

This ambience was best expressed in the existence of *burrukalariak* (fighters) among the youth, those with the determination to carry out the work of organizing the youth and pushing for the required changes. This fighting spirit was aimed initially at the parish priest because of the restrictions he was accused of imposing on the organization. The new young priest of Itziar attended the meetings. He was seen by the youths as an emissary of the parish priest to control what was going on and to report back. The incident that signaled the end of any church participation in Herri Gaztedi was the priest's walking away from a meeting, infuriated, charging that "this is all Marxism." An open confrontation between the church and Herri Gaztedi followed. The same social movement that only ten years earlier was an example of religious militancy in 1970 launched an active campaign to discredit the local priests in the eyes of the villagers and to stop the youths from going to church. Itziar's practicing parents were upset by their children's desertion of religion.

Meetings of Herri Gaztedi differed according to whether their purpose was one of ideologization, action, or critique and self-critique. The meetings consisted basically in reading and discussing *Gazte*, the organization's official publication. The leaders at the zonal level met twice a month; their agenda focused on how to lead a group and how to fight. Practical ekintzak were emphasized—provoking labor conflicts, finding solutions to town issues, writing graffiti, antiauthoritarian acts in the family, and so on. Literacy campaigns to encourage fluency in Basque were also launched during these years.

Literature that Herri Gaztedi was reading at the time included the works of French philosophers Garaudy and Althusser and those of Freud, Marx, Mao, and Lenin. However, the basic literature was provided by *Gazte*, the mimeographed, bimonthly publication in which the organization expounded its ideology and goals. A review of *Gazte* becomes essential to understanding the thinking of Itziar's activist group during the late sixties and early seventies. It is in this short period between 1969 and 1974 that apparently radical changes concerning religious practice, sexuality, and political ideology were adopted by Itziar's youth.

Gazte had primarily a pedagogical purpose. An important theme was to explicate the meanings, goals, and techniques of the ekintzak. It constantly reminded that action and reflection should be coupled. There were articles dedicated to schooling. Commitment was seen as inseparable from personal fulfillment. As a backdrop against which to measure the abnormalcy of the Spanish political situation, the United Nations International Charter of Human Rights was constantly invoked. The first criticisms of the capitalist system appeared.

In the summer of 1968, ETA assassinated the chief police inspector of Guipúzcoa, Melitón Manzanas, in retaliation for the killing of ETA's top leader, Txabi Etxebarrieta. Madrid imposed martial law, and hundreds of suspects were imprisoned amid rumors of police brutality. The December issue of *Gazte* dedicated nine pages to the issue of violence, which was becoming a major social problem. Its logic was stated as follows: "If the situation is to be defined in terms of violence, there is already an ever-present institutional violence; any response to it, even pacifism, is violence. Violence therefore is the basic agent of social change; and whoever refuses to participate in it lacks personal commitment."

As simple as this logic of polarization could be, it was also an intimately persuasive one after thirty years of dictatorship in which all political and linguistic rights were indefinitely suspended. The same issue of *Gazte* has an article, "The Present Situation and the Christian," that begins by quoting Jesus: "If any man would come after me, let him deny himself and take up his cross daily and follow me. For whoever would save his life will lose it; and whoever loses his life for my sake, he will save it" (Luke 9:23–24). The text is a clear indication of the bridge between the appeal to resist institutional oppression and the Christian models of sacrifice and martyrdom.

By 1969 *Gazte*'s pages were dedicated increasingly to ideological topics. The April–May issue was devoted almost entirely (forty-five pages) to socialism: its mentality, its history, why socialism, socialism today, socialism and Christianity. The issue of June–July continued in another thirty pages the history of socialism and Soviet communism. It also contained a significant section on socialism and sin, which made the connection between Christian mentality and the new ideology strikingly clear. It was socialism invested with the religious morality of sin and salvation. Socialism was not seen as an optional ideological system. Not to fight for socialism equals being an accomplice of sinful structures and actually being in a state of sin by omission. Grace, fight, and socialism were lined up together against sin, apathy, and capitalism. Another article in the same issue, "God and Matter," defined God in Teilhard de Chardin's terms as a "spirit," as the alpha and omega that imposes energy and direction on evolution.

From there on *Gazte* divided its pages roughly into the following sections: social philosophy, basic concepts of Marxist economy, psychology and sexuality, Christianity and world commitment, methodology of action, and news. Freud, L. H. Morgan, Malinowski, Simone de Beauvoir are some of the authors quoted in explanations of basic psychological concepts, the institution of the family, or female inequality. The world-news section paid attention to major liberation movements or conflicts that might apply to the Basque situation, such as the conflict in Ireland and the Vietnam War against United States imperialism.

By the fall of 1971 "the pedagogy of liberation" became a fashionable topic. I. Illich and P. Freire, to whom *Gazte* dedicated a long interview in the February 1972 issue, were widely quoted. E. Osa's timely book *Pedogogia eta Gizartea* (Pedagogy and Society) popularized Freire's ideas and became the textbook for cultural activists working on evening literacy campaigns or in children's *ikastolak* (Basque schools).

Radicalization and Collapse of Herri Gaztedi

The zenith of Herri Gaztedi was marked in December 1970 by the Burgos trial, the most significant political event in Euskadi since the civil war. Sixteen ETA people were tried militarily in the Castilian capital of Burgos on charges of illegal organization and the murder of the police officer Manzanas. Six of the accused were given death penalties, later commuted by Franco in response to protests and appeals of leniency from many world capitals, and the others were sentenced to a total of 519 years in prison. General strikes and street demonstrations were staged in Basque cities during the trial; demonstrators attacked Spanish embassies in Western Europe; and intellectuals and artists endorsed ETA's struggle. Sartre, for instance, wrote: "The Basque issue imposed itself at Burgos by *necessity*" (1971 : xi); "All over the world . . . Euskadi has become known . . . as a martyr country fighting for its national independence" (ibid. : xxix).

For the first time, an international airing was given to ETA's political claims. At this crucial moment Herri Gaztedi took upon itself the organization of the previously mentioned general strike and mass demonstrations in the Basque area as a protest against the Burgos trial. This proved for Herri Gaztedi an enormous success that bolstered its morale. The message that the masses could be organized was unmistakable, and Herri Gaztedi had shown itself to be the organization with the most effective apparatus at the regional level.

During 1970 and 1971 Itziar's Herri Gaztedi met regularly and maintained close ties with district headquarters in Zumaia. A most important element in this last stage of Herri Gaztedi was "ideological commitment." The following incident illustrates the manner in which this commitment was induced as well as its potential for conflict. One of the members of Herri Gaztedi was Martin's younger brother, who was working in the baserri cooperative. The responsable from Zumaia in a meeting told him that since he was working in a cooperative he should analyze the relationship between cooperativism and capitalism. The latter was considered the sum of all social and economic evils by Herri Gaztedi. When he refused, the responsable insisted he leave the group, which he did. As a result, the very continuity of the entire group was put at risk.

The Burgos trial had resulted in an enormous organizational success for Herri Gaztedi. And yet, ironically, as Koldo (a liberado and key figure in Herri Gaztedi between 1968 and 1972) later explained to me, "After the role played in the Burgos trial a big crisis arose within the organization. We couldn't see a clear course; we didn't know what to do with the organization." The problem was that there were many initiatives but no real coordination. They had a network of seventy responsables throughout the entire province, each of them in charge of a group such as Itziar. "But what for? The basic contradiction," Koldo pointed out, "was between religious faith and political action."

The Herri Gaztedi group in Itziar was very active in this period. The establishment of an ikastola for Itziar's nursery school was achieved. The literacy campaign continued. The village fiestas provided an important occasion to display the newly emerging folk singers and artists as well as the traditional *bertsolariak* (troubadours). Special youth days continued to be organized.

In 1971 ETA split into two factions known as the Fifth Assembly and the Sixth Assembly. The Fifth Assembly advocated a hard-line activist and militaristic course and accused the Sixth Assembly of *españolismo* (Spanishness) and of watering down or compromising the Basque ideal of national independence. The Sixth Assembly, inspired by international socialist ideals, stressed social revolution over ethnic nationalism. Through Herri Gaztedi, ETA's major split over the priority of social or national struggle became the dominant ideological theme in Itziar. This ideological controversy covered, in fact, a much more pragmatic and consequential stance regarding armed struggle. Emphasis on class struggle lent itself to giving priority to the organization of workers. Emphasis on national liberation inevitably led to advocating armed struggle's undisputed primacy. *Gazte*'s spirited rhetoric was filtered (in Itziar) through these compelling dichotomies.

Herri Gaztedi's crisis had been generated by its apparent inefficiency vis-à-vis ETA's much more consequential ekintzak. ETA defendants' unambiguous acceptance of armed struggle and a Marxist-Leninist ideology in the Burgos trial made it seem that Herri Gaztedi was a group of devout believers unable to step out of the church's lap and biblical rhetoric. As Mari Tere put it, "It was ETA that was clearly uncovering the contradictions within society." Compared to ETA theirs seemed like a rosary of reunions and mere analytical discussions. The old problem was still alive. Mari Tere pointed out, "The low political consciousness was combined with the momentous efficacy of the ekintza."

Meanwhile the church's repressive attitudes were becoming unbearable. Permission to meet had to be obtained continuously. Organization of any festival was plagued with censorship problems. When relations with the parish priest were strained, festivals might be kept unauthorized until the last minute. Sometimes permission was denied. *Gazte* began to insist upon direct action, noting that "talk is cheap." Something else was plainly required.

In this period an event occurred at Herri Gaztedi's provincial level that reflected the magnitude of the organization's crisis. Koldo's question "But what for?" was directed at the whole organization. A crisis of institutional backing was combined with a crisis of purpose. Without the church's nominal protection, could an organization with such blatantly Marxist revolutionary rhetoric stand by itself in such a politically repressive period? The organization had no problem in setting eschatological and humanitarian goals or preaching social and political liberation. Yet in practice this amounted to simple and alarming decisions such as having to accept a clandestine life-style or armed struggle.

An influential liberado of Herri Gaztedi at the time tells the story of a crucial event:

> We decided to give the entire organization to ETA-Sixth. We didn't feel that we ourselves were able to handle it. We convened seventy responsables in Santa Teresa for two days so that the people of ETA could talk to them and take over the entire organization. They came, talked for an hour, and left saying that they had other things to do. If we had little capacity to handle the organization under those circumstances, ETA-Sixth had even less. This was a terrible dirty trick, one that I will never forget.
>
> There was an urgent need to find a way out, and having become too worried about what might happen, each one started doing whatever he thought was most appropriate. This was a tremendous error, one that I have regretted a thousand times; that is, not to have preserved the unity of the organization.

Someone proposed the creation of clandestine committees within factories, schools, and towns. It should also be noted that within ETA's internal division the Sixth Assembly tendency stressed first the social revolution.

In Itziar the collapse of Herri Gaztedi signaled the end of a unitary youth movement in which village solidarity prevailed over ideological differences. By 1974, Manolo and Mari Tere joined OIC (Organización Internacional Comunista [International Communist

Organization]). Isidro became affiliated with LKI (Langileria Komunista Iraultzailea [Revolutionary Communist Workers]). Another influential member, Martin Txiki, became a member of LAIA (Langile Abertzale Iraultzaileen Alderdia [Patriotic Revolutionary Workers' Party]). Others, such as Xili, Bixente, Arrate, and José Antonio, were not affiliated with any party. The notion itself of party was indeed a new element to those used to Herri Gaztedi's pedagogical and nonpartisan dynamics.

It was in Santa Teresa (the church's provincial house for spiritual exercises) that Itziar youths had their initial spiritual conversion in 1956. That commitment to social and religious reform materialized in Itziar in the organization of the Baserri Gaztedi, which later evolved into Herri Gaztedi. For almost two decades this organization promoted and channeled the ekintzak of Itziar's youth. This same building of Santa Teresa was now housing the end of the religious organization and witnessing again a crucial conversion: the former religious rhetoric and pedagogical goals had to be dismissed for the youth to plainly assume the politico-military goals of an armed group seeking national liberation—Herri Gaztedi had been converted into ETA.

ETA

What ETA reveals to us is the need which all *men have, including centralists, to reaffirm their particularities against abstract universality. Sartre*

I rebel—*therefore we* exist. *Camus,* The Rebel

Even while Herri Gaztedi was collapsing and losing older members, a new generation of the Gaztetxoak continued. Arrate and Xili, members of Herri Gaztedi, took charge of the group. *Gazte,* as in the past, provided an agenda and the literature for the meetings. Sexuality was the hottest topic in these meetings. Mountain picnics and other activities were also organized. By the end of 1973, Manolo was still the main leader in Itziar's Herri Gaztedi while he was following step by step its disintegration. Among the Herri Gaztedi Itziar youths were Atxega, Juan Mari, José Ignacio, and Iñaki. Talking of them, Manolo observes, "They had a terrible rebelliousness within them, they wanted activism at any cost."

The one issue that in the view of these youths radically separated the nature and methods of any sort of political struggle was the acceptance or rejection of armed resistance. This amounted to involvement or not with ETA. Manolo, their mentor, was against giving priority to the activities of a small nucleus of fighters. Rather, he argued for the organization of the working masses. In this respect he remained true to the philosophy of the recently dissolved Herri Gaztedi organization, which contended that the social contradictions emanated from economic oppression. The true revolution, therefore, would have to come from the working class itself. The counterargument was that this was fine in theory but what about practice?

In case there were doubts as to the efficacy of armed struggle, on December 22, 1973, ETA carried out the most spectacular action in its entire history: the Spanish prime minister, Carrero Blanco, was killed in an explosion that sent his car skyrocketing over the roof of an apartment building. As Franco's right-hand man, Carrero Blanco had been expected to prolong Francoism when the aging dictator died. The Spanish Left was delighted and Basques were jubilant. ETA had reached new heights.

In Itziar, Manolo could not convince his young group that the organization of the masses was a more urgent task than ETA's ekintza. They were definitely uninterested in political groupings and polemics. They were bored with what seemed just rhetorical subtleties. One youth said, "We told him to go shove it, since we wanted a contact with ETA." Manolo wasn't the only opinion maker in Itziar who disagreed with ETA's militant approach. Isidro, who was also an ex-seminarian and was affiliated with a communist minority group on the radical Left, was against giving tactical priority to armed struggle. His younger brother Iñaki was in the group seeking contacts with ETA, and the two brothers argued intensely over the issue.

Herri Gaztedi offered a platform to raise political consciousness. The beneficiary was ETA. Dozens of militants, once they were ready, left Herri Gaztedi to join ETA. As Manolo put it, "In the 1970 to 1975 years the youth that didn't get into ETA in Itziar was simply lacking balls, for ideologically everybody agreed with ETA's premises." Manolo's own case, as well as Isidro's or Mari Tere's, is a significant qualification of this statement. Nevertheless, it accurately reflects the most salient political perception among youths at that period after the Burgos trial: "Here the only one who does anything is ETA." Carrero's killing had taken this belief a step further. It was a *real* ekintza.

ETA had had internal divisions between its Fifth and Sixth assemblies, ideological discussions on the priority of the working-class problem or the national problem and, accordingly, over the tactical uses of armed struggle. Yet the local reading of ETA stemmed largely from reaction to the media. What the state-controlled TV and newspapers deemed "criminal" and "terrorist" was believed to be precisely what was hurting the enemy. The history of ETA seemed to offer the lesson that political efficacy can best be measured by the degree of denunciation of an action in the media. The media reported on ETA's endemic violence. It did not report on ETA's internal debates over conflicting alternatives.

Atxega, José Ignacio, Iñaki, and Juan Mari decided to form an ETA cell. They had first participated for about three years in the Gaztetxoak junior organization, and then in Herri Gaztedi under Manolo's guidance in Itziar and under Sakone's in Eibar. Despite Itziar's tradition of activist involvement, theirs was going to be an entirely new start, a thoroughly ETA commando unity with an unambiguous acceptance of armed struggle.

They were still very young—in their mid teens—but they thought they had already had their share of ideological instruction. Their alternatives were clearly Manolo's OIC silent organizational and theoretically loaded type of involvement or ETA's bold ekintza. As Mari Tere observed in talking of their motivations, "There was, on the one hand, the issue of heroism and adventurism and, on the other hand, the alternative between active and passive militantism. The active [that is, ETA] is easier and has rewards that the passive [that is, organization of the masses] has not." Juan Mari and José Ignacio recognized that ETA's type of action was easier for them to understand at the time, adding that it was also more efficacious. Manolo, despite his disagreement over their joining ETA, especially because they were so young, nevertheless stressed that the four youths did take the responsibility for their political decisions seriously.

The mutual selection of the four shows that they wanted to inoculate themselves from any danger of undisciplined excess in their midst. They did not invite another close companion because "he sometimes would like to be on his own, and also he could be a bit of a *quinqui* [bandit] sometimes." Despite their closest friendship in recreational outings, this youth was excluded because he had not given signs of political motivation. They pointed as an example to his not having participated in Herri Gaztedi.

Juan Mari, José Ignacio, and Iñaki were at the time studying in Deba and Zarautz in secondary technical schools. Their teachers in Deba told me that José Ignacio and Juan Mari were considered top students in their classes because of their grades and industriousness. Earlier the three of them had been altar boys in Itziar. When asked about their reactions on reading in the newspapers about their ex–altar boys being involved in ETA activities, Itziar's priests expressed astonishment and lack of understanding. The three, because of their records as altar boys, school performance, and group leadership, had seemed the most promising youths of the village.

These three invited Atxega, who was then twenty, to join them. While he had been working in a factory in Deba, which produced padlocks, he had participated in a strike and had been fired. He and the workers took the factory to court and won the case, but Atxega was never rehired. As a consequence he started working as a waiter, his occupation when he joined ETA.

The four unexpectedly made their first contact with an ETA member during the fiestas of Bergara. But the connection did not work this time and "the contact was lost." They insisted that Manolo find them another contact with ETA. An appointment was made for a Saturday afternoon in one of Itziar's bars with someone coming from Zarautz. The secret mark was that he would have a cigarette over his ear. It was top secret and utmost precautions were required—they were already in ETA.

A personal account of these processes was given to me in February 1981 by Juan Mari:

J. Z.: Could you describe for me the mental context in which you entered ETA?

J. M.: Well, the village tradition was a big influence. When we were twelve years old we had started already with Arrate [in Herri Gaztedi]. We could go to the mountains; we would discuss sexuality. On the other hand, there was a certain ambience in the village—political, social. There was a certain movement going on. What previously had been created by the church and so on. We ourselves had an enormous component of the church, the idealism, there was a lot of that: justice and equality, or things like that. Right away we connected our ethical-religious concerns with Marxism, as if saying, there is nothing more religious than Marxism. In a way that was the first simple connection. That was supposed to be the most authentic. That was the true mode of struggle. And on the other hand it must have been our desire to become men. Also, that was the easiest way. Compared with the theoretical tedious discussions of OIC of course it was; it was easier because we wouldn't see things too much. And also probably because then it [involvement in ETA] was more efficacious, although nowadays maybe not. Our affair, deep down, was unconscious: we didn't even know what we were doing, you never know what you are doing. I am not sorry for anything we did, it was great, but we weren't very conscious of what we were doing. We were young.

J. Z.: It must have been an almost mythical thing.

J. M.: It was a complete thing that would include everything, a religion, a total thing.

J. Z.: Total in which sense? Easiest in which sense? For getting into ETA seems the hardest thing. You mean easier than OIC.

J. M.: Yes. Then you know there was always a downgrading of theories, the primacy of praxis. Also it was most likely that ETA was more worthwhile then. Everything is interconnected. I remember I used to read about an arrest in the newspapers, and how it would enrage me. It was maybe as when you saw on the TV, cowboys against the Indians, and you were always on the side of the Indians, weren't you? There was something of that sort. Well, I was always on ETA's side, since I was eleven, or since I was nine, I don't know since when because I would see a certain thing, an "aureole." Then it would attract me at the level of adventure as well. There were all those things. And then, our political stories [*rollos*], and Marxism, and values, and an egalitarian society, and all those stories as well, of course. Also at that time [when they were involved in ETA] we worked in a workshop, and we used to live the boss/worker issue more vividly than now. In sum, we lived another idealism, we experienced it much more than now. But it seems to me now that it was partly absurd, that it all couldn't be very real.

J. Z.: You attended the Professional School, but that had no incentives?

J. M.: We used to go to the school, I don't know what for. On the other hand, I used to come out very well in the school. Since we had to go we would study a little bit as well. But otherwise it had no appeal, it had lost any incentive at all for me, surely because of the political business. Our only value in life was the political matter. I was also rather religious when I was ten or twelve years old: I used to believe in God and those stories quite a bit.

(Zuriko, younger than Juan Mari, himself having been unsuccessful in carrying out his intention to join ETA, takes part in the conversation.)

Z.: For me the story of ETA has been adventurism and heroism.

J. M.: Of course there was heroism, but you always have behind that an idealism, something for justice. I don't see clearly that there was any desire for sacrifice, but I can see that there was a religious matter.

Z.: What we knew about what socialism was, or what Marxism was, was about one-tenth of what someone from OIC knew.

J. M.: We [Juan Mari and his three friends] knew a lot more than you did.[7] We used to take great responsibility. I think our business was deeper than that. There has always been a certain inferiority compared with the "españolistas" up to now.[8] It would seem that the abertzaleak were stupid, and people such as those of OIC were more intelligent. What I know of Marxism I know from that period. I wouldn't pick up one-tenth, but we would read and read. When we were thirteen we were reading Marta Haneker, Althusser, Lenin, and so on. I remember we were pro–working class. It is incredible, it is something to cry about, or to laugh about, that when we went to Martutene [San Sebastián's prison] there were there forty-two ETA people and that, with the exception of

> Ezkerra[9] and someone else, I am pretty sure we were the best informed. There were some who didn't even know Marx existed.

José Ignacio was the other member of the ETA cell living in Itziar when I did my fieldwork. He insisted on the normalcy of their joining ETA: "I am sure that there were in the Basque Country a thousand youths who would do the same thing we did. Only that we were lucky that during a town fiesta we stumbled upon a connection, and that's all."

The postwar generation of social activists was preceded in Itziar by a religious conversion that called for an exemplary life in order to transform the village. Two decades later an analogous transformation at a similar age had taken place once again among Itziar's most conscientious youth. José Ignacio insisted on the importance of idealism in their decision to join ETA: "Things such as the history of Che Guevara were fundamental. We, too, had to be models in the village." Talking about the factors that counted for their ETA involvement, his observation is revealing: "By far the most important among those was the village ambience." It was not the school milieu, or the factory, or the family that was seen as decisive in shaping their view of politics, but companionship (*lagunartea*).

Talking generally about the dangers and rewards involved in ETA, José Ignacio once summarized it all with this analogy: "It is a *joko* [game].[10] You don't conduct a robbery without preparation; you do it after a careful calculation. It is a joko. Life too is a joko, isn't it?"

On another occasion, while we were discussing heroism, he remarked:

> J. I.: I think that what matters there is that it is an unconscious act. I think that a conscious act is not heroic. For me an example was Ondarru; he was a hero in his unconsciousness.[11]
>
> J. Z.: What do you mean that he was not conscious?
>
> J. I.: Imagine now I am someone from ETA and I have to kill a guy, and you do it although you don't like it. And because of it you put your life in danger. And it is not that because your life is in danger you take the right to take someone else's life. It is entirely apart from your personal interest.

Juan Mari also remarked on this notion of unconsciousness and forced duty becoming aspects of heroic action. In another conversation he insisted, "We had no fear at all while we were in ETA. The day we kidnapped Berazadi I had less fear than now going through a police roadblock."[12] This quality of unconsciousness, to the point of psychological fearlessness, could, in fact, turn membership in ETA into a source of *juerga* (fun time), as they pointed out to me.

Tied to this enjoyment is the other crucial element of "group mystique." José Ignacio says, "We had an indescribable friendship among the four of us. In the presence of each other we used to feel an enormous protection. I still miss Iñaki [he was killed by a civil guard]; I dream of him constantly." I asked him what was so special about Iñaki, was it perhaps his capacity to give himself up totally to something? He replied: "No, it wasn't that. It is as when you like a girl, you don't know why you like her so much. It is sympathy, sincerity, humbleness . . ." Juan Mari similarly emphasized the sentimental bonds among themselves: "In an ekintza you become like brothers." However, despite this feast of comradeship, there were "painful steps to take such as breaking up the family bonds and leaving the village."

The Ekintzak

> *Who were we? What did we represent? Of what new ideas were we the heralds? . . . We wanted to act, act, act. Gramsci,* The Programme of Ordine Nuovo

> *There are criminals even more terrible than that one, men who have murdered a dozen people and feel no remorse at all. But this is what I noticed: the most hardened and unrepentant killer still knows that he is a "criminal"; that is, he realizes in his conscience that he has not acted rightly; but those Yevgeny Pavlovitch was speaking of refuse even to consider themselves criminals and they think they are in the right and—that*

> *they have even acted well, it almost comes to that. This seems to me where the terrible difference lies. And notice they are all young. Dostoevsky,* The Idiot

José Ignacio told me repeatedly, "Making ekintzak was our thing." He gave me this definition of an ekintza within ETA: "The ekintza is the ordeal by fire in which you test your personality." Within ETA an ekintza is an armed action, usually against the Spanish police, for military objectives. An ekintza implies a ritual condensation of action invested with premises of almost magical efficacy (see chapter 13). José Ignacio conceded that there was fear involved, "but this was a substantial aspect of the ekintza, one that would give satisfaction afterwards." It could be likened to an initiation ritual for the acquisition of a warrior identity. The singular importance of performing ekintzak was constantly reiterated by José Ignacio and Juan Mari: "There was nothing worse than having to wait without doing an ekintza." On one occasion they had to wait for a month until they were ordered to perform a given ekintza. They both told me, "We were burnt out, we had an awful time." José Ignacio spoke to me about the punishment inflicted by Che Guevara upon his guerrillas: "He would not allow them to participate in a combat; it yielded good results."

The "ordeal by fire" that the ekintza implies became the backdrop against which everything was measured. As such, it was the constant challenge that "either made you tougher or the opposite." It was never a conquered state of behavior but a "no-man's-land," which gave one either renewed courage to jump forward or shrink back. The "fire" aspect of ekintza is in telling contradiction with the features of unawareness and even fearlessness mentioned above. The obvious risks involved in their ekintzak were ominous, yet it all seemed to them in retrospect to be pervaded by unconsciousness.

When the liaison from Zarautz arrived in Itziar one Saturday afternoon in February at 4:00 P.M. with the cigarette behind his ear, the four young men proposed the first ekintza to him immediately. It was stealing dynamite from the construction works of an industrial estate in Itziar. They urged the liaison to bring them a truck for this ekintza; otherwise they would do it completely on their own, even if they had to carry dynamite from the storage site to some attic on their shoulders. This was their first successful and serious ekintza, and afterward a succession of others followed.

There is nothing much to be said about ETA's organizational structure from the descriptions offered by these former members, except perhaps about its insignificance in their daily activism. In theory ETA had an organic structure similar to that of Herri Gaztedi (described above). In practice the Itziar cell did not conform to such a scheme and, depending on practical needs, developed its own pattern within ETA. Initially, their link with the organization was their contact from Zarautz. After a few actions had been performed the contact was lost. By then they had earned their own status within the organization and, dismissing the intermediary they should have had at the provincial level, put themselves directly under Apala, a top ETA leader living in southern France, after spending a week with him at his hideout. The cell would choose objectives on its own initiative and simply ask permission to carry them out; a phone call was sufficient for that. The organizational apparatus relied entirely on the actual ekintza. Ironically, it was when they were arrested and had to be situated somewhere within ETA's structure that they learned most about it from the police. (Readers interested in ETA's history and organizational patterns should look at the works of Garmendia [1979], Jauregui [1981], and Clark [1984].)

In the summer of 1975 an event occurred that was crucial to the radicalization of Itziar's ETA quartet. In their first serious ekintza of February they had met Txiki, who had come with a truck to pick up the dynamite. In June, Txiki was caught by the police in Barcelona precisely the day he had an appointment with the Itziar cell. In September, he and Otaegi (another ETA operative) were tried, sentenced to death, and executed by a firing squad. The executions were protested by huge crowds of demonstrators throughout European capitals. Olof Palme, the Swedish prime minister, was seen in the street collecting money for the Spanish opposition to Francoism.

After the execution the details of Txiki's death were vividly described by Itziar's youth. In the presence of his mother and brother, Txiki had raised his left fist and shouted "Gora Euskadi Askatuta!" (Long life to a free Euskadi!). Then he, who was an emigrant from Extremadura in southern Spain, had started singing the Basque soldiers' song "Eusko Gudariak Gara" (We are Basque soldiers). After he was shot by the firing squad and fell, he went on singing the song "Eusko Gudariak Gara" until he died. The distribution of the bullets in Txiki's body was recounted with precision, as if it were the exact map of heroic martyrdom. During the final night awaiting execution, Txiki had written a few words, which soon became song and sacramental memory: "Tomorrow when I die, don't come to cry over me; I won't be beneath the ground, I am wind of freedom." Txiki had set a conclusive model of heroism for Itziar's youth, especially for those four teenage youths in Itziar for whom Txiki's death was not only a moving example of sacrificial offering but also the execution of a friend that demanded revenge out of loyalty to him.

They told me that "after Txiki and Otaegi's [death] we became much more radical." During the fall of 1975 they rented an apartment in Bilbao and began preparations for major operations. They became the most efficient cell of ETA. They told me with pride, "Most of what ETA did during that year was carried out by us." In the spring of 1976, as a consequence of the tragic ekintza that ended in the killing of a kidnapped industrialist, which will be described in the next chapter, they were arrested.

After the initial three days of torture and terror in the police station, on the fourth day Juan Mari heard a tune being whistled; it was one of their favorite songs. The words of the song (by the poet Artze) went: "If I had cut her wings / she wouldn't go away, / she would be mine; / but then she would never be a bird, / but then she would never be a bird / and I loved the bird / and I loved the bird." It was José Ignacio at the other end of the corridor. There were no words to describe the tune's effect in uplifting Juan Mari's spirit. He replied with another tune, "Eusko Gudariak Gara." Atxega was still lying on the ground in the corridor, unable to stand or speak. High-voltage electrical charges had been repeatedly applied to his testicles. Iñaki had barely escaped by taking the bus to San Sebastián, and Atxega had been arrested the same afternoon in Itziar. In a few days, Atxega would join the new choir in the police quarters. From there they passed to Martutene's prison. Their spirits were high again.

The Return of the Heroes

Franco had died the previous November (1975), and King Juan Carlos had replaced him without issuing a general amnesty. The Basque region increasingly became involved in a petition of amnesty for its *gudariak* (soldiers). In Itziar, two months after the young commandos were arrested, there was an "Amnesty Week" organized by the local youth that included speakers, ex-prisoners, movies on the prisoners' lives, and so on. The parents of Itziar's prisoners were present during the events. At the end of the week, a sit-in and lock-out were staged in the church to demand the release of the prisoners. A demonstration with big photographs of the jailed Juan Mari, José Ignacio, and Atxega and the exiled Iñaki was headed by their parents and went through Itziar's streets. When the demonstration passed the house of one of the four young men, his name was shouted with the words "Out!" or "Back home!" The impressive silence of the demonstration echoed even larger after these sporadic shouts. Faces could not hide the deeply felt emotion of the dramatic event. The village was performing something akin to an incorporation ritual of its crimes and prisoners. The significance of this "Amnesty Week" and demonstration was crucial in dissipating any sense of community guilt from the village. A few months later another "Amnesty Week" was organized with the assistance of many outsiders from the surrounding towns.

During the fall and spring of 1976–77 the petitions for amnesty spread throughout the Basque region like a frenzy. Several people died in demonstrations. By June 1977, before the general elections, even the ETA convicts, who only a few months earlier had been awaiting death penalties, were released from their prisons. Atxega, José Ignacio, and Juan Mari were among those released in European countries as political exiles. And in a month they were back in Euskadi, hailed as heroes, occupying the front pages of newspapers, and participating in packed, delirious demonstrations. They were now in the pantheon of Basque resistance leaders such as Monzon and the Burgos trial's ETA figures.

But all that popularity was worthless compared with another situation. Upon their return from Denmark, where they had been exiled, they met again in southern France—Atxega, José Ignacio, Juan Mari, Iñaki, and an ETA companion from Zarautz named Aitor. As one of them explained, "We could not be sure whether that was real. Only five months earlier we were in prisons wondering whether they would cut off our heads, and there we were as if nothing had happened." All they could do was laugh and laugh and laugh.

The laughter did not last long, however. In 1974, ETA had split between the military (hard-line militarists) and the politico-military (those who placed some faith in the political process) branches. The Itziar youths had formed one of the *berezi,* or special-action cells, which were part of ETA politico-military. After the arrest of the Itziar cell the berezi commandos, and Iñaki with them, had decided to join the military branch, while the three arrested remained in the politico-military. Both branches became increasingly alienated from each other. In meetings after that first unforgettable one following their release, argument was unavoidable; their parties were following divergent lines. Juan Mari said to me more than once, "All the other times that we met were hell; we would end up arguing, and either he [Iñaki] or me crying."

In 1977 the first democratic elections were held in Spain after forty years of dictatorship. Two political coalitions seeking Basque independence were formed: Euskadiko Ezkerra (Euskadi's Left), the only group on the Left to participate in the 1977 elections, and Herri Batasuna (People's Unity), which was formed in 1978 and contested elections in 1979. The two groups were supported by about 25 percent of the Basque electorate. (This percentage is increasing.) The latter supports ETA military and, while contesting elections, fails to participate in the process by filling the posts that it wins. Euskadiko Ezkerra was formerly the political arm of ETA politico-military (this branch is almost extinct after most of its members decided to abandon the armed struggle in 1982) and participates in the parliamentary political process. The PNV, however, has remained the dominant force within Basque nationalism. Itziar's votes go almost exclusively to these nationalist parties; as an instance of a typical voting pattern in Itziar, these are the results of the elections of March 9, 1980: PNV, 364; Herri Batasuna, 154; Euskadiko Ezkerra, 42; others, 19.

Since 1980 the Basque provinces of Guipúzcoa, Vizcaya, and Alava have enjoyed a degree of autonomy within Spain. The autonomous region of Euskadi has its own parliament, president, and ministries. It is still in the process of negotiating with Madrid its spheres of influence. The democratization of Spanish politics and the creation of the Basque autonomous region have both complicated and, for some, compromised ETA's position. When the adversary was a fascist dictatorship overtly committed to the abolition of Basque distinctiveness within Spain, ETA was a courageous David prepared to do battle with Goliath to save his people. Today, the issues are no longer framed in such black-and-white terms.

In the summer of 1977, at the same time that Atxega, Juan Mari, and José Ignacio were being hailed as political stars at the regional level, they were being ostracized by Itziar's youth. They had taken the Euskadiko Ezkerra line by participating in the June 1977 elections. Participation in the electoral process was deemed by the most radical abstentionist position as an unpardonable breaking-off of the union of the Basque Left and as downright treason. Suddenly, therefore, the ETA heroes from Itziar were themselves "traitors" to their closest followers in the village. For the most radicalized sector of Itziar, operating strictly in a politically polarized scheme, the actions of the idolized fighters just released from prison were no longer revolutionary ekintzak of liberating power. The heroes had returned to their original home. They were about to learn the meaning of treachery and tragedy.

CHAPTER FOUR

History as Tragedy

The events narrated here are strictly historical. Yet the particular perspective in which I have placed them is mine, and some Itziar villagers are not likely to agree with parts of my exposition. Being myself a participant in these events allows me the freedom to give an account of the recent history of Itziar without committing to it any of my co-villagers. Clear differences in interpretive frames can be observed from within the village. Mine is only one more chapter in the mythmaking process of Itziar villagers about themselves.

The Action: "But How Can That Be?"

One Saturday morning in the summer of 1975 I was at home in Itziar when I suddenly heard women crying in the street. As I ran out to see what had occurred, I found my mother, pale, sitting on the stairs and unable to walk up to the first floor. With frightened eyes and holding her stomach she breathlessly exclaimed, "They have killed Carlos on the bus." Carlos was the alleged official *chivato,* or police informer, of Itziar as well as the bus driver. Every Saturday morning Itziar women used to go to Deba shopping. That day, when they were returning home at noon and were two miles away from the village, two ETA militants stood up, walked toward Carlos, and forced him to drive off the main road. After shouting at him, "Hi txakur bat haiz!" ("You are a dog!"), they shot him to death in front of his brother and sister and the horrified women, who were screaming while scrambling out of the bus. While Carlos's body was lying on the steering wheel the bus began to roll backwards, nearly running over one woman who had fallen to the ground in her haste during the moment of terror. It came to a stop by colliding with a wall. Carlos's blood, spilled on the public road, remained visible for days.

The women were taken to Itziar, still crying and sobbing, by drivers passing by. My mother observed, "When I saw the two boys advancing toward him I knew immediately what was going to happen, and my stomach turned." After I walked her upstairs I went out into the street. Several women surrounded me in a daze and with bewildered faces asked me, "Baina ori nola leike?" (But how can that be?). Their eyes were spearing me, pleading for an answer. I remained mute. "But how can that be?" It was not a question. It was the inexpressible.

Milk Brothers

When I was a child in Itziar during the fifties I was influenced by the teachings of two men. One was Martin and the other Carlos. Martin and Carlos, who later emerged in the eyes of the villagers as the leaders of two adversarial factions, were milk brothers. Both had been nursed by Carlos's mother after Martin's mother had died. Carlos's family was of Carlist persuasion and, therefore, when the Spanish civil war broke out in the summer of 1936, sided with the anti-Republican forces led by Franco. His family was in charge of services that were marginal in a farming society, such as postman, gravedigger, constable, and carpenter; they were the mediators between Itziar and the larger municipal life of Deba. In Martin's family, two brothers, including his father, fought for the Basque nationalists (PNV) and two others with the socialists, all opposed to Franco's military uprising. While their menfolk were battling each other at the war front, the babies of the two families shared milk brotherhood at the breast of Carlos's mother. As they grew up, Martin and Carlos, aware of their past intimate kinship, were closest friends while involved in the various social and cultural activities in Itziar during the middle fifties.

It was a period in which overt political action was all but impossible, indeed, inconceivable. For idealistic youths the surrogates for political activism were involvement in religion, on the one hand,

and the preservation of the Basque language and folkloristic aspects of Basque culture on the other. These were not mutually exclusive approaches since many persons were involved in both. However, it is also true that there was a sense in which they were alternatives with greater or lesser appeal to each individual according to personal predilections.

The religious approach, which implied asceticism, was personified by Martin; Carlos represented more worldly interests. Martin would lecture to small groups of ten-year-old boys about moral rectitude and Christian duty. His message to us was straightforward: lead a righteous and religious life. He extolled the model of true commitment represented by the example of a well-known soccer player who, when asked to give a speech in a tavern where pictures of naked women were hanging on the walls, refused with the explanation: "In a place where God is offended, Jesús Garay shall not speak." Martin's dedication was to us admirable. Born on a baserria, he had no formal education, yet he was articulate and persuasive. He was also a marvelous actor in the plays staged by the village youth. Above all he was a man of undisputed religious convictions. A word that summed him up was *benetakoa* (truthful).

As reported in the previous chapter, during the middle fifties a young priest, Don José María, was assigned to Itziar. In addition to religious doctrine he imparted a message of social and civic responsibility and personal integrity. Martin, Carlos, and their good friend José Mari were among eight youths most influenced by the message. All became dedicated members of the local group Baserri Gaztedi, founded by Don José María as a vehicle for realizing religious and social goals. In Martin's case it is not an exaggeration to say that he experienced a genuine conversion. He emerged as a major figure in the Acción Católica group and in this capacity was influential throughout the region. He spearheaded a cooperative movement among several farmers of Itziar, urging each to subordinate personal and household interests to the well-being of all. In his personal comportment Martin was a model of the good Christian. He forsook swearing and social dancing. He married a girl from the village and became a respected and admired family man.

Carlos taught me the *aurresku,* the favorite dance of Itziar boys, which is performed ceremoniously on special occasions such as the annual village fiestas. He was an elegant dancer and a fine instructor who still holds the record for dancing the greatest number of aurreskus in Itziar. For weeks my friend Juan Kruz and I rehearsed under Carlos's guidance. When we danced the aurresku in the plaza of Itziar I was eleven.

Carlos was from an unusual family. His father was not born in Itziar; he was an illegitimate child adopted from an orphanage. The family was not involved in agriculture or factory work, the two most common occupations in the village. Rather, Carlos's father worked as a gravedigger, carpenter and mail carrier. Carlos himself was the village shoemaker. He was a glib and charming man, and his shoe shop became a meeting place for the youth. He was fond of me; I recall him offering me career advice. He helped me to collect the pictures of soccer players that came with chocolate bars and could be redeemed for footballs.

In the group of young activists, Carlos excelled at organizing hikes in the mountains, Sunday evening dances, village festivities, and the like. He incurred the wrath of one priest when he opposed the dictate that prohibited girls belonging to the religious sodality Daughters of Mary from engaging in social dancing on the Sunday of their monthly meeting. Despite his full participation in the group's religious devotional life, Carlos was more given than the rest to courting girls. In the traditional culture's ambience of marked segregation of the sexes and a repressive morality imposed by the church, Carlos stood out as liberal.

In 1959 Itziar's youth staged a play called *Eun Dukat* (A Hundred Ducats),[1] the story of a blind uncle whose savings are stolen by his wretched nephew. Unaware that the thief is spying on him, the blind man reveals in a sung verse that he has a hundred ducats hidden under a fig tree. The wretchedness of the betrayal is magnified by the cultural resonances it evokes. The uncle is a man who lives on a baserria and pursues a traditional way of life, whereas the nephew resides in town and has been educated in an urban milieu. The golden ducats become a symbol of the former culture now polluted by the perfidy of modernity. A third key figure is a sorcerer who engages in traditional formulas and curing practices. Who was chosen to play the role of the blind uncle, embodiment of the ideal man according to traditional values? Martin, of course. Who played the role of the villainous nephew? Carlos. The sorcerer's role went to their intimate friend José Mari. The performance was so intense that many spectators were moved to tears. Itziar's theater group was requested to perform it in nearby towns. The play was a rehearsal of the roles that each was soon to play in real life, a harbinger of impending treachery and tragedy.

The Isolation and Alienation of Carlos

In order to understand the subsequent events it is first necessary to consider further the climate of opinion in the village during the fifties described in the previous chapter. Like other communities of the region, Itziar was poised between the Basque nationalist sentiment of the majority of villagers and the consequences of having been on the losing side during the recent civil war. Opposition to Francoism was shrouded in a privacy imposed by fear, frustration, and exhaustion. In the harsh reality of the times, village affairs were dominated by local officials deemed "safe" by higher authorities and hence regarded as puppets by most villagers. The very essence of one's Basqueness could be challenged on a daily basis. Martin, Carlos, and José Mari all attended Itziar's public school, which taught the official curriculum.

The only possible counterbalance to overt authoritarian assaults upon one's self-identity and cultural pride was the church. At a national level the Franco regime courted the Catholic hierarchy; at the local level this provided individual priests with the flexibility to become guardians of human rights were they so inclined. Many Basque clergymen, such as Don José María, accepted this responsibility.

Don José María's efforts to organize the youth of Itziar were viewed with alarm by the mayor. He tried to recruit Carlos as an informer regarding the activities of Baserri Gaztedi. Possibly out of fear and an unwillingness to inform on his friends, Carlos left the group. A short time thereafter, Don José María was removed from his post and sent to a different town. The people of Itziar were incensed. In their need for an explanation the rumor spread that Carlos had denounced the priest to the authorities.

It was the policy of the ecclesiastical machinery to give priests new "destinations" from time to time. In the case of a priest as dynamic and exemplary as Don José María it was normal that the bishop should decide to move him to a larger town with greater responsibilities. But in Itziar, where Don José María was intensely liked, his removal could not be taken as an impersonal ordinary event; there had to be a cause for it, and the alleged cause was that Carlos had secretly made a *denuncia* (accusation) against Don José María. This conspiracy theory had been applied already to a lesser degree with Don Joakin, another popular priest, who served in Itziar prior to Don José María. With Don José María the theory took on major credibility because of the accusations of "doing politics" previously aimed at the group formed by him. The pattern was simple: when a well-appreciated priest was ordered to move to another post, he had been "thrown out" because of internal reporting against him. When a priest was not particularly esteemed and was given a new post, it was an ordinary move. Thus, in the 1955 to 1965 decade five priests were "thrown out" of Itziar, yet each of these priests categorically denies any conspiracy or denuncia against him.

Carlos was blamed as the treacherous chivato in the case of Don José María. It was said that because Carlos had abandoned the meetings of Baserri Gaztedi he must have reported their content to the authorities. By all accounts there was no truth to such rumors. In the decisive year of 1960, the combination of Don Antonio being removed from Itziar and José Mari from Andutzene being imprisoned marked a turning point for Carlos. Although he had no direct implication in these events, he was again blamed. It had been wise to recruit him again for the Baserri Gaztedi group. Under questioning he had to say that nothing strange had been going on in their meetings. Carlos claimed instead that it was during the one-on-one private discussions with Don Antonio that politics went on.

Upon the discovery of José Mari's and Martin's clandestine political involvement, Carlos felt utterly betrayed. He confronted Martin with a single question, repeated over and over: "But weren't we friends? Why then did you keep things secret from me?" Martin kept explaining in vain that they hadn't told any of their companions from the Baserri Gaztedi group because of the nature of the enterprise. However, for Carlos the secrecy was a betrayal that terminated the friendship as well as any support that he might have felt for their cause. To many villagers, Carlos was the agent of José Mari's downfall. Unaware of the true chain of events, the presence of Carlos, a chivato, provided a ready explanation.

In objective terms the factual grounds of the abominable treachery on both sides were indeed insubstantial to the point, one might argue, of being pure invention. Carlos's unwillingness to recognize Martin's reasons for secrecy was tantamount to ignoring the nature of underground activism and to disallowing the political option of resisting a dictatorship—hence the "betrayal" was nothing but Carlos's own misapplication of a friendship premise. Conversely, charging Carlos with responsibility for the events of the summer of 1960 was plainly a fabrication with no basis in fact. Carlos simply had not informed against his friends any more than he had against the priest two years earlier.

Reality notwithstanding, within the group of young social activists as well as the wider echo of Itziar public opinion as a whole the perception of intolerable acts of either withholding or disclosing information committed among friends became a source of factionalism. The lines of communication were broken and each faction assumed the inimical role ascribed to it by the other.

After the summer of 1960 the two milk brothers Carlos and Martin were seen to be irreconcilable enemies in the eyes of the villagers. José Mari, Martin's companion in underground activism, had been arrested, tortured, and put in jail. Their religious-political mentor, the priest Don Antonio, had been removed from Itziar as punishment by the bishop. Of course, none of this repression would affect Carlos, who was viewed as belonging to a family supportive of Franco. Ecclesiastical punishment of a dynamic priest and police brutality toward an exemplary youth had brought to the village a sense of pathos. The elements of tragedy, with its concomitants of heroism and villainy, were in place.

The recent political history of Itziar is a resolution of the enmity bred between Martin and Carlos. The story of the two milk brothers is based on factual events yet vested with the dimension of a mythical narrative. They represent the factions that either embraced or opposed the new wave of Basque nationalism. It was a role partly imposed on them by the village, partly sought by them personally. It was by negating one another that the figures of Martin and Carlos gave to each other a clear public profile. For those who supported the nationalist cause, José Mari's and Martin's commitment was of a heroic nature. They had endured suffering not for personal gain but in the legitimate defense of the country; their suffering had been caused by Carlos's treason, which, in archetypal opposition, was also magnified into a wickedness beyond personal conditions. For those unsympathetic to the nationalist cause, Carlos's nobility consisted in his imperviousness to the alarming error of undercover political maneuvering into which his friends had fallen.

The enmity between Martin and Carlos was not of a personal nature for, as Martin insisted, they knew each other too well. Their special relationship and the devout religiosity they shared for years did not leave room for feelings of contempt or hatred. Soon after their falling out, Martin attempted reconciliation with Carlos on two occasions. Martin argued that despite differing political views they should remain friends. Carlos precluded any such possibility by stating that above all else he was a supporter of Franco. But then, too, Carlos sought reconciliation when in the late sixties he repeatedly asked José Mari to play with him as a team in a *mus* (card game) championship, a clear sign of friendship that anybody in the village would have interpreted as the end of their enmity. José Mari refused.

The Chivato Scapegoat

Thus the figure of a typical or random victim begins to crystallize in domestic tragedy as it deepens in ironic tone. We may call this typical victim the pharmakos *or scapegoat. . . . [He] is neither innocent nor guilty. He is innocent in the sense that what happens to him is far greater than anything he has done provokes, like the mountaineer whose shout brings down an avalanche. He is guilty in the sense that he is a member of a guilty society, or living in a world where such injustices are an inescapable part of existence. The two facts do not come together; they remain ironically apart.*
N. Frye, Anatomy of Criticism

José Mari was brutally tortured and his life put in serious danger. A similar fate possibly awaited Martin. Yet they were not shamed in the eyes of the village. To the contrary, more than ever they were seen as honorable men whose suffering was a further proof of their moral commitment. Among Acción Católica activists José Mari became a living example of absolute dedication to a righteous cause. The social standing of both Martin and José Mari soared to new heights.

Unlike Martin and José Mari, who were heroes to many villagers, no aura of heroism surrounded Carlos. Despite his earlier difficulties, throughout the sixties he continued to have a high profile in Itziar affairs. He was a regular organizer of the village festivals. At one point he was the only, and hence successful, candidate for town councillor. However, he assumed his post on the town council when that body was highly suspect and a symbol of collaboration with the hated Franco authorities. He bought a bus and secured the franchise for the Itziar-Deba run. The local open-air dances were being abandoned, and in 1965 Carlos enclosed the dancing place and tried to liven it up with red lights. This was the first scandalous attempt at initiating a dance hall in Itziar, and the dance hall was boycotted by the village youths, who, however, frequented just such an enclosed dance hall six kilometers away. Around 1968 Carlos drove groups of Itziar and Lastur youngsters to Deba on Sunday afternoons, and he enjoyed the complicity of allowing his bus to become a place for pairing off of boys and girls while returning home. He was not the moralist in Itziar.

Over the years his reputation as a police informer grew to the point that it became an unquestioned assumption in the village. As if by contagion, any contact with Carlos brought the immediate suspicion that one was a chivato as well. A score of people suffered this accusation. Despite his charm and outgoing personality, Carlos never succeeded in having a girlfriend or marrying. Parents discouraged their daughters from getting involved with him. Progressively, then, Carlos became a pariah in Itziar. In the late sixties, on one occasion, ETA set fire to his bus. Villagers were given the clear message that he was no longer a private man with whom normal neighborly relationships could be maintained innocuously.

The case of Carlos is reminiscent of its historical precedent in Itziar during the prewar period. In the twenties and thirties several peasants and townspeople from the village became chroniclers in a weekly periodical called *Argia*. The pseudonym of one of them was "Atxurra," which means "hoe." In talking with Atxurra about the politics of the day, perhaps the most revelatory incident had to do with one of the chroniclers taking a pro-Franco stance during the civil war. The dilemma consisted in either pursuing strict religious posture by adopting Carlism's anti-Republican stance or giving priority to political allegiance by supporting the PNV (which had sided with the Republic). There were two Carlist priests in Itziar at the time, and apparently one of the chroniclers followed their pro-Franco orientation. Atxurra recounted this with deep sadness and disgust. It had been a total "betrayal," the lowest thing a man could do. He recalled to me: "We were five people who used to write in *Argia;* we used to be around the *batzokia* [PNV's meeting place]; we were all abertzaleak. But one of us turned out to be a worthless man. He betrayed us. He used to work on the railroad, and from there he could see the people leaving the village to escape and he would denounce them."

In Atxurra's terms, this man became an *espia* (spy). He offered this fateful explanation of how a spy originates: "If you belong to the side of the losers, you have only one possibility of passing to the winners' side—to inform against your friends. In this way you gain power over them, and money." "Spy," the term of the thirties, was replaced in the sixties by "chivato," but the social logic was similar.

The accusation of chivato, as with the accusation of witchcraft in earlier times, was one with grave consequences.[2] The individual himself, and his family by association, was segregated from the community's ordinary interaction. Once the rumor was spread that someone was a chivato, he was likely to be the object of ETA's death threats or to become the target of such loathsome acts as having a dead black cat hung over his doorway. By the late sixties Carlos's only friends were civil guards and "declared" chivatos. Much like the idea of witchcraft, the chivato complex is a collective representation and one that demands expurgation. However, it is not necessary that the local community take direct action; rather, ETA provides the punitive means.

One day in 1972 Itziar awoke to white graffiti. The two-word message was a statement beyond commentary: "Karlos Hil" (Death to Carlos). Villagers did not know who had painted it—it was an ekintza approved at a trial-like meeting of the Catholic group Herri Gaztedi. The youth of Itziar had passed a judgment that was to negate Carlos's right to life.

Negation is a conspicuous theme in Basque culture, as will be shown in chapter 13. Rigid self-denial expresses the moral dimension of the negative. All the fuss made by priests and the activist youth in Itziar about social dancing is merely an example of that moral rigidity. Nobody more authentically exemplified the power to negate than Martin. In an archetypal opposition, it befitted the role of Carlos to refute the negations personified by Martin, that is, the plot required that what was denied by Martin should be affirmed by Carlos.

Discussing the crucial reunions of Itziar's youth during the late fifties, priests and friends of Carlos at that time, when pressed for an explanation of his actions, point out the weakness of his character. He would rely on the advice of his brother, for instance. Unfortunately, by the time I conducted field research Carlos was dead. Yet, in a cultural and moral context in which strength was characterized by the power to negate, weakness had to derive from a deficient capacity for saying no. When Martin and José Mari decided not to include Carlos as a partner in their covert political activities, they assumed that he had not given sufficient proofs of personal strength by self-renunciation. The deep sense of betrayal experienced by Carlos in his friendship was ultimately based on their secret judgment of his unworthiness for such action. Carlos was led to show his capacity for denial by breaking off his friendship with Martin. While José Mari was in jail in Martutene, Carlos went as far as organizing an open-air dance to commemorate the anniversary of Itziar's "liberation" by Franco's forces during the civil war. The village was now polarized.

Before the fatal shots he had been called a *txakurra* (dog) and accused of treachery to the country. His funeral revealed who his real friends were: civil guards, police informers, and Spanish military men. Carlos paid for his loyalty to them with his own life. To the extent that he belonged to "them," he had been removed from his village community. People from Itziar attended his funeral for he was, after all, a son of the village, but they were overwhelmed by the swarm of outsiders in military dress or looking non-Basque. Even after his death he seemed to belong to "them."

The killing of Carlos was an unmistakable statement about the very foundations of the political and social order. In Itziar it was imperative for everybody either to take sides in favor or against or to make an assertion of unawareness—"He must have known what he was doing" was an expedient way out. If for the women who witnessed it the sights and sounds of the killing were sheer fright beyond reason, the killing for the rest of us was hearsay and a front-page newspaper story next morning.

No disapproval of the killing was voiced among my young Itziar friends. On the walls of the church the graffiti "Death to Carlos" had stayed for three years. The killing was an act committed a long time ago in thought and conversations. It triggered champagne celebrations by some. Still impressed by the shock of my mother and other Itziar women, I showed disapproval of the killing and was reproached by my friends. People from the older generations kept their opinion to themselves. As if it were a secret ballot, to query about the event was most inappropriate. It seemed that generally the villagers repudiated the act on moral grounds but were perplexed as to its political motivations. After all, "He was into politics," and politics is something closely associated with the civil war and indiscriminate killing. Although morally unacceptable, once the killing was situated in the antagonistic frame inherited from the war, reprobation of it seemed to imply an acceptance of Franco's already forty-year-old dictatorship. Any doubt as to Carlos's political personality was dispelled by seeing a large crowd of civil guards and police attend his funeral. The military governor of the province had an attack of hysteria in the cemetery during the eulogy speech. Later on, a right-wing commando team that was to perpetrate several killings was formed in Carlos's name. The youths were relieved that nobody could entertain any uncertainty as to his political associates.

Carlos was the first in an ongoing series of indiscriminate killings of chivatos and civil guards carried out by ETA. In some cases, as with a young man popular in Itziar, ETA simply confused the victim with somebody else and killed him by mistake. With the coming of democracy and legalized parties, accusations of treachery shifted to political options adopted by concrete groups. The young Itziar ETA heroes of the middle seventies, whose lives were spared because of the 1977 forced amnesty that followed Franco's death, found themselves ostracized in the village when they returned from prison and turned into "traitors" for participating in the elections. Occasionally, I have heard these ex-ETA members of Itziar, who played their part in intimidating and castigating alleged police informers, wonder aloud if there was any truth to the whole chivato craze. Finally they were realizing they had acted under the spell of a collective representation whose very existence was subsequently a source of puzzlement.

The Hero's Error: From Carlos to Iñaki

The hero's error . . . is really an error, yet it is the sort of error a good man would make. It is thus an act both free and conditioned. The hero's error is not forced upon him, but he makes it under conditions so adverse that we watch him with compassion. Tragedy is thus grounded in meditation on action and the conditions of action, and these two can be understood only in relation to each other. Hector's freedom can be understood only in relation to the imperfections of his power and knowledge; these define his acts. Redfield, Nature and Culture in the Iliad

Carlos committed such error by reacting negatively to Martin's and José Mari's covert political involvement. He compounded it by organizing out of revenge a pro-Franco festival in Itziar while José Mari was incarcerated. Carlos should have learned from *Eun Dukat* that definitions of heroism and villainy are culture-dependent. Yet Martin's legacy is no less susceptible to error. In Martin's judgment, the killing of Carlos was, for instance, one such tragic error; yet in retrospect it was Martin's own legacy of ekintza and sacramental identification with the cause of the country that led a decade later to Herri Gaztedi's graffiti "Death to Carlos" and to ETA's final fulfillment of it.

If anything, it is the heroic ethic advanced by Martin that has become problematic to Itziar as a community. This is the ethic that, since the death of Carlos, has produced five other political killings in Itziar between 1975 and 1980. These include another alleged chivato, a civil guard married to a woman from Itziar, an innocent worker also married to a local woman that ETA mistook for a third alleged chivato, the industrialist Berazadi, and Iñaki, the ETA member from Itziar. These killings seem to pose no problem for ETA sympathizers. Yet, as the description of Carlos's death reported at the beginning suggests, they are deeply perplexing for Itziar villagers as a whole. My own parents, for instance, are by family loyalty supportive of Basque radical politics; yet they have frequently expressed unmistakable signs of moral uncertainty. "But how can that be?" is a question pointing to the contradictory foundations of the political order.

The case of Berazadi is a compelling one. He was a Basque industrialist supportive of the nationalist PNV. ETA decided to relieve its financial problems by kidnapping him and asking for ransom money. Itziar's young ETA cell had just completed a similar action successfully with respect to another industrialist. However, the kidnapping of Berazadi ended in tragedy. Negotiations with his family, carried out by ETA's leadership in southern France, did not progress in timely fashion. In the meantime, some villagers discovered that the kidnappers were keeping Berazadi in the attic of an abandoned baserria in Itziar's center. The situation was precarious and, upon orders from ETA, the four activists from Itziar killed the man. For large segments of the population of Euskadi sympathetic to the PNV but tacitly supporting ETA, Berazadi's killing was a turning point. They became alienated from ETA.

The reaction in the village to the news that Itziar's young men had kidnapped Arrasate and kidnapped and killed Berazadi was one of incredulity. ETA had always been imagined as being made up of supermen operating in distant ultrasecret milieus. When the villagers were told that ETA was their seventeen- and eighteen-year-olds holding a kidnapped industrialist in the middle of the village center, initially they simply refused to believe it. But there was no doubt that these four had been the ones; even their families were witnesses. Personal knowledge of the actors put their actions into a different perspective. If they had been distant supermen they might be wrong, but it all would be part of "their" war. Since the actors were from one's own community a moral judgment was inescapable. With the exception of the village youth, the general consensus in the village was to deplore the Berazadi tragedy.

After Berazadi's killing, the public invented all sorts of rumors to discredit the young Itziar cell. They were said to be unemployed youth who had done it to get money for themselves. It was asserted that they had treated him inhumanely during the captivity; Berazadi was filthy when he was found. The alleged depravity of the kidnappers was a way of diminishing the affront that his cold-blooded killing represented. In fact, kidnappers and victim had become good friends. They had spoken at length and joked with each other. Berazadi had cooked their meals and shared their sleeping quarters. Captors and prisoner had made plans to meet somewhere in southern France to share a banquet and celebrate their forced comradeship after the affair was resolved.[3] As one of them told me, "The worst thing is that you become friends, and then . . ." This matter-of-fact intimacy between captors and captive is the hardest thing for any spectator to digest. It is less disconcerting to view the killers as psychopaths or perverts or to imagine them overburdened with guilt than to face their normalcy.

After leaving Berazadi in the ditch with a bullet in his head, the four retired to their Bilbao apartment. Enormous tension grew following the final days of the event. They had been besieged, literally, by the manhunt and then by family disclosure. The Saturday afternoon after the killing they had planned to meet their girlfriends in San Sebastián to decide whether they should disappear underground altogether or go into exile. Before leaving Bilbao they heard Mr. Fraga's voice on the national news: "If they want war, they will have it." It was the Spanish minister of the interior talking to them directly. Soon afterward they were stopped routinely by a police roadblock. The police looked inside the car and found the cartridge case of the bullet they had used only three nights earlier to shoot Berazadi. Juan Mari and José Ignacio could not believe their own oversight. It seemed to be the end of everything.

Iñaki was the only member of the commando group who escaped arrest after Berazadi's killing. He joined the military wing of ETA and became an exemplary warrior. Iñaki, alias "Donibane," was killed by a civil guard in June of 1980. He was considered by the police to be the toughest ETA activist, and his death was hailed by the minister of the interior as a decisive blow to ETA's military branch. However, none of his cold-bloodedness ever surfaced in his relationship with his mother. The intense affective bonds between the deeply religious woman and her ETA son did not pass unnoticed by many Itziar villagers.

A few months after Iñaki's death I was riding with José Ignacio when we passed by Orio, thirty kilometers from Itziar, and decided to see the spot where Iñaki had died. José Ignacio had participated in the famous Itziar commando group until his arrest in the spring of 1976 and was a particularly close friend of Iñaki. Later their political strategies had diverged as the result of different courses forced upon them, the one by prison life and the other by militant activism. José Ignacio, before and after Iñaki's death, spoke of him with the highest regard. José Ignacio is an intelligent and good-natured person, so I respected his high esteem of Iñaki. However, each time I tried to make him spell out what made Iñaki so special, he would simply hint at their intense bonds and add something like, "There is no explanation for it." I pressed him to articulate the basis for the aura of heroism that surrounded Iñaki. I knew that José Ignacio did not agree at the time with the ETA military wing's violent course. I baited him by arguing that certain kinds of heroism are entirely beside the point and can constitute foolish stupidity. José Ignacio would readily admit the possibility of a mistaken course but still found something uniquely great and heroic about Iñaki. His actions might have been politically disputable, but there was an ultimate truth about Iñaki's person. The hero's error can be deplored, yet those bound to him by ties of friendship or community know that his truth does not depend on the correctness of his ideological or strategic premises. Understanding of tragedy requires a vision of the relationship between action and the conditions of action.

Martin never approved of Carlos's killing, yet he revered ETA's martyrdom ethics. The ethos of militantism and primacy of ekintza formed within the Catholic movement evolved naturally into the *burruka* (fighting) mentality, which perceives combat to be the necessary business of life. A Homeric view of man and society develops in which war is seen as the background condition of life. A few leading men—the heroes—must shoulder the burden of battle. And a new sense of community is generated by combat: "A Homeric community consists, in effect, of those who are ready to die for one another; the perimeter of each community is a potential battlefield. Under these social conditions, war is perceived as the most important human activity because the community's ability to wage defensive war is perceived as the precondition of all communal values" (Redfield 1975:94). Heroism is thus for Homer "a definite social task, and the heroes are a definite social stratum" (ibid.).

This was well known to Martin. In his premarital period of heroism, his combat was fought on religious and social grounds; subsequently he got involved in clandestine patriotic and syndical activities that implied serious personal danger, and there was no question in his mind that, had he been born a few years later, he would have been involved in ETA's armed war against the Spanish military. It was only through total commitment, to the point of a readiness to die, that Martin felt fully a man, even if that might mean falling into the hero's errors.

Iñaki embodied the warrior ethic to perfection. More than anyone in Itziar he was the one sustained by the village while it contemplated his inevitable destruction. No other man was so completely given to his community, yet nobody was so removed from his society and culture. When friends occasionally visited him in his southern France hideouts, they were disturbed by his cold distance. Any show of emotion by his visitors could easily become a matter of scorn for him. Iñaki's example would point out disturbingly the insignificance of their lives. He was utterly outside anything that made sense in Itziar: family, village community, church services, regular work and leisure, traditional norms and values. The ordinary affairs of life could not make much sense to somebody who was dead to them. Iñaki's reality transcended personal life. His only occupation was war, the unruly war of a handful of young men battling with a few guns against the powerful Spanish military. Any sense of personal or cultural limits could only arouse disdain in him. He had fully assumed the war obligations of his community, including killing. His only real place was the underground battlefield and there, as another Achilles, he acted "not as a leader of men but as an isolated destroyer—a kind of natural force, like fire or blood" (Redfield 1975 : 107). To the passive impurity of Carlos is contrasted the active impurity of Iñaki, for, in the end, "Whereas Hector can do nothing but die, Achilles can do nothing but kill" (ibid.:222). The warrior must assume the community's impurity for others to remain pure. The perplexing question "But how can that be?" is only an expression of the contradiction inherent in the warrior's role.

Looking at Carlos through Martin's Eyes

In the light of the polarization that has split Itziar since the summer of 1960, the milk brothers Martin and Carlos turned into adversarial agents of each other's fate. Theirs had been one more instance of the old theme of enemy brothers in which "it becomes impossible to distinguish history from ritual" (Girard 1977 : 110). In a later period the tragic enmity centered at the village level between Carlos and the ETA youth—the subhuman condition of Carlos as txakurra turned his ETA co-villagers into supermen defenders of the country. Iñaki epitomized this ETA militancy. They were given by their society antagonistic roles in a heroic plot reminiscent of a Homeric tragedy. Of them it can be said, as of the great Achilles and Hector, that "these two heroes, driven by fate into a duel, descend together into the pit of impurity—together, but differently. Hector changes from man to dog to meat for dogs; Achilles, from man to devourer of men" (Redfield 1975 : 222).

Achilles and Hector did not know each other; Martin and Carlos were intimates. Before his death in 1981 I was fortunate to hear Martin talk about Carlos. In writing this chapter I feel I am merely fulfilling a debt I contracted with Martin when he shared with me his perception of Carlos. That it is Martin's view makes it particularly significant.

Since my childhood I have harbored deep respect for Martin. When polarization split Itziar, I was naturally for his social and political ideals. Carlos became a scandal for those of us supportive of the cultural and cooperativist movement taking shape in the village. By the late sixties Carlos was the declared enemy of the progressive youth's goals. Repudiation of Carlos was a precondition for any conscientious patriot. Still, his killing, which horrified Itziar women, could not become for me an occasion for celebration. It was only recently, however, while writing this ethnography of the political violence in Itziar, that I came to realize the full significance of the tragedy of Carlos. Great errors, not arbitrary murders, are the stuff of tragedy. In my research I found that solidly established "facts" about him, such as his traitor role in the events of 1960, were plainly false. Most of all I was affected by hearing a portrait of Carlos given by the man who claimed to know him better than anyone else—Martin. Nobody in Itziar had more obvious motives to fear Carlos's perfidy than Martin and José Mari. Yet Martin insisted on minimizing the danger posed by Carlos. He kept telling me he knew the man too well. Martin's conviction as to Carlos's innocence was beyond the level of concrete acts. He knew, of course, that Carlos had assumed his role of chivato. Yet, Martin argued, Carlos simply did not have the capacity for such evildoing as to deserve being killed. It was Martin's secrecy that had provoked Carlos's treachery; now it seemed that Martin was again burdened with a secret about Carlos's humanity that he wished everybody could share. All he could say was that he knew the man too well; he knew him better than the civil guards or ETA. His knowledge was based on the years of close upbringing in Itziar during their childhood, adolescence, and the period of moral and social activism of the fifties. He looked at me dramatically as if involving my position as Itziar villager to make me understand that the core of a man can be known within his community's boundaries. Through Martin's eyes I, too, felt I knew Carlos differently.

As I thought more about Carlos, I began to realize that no other man concentrates as forcefully the pathos of Itziar's recent political history. The tragedy of what happened to Carlos has no equivalent in all the willful activity of the Acción Católica and ETA's ekintzak. If one decides to watch the fateful event that stopped his last bus ride with the eyes of the women who were present, what remains indelible in their "But how can that be?" is not primarily the determination of the two men walking down the aisle with pistols in their hands, but the blood of Carlos running down the aisle, preceded by the impotent gestures of his brother raising his hand to stop them and followed by the weeping of his sister left alone with her dead brother while everybody was hurrying to escape the site of terror. Carlos was the one to endure the beastly condition of txakurra and the separation from the community. The inhumanity predicated on Carlos was a condition for his killers to be patriotic heroes. His death was a necessity for the political drama of Itziar.

Unlike Carlos, Martin died a natural death outside the battlefield; he died of leukemia in the summer of 1981. It is Carlos's death that concentrates the drama of their rivalry. Yet it was Martin's fortune to have been able to see the life of Carlos in its entirety when he learned of the bullet-ridden body resting on the steering wheel of the bus. Martin strongly disapproved of the killing. The act did not absolve Carlos from what Martin saw as his "weaknesses," yet the injustice of his death was inexcusable. Martin emphatically insisted that Carlos did not pose a sufficient threat to merit death. Although Martin had vigorously pursued a course of action opposite to Carlos's since their split in 1960, he was able to understand the conditions under which Carlos had acted. Consequently, he could not establish a categorical distinction that demanded the sacrifice of Carlos's humanity. In this Martin was performing the basic ethical act of recognition in which "what is human falls beyond all mediation and all instrumentality" (Savater 1981 : 83). By turning Carlos into an object of intelligibility, Martin developed a new vision of their common fate. That synthesis of action and comprehension made Martin great.

Conclusion: Culture as Tragedy

That Saturday morning in the summer of 1975 I had been jolted by Itziar women's unanswerable question. Five years later, in the middle of June 1980, I was returning to Itziar from Princeton to continue my fieldwork on Basque political violence. While flying over the Atlantic I began to skip through a Madrid newspaper and, as I found news about Itziar, sprang back on my seat. Iñaki had just been killed by civil guards in an ambush in the nearby town of Orio. A town meeting had been held in Itziar, the newspaper continued, headed by my brother Bixente, who was at the time the town councillor elected for Herri Batasuna, to decide the course of action to take regarding the killing of a villager. Still flying between two worlds, I was back in Itziar sooner than I had anticipated.

Upon arrival in the village I went to Iñaki's home. After expressing my condolences to his father, who was then alone, I headed to the cemetery, where I found Iñaki's mother and two sisters putting flowers on the grave. As I approached and offered my sympathy, his mother replied: "Our Iñazio Mari is gone. I still cannot even believe it. We used to be waiting for his phone calls all the time. I still find myself waiting at moments. I feel he is going to call. I will realize in time." Several friends of his told me they were having the same difficulty in believing that Iñaki actually was dead and buried. Three young girlfriends of his came to Itziar from a Vizcayan town to visit his grave shortly after hearing of his death. They had recently been in prison for several weeks because of their connections with him. At Iñaki's grave they said, "He cannot be down there under the earth; he must be somewhere else." Then their eyes lifted toward the sky. His absence exceeded any reason or belief.

On the afternoon of Iñaki's burial his body had been taken directly to the cemetery and was not in the church during the service. Itziar had been literally overrun by police forces, who denied entry to any outsider. During the sermon the priest spoke about the need for peace; he also stated the value of giving one's own life for a belief. In the cemetery the lid of the coffin was removed and relatives and friends could finally contemplate his face. Pictures were taken and the general commentary was that his face looked *polita* (pretty). Some observed on it that everlasting smile, partly candor, partly sarcasm, that was typical of him and that had earned him the nickname of "Amabirjina" among his friends.

Before he was buried his brother Isidro broke the utter silence to speak of the ideological differences between the two of them and of the divergent strategies they had chosen. Nevertheless, he considered his brother a total revolutionary who had committed himself as far as giving his own life for what he believed in. Isidro belongs to the radical internationalist party LKI. With his left hand raised, he swore to work for the oppressed workers and to give his own life if necessary. When after the speech Isidro intoned the Basque militia song "Eusko Gudariak Gara," emotion swallowed the people's voices and there was hardly anyone who could sing—"We were all mute," I heard someone report.

One November evening I was talking to four young people in Itziar's youth center. When Iñaki was brought into the conversation, three out of four recalled having had dreams about him that week. José Ignacio was one of them. He realized that he was dreaming about Iñaki quite frequently. But recently he had spent an entire night with him in a particularly vivid dream experience in which they talked and argued and he asked Iñaki over and over, "But what happened to you in Orio? But what happened to you in Orio?" He woke up rested and content. Then he realized it was just a dream and became enraged. Not even a dream could capture the enormity of the event or dare offer a response to that simple question. It could not be resolved by a dream.

Martin could not sacrifice the life of Carlos to a history of polarization. He did not relinquish his claim that he knew Carlos better than did ETA or the military friends who stole his funeral. Martin could not conceive of Carlos being buried anywhere but in Itziar's cemetery. Yet those who carry Martin's legacy of patriotic commitment may find it hard to be so generous. Friends of Iñaki raised money to erect a funerary statue in the cemetery over his burial plot. I joined other youths from Itziar on a visit to the cemetery to see Iñaki's monument. The conversation took an odd turn; somebody had been buried a few months earlier right next to Iñaki. The peaceful and definitive fellowship between the graves was grotesquely incongruous and offensive to Iñaki's admirers. The other grave belonged to Benito, the Castilian civil guard who had arrested José Mari in 1960. Later on he had married a woman from Itziar, where he was well liked for his personal charm; people recall about him that in the troublesome years he lived in Itziar nobody from the village was ever arrested. Benito had been killed in Itziar by ETA that winter. One of the visitors remarked, "There is nothing I hate more than seeing them one beside the other here." Not even death could reconcile them.

These chapters on Itziar's history were written in the spring of 1981, and the narratives incorporated in this book conclude at that time. However, lest the reader think the historical sequence is now closed, we must mention events that happened in October of 1986, developments that could serve as material for the next, as yet unwritten chapter. Inevitably they are intimately linked to the previous narratives and highlight the dramatic contradictions within Basque nationalism. On October 15, 1986, ETA kidnapped a retired Basque industrialist, part-owner of a small costume-jewelry factory employing thirty-five workers. He was Luzio Aguinalde, the brother of Abene mentioned in chapter 2, who had moved to the provincial capital of Vitoria in 1956. The irony of the historical sequence could hardly be more striking. As we know from Abene's war story, it was Luzio's family that volunteered an apartment to house the PNV's batzokia in the 1930s, which became the bastion of Basque nationalism in Itziar. This cost both Luzio and his father three years of confinement in Franco's prisons. When, with the exception of Abene, the family moved to Vitoria, it continued promoting Basque initiatives. Luzio was the oldest member of the PNV in the province and held a position within the party. Now Luzio was the target of nationalist aspirations turned into armed struggle by ETA. The reason adduced was that he had refused to pay the "revolutionary tax" that ETA demands from Basque industrialists, but his kidnapping was widely perceived as ETA's defiant signal to the majority PNV political party. In Itziar I wrote and distributed in the bars a leaflet pointing out Luzio's role in the village's past nationalist history and arguing that so long as we wanted to remain free men and women we should oppose such senseless and dishonorable action against the life and family of our neighbor. I urged people from Itziar to show our condemnation by participating in a demonstration that was going to take place in Vitoria demanding his release. Previously, Herri Batasuna had called for another demonstration in Bilbao at the same day and hour, demanding that Madrid begin political negotiations. People from Itziar were torn between the two events.

The chain of events continued its course, and after eighteen days the kidnapping incident came to a head. It was Sunday afternoon, and I was in Itziar sharing a meal with twenty-two young villagers. The news that Luzio had been released reached us as we shared coffee and a game of cards. Isidro, Iñaki's brother, was by my side, and at one point he left the table to congratulate Andoni, Luzio's nephew. Fifteen minutes later, however, Isidro's girlfriend arrived with a frightened face and told him the news that his younger brother, in exile since 1982, had been badly injured. He had followed in the footsteps of their dead brother Iñaki and joined ETA. Our after-dinner recreation was instantly over. What had happened was that the Ertzantza, the Basque police to which Luzio belonged in his wartime youth, had found the hideout (a mountain cave) where he was being held captive and had released him after a gunfight with the kidnappers. The head of the police had died and one of the kidnappers, Isidro's brother, was seriously wounded. Not only the kidnapped but one of the kidnappers as well was from Itziar. Isidro and Andoni, then, were brother and nephew of the kidnapper and the kidnapped. Both were from Itziar, and their mutual respect and companionship is revelatory of the social contradictions in the village.

And what about the relationship between kidnapper and kidnapped? After the shooting, both men were taken together to the hospital. Luzio, who had not recognized his young co-villager's identity during his days of captivity, urged the doctors to take care of his wounded captor first. At their farewell, Luzio extended his best regards to the young man's mother, who reciprocated with greetings to Luzio's wife. The exchange was as sincere and normal as it would have been in any casual situation. During the days of captivity this "normalcy" had been clouded by the antagonistic roles they had been led to play in a plot neither could fully master, but now they were again friendly co-villagers. The incident epitomizes the internal paradox of the nationalist struggle.

For the combat to be meaningful, enemy and ally must stand for different causes; for the justification of killing, slayer and victim must belong to different categories; for enmity to be perpetual, alienation of will and separation of minds become a condition. What the recent history of Itziar shows is that a categorical distancing of one person from another and ignorance of or insensitivity to each other's life conditions can be effected in the cradle of supreme intimacy of a small village. In life and in death, the intimacy of slayer and victim, hero and villain, is startling in the above cases. Carlos and Martin, leaders of the opposing factions, were milk brothers and confidants. The civil guard Benito and José Mari, whom he arrested, each married a daughter of a local restaurateur. Berazadi and his kidnappers, before they killed him, ate, conversed, and slept together in a farmstead attic for twenty days. Iñaki was killed by a civil guard whom he had already fatally wounded when Iñaki approached to finish him off—both men, mutual slayers and victims, were found lying dead next to each other. Removed from the fateful spot to the peace of Itziar's cemetery, Iñaki found another civil guard, Benito, waiting for his fellowship.

The people of Itziar have all had an ineludible experience of political violence. The civil war presented for the older generations the exemplary case of such military violence in the form of fratricidal killing. During the two decades of the postwar period, the suppression of civil liberties and cultural rights was endured as a direct consequence of the war confrontation and the subsequent establishment of a military regime in Madrid. The newly awakened political awareness of Itziar's youth in the late 1950s led rapidly to participation in organizational forms deemed illegal by the established order. The imprisonment of José Mari and expulsion of the priest Don Antonio from Itziar in the summer of 1960 were only inevitable eruptions of such subterranean enmity. The political participation was in intimate relationship historically and morally to a religious conversion that called for the promotion of justice in world affairs. A mentality of action fostered a course of ekintza activism that became, throughout the sixties and early seventies, the "trial by fire" for the youth. Between 1975 and 1980, six political murders occurred in Itziar. The climate of polarization and political violence is darkly condensed by these killings. They are, literally and symbolically, the major events that have taken place in Itziar during these years.

Yet, were I to project an image of Itziar in which the presence of violence is the paramount reality in everyday life, this would be a distorted picture in which the villagers would not recognize themselves. Regarding violent behavior in general, the social experience of Itziar supports the stereotype of Basques being a peace-loving people, a view that seems to run directly against this ethnographic description. In Itziar I have never seen an actual fight or public verbal insults between two adults. A rowdy argument in a bar creates extreme tension among those present and is therefore much disliked. The notion itself of violence in Itziar's rural society belongs, for the most part, to a burruka level of conflict that can be dealt with locally within native cultural frames.

This ethnography deals, therefore, with one very restricted aspect of Itziar's history and social reality. Nevertheless, in the recent course of events it is an aspect that has acquired a stark centrality in Itziar's everyday life. Faced with political homicides for whose justification the ordinary cultural premises and social rules do not seem to apply, the violence itself tends to become an intractable phenomenon that generates deep moral and political disorientation. As the Basque poet and philosopher Unamuno phrased it, "a tragic sense of life in men and in countries, or at least in me—who am a man—and the soul of my country, as is reflected in mine" derives from these perplexing situations (1931 : 323–24).

In February 1984 I had the opportunity to visit the top security prison of Herrera de la Mancha in the capacity of professor at the Basque University. Atxega, one of the four members of the commando unit from Itziar arrested for the Berazadi affair, was there. After the 1977 de facto amnesty, he had again joined ETA. In 1978 he was arrested and tortured, but the police could not get any information from him and he was released. In the spring of 1983 he was arrested, tortured, and imprisoned again. He is one of the hard-core "terrorists" who have participated in countless actions. When we embraced we were just old friends from Itziar. Another youth from Itziar in his teens, Vitoriano, arrested in the summer of 1983, was there as well. In Herrera de la Mancha alone there were about two hundred ETA members imprisoned. In all Spanish prisons there were over four hundred of them imprisoned by April 1984. Their crime is to believe that the Basque Country requires national sovereignty as an indispensable guarantor for preserving its ancestral language and cultural heritage. This belief is acted out in assuming the slogan for which the acronym of ETA stands, Euskadi and Freedom, and in pursuing it through an organization that practices armed struggle. Sartre stated forcefully ETA's ultimate dilemma after the Burgos trial: "Independence or death: these words that were proclaimed yesterday in Cuba and Algeria, are today repeated in Euskadi, this is the full exigency of the present situation. It is this or submission—which is impossible" (1971 : xxiv). To those who do not share their nationalist belief, ETA men are heartless terrorists; to those who are Basque nationalists but do not support ETA, their misguided course is a dead end with dramatic consequences; to their supporters they are heroic fighters.

The practice of torture on the nationalist population supportive of ETA is widespread. An antiterrorist law allows for any arrested citizen to be held incommunicado for nine days prior to seeing a lawyer. Every year, even after the Socialists came to power, the Amnesty International report finds a "systematic use of torture" against Basque nationalists.[4] In 1981, and again in 1985, a presumed ETA member was tortured to death. Grisly descriptions of torture are commonplace in the Basque media; macabre photographs of tortured bodies are part of the recent political iconography. The hundreds of cases of torture per year mean that many people and their families and friends experience in personal terms the horror that one may incur for patriotism.[5] It is a Dantesque initiation ceremony that nurtures Basque collectivity into resistance and martyrdom. This "theater of hell" operates both ways as "a torture of the truth" (Foucalt 1977 : 40): for the police it is the final test that will reveal hidden plans and connect events to their authors; for the victims it is the ultimate proof of their own righteousness against the hated inhumanity of their torturers. In the cases of various friends of mine I have verified how the atrocity of torture leaves indelible physical and, above all, psychological marks.

It is frequently remarked that no other "terrorist" organization in a democratic state receives the popular support enjoyed by ETA.

During Franco's dictatorship ETA was widely supported by the Basque population, as reflected by the reactions of general strikes to the Burgos trial. But, contrary to what political logic might have predicted, even after the advent of democracy in 1977 a substantial backing for ETA remains. An opinion poll in November of 1979 showed that 54 percent of Basques thought that ETA people were "patriots or idealists" and only 14 percent considered them "madmen or criminals" (*Egin* 1982 : 195). In electoral terms, summing up the votes of Herri Batasuna and Euskadiko Ezkerra, which were perceived as political screens of ETA's two branches, about 25 percent of the Basque electorate opted for ETA's goals. Although these goals ultimately point toward independence for the Basque Country, it should be noted that ETA's maximum political demand for ceasing the armed struggle is not Basque national independence but the right of self-determination. According to polls, only about 30 percent of the Basques are pro-independence. Self-determination is not senseless utopianism but a right proclaimed by all Basque political parties, one that even the Spanish Socialists, in power since 1982, favored when they were in the opposition. Buttressed by the 1976 Spanish constitution, which was approved by only one-third of the Basque electorate, and amid rumors of military threats and pressures, Madrid offers deaf ears to such Basque claims. This constitutional stalemate is the key to the current Basque political drama.

In Itziar, neither the strongly Catholic groups at the beginning of the ongoing political revolt nor ETA is believed to be any sort of organized criminal association. The Spanish media notwithstanding, they are not perceived within their community as vicious murderers. Still, as Martin observed, error is not necessarily absent from heroes. In fact, in the Aristotelian sense of tragedy, "the typical tragic hero . . . is a good man who falls into vice and error" (Redfield 1975 : 84). Vice and crime are uninteresting per se; a good tragic plot rests on a great error. The deeply perplexing question "But how can that be?" indicates that at critical moments members of the community cannot avoid perceiving the tragic consequences of their own everyday life. That question allows for casting Itziar's recent political history as the ritual enactment of an ongoing tragedy. And, since the end of tragedy marks the step to history, in that respect the village enactment of tragedy is, in its repetition, an attempt to preclude competing historical representations. It therefore negates the existence of fundamental historical changes in Basque society; the advent of democracy in Spain could be seen as an instance of such basic historical change, but this happens to be irrelevant for a political experience that perceives the extinction of Basque language and culture as a tragic loss. Itziar's history, archetypically concentrated in the relationship between Carlos and Martin, ultimately poses an enigma for the cultural order in which it is couched.

Martin would not have regretted being next to Carlos in Itziar's cemetery. As an individual born and raised in Itziar, someday I will join them in the same beautiful land under Mount Andutz and overlooking the Cantabrian sea. I can aspire to no better companionship than Martin, who in my childhood taught me moral commitment, and Carlos, who taught me dancing.

Part 2

Baserri Society and Culture

Introduction

Part 1 described representations of history made by and for the ongoing violence; part 2 presents the continuity and transformations of traditional social forms as constitutive of that violence. It examines the baserri farmstead (*caserio* in Spanish) as the basic institutional grounding of Basque rural society. Itziar is, for the most part, a baserri society, and any account of political violence there must take into consideration this fundamental social structure. Regarding the extension of the baserria's[1] import in generating violence, a clear distinction should be made between its sociological insignificance (about 10 percent of Basques are farmers) and its crucial role as the reservoir of a past society's idealized culture. The fading economic reality of the baserria does not preclude its becoming a fitting symbol of an autochthonous Basque institution. The imagination of an original Basque environment finds its home in the baserri organization of space. The decline of the baserri lifestyle has been viewed by many as the decline of Basque language and culture. Recent industrialization has imposed on rural society radical departures from the "traditional" modes of life.[2] Basque perception of a survival threat to their collective identity and the fight to preserve that identity are intrinsically connected to this dramatic transformation. Since the foundation of Basque nationalism by Sabino Arana at the turn of the century, "the idealization of the rural world [has become] the cornerstone of the nationalist argumentation" in which "the *baserritarra* turns into the archetype of the primitive Basque" (Elorza 1978 : 186). These chapters on baserri society and culture provide, therefore, an indispensable frame for understanding the ongoing violence. Yet, the obstinate perpetuation of these institutional and ideological forms is in itself something to be explained within the overall cultural process of being Basque. Part 2 describes a basic dimension of that culturally constituted reality from which political violence derives its arguments and objectives.

CHAPTER FIVE

The Baserria

A Social and Economic Institution

This chapter examines the baserri farmstead as the fundamental socioeconomic institution of Basque rural society. Itziar is still a typically baserri society in the Basque countryside. Despite the heavy rural exodus during the last two decades, in the summer of 1980, out of Itziar's 184 households, 128 were operating as baserriak; of the remaining 56 households, 43 are situated in Itziar's semiurban center.[1] The analysis of the baserri institution is, therefore, central to the description of Itziar's social structure and economy and forms part of the context for an ethnographic account of political violence in Itziar.

The dramatic economic collapse of the baserri institution is emphasized in the present chapter. Its social reproduction has become a key generational issue. What is at stake is the continued existence of the institution as such in the face of its economic unviability and social drawbacks. The consequences of such an untenable situation are reflected in the large number of baserriak that have ceased to operate as such.

The fundamental significance of this factor in creating social discontent is only too obvious. For the Itziar youth who became committed to ETA activism the perception of capitalist aggression, condoned and facilitated by Madrid's politico-military rule, could not find clearer expression than in the industrial development and the siting of a nuclear power plant in Itziar in the early 1970s. A third major transformation consisted of the construction of the Bilbao-

Behobia freeway right through the middle of Itziar's territory. These projects were only possible through the sale and demolition of many baserri farmsteads.

It can be generalized that the main actors of Itziar's social and political history during the last twenty-five years have been, in practically all cases, baserritarrak themselves or people whose parents were baserritarrak. The first political involvement in Itziar at the turn of the 1950s was produced within an organization that was called, significantly, Baserri Gaztedi (Baserri Youth). Subsequently, the same social movement became the platform for political indoctrination and ETA recruitment; the *liberados*,[2] or activist leaders of the movement, were all from baserri families.

It is hard to overestimate the significance of the relationship between baserri culture and political insurgency in Itziar and, by extension, in Basque rural society. Yet the link should not be made primarily in direct sociological terms. The following examples taken from Itziar illustrate how the connection between ETA and the baserria may better be understood. ETA began as an organization in 1959. Only a year later, in the summer of 1960, an underground cell (nominally affiliated with EGI) was uncovered in Itziar with the arrest of José Mari Andutzene. At the time José Mari was a machinist. However, by birth, family, education, friendships, and worldview he was a baserritar. He would never have considered himself to be a *kaletar* (street person; that is, townsman). It was decisive for his underground political involvement that his family fought with the Basque nationalist PNV party during the civil war and that his religious teachers in Deba used to punish him during his school years for not speaking Spanish. In his baserri home they spoke only Basque.

Another instance of the baserri connection to ETA was given to me by an Itziar seminarian. Two broad groups could be distinguished in the seminary of San Sebastián in the early sixties: the more urban seminarians coming from the provincial capital or urban centers and the more baserritar seminarians belonging mostly to rural small towns. According to the Itziar seminarian, in 1965, when he left for Paris to study folklore, all the half-dozen ETA liberados of Guipúzcoa were living in the seminary and they were all from among the baserritar seminarians. These seminarians were no longer peasants by virtue of their occupation or social class, but they were profoundly baserritar in their social and family origins.

Still a third example comes from Itziar's famous cell of the middle seventies comprising four young members. One of them was finishing secondary school, two others had finished it recently and were working in small workshops, while the fourth was working as a waiter. None of them was baserritar by occupation, but two of them were born and raised in a baserria, and the fathers of the other two were baserritarrak who married in Itziar's center and took jobs as a quarry worker and a blacksmith. Their social origin and family background were again deeply baserritar.

These illustrative cases from Itziar point to an interesting phenomenon. It is not primarily the youth who inherit the baserria and consequently have to remain within its occupational and mental strictures who participate in underground insurgency. The baserria's all-embracing nature is, in fact, a most serious obstacle to such participation. It is rather baserri-born youths who are excluded, by virtue of the single-heir inheritance system, and cast away from their natal rural milieu into the seminary, factory, or urban center who become prone to such rebellious activity. The broad sociological equivalent of this first level of removal from the baserria can be seen in the small towns of recent industrialization, which are credited by Garmendia (1979), the historian of ETA, as being the main recruitment base of the organization. Clark (1984) likewise insists on the strong ties ETA members keep with their original baserri villages.[3] It is the individual "once removed" baserritar who, from the vantage point of his consecrated priesthood, industrial job, or urban enlightenment, can look back at his *etxe* (household) of birth now threatened by extinction and perceive fully the waning strength of his own original roots. Only by virtue of a revolutionary act of liberation can he save his natal household and, by extension, himself from disgrace. The resonance of the symbolic affront to Basque identity implied in the demolition of a baserria will be discussed in chapter 6.

The Institutional Aspects of the Baserria

In daily use the term *baserria* refers both to the farm building and to the entire unit of production, including people, livestock, and lands. Just as each *bailara* (neighborhood) tends to be a relatively autonomous geographical and social unit, reproducing within its limits the larger *herri* (village) identity, in a more circumscribed sense there is the tendency toward the autonomy and self-sufficiency of each baserria.

Architecturally, despite the existence of variations, the Atlantic baserri type is considered "the Basque house" par excellence (Caro Baroja 1971 : 112). Prominent features include the low incline of the two-sided roof, due partly to the curling of the edges; the ridge perpendicular to the main front; prominent eaves; orientation toward the south in order to avoid the cold north wind; and the large porch entrance, which is an open shelter in front of the inner dwellings.[4]

In its simplest distribution of internal space, the baserria has the kitchen and the stable on the first floor and rooms and attic on the second floor. The architecture of the baserri house is thus adjusted to the residence and nurturance of humans and animals alike. The house becomes the walled enclosure where people, cattle, and lands are brought together for the performance of the vital functions of breeding, nurturing, and protection. The tangible interplay between the three areas for persons, animals, and storage has resulted from a dynamic relationship between ecological constraints, functional needs, and a specific architectural style. The etxe is therefore an architectural mirror reflecting the actual relationships that constitute the all-encompassing institutional nature of the system.[5]

A feature that immediately stands out in baserri ecology is the dispersion of the households (García Fernández 1974 : 55).[6] This is certainly the case in Itziar, where the farmsteads dotting the countryside stand in contrast to the small nucleus of street houses and buildings of the center.

The baserri household is a typical example of the stem family as described, among others, by Douglass (1969, 1975, 1981). Customary law has reinforced the stem family system and ethos (Caro Baroja 1978). The traditional baserri household consists of two families: the *guraso zarrak* (old parents), whose heir and other unmarried children have the right to reside in the natal baserria; and the *guraso gazteak* (young parents) with their children.[7] The *etxekoak* (literally, those of the house) domestic group includes members gained through descent, marriage, and adoption; at the same time, consent can be used as a criterion to incorporate distant relatives, nonkin, and servants. Thus, the pronoun *gure* (our), as a shortened version of *gure etxekoak* (those of our house), may acquire an extended or a restricted sense. In its more restricted meaning it refers to the resident domestic group living at home; in its extended meaning it is equivalent to *senide* (relation) and can be applied to anybody who originally was a member of that baserria and to affinal relatives as well. The corporate nature of the baserri domestic group can be observed in that the etxekoak encompasses consanguineous and affinal relatives present in the household and persons unrelated to the head either by blood or by marriage who are, nevertheless, in residence, such as *morroiak* (agricultural servants). Etxe is invested with the notion of a person's original and immutable identity.

Dispersion of the baserria correlates with other fundamental traits inherent in the institution. The isolated farmhouse is surrounded by its farmlands, an average of five to ten hectares, which geographically enclose it. The house and the lands juridically and materially are a single unit of exploitation constituting a unitary whole of immovable property and income. Indeed, indivisibility of the baserri house and indivisibility of its farmlands are fundamental rules of Basque peasant land distribution and social structure. The rule of one family for one baserria is observed in almost every case in Itziar. In each generation the farmstead is inherited by a single heir.

As residential dwelling place for humans and animals, as main storage area for supplies and harvest, and as an integral part of the rural ecosystem, the baserri house symbolizes the entire agrarian production and culture. In this respect, the identification of the baserria, the traditional Basque peasant livelihood, and Basque culture itself is complete.

Luxio, raised in a baserria and now living in Itziar's center, pointed out the totalistic dimension of the institution:

> A baserria is like a small village. It has its own name, its own personality, just as does Itziar or Deba or Lastur or Elorriaga. And in this respect to demolish a baserria is for me comparable to demolishing all of Itziar. Itziar has a name and so does Itxistan [one of the baserria demolished in 1973 for the industrial development]. Itziar has a personality and so does Itxistan. A baserria is very small compared to Itziar, but so is Itziar compared to Deba. But for me the street etxeak are different, I don't know how to explain it. A baserria is a name and a community unto itself; it is part of the land. A street house, to the contrary, well,

> it may have four floors or eight, and it has numbers. A street house may have a name as well, but that is different, there is something else to a baserria. I have always seen the baserri way of life and the street life as different. The street life does not have the hardships of a baserria. A baserria is a workplace similar to an industry.

The literature on "total institutions" characterizes them as ones in which the ordinary separation of work, play, and residence breaks down (Goffman 1961). The baserria largely shares the institutional feature of being simultaneously a place of residence and work, with no other co-participants but the household members, under the same authority and with an overall self-perpetuating design. In a baserria the images that serve as closure are geographical boundaries, the architecture of the house, and the domestic group—territorially, architecturally, and socially the boundaries are presumed to be established by nature. It is the landscape itself, the architectural needs of the household, and the procreative limits of a couple that establish closure in a baserria.

A more effective perspective on the baserria's totality derives from the diverse functions it realizes, for it is at the same time a system of production, an extended family, a residential place, and the proclaimed womb and carrier of Basque culture. This blending of social, economic, and cultural factors in mutual reinforcement and dependence is essential for an adequate description of the baserri institution.

In sharp contrast to the social closure of the baserria, in which outsiders rarely penetrate beyond the porch into the interior of the house, the taverns of the village present the opposite model of openness. "Our house is becoming a tavern" is a comment that can be heard when peasants occasionally gather in a baserri interior to socialize.

An opposition of public versus private could be established between the domain of the plaza and the tavern and the domain of the baserri house and property. This overall division of private and public domains in baserri society has a definite effect in determining female and male roles. Traditionally the plaza and the tavern are male domains in which females do not participate actively. In the private baserri domain, men are associated with the outside work of laboring in the fields or raising cattle, whereas the etxe is conspicuously female territory.

For a population of eleven hundred, Itziar and Lastur have twenty locations that serve as taverns, discotheques and eating societies included. In the past, taverns were the places for drinking, singing *bertso,* and playing the mus, all of which were male performances. Itziar and Lastur both have a plaza, which is still the locus for *joko* (games), *zezen* (bulls), and singing bertso, all of them again male activities.[8] In brief, the plaza and the tavern are sanctioned as public male domains in which women participate only as spectators.

Farmers themselves make continuous use of the opposition between *kale* (street) and baserria, implying two entirely different modes of life. According to this dichotomy, the baserria is primarily nonurban, and its life-style is sharply different from that of the urbanized collectivity of the street. When a baserri house is modified by converting the stable and the granary into rooms or other dependencies, the baserria is said to have turned *kaleko* (of the street).

The total-environment nature of the baserria gives it a character of its own. Thus, contrary to the urban residential *piso* (flat), in the baserria one lives side by side with animals and the stored harvest. Odors, views, sounds create a different relationship to nature. Social interaction is balanced with animal interaction. The perception of personal life cycles is related to other seasonal biological cycles.

The occupational settings offered by a baserria and a factory are quite dissimilar. Antonio, a middle-aged husband who, due to monetary needs, mixed baserri responsibilities with a part-time job in a factory, was vocal about the difference. He enjoyed working in his baserria with the animals and in the open field, he said, but to work in the factory for somebody else was quite another matter. The working space, time schedules, sense of property, home's proximity, nature of authority and decisionmaking, and so on were obviously different in the two work settings. Back home from the factory, while others watch television Antonio spends from seven or eight until about midnight in the stable feeding and milking the animals despite having to get up at six the next morning. He readily admits that he does not need all those hours in the stable, but, as his family members say jokingly, "He enjoys himself in the contemplation of the animals." Baserri "home" work and factory "alien" work are two different worlds for Antonio.

Concrete limits on the amount and rhythm of production help to create a self-enclosure that adds to the holistic character of the baserri life. No workers are hired in a baserria except for an occasional servant. Being a family enterprise, there is no sense of baserria unless the family resides in the farmhouse and carries out the farming. Both people and cattle are nourished by the same farmlands, and in their subsistence mentality the primary purpose of animal products is the direct maintenance of the domestic group itself.

Certain baserriak have evolved into pig farms, cooperative stables, greenhouses, taverns, and even small factories in recent years. All contrast with the baserri mode and intrude upon the sense of totality inherent in the baserri institution. Each one is an elaboration of a single element or a single independent function, or has no discrete social boundaries. In contrast, the traditional baserria combines those interdependent elements into a clearly bounded whole.

The Economic Collapse of the Baserria

The downfall of the baserria as an agrarian economic institution has been described most dramatically by the economist Etxezarreta, who, after a team study carried out over four years, reached the conclusion that "the baserria is not feasible in the future . . . we have no other option than to conclude that the baserria is disappearing, it is going to disappear entirely as an economic unit of production" (1977 : 384). This hardly comes as news to the baserritarrak themselves, from whom one can repeatedly hear the discouraged comment, "There is nothing left to do with the baserria."

With its family-based scale of production, the baserria finds itself submerged by the unrestrained industrial development of the Basque region. The baserria type of production is at a disadvantage in competing with other national and international producers in supplying milk, meat, and vegetables to the urban centers.

In order to illustrate the complete unviability of the baserria as a modern form of agricultural production, Etxezarreta's formal analysis offers some figures on the gross income and net profits of baserriak of diverse sizes. The yearly profit of a baserria of five hectares devoted mostly to cattle-raising and selling milk to a dairy company comes to less than the monthly wages of an industrial worker. Over 50 percent of all Guipúzcoan and Vizcayan baserriak are under five hectares.[9] No amount of modernization or mechanization could make a farm of this size profitable.[10] Despite the element of high risk, gardening presents a better prospect than dairy production, provided that technical competence and continuous care are guaranteed.

A table presented by TALDE (1978: 115) on the two reference years of 1962 and 1972 clearly shows the dramatic reduction in numbers of small baserri units in just a decade in Itziar-Deba. It also shows that the larger ones are still viable.

Scale of Exploitation	1962	1972
Fewer than 5 hectares	102	24
Between 5 and 9.9 hectares	45	39
Between 10 and 29.9 hectares	130	135
More than 30 hectares	30	22
Total	307	220

A note on baserri property ownership is appropriate here. It has been estimated by Etxezarreta that at the beginning of the century only 10 percent of the baserriak were owned by the peasants themselves. These data on baserri tenancy openly contradict at first glance the previous description of its self-sufficiency and totalistic enclosure. It should be borne in mind, nevertheless, that owners and tenants historically had a similar subservience to the ecclesiastical organization (Arpal 1979: 134) and that the formal ownership of the land as such did not mark a difference in status group. Caro Baroja's observation that "the farm is an *entity of exploitation* and not so much an *entity of ownership*" (1974a: 115; his emphasis) establishes the appropriate perspective from which the baserri property relationships should be contemplated. The data from Itziar support this view.[11]

A widespread response to the baserria's economic stalemate, particularly in Vizcaya, has been the planting of pine trees. Another solution, common in Itziar, has been to combine industrial work and baserri farming. According to this solution, while old parents and younger housewives keep the baserri lands cultivated and take care of the cattle, the younger men mostly earn a salary in the factories and help at home during their free time. It is estimated that over 76 percent of the baserriak of Guipúzcoa and Vizcaya operate in this "mixed system" economy. Etxezarreta poignantly notes that this combined production, although viewed as an attractive situation, demands from a married couple with aged parents and children in school the yearly equivalent of 3.8 years of industry hours of the man's work. Needless to say, the persistent effort to keep up baserri production even while earning an industrial salary should not be viewed as motivated only by economic necessity. As I have heard from some baserritarrak, "To abandon forever a baserri property and livelihood that has been handed down to you from your forefathers is not an easy thing to do."

In fact, a purely economic view of the baserria as a unit of production fails to explain why the institution continues at all and why the prospect of its disappearance still arouses intense emotions. This profound identification of the baserri people with their natal home and, vicariously, with the ancient institution itself was articulated by Luxio, a second son now living in Itziar's center:

> Take my case. I was born in a baserria and now I have my own house here in the street where I live. But if I was faced with the dilemma of one of the two houses having to disappear, I certainly would give up my own street house. Maybe I am a bit sentimental, but the baserria is the product of my father's and mother's sacrifice. I have a feeling for that, and thus I regard what they gave me as being worthier than what I have made on my own. I see theirs differently, I love and appreciate their way more, and I will always resist the destruction of it more vigorously. I was born there and I will always be known by the name of that baserria. That is my name.

It would be misleading to think that the farmer has failed to make an effort to adapt his baserria to the changing economic situation. In that respect it should not be forgotten that in the regional economy of Guipúzcoa and Vizcaya agriculture represents a very minor sector: 2.4 percent in 1973. All but a negligible part of baserri production of milk and meat from cattle raising is nowadays commercialized. This production has, in fact, increased through mechanization, better selection of breeds, feeding, and sanitary improvements. All this is meant as an indication that a regional and national analysis is required to make sense of the economic downfall of the baserria.

The Maiorazkoa and the Segundón

In the rural area of Itziar during the last twenty-five years alone over seventy baserriak have been abandoned; over one hundred still operate. Confronted with the obviously disadvantageous productivity of the baserria as compared with industrial salaries, the issue of the very continuity of the baserria itself has become the center of family conflict.

Marriage and the problem of succession are the main catalysts of the difficulties of the baserria as an institution. Greenwood (1976a: 122–25) and Douglass (1971 : 45) discuss the extent to which the traditional access to baserri property through marriage and inheritance is in crisis. In the Vizcayan town of Mendata,[12] where I did fieldwork in the summer of 1978, out of the more than 100 baserriak only one marriage to a baserritarra had taken place during the past fifteen years. In the same period, from the more than 120 baserriak in Itziar, only fifteen women married onto a farmstead.

Although Basque customary law permitted women to inherit, this was rarely the practice. The tendency has been to give the estate to males, admitting the validity of the female line only when males are absent. Inheritance is governed by the institution of *maiorazkoa* (heir), or entailed estate, by which the successor, usually the first-born son, inherits the immovable wealth and livestock of the baserria. The house, furnishings, agricultural implements, lands, and cattle are indivisible. The complementary rule is that of the *mejora* (improvement), by which one-third of the wealth assembled by the parents goes to the maiorazkoa, the second third is for the other siblings, and the remaining part is held by the parents. The maiorazkoa has to discharge certain family responsibilities, such as supporting the parents. Furthermore, he cannot enjoy the usufruct of the baserria estate until the death of his parents. Most critically, despite the present situation of economic collapse, the maiorazkoa still has to endow his brothers with hard cash and his sisters with dowries when he inherits the baserria.

In the sometimes dramatic bargaining that transpires, different notions concerning production, family roles, authority, law, generational succession, and cultural values are invoked. Martin, who until his death in the summer of 1981 was a baserri adviser at the provincial level, commented on the central focus of baserri conflicts from his vantage point:

> What breaks down many baserriak is the *senide partia* [the share of the siblings in the inheritance]. The old parents can keep the property and not give it to the maiorazkoa [until they die]. Or they may demand from the heir excessive duties toward the other siblings. In these cases, many times the oldest brother abandons everything, he plants pine trees and goes to the street. . . . In Navarre the inheritance law is different. There the entire property is handed down to the one who stays at home. But in Guipúzcoa this is a crucial issue. Right now I know of many families that are in a complete *jaleo* [turmoil] because of this.[13]

Furthermore, baserri conflict may emerge as a mental gap between two successive generations that appears insurmountable. The differences between the two generations concerning the notions of family roles, authority, property, management, and production become too antithetical to be negotiable without one or the other having to cede what is considered an inalienable right as present proprietor or as future heir. The new generation is faced with the dilemma of either continuing with the baserria or deserting it.

The maiorazkoa rule of inheritance is intrinsically related to the preservation of the baserri system as an indivisible unit. The consequence of the firstborn son inheriting the entire baserria is the high proportion of brothers and sisters who need to be pushed out of the home to seek their own living elsewhere. This creates the classic role of the *segundón,* or younger son. Traditionally there were several ways out for non-firstborn sons: the religious or military life and entry into the government bureaucracy were options. This was also the social rationale underlying the early participation of Basques in seafaring enterprises, colonization of the New World, and overseas emigration.

The institutionalized migration of the secondborn is "a general social structure" (Arpal 1979:227) and thus provides "an elementary structuring of reproduction" (Arpal 1982: 107) that feeds back into the maiorazkoa system. As remarked by Otazu y Llana, the acquisition of Basque capital "is intimately tied to the fortunes of the emigrants . . . accumulation is perpetuated by linking it to the family through the *maiorazkoa*" (1973: 95). Douglass and Bilbao (1975) discuss the image and social status of the *Amerikanua* (American) who returns to the Basque Country enriched by his New World sojourn. By this century, in Itziar as elsewhere the excess baserri population was absorbed mostly by Basque industrial centers.

Conclusion: The Baserria Violated and Baserri Violence

As elsewhere in the Basque Country, in Itziar rural exodus has been a dramatic social phenomenon since the late fifties. During the 1962 to 1972 decade alone, the number of baserriak diminished by approximately 30 percent. After 1972 twenty baserriak from Itziar were sold and some demolished for an industrial development and a nuclear power plant. According to my own statistics, in Itziar in the summer of 1980 there were eighty-five baserriak that were either empty, had fallen to the ground, or had altogether disappeared in recent years. In the bailarak of Itziar, for instance, out of a total of eighty-seven inhabited houses there were thirty-six empty baserriak; in the bailarak of Lastur, for the forty-two occupied baserriak there were thirty-five empty ones. In Luxio's words, "A baserria is a name and a community unto itself, it is part of a land." For Itziar villagers the eighty-five nonoperating baserriak are eighty-five names made obsolete, eighty-five lands become sterile, eighty-five communities extinct. Although absent from the socioeconomic order, they are nevertheless very present in the village imagination and speech. The farmer cannot avoid perceiving these empty or collapsed baserriak as an offense to his way of life. Watching a baserria being demolished, as has transpired repeatedly in the 1970s, is for baserritarrak a very hard thing. So is being surrounded by empty ones, the obvious expression of the vacuum and the helplessness into which the institution has fallen. It is a sight that marks the violence done to baserri life in all its existential dimensions.

Itziar's recent history is inextricably related to the fate of the baserri institution. The reformist ideals of the Baserri Gaztedi movement since the middle 1950s were aimed primarily at resolving the social and economic problems posed by the crisis of the baserria. Speakers and night classes were organized regularly to meet the baserritarra's need for better information and acquisition of new skills. Itziar's cooperative movement, to be studied in the next chapter, was the outstanding result of this reformist movement. Commitment to the reform of the baserria and political involvement went hand in hand in the experience of activists like Martin. The same was true at the turn of the 1960s when Herri Gaztedi was at the peak of its influence in Itziar—the youths who were exploring the institutional feasibility of the baserria were also at the forefront of the political activism. It cannot be accidental that, of the four members who formed an ETA cell during the middle 1970s, the baserri house of one of them was demolished for the construction of the Bilbao-Behobia freeway and rebuilt nearby; the baserri family of another of them sold its lands to industry and moved into a newly built apartment in Itziar's center. The brother of one of them, heir of the baserria, who for years experienced the typical situation of being unable to find a wife, committed suicide. In a baserri society such as Itziar the collapse of the traditional institutions becomes the clearest sign of the irreversible transformation brought about by recent industrialization. The perceived need for reconstructing an autochthonous Basque society, in which the baserria is projected as a natural institution, is translated into the revolutionary project of freeing the country from foreign political and economic domination.

An immediate requirement of the new political awareness is to establish a certain distance from the baserri life so as to have room for action. Residence in the totalistic baserria imposes on its dwellers an enclosure that hampers the freedom of movement required by political activists. Members of ETA, for instance, can hardly take on the responsibilities of inheriting a baserria. The baserria's holistic aspects work against such underground participation. The personal cases from Itziar's recent history illustrate that political involvement is higher among those born and raised in baserriak but who left it for a seminary education or an industrial occupation in a nearby town.

In former times it was the segundón who, deprived of the baserria's limited resources, became the priest, secretary, or soldier seeking his fortune in foreign ventures. In a social role that is reminiscent of the segundón, present-day political activism demands an occupational and ideological distance from the inherited responsibilities of perpetuating the baserri livelihood. Active political involvement is correlated typically with the loss of the former rootedness imposed by identification with a baserria and family allegiance.

A clear case of this incompatibility can be observed in Itziar in the baserria Isasi during the thirties. The firstborn son, who would normally have inherited the baserri estate, became a socialist and decided to resign his maiorazkoa rights. When I asked his brother José Mari, whose war story was recorded in chapter 2, how his brother became the first socialist of Itziar in those early years, he replied:

> I couldn't tell you why that happened. In our home there were no reasons whatsoever to become a socialist. As you well know we have been strong practicing Catholics. And then my brother said that instead of becoming the maiorazkoa of Isasi, he preferred to have a dog's job. He was the maiorazkoa. He said that he preferred a dog's job because in the baserria there was a lot of work and little food. And he left.

José Mari himself joined his older brother in his socialist militancy. In the subsequent postwar generation, Martin from Isasi, nephew of the socialist fighters and milk brother of the Francoist Carlos, became the respected Basque nationalist we know from part 1. Martin was the next maiorazkoa from Isasi to inherit the baserri estate that had been rejected by his socialist uncle and subsequently taken on by his father, who fought with the Basque nationalists on the Republican side during the war. Despite his political involvement, Martin did not resign his baserri responsibilities, but I find it significant that he was a principal force behind a subsequent cooperative movement in Itziar. He himself joined his baserria with three others in a single cooperative enterprise. Thus, Martin fulfilled his maiorazkoa role, but only at the expense of breaking down the institutional enclosure of the baserria. In the sixties and seventies, although most of the youth of Itziar who engaged in political activism were born and raised in baserriak, their involvement has been coupled with a distancing from their baserri duties.

As the self-enclosed baserri world—with its economic sufficiency, extended family pattern, and undisputed personal and social reference point of etxe—was losing its power as guarantor of primary identity, the new generations of youths were replacing it with new modes of personal and group identification. The totalistic tendencies of the baserri form of enclosure were apt to be transferred into the new socioreligious attitudes and ethnopolitical ideology of Itziar's recent history.

The gure dimension of baserri family life was pointed out earlier. Gure stands for the senide category that includes consanguineous and affinal relationships. This mode of collective household identification is well suited for application to the broader collectivity of the country. A metaphoric extension of the gure possessive pronoun became most popular during the seventies in a song that repeated four times in each chorus and strophe "gurea da ta gurea da" (it is ours and it is ours). The song concluded with *eta* (and) repeated four times plus the words "Euskal Herria" (Basque Homeland). *Eta* is a conjunction, but its metaphoric use in the song clearly refers to ETA. Gure is not only the household members; the country and its fighters are also, in a primordial sense, gure.

A fundamental aspect of gure possession is, of course, ownership of the native land. Even if the baserria was deemed to be primarily not an entity of ownership but of production, in recent times the baserritarra has had a good deal of experience regarding the vast difference between owning and simply exploiting a baserria. When the industrial developers and the nuclear power company purchased twenty baserriak in Itziar during the early seventies, ownership or tenancy of the baserri estate made a big difference. Tenants were given an apartment in Itziar center, whereas owners secured, besides their apartments, substantial monetary repayments.

The relationship between Basque nationalism and a capital mode of production is complex. Although the earlier Carlist wars were preindustrial, the nationalist movement founded by Sabino Arana was born at the turn of the century, a period of intense industrialization and immigration. Presently, approximately 40 percent of the Basque population are migrants from non-Basque areas of Iberia, a fact that must necessarily be of singular relevance to Basque self-perceptions. The ambiguity between national sentiment and commercial interests that formerly characterized Basque participation in Spain's colonial venture became more pronounced with an industrialization that required access to larger markets and workers from other Spanish regions. The PNV is frequently charged with being the main beneficiary of this state of "indefinition" regarding pro-Basque policies.

The relationship between the classical nationalism of the PNV, which lost the war, and the nationalism of ETA, which rekindled the torch of total independence from Spain, has been perceived in critical moments as one of both tension and accommodation. Thus, while attacking the interests of the pro-Spanish wealthy aristocracy of Neguri-Bilbao does not seem to present for ETA any legitimation problem, a very different situation obtains when the PNV becomes ETA's target. ETA regularly collects a so-called revolutionary tax from the Basque bourgeoisie and occasionally kidnaps some industrialist for ransom money; this is easily justifiable from a nationalist revolutionary perspective, for the bourgeoisie's goals are seen as mere profiteering—they are potential Judas-like Basques who would consider trading their national-cultural identity for monetary gains.

ETA's kidnapping and/or killing of a PNV middle-class affiliate for monetary benefit smacks of fratricide and forebodes civil war. This was the case with Berazadi, a PNV affiliate whose killing marked a turning point for the PNV and provoked deep tension within ETA itself. One can read in the media of ETA kidnappers and a Basque industrialist embracing each other in relief when the negotiations have concluded satisfactorily and the order comes from the top to release the captive. The Itziar ETA youths had to confront the hardest situation possible when they were ordered to kill Berazadi, a man they knew only too well was innocent, pro-Basque, by then even a friend.

Herri Gaztedi's ideological stance in the early seventies emphasized in Itziar and elsewhere the "devilish" nature of capitalism. When Herri Gaztedi dissolved in 1973 most of its leaders in Itziar joined the organization OIC and were known locally as "the anticapitalists." Membership in ETA and anticapitalism, although ideologically distinguishable, were in fact inextricable in the experience of the activists. Perceiving the baserri property of their parents at the complete mercy of capitalism, the revolutionary goal became evident: the motherland—"our" land—had to be rescued from the greed of outsiders and given the *askatasuna* (freedom) of a native and collective ownership.

CHAPTER SIX

Baserri Culture

Obsolescence and Symbolization

An Autobiographical Image: Mount Andutz

Two men from the Itziar-Lastur area, both brought up in a baserria, have written autobiographies—a most unusual event. These are orally structured narratives transcribed into literary form. One is by the renowned versifier Manuel Olaizola, alias "Uztapide." The other is by José Manuel Arrizabalo, alias "Arbalitz," who narrated his life history with the help of a transcriber. Both aliases are the names of their natal baserriak. These two books are paradigmatic descriptions of the older generation's images, meaningful events, life cycle, and customs.

As elsewhere, among Basque peasants *lurra* (land) provides a primordial cultural map. Images of lurra and the modes in which they are articulated into a visual sequence are a significant aspect of cultural construct. Mount Andutz, next to which Arbalitz was born, is the principal mountain of Itziar, and it serves for him as a root image for personal and group identification. The first chapter of his book *Baso-Mutillak* (Forest Boys), published in 1979 when he was seventy-three, is entitled "Andutz Mendia" (Mount Andutz). (The metaphoric uses of the images of *baso* [forest] and *mendi* [mountain] are described in chapter 11). Arbalitz's narrative proceeds by dividing the geography portion by portion into distinctly separated and named units. Each of these units is a particular piece of terrain situated in relationship to a baserri house. Arbalitz describes the spatial connotations and orientation of each place, natural elements such as stones and trees, and land features such as peaks and their ruggedness or smoothness. Mount Andutz is the overall entity that integrates the partial "views."

This internal description of the mountain is followed by its placement in a wider geography that includes the sea. After Andutz has been situated in its broader setting, the description continues with its animal life, which reminds Arbalitz of his passion for hunting. He completes his first chapter in a way revelatory of the older generation's mental configuration by giving a specific description of each baserri house situated on Andutz:

> I will begin with the baserria of Santuaran Goiko. They demolished it to build the freeway. Later on they made a new one nearby, a very beautiful baserria. The family lives there. Let them live well under the protection of Andutz. (1979: 15)

Arbalitz describes twenty-nine baserriak in this manner. Each of these descriptions includes the spatial relationship of the baserria to the one previously described, the name of the baserria in question, whether or not it is inhabited, and, if so, a statement of good will toward that family.

Arbalitz's description is limited to Andutz. No other baserriak, lands, or animals belonging to Itziar or Lastur are reported. The map that delimits the geographical, ecological, and social unit is the image of Mount Andutz itself and nothing else. At the very end of the chapter, after a strophe of verses dedicated to the baserriak of Andutz, it is said, however, that "the street side of Itziar is also a very beautiful place; and pleasant too. Let their Amabirjina help and protect those who live there for many years" (ibid.: 19–20).

In Arbalitz's narrative Mount Andutz articulates the geographical and social territory to which he himself belongs. Arbalitz's personal history is also encompassed by Andutz. He does not start his memories by saying, "I was born in . . . " It is Andutz and its area that he describes. It is only later on, when he is describing Arbalitz, his natal baserria, that he offers a more personal note:

> At the level of the baserria Soldauso, a little further below, there is the baserria called Arbalitz. A white house. Now it has been remodelled. I was born there, the 20th of November, 1906; I

> was brought up there as well. The family lives there. Let my beloved relatives and nephews live there in happiness for many good years. (Ibid.:16)

"I, in the Mount Andutz . . ." states a relationship between the person of Arbalitz and Andutz that is not experienced by younger generations of Itziar. For the latter, Andutz can only be a reference point, an object of passive observation, a picnic place for an accidental and transitory stay. But when Arbalitz says "I, in the Mount Andutz . . ." he is implicitly stating a relationship of inclusion between the "I" that was born and brought up in Andutz and the mountain itself. The life stage where this "I" was developed is the mountain Andutz, which therefore becomes its natural and social milieu. Filled with people and animals, Andutz is for him an alive territory with its microclimates and ecologies.

Similarly, the first chapter of Uztapide's book (1975) is entitled "News about the House of Uztapide." In it the only description is geographical and centered upon his natal baserria. Uztapide describes the lands of the baserria, animals, woods, mushroom locations, hunting spots, and the seasonal variations in the weather. For him the baserri lands and their wider setting are the bounded ecological locus of his origins, just as Arbalitz belongs in Andutz.

Uztapide's naming strategy is consistent with the narrative form used by Arbalitz to describe Mount Andutz. The baserri names of Itziar show the extent to which they are a mapping out of the territory of Itziar with geographic features taken as reference points. The signification of these names is primarily a locational one, and as such they are relative to certain natural or historical reference points. Each name designates a certain ecological and social feature such as a hill, a fountain, a cave, a tree, an occupation, or a previous name to which further locational description is added. The name primarily points to the baserri house, but it also encompasses the entirety of its landholdings and occupants. The act of naming the land becomes a basic cognitive process. Not surprisingly, the study of toponomy and surnames—inextricably bound together in such a culture—becomes an essential source of linguistic and anthropological information (Michelena 1973; Caro Baroja 1945).

For a Basque speaker the presence of names of natural objects in the composition of baserri or bailara names is quite explicit. Thus, the word *mendi* (mountain) forms part of some baserri names: Menditxo, Mendata, Murgimendi, Menitxosoro. Andutz appears in the baserri names Andutzene and Andusoro; *Itxaso* (sea) forms part of Itxaspe, Itxasburu, Itxistan, and Itsaiz.

Natural images are also associated with the names of the baserriak such as Sakoneta (deep hollow), Itxasburu (head of the sea), or Gaztanegi (a place of chestnuts), implying a visual description of Sakoneta being in a hollow, Itxasburu being at the border of a cliff overlooking the sea, and Gaztanegi being, in the present or in the past, the place of a chestnut grove. The personal identity granted by these names not only links an individual to a baserri house but also connects the individual, his family, and his natal house to the image of a concrete ecological unit. The territory is made into an ordinary source of locational images that, with their names attached, constitute a primordial cognitive map in which family households are embedded and to which individuals project their root identity.[1]

The Baserri Idea of Society

Characteristics of the basic idea of society emerging from Arbalitz's chapter on Andutz include the following: (1) Society is founded in close dependence upon the natural habitat; as the Paleolithic painter may draw figures by merely adding partial lines to already present shapes in the cave wall, likewise in Arbalitz's description of Andutz a house is juxtaposed to a rock, a rock to a quarry, a quarry to a cave, and the cave to another house. (2) The basic structural unit is given by the house, where family life, generational succession, authority, and storing of supplies take place. (3) There is no clear picture of a differentiated administrative structure or institutional organization above the elementary kinship one found in the baserria. (4) The immediate social boundaries and group affiliations are largely traced according to territorial boundaries that can be walked.

In this mentality an individual baserria is the basic structural community. It is the nonhierarchical nature of territorially based communities that is of significance in the social structure of the baserria. The absence of suprahousehold institutions at the village level, except for the church, contributes to the persistence of the traditional outlook on society. In such a worldview the primordial image is not one of a stratified social structure; it is instead an image of contiguous baserriak, each a self-contained social cell. Each is perceived as being fundamentally equal to the next. The basic supra-baserri institutions forced on Itziar villagers have to do, of course, with the economy, since industrial work in the factories and workshops of the surrounding towns has become the mainstay of the local economy. Yet having work in the factory of a nearby town may be largely experienced as a mere occupational extension of the fundamental baserri structure, from which people go daily to work but to which they return to live.

A significant cultural consequence derived from the baserri-centered social configuration has been suggested by Caro Baroja: "A fundamental issue for future investigation will be the relationship between the idea of freedom that the Basque has since quite some time ago, and the history of the family property" (1974a:117). It is in the investigation of such relationships that an appreciation of culture-specific themes emerges. The notion of honor is a prime example in the Mediterranean area (Campbell 1964; Peristiany 1966). The historically fundamental theme of "collective nobility" is the Basque counterpart to this notion of honor. The relevance of ideas such as freedom or ideologies of collective nobility need to be related to the basic baserri social structure in rural society. Family lineage and collective nobility became central institutions in traditional Basque society from the sixteenth century on. This is "a nobility that is produced from the lineage, from the family structures, but with the peculiar placing of residence (original inhabitants) synthesized in the house, in the *solar* 'ancestral home'" (Arpal 1982:104). In Basque agrarian society this "ancestral home," seat of status and honor, is the baserria.

The different historical usages of the Spanish concept of honor are sketched by Caro Baroja in his essay "Honour and Shame" (1966a).[2] Arpal has also given a summary of the "status honor" arguments of the Basque nobility during this period.[3] He notes that nobility was seen as being based on honor that springs from worth, from a spirit of independence and solidarity. Honor was seen as flowing from ancestry—language, residence, the land on which one lived were also honorable. Honor was transmitted through inheritance and within the territory. Time, territory, language, blood, and worth appear inextricably blended into a global notion.

The Jesuit Larramendi, writing in the eighteenth century, eulogized this sort of popular collective nobility. He wrote:

> Every Guipuzcoan who comes from any of the ancestral homes (*solar*) of Guipúzcoa has always been noble, always is, and always will be, unless he is degraded from it because of his "infamies." This nobility of blood comes to them by inheritance. (1969: 135)

What else can these *solares*, or ancestral homes, be but the baserriak? Larramendi is saying that any baserritarra is noble and that no debasement is attached to his menial labor.

The baserri concept of society was not completely abandoned in the formation of urban centers. Indeed, here a rural/urban distinction may not be decisive. Caro Baroja points out: "The dichotomy [town and country] so fruitful in the historical, geographical and ethical fields, is not so in the social one." He adds: "What was born in the country, as the result of an eminently rural social structure [the lineage], was transformed into a political instrument of urban nuclei, traditionally considered enemies of the peasantry" (1957: 41). He concludes that this system of coequal lineages has prevailed for a long time.

In the complex of honor and shame it is *lotsa* (shame) that is pervasive in Itziar's daily speech. The standard negative blame leveled at anyone failing to fulfill customary social or personal rules is *lotsagabe* (shameless). Children and adolescents are particularly liable to such indictment by older people.

Despite the notion of honor as such not being operative nowadays, people are cognizant of the notion of collective nobility. The Larramendi type of praise for it was popularized most recently at the turn of the century in the nationalist ideology of Sabino Arana. The ideology of egalitarian familism and of all people being fundamentally equal has still a powerful hold upon baserritar mentality. The ideological commitment to egalitarianism has given rise to the widespread stereotype of "the pride of the Basques," which has been eloquently spelled out by Ortega y Gasset.[4]

The Obsolescence of Baserritarra's Knowledge

"Etziok konparaziorik ere" (There is no point of comparison) and "Etziok sinisterik ere" (You can't even believe it) are common expressions that members of the older generations employ when they are asked to relate the present to the immediate past. Changes in the socioeconomic and cultural orders are of such magnitude that they present problems of recognition and credibility. The transformations resulting from rapid industrialization and increased exposure to mass media permeate and easily disturb the basic elements of the baserri cultural structure. Male/female roles, public/private domains, authority patterns, nonhierarchical social ideology, and orally based communication have all been affected. The changes tend to be perceived as creating such differences that intergenerational estrangement is an inevitable result.

The Marxist concepts of alienation and estrangement are of help in describing this process. The emphasis on the former rests on what "man has given up and its subsequent relations to the donor," whereas the second stresses "the state of the individual upon and after giving" (Ollman 1971 : 299, n. 20). The phenomenon of estrangement may be seen to arise when what was the core becomes peripheral or when native cultural forms are no longer effective. The baserri farmer is now going through this estrangement vis-à-vis his own modes of relationship and organization to the point that the very perpetuation of the institution is at stake.

It is in the "street," or urban center, where the baserritarra is perceived by others and himself as baserritarra. His dealings with banks, doctors, and lawyers are seriously handicapped unless he is accompanied by somebody who knows the urban milieu. By his style of dressing and walking he is easily distinguishable. His economic transactions are governed by the oral information that somebody "of confidence" eventually offers him or reduced to market days when he personally will buy or sell something with "money in hand." Newspapers, journals, and books are normally not for him. Not only is Spanish a foreign language, but even in Basque he is most likely illiterate and ready to admit that "my Basque is bad." He will easily feel ashamed or insecure in an environment where he knows people look down on him as backward.

Despite the street life being another world for him, the baserritarra usually comes to the conclusion that his own safety resides there. The doctor, the pharmacy, the shop, the butcher, the factory, the children's school, the married younger generation's flat—all belong to the street now. The elderly, too, have to buy a flat in town to which they can retire. The baserri house is no longer safe.

Yet the baserritarra does a real violence to himself in abandoning his own ecosystem and life-style. It is not uncommon to find cases such as the aged mother who refuses to follow her three sons to an urban apartment and stays in the baserria taking care of a few animals. In this regard the remark made by the doctor in Deba is dramatically poignant. He speaks bluntly of the baserritarrak who are leaving farms: "After coming to town, in three or four years they will be dead." He added that his prediction was backed up by twenty-five years of medical experience with them. This view was corroborated by other people.

The phenomenon of estrangement is extended to all the baserritarra's knowledge. If he is lucky enough to have a son who wants to carry on with the farm, he is likely to be in the position to hear from him that all his traditional farming practices are obsolete. The schooled son can tell him what should be cultivated and even give him lessons on how it should be done. The son's disdain of traditional farming threatens the old man's sense of authority. If he always thought the people who were robbing him were the middlemen, the veterinarians, and the milk dairies, he is now told that the real enemies are somewhere else. The enemies are now said to be bad distribution of land, lack of technical aid, limits on credits, and the nonexistence of unions. When the legitimation of knowledge has shifted from customary experience to economic planning and specialized information, the baserritarra's confidence in his own farming competence becomes eroded. Supposedly he does not even know his own job.

"School" is the magical word that epitomizes knowledge. A baserritarra may be able to describe thirty-one different kinds of trees around his house, each with its own distinctive qualities of shape, straightness, weight, touch, resistance, flexibility, internal structure, color, smell, quantity of heat produced when burned, preferred environment, suitability for making certain implements, and so on. It never occurs to him that this is knowledge of any value. Schools, books, elegant writing, counting—only they are proper knowledge. By definition knowledge is something formal, technical, literate, alien from everyday life.

Official agrarian experts spoke to me of the farmer's "complete lack of culture." They felt that the baserritarra "does not know anything" about diseases affecting trees or about the new sulphates that are needed to combat the changes in the bacteriological fauna or in general about how to take care of his land. For the baserritarra, after observing the increasing numbers of new diseases, the conclusion is that "the land is sick." He is unprepared to fight new diseases produced by mounting pollution, the planting of pine trees, soil acidity caused by the increased use of chemical fertilizers instead of the traditional lime, and so on.

The baserritarra's estrangement from his own way of life can reach the point where, as I witnessed in a baserri village, he has to watch his work tools hanging in an exhibit specially prepared for the yearly festival. Implements, both obsolete and still in use, and photographs of baserriak were shown in the exhibit. His house, his tools, the culture of his own rural village are treated as quaint objects of ethnographic interest. Before his eyes, his very livelihood becomes a museum object. That which was the locus of family life, work, and culture now appears as incapable of adapting itself to new forms of human experience, a matter of public curiosity.

The Rise of the Baserria as a Symbol of Basque Culture

An integral part of baserri experience in recent years is its having become a symbol of Basque traditional culture. It is this rather than its economic potential that makes the baserri institution still significant for the Basques. In the largely urbanized Basque Country, the baserria affords an image of a past social organization and culture that identifies the primal "we." With the acute need for national symbols of identity in the new nationalist revival, the baserria becomes indisputedly the most genuine of Basque institutions.

In the poetry of the late poet Aresti, one poem has been singled out by other writers and singers as containing a legacy of particular significance. The poem, entitled *Nire aitaren etxea* (The house of my father) and published in 1963, reads:

Nire aitaren etxea	My father's house
defendituko dut.	I will defend.
Otsoen kontra,	Against wolves,
sikatearen kontra,	against drought,
lukurreriaren kontra,	against usury,
justiziaren kontra,	against "justice,"
defenditu	defend
eginen dut	I will
nire aitaren etxea.	my father's house.
Galduko ditut	I will lose
aziendak,	property,
soloak,	fields,
pinudiak;	stands of pines;
galduko ditut	I will lose
korrituak,	income,
errentak,	rents,
interesak,	interests,
baina nire aitaren etxea defendituko dut.	but I will defend my father's house.
Harmak kenduko dizkidate,	They will take away my weapons,
eta eskuarekin defendituko dut	and with my hand I will defend
nire aitaren etxea;	my father's house;
eskuak ebakiko dizkidate,	they will cut off my hands,
eta besoarekin defendituko dut	and with my arms I will defend
nire aitaren etxea;	my father's house;
besorik gabe,	left without arms,
bularrik gabe,	left without shoulders,
utziko naute,	left without chest,
eta arimarekin defendituko dut	with my soul I will defend
nire aitaren etxea.	my father's house.
Ni hilen naiz,	I will die,
nire arima galduko da,	my soul shall be lost,

nire askazia galduko da,	my descendants will be lost,
baina nire aitaren etxeak	but my father's house
iraunen du	will remain
zutik.	standing.[5]

Which actual architectural image of the Basque past does this symbolic house designate? No other image is as tangible and by now symbolically invested as the baserria.

In the common view of Basques, the baserria is the reservoir of that which most genuinely makes up Basque culture—its language, customs, worldview. During town festivals and on special occasions, when parents want to dress their children in typically Basque costumes, they are likely to turn them into baserritarrak. No urban parents would want their daughter married to a baserritar, nor would they enjoy being taken themselves as baserritarrak (or what their forefathers were until a few decades ago). Yet despite the collapse of the rural economy, society, familial organization, and life-style, the baserria is now enshrined as the taproot of genuine Basque culture.

The world of the farmer living in the baserria is falling apart. His organization of family life, daily work, and seasonal economy is not what it used to be. Though he has lost these, he has nothing with which to replace them. He learned his basic cosmology watching the changes from summer to winter: the direction, force, and temperature of the winds; the shape, color, and velocity of the clouds; the phases of the moon; the seasonal appearance and disappearance of birds, plants, buds. His sense of self developed year after year intimately intertwined with his crops. With maize in May it was the seeding, around June it sprouted, in October there was grain. With turnips in August there was the seeding and in December there was harvest. As one farmer told me, land for him is "like a living thing" replete with biological cycles, different rhythms, seasonal needs, and sensitivity to the environment. It has definite qualities such as weight, color, thickness, age, savor, abundance. His main metaphors are animals, trees, weather variations, land, and topography. Extending his hands toward his house, lands, trees, and the stream flowing beside us a farmer said, "Some people in the city like to go to the theater, and they have to pay for it. This is my theater. I don't have to pay anything for it. I am chained here by all this." The only textbook he reads daily is the land he walks upon. His only map is the sky with its "treacherous" clouds, "beautiful" sun, or "unexpected" winds.

For the urban Basque who is trying to recover the language forgotten after his childhood or lost by his parents' generation, the baserria is the locus of Basque language and traditions that were shamefully abandoned. During my stay in Mendata the children of an *ikastola* (Basque school) near Bilbao came for two weeks of country life and practice of the Basque language. Although housed in the public school, they referred to it as a baserria, for so they had been told by their parents, who identified rural environment and learning Basque with the baserria. Individually or in groups, staying in a baserria to learn Basque has become a common practice for urbanites. In the meantime, as is well known in towns with an ikastola, those among the Basques least interested in sending their children to a Basque school are the baserritar parents. They simply say that their children know enough Basque already and are afraid that they may remain enclosed in their baserri world, ill equipped for modern life.

The theme of the baserria as a cultural reservoir has a long history among Basque writers and artists. Until the 1950s, impressionist painters portrayed farmers and fishermen in much of their work. Praise of the baserri life-style is the central message of the work of Domingo Agirre and Orixe, who are viewed as the best exponent writers of the first half of this century (Azurmendi 1976, 1977). A strong literary reaction against peasant idealization and in favor of urban literature took place in the sixties (Sarasola 1971). Basque cultural revitalization relies heavily on the pivotal element of the Basque language, whose unification, technical standardization, and literary modernization are absorbing most Basque intellectual energies. The lexicon and expressive idioms of the Basque language are almost exclusively agrarian. Its literature, popular sayings, oral tradition, folklore, and mythology bear continuous reference to the peasant way of life. For anyone interested in Basque language and conceptual worldview, an acquaintance with baserri culture is therefore essential.

Political groups have largely ignored the baserria, which is economically insignificant, in their programs. Nevertheless, it is commonplace to state the ideological attraction of the baserria for Basque society. Etxezarreta mentions "the contradiction between the economic and the ideological bases" (1977: 173). As is to be expected, this mixture of political abandonment and cultural idealization, which wants the baserriak to remain as they were in the past, irritates the farmers. They do not like becoming quaint assets embellishing Basque geography.

The industrial development and nuclear reactor of Itziar are extreme cases of the dilemma in which the baserritarrak are increasingly caught up of choosing between either monetary impoverishment or abandonment of the baserria. The case of Itziar is telling in that in order for the baserri population not to migrate to urban centers the demolition of some of the baserriak was thought to be necessary. At least this has been the view of the local people who supported the establishment of the industrial complex. Previously two small industries employing about twenty workers each had left Itziar because of infrastructural disadvantages. A new major industrial park was proposed. In the process, however, Itziar suddenly had to face the unprecedented dilemma of becoming estranged from its natural environment and centuries-old village form. Everybody's question was, "Shall we be able to recognize Itziar in a few years?" Despite the farmers' willingness to sell their baserriak for economic reasons, the prospect of Itziar—a major center of Marian pilgrimage and outings—being "lost" to industry generated a wave of discontent.

A fundamental dimension of ETA's violence consists in promising a revolutionary solution to the political estrangement of Basque society by creating the images of an independent Basque nation. The premise is that after the achievement of this radical "freedom" Basques will be in a position to build their own political institutions, which can alone prevent the country from falling into historical and cultural alienation. Recapturing the original Basque identity is portrayed as the raison d'être of the ongoing violence. This identity is best pictured through the central images of the traditional society.

The model of society put forward by ETA in its origins inevitably assimilated basic contents of the Basque nationalism founded by Sabino Arana. This nationalist argumentation is based on a "ruralist orientation . . . as a logical consequence of opposition to the consequences of industrialization" (Elorza 1978: 174–75). It is a matter not of protecting the interests of rural society but of creating a mythical model to set against the negative aspects of the conflictive industrialization around Bilbao; indirectly ruralism was helping the interests of the urban middle class. Sabino Arana anchored his political thought in the slogan God and Ancient Law. His vision of recovering ancient religious and political rights for the Basques has been expressed by Larronde: "It is obvious that in Arana-Goiri's mind this Vizcaya ruled by the *fueros* is nothing but rural Vizcaya, attached to Basque values and traditions (language, Catholic religion), the Vizcaya before the Industrial Revolution" (1972: 107).

Larronde addresses the Aranist ideology that reached Itziar during the twenties and thirties in the prewar Republican period. By the late fifties, the aims of the newly founded Basque Revolutionary Movement of National Liberation, ETA, were phrased in a different vocabulary. Yet the continuities are substantial if one examines ETA's publications of that time. For example, ETA is most explicit in recognizing the validity of traditional political institutions. Its members consider the family institution to be the foundation of civil society. Family heads in the past were key figures in the municipalities. They were united in district and provincial Assemblies of Elderly as the supreme Basque authority. In its first pamphlets, ETA invoked the model of those past institutions: "Among Basques, democracy has not been either a discovery or a bloody conquest; it has been a practice centuries old . . . the Basque democratic system was based on the *etxeko-jaun* 'lord of the house' as the holder of active suffrage" (Hordago 1979: 2: 68). Basque ancient consuetudinary laws, lost to Madrid's military power only during the Carlist wars of the last century, are elaborated into an ideal charter. The imagery of this timeless native idiosyncratic democracy necessarily required the baserria as its focal point.

In a significant shift from Sabino Arana's first nationalism, ETA abandoned any racist overtones in its ideological program. Basque language—euskera—is proclaimed to be the essential condition for Basque identity: "A Basque for whom the problem of *euskera* is not DECISIVE is a traitor" (Hordago 1979: 2: 40; his emphasis). For the youth of Itziar, born and raised in Basque-speaking baserri society, ETA's cultural and political goals presented an adequate articulation of the stance that local institutions and collective ideals require urgent rescue.

If the reduced but significant impact of baserri society on political violence may escape a macrosociological analysis, the cultural import of the baserria in the Basque revitalization movement is even harder to pin down. As I have often heard, ETA members have a dream in the midst of their arduous fight—they envision retiring to a baserria after freedom has been achieved. The ETA activist has a problem in distinguishing metaphoric and literal meanings when he dreams of returning to the baserria. His struggle is partly one for the resuscitation of the collapsing images of traditional identity and their conversion into new forms that will project a continuity toward the future. This requires from the activist that he obliterate from his perception most of what is actually the case and replace it in his mind with a reality that transcends the status quo. Fittingly, in the massive volumes of documents on ETA being published by Hordago, the artist has inserted small baserri pictures on the covers and throughout the texts. At the other end of the dark underground tunnel, there it stands, silhouetted against the light, an imaginary baserri mansion.

CHAPTER SEVEN

Baserri Cooperativism

Testing the Limits of Communal Ideas

This chapter examines the continuities and the incompatibilities between traditional and modern forms of baserri cooperation in Itziar. Furthermore, this case is intended as an "ethnographic allegory" (Clifford 1986) of realities taking place in other domains of public cooperation such as the political arena. Cultural premises that hold fast to obsolete modes of production as well as deeper structural problems plaguing the agrarian sector within the national economy militate against reinventing new forms of baserri cooperation. The allegorical casting of this story helps us understand how parallel cultural premises, as well as global structural impediments, prevent the recreation of new political forms.

By revisiting Itziar's history during the late 1950s, when a dynamic group of youths was involved in religious and social reforms, we will recapture a less politicized aspect of the revival sought at that time. In an ambience of cultural and educational fervor, the issues of the baserria's economic stagnation could not be avoided. During one of the Sunday after-Mass meetings in which Itziar farmers received instruction on agriculture and animal husbandry, a speaker was brought in to explain the nature and possibilities of cooperatives.[1] One of the older farmers, the head of a baserria, proposed in the meeting that a feed cooperative be formed. Other meetings ensued and soon the cooperative was a reality. The year was 1960. But the real cooperative adventure was to come in 1966 when three baserriak merged into a single unit of production. They jointly built with their own hands a communal stable in which they put their cattle, about fifty cows and eighty calves. This implied a radical departure from the institutional self-sufficiency of the baserria. The three partners in the venture were the baserriak of Isasi, Ipiola, and Larrabiel. A year later a fourth baserria, Beliosoro, affiliated. It is significant that people like Martin were decisive agents behind this cooperative movement; Martin was the heir of Isasi, and his wife was from Beliosoro. The cooperative stable was proposed as a daring solution to the institutional difficulties of the baserria and was replete with the risks of complete novelty.

For years Itziar's baserri cooperative was considered the pioneer and model of such agrarian cooperatives throughout the district. Out of the approximately two hundred baserriak at the time in the Itziar-Lastur area, the cooperative merging of four units might appear to be a minor event. This venture was, however, unquestionably the single most consequential development in Itziar's rural economy since the war. The feed and the baserri cooperatives were later complemented by a consumer cooperative. The feed cooperative not only quickly embraced most of Itziar's baserriak but also has come to dominate the provincial market. The consumer cooperative is likewise successful. But it is the merging of four baserri farmsteads that is by far the most interesting phenomenon for the purpose of analyzing the principles of communal cooperation, and we shall restrict our investigation to it.

In similar fashion a few other agrarian cooperatives began to appear in the Basque countryside in the early 1960s. Cooperatives were presented as the best solution to the baserria's economic dilemma. The incentive to form cooperatives originated in a highly successful industrial cooperative movement centered in the Guipuzcoan town of Mondragon.[2] Despite the success of industrial cooperatives and though this movement was seemingly in keeping with the ancient tradition of rural collectivism as reflected in the village commons and communal practices, the number of agrarian cooperatives remained surprisingly small. Out of the approximately twenty thousand baserriak existing in the provinces of Guipúzcoa and Vizcaya, in the year 1979 no more than twenty-nine had joined cooperatives.[3] Furthermore, about half of the few cooperatives that were formed failed within a short period. The question is why the agricultural cooperative movement engendered so little enthusiasm in rural Basque society.

My argument will be a systemic one: while the traditional communal system and the recent agrarian cooperative model share apparent similarities of ideological egalitarianism and collective work practices, they differ substantively in their guiding notions and principles of organization. That is, the central ideas regarding economy, authority, property, work organization, women's participation, and the nature of cooperation itself are situated in the two communal systems at different levels of abstraction and application. I will argue, based on my own fieldwork in the village of Itziar and from the ethnographic literature on Basque communal institutions, that the perception of differences in the underlying notions is the main reason farmers rejected the cooperative movement. Certain forms of a communal nature may, in fact, preclude the acceptance of others.

Village Commons and Other Traditional Modes of Association

As have other regions of Spain (Costa 1902), the Basque Country has enjoyed an ancient tradition of communal lands and practices. An extensive literature documents the articulation of the baserria with the village commons.[4] The impact of the commons on individual baserri households varies significantly, however, from village to village. Douglass (1975) has studied the commons in Echalar and Murelaga, where, respectively, 2,880 hectares out of 4,732 and 447 hectares out of 2,436 are communally held and administered by the village council. He finds that "in Echalar the communal reserves currently play a significant role in the household economies of all rural domestic groups" (ibid.: 71); the benefits provided by the village commons are wood, pasturage, ferns, and tax breaks. Compared with Echalar, the effect of the commons in Murelaga's baserriak is minor. Still, "while the village commons presently provides little direct supplementation to the household economies of Murelaga, this was not always the case. Informants note that until about thirty years ago villagers took much greater advantage of communal resources" (ibid.: 74). At the other end of the spectrum, Itziar currently has no lands held communally, though there was a commons in former times.

Moving from the commons to communal labor, in Itziar as elsewhere the practice of *hauzolan* (from *hauzo* [neighborhood] and *lan* [work]), or communal work, has been in effect down to the present among the baserritarrak. Farmers participated in obligatory collective roadwork and cemetery repairs. Each neighbor was bound to share in hauzolan. The road from Itziar to Lastur, for instance, completed during the early fifties, was built largely by hauzolan; the cemetery of Itziar was likewise constructed in the twenties; periodical church repairs, the last ones taking place in 1986, are carried out partly through hauzolan. Major and minor hauzolan were distinguished depending on whether the neighbors had to provide cartage or only hoes and picks. A small political group on the radical Left is named Auzolan.

In the past each hauzoa was in charge of the preservation and maintenance of its local roads. There was ordinary hauzolan in September of each year and supplementary hauzolan during spring or at any time the roads required repairs. The collective participation was organized by a village committee, which assigned the day, place, and time for each neighbor. The municipality contributed to hauzolan by providing meals and utensils as well as by collecting fines from neighbors who did not attend to their assigned tasks. For such necessities as house repairs or construction there was likewise a custom called *totuen*, according to which all the tenants of the same landlord were obliged to help each other.

Both Unamuno (1902) and Echegaray (1933) describe other forms of mutual service among neighbors.[5] Still in effect during the youth of Itziar's older generations was the custom of collective *artazuriketa*, or husking of maize. Around Christmas the killing of a pig was followed by the partition of pork parts (*txerri puskak*) or sausages (*odolkiak*) along an hauzoa network of close neighbors and households related by kinship. In Lastur, when an animal died a similar network of eight baserriak was activated for the distribution of exact portions of the meat; two commissioners would establish the price of each portion. Likewise, one stud bull was held communally by a brotherhood of sixteen baserriak among which it rotated annually.

No traditional forms of cooperation would endure, however, if the moral demands for mutual assistance were not situated in an institutional framework of hauzoa reciprocity. Of prime significance is the "first-neighbor" institution to which Douglass (1969, 1975) and Ott (1981) have paid due attention. They have argued that these first-neighbor relationships are systematically ordered. In her ethnography of Sainte-Engrâce, Ott described two asymmetric systems of exchange having to do with the prestation of blessed bread and mortuary services. The baserri pattern of independent dispersed houses and self-contained institutional units stressed in the previous chapter is thus balanced by an ideology of neighborhood reciprocity and by concrete frameworks of cooperation. Particularly significant occasions for formalized exchange among hauzoa members are provided by the ritual cycles of birth, marriage, and death. The formal and obligatory nature of the hauzoa ritual transactions reached its highest expression with death (Douglass 1969).

In summary, in the past the village commons, communal work practices, systematically ordered neighborhood networks, and religious brotherhoods provided extensive frameworks of cooperation in baserri society. This tradition dramatizes all the more the recent failure of baserri economic cooperatives. If the baserritarrak elaborated effective approaches to traditional problems, why have they been so ineffectual in forging a common front with which to meet the current challenge?

The Baserria in Crisis and the Search for a Solution

The previous chapters indicated clearly that the crisis of the baserria cannot be blamed entirely on or analyzed solely from the macroeconomic frame of national and regional markets. A cultural outlook is essential to understanding the baserri system's inability to adapt to new social and economic needs. A close look at the cultural dimension reveals that the baserri institution is aiming at self-perpetuation despite its economic inviability. Douglass (1971) and Greenwood (1976a) have argued forcefully for the centrality of the cultural outlook in understanding the present state of the baserria.

As described earlier, the baserria fulfills the functions of a total institution where familial, social, economic, juridical, and educational needs are simultaneously met. In this view the baserria has been not only an economic institution but also a way of life with a culture of its own. The economic dimension itself has been conceived differently from the monetized mentality of capitalist exchange.

With the typical baserri dispersed settlement pattern and the small size of each unit, intensive mixed farming had been the norm. Twentieth-century industrialization and the necessity of serving the urban centers eventually provoked the replacement of the traditional agricultural crops by a cattle-raising economy. The baserria's small size, immovable property rules, and home-centered mentality did not easily adapt to this change in orientation. Consequently, although the insertion of the baserria into the regional industrial economy can be dated back to the beginning of the century, its development has been slow.

The economic concepts of the baserritarra are still largely anchored in the yearly agricultural cycle, according to which preparation for the winter season is the main concern during the summer. In this mentality, food is the basic measure of prosperity. In such an economy one is either saving or is in a state of debt. Debt in a subsistence mentality means begging for food. Any debt becomes total debt. It is no surprise, then, that the baserritarra suffers from an "allergy to loans." Leaving aside the policy errors of agrarian institutions,[6] to depend on money borrowed from a bank is like being indebted. He is sure that all the bank wants to do is "to eat off him." This monetary knowledge does not transcend the use of cash in hand.

Self-sufficiency in disposing of all the means of production is correlated with the holistic features of the baserria. The peculiar risk inherent in farming production because of weather conditions, soil diseases, or market variations enhances the need for self-reliance. An unfortunate consequence of this self-reliance is the wasteful individualistic approach to mechanization. I found forty tractors in one community near Mendata; according to one of the farmers, three would have been enough were the farms collectivized.

When the cooperative was presented as a solution to the baserria's economic stalemate, its radical novelty could only be appreciated against the backdrop of baserritar conservatism and worldview. The decision to form a cooperative by merging the land, cattle, and labor of several baserriak was truly a call to explore new modes of relationships and production within agrarian life. Itziar was an outstanding exception to the previously mentioned unwillingness of farmers to engage in cooperative enterprises. Two Catholic priests of the village played a key role in overruling the town council's suspicions regarding the new venture by providing church protection for the meetings leading to the formation of the cooperative. But more significantly, despite the strong gerontocratic emphasis among baserri farmers, the impulse for the new mode of cooperation was nourished by the existence in Itziar of a group of reformist youths. The presence of these young men on the farms that merged cooperatively was decisive. For these youths it was a proclaimed goal that the cooperative would provide a more satisfying mode of production consistent with their social and spiritual ideals.

The principles of the cooperative movement were borrowed from the Mondragon movement. Inspired by the priest Arizmendiarrieta, these "are that the operatives of an enterprise shall be its owners, exercising its control and disposing of its variable income, and that the suppliers of its capital shall be limited to a fixed interest return on their money" (Campbell and Foster 1974:3). The agrarian cooperatives copied from Mondragon several basic principles of operation as well: ownership and control is vested in the general assembly, of which all operatives are members; membership depends on the payment of entrance capital; business direction is the responsibility of a general manager elected by a control board; remuneration depends on the earnings; a member is paid back his or her increased or decreased capital investment on withdrawing.

The actual translation of these principles into baserri cooperatives takes the following forms: the lands are handed over to the cooperative for a given period of collective farming; proximity of lands is a strong desideratum; the leasing of lands from third parties is done collectively; an initial fund is established in goods or money; all new investments are made collectively by using agrarian credits; the operations are regulated by the statutes of the cooperative.

Failure of the Cooperative

A major question remains. Despite recognition of the stated forms of cooperativism, plus the reassuring presence of positive models such as the one of Itziar, most farmers were not attracted by baserri cooperatives. In Itziar the cooperative never expanded beyond four members; in fact, one of the original members withdrew in 1973. The desperate economic situation of the baserria is demonstrated by the abandonment in Itziar of seventy out of the nearly two hundred baserriak since the formation of the cooperative. Outside Itziar in the Basque countryside only a handful of farmers felt inclined to join in cooperatives. About half of the few cooperatives formed quickly failed.

Reasons given for the failures included an excessive initial investment, lack of technical advice, and disproportionate expectations as to profits and freedom from work. But the main argument given by experts, promoters of cooperatives, and the farmers themselves is always "the difficulty in getting along." Technical and economic problems aside, we are most interested here in understanding what lies behind these relational difficulties. This analysis will focus on the different systemic orders of participation in the traditional baserria/village-commons articulation on the one hand and the new cooperative model on the other. In a different domain of meaning, the reasons given for the failure of the cooperative movement can be taken as allegories for parallel developments and incompatibilities, left unarticulated here, in the tension existing between either more assembly-oriented or more party-oriented political organizations.

One must start by examining the profoundly differing nature of communal organization in the two systems. The distinction by Durkheim (1964) between mechanical and organic solidarity provides a paradigm of the differences involved: typically, a mechanical society is based on an aggregate structure of juxtaposed familial groups dominated by the existence of a strongly formed set of sentiments in which property is communal and each individual is a microcosm of the whole; functional interdependence in the division of labor characterizes the growth of organic solidarity, which presupposes not similarity but difference between individuals (Giddens 1971 : 70–79). Basically, the traditional form of communal cooperation is structured as a segmented juxtapositioning of self-sufficient baserriak, whereas the new baserri cooperative implies an organic interdependence of an altogether different order.

Traditionally, the communally held pasturage was an essential component of the farming economy, but the basic unit of participation in the traditional commons was the baserri primary institution itself. Whether using the common pasturage or working in hauzolan, the unit of production remained always each individual baserri farm. In the agrarian cooperatives, by contrast, the corporate unit had to be disassembled if several baserriak were to merge into a larger single socioeconomic system. When the four baserriak of Itziar united in a cooperative, this implied that their cattle were collectivized in a single herd, that the produce of their lands was shared, and that labor had to be integrated into a single overall schedule and strategy. This very simple systemic difference of breaking down the unit of participation was perceived as implying, and rightly so, a most radical departure from the baserri-based order.

It is easy to point out other key departures from the notions guiding the traditional communal system. Property ownership versus usufruct is a good case in point. We have noted that traditionally the farmer was the tenant, not the owner, of his baserria. We nevertheless emphasized that the baserria should be regarded as a unit of exploitation rather than a piece of property. Either owned or in tenancy, what is distinctive about the baserria is its fixed property boundaries, considered inviolable by customary law and respected as indivisible by the inheritance rules. The cooperative system breaks down these boundaries. But again, it is significant for our argument that the cooperative does not require from its members the alienation of their property rights: each member keeps intact his property and may abandon the cooperative if he so wishes. The issue is not, therefore, one of private property versus collective property. The real issue concerns the fixed boundaries of the baserria as a unit of production and the use made of them. The cattle, labor, and lands of one baserria—a self-sufficient unit of production—become in the cooperative only a part of a larger system of production. The farmer's freedom from dependency is lost. Thus, it is not the private nature of the property that is at stake but how it is systematically distributed and subsequently used.

Another drastic difference between commons and cooperatives as communal systems has to do with the very economic concepts that regulate them. A cooperative enterprise demands from the outset a radical transformation of the farmer's economic notions, which are largely anchored in the yearly agricultural cycle; an initial investment and long-term dependency upon bank loans is only the beginning of a cooperative system in modern terms. This is equivalent to a state of indefinite debt for the baserritarra, who is used to operating on a year-to-year basis. Besides, a Basque farmer, like a rancher in the American West, may pursue a traditional way of life partly on sentimental or moral grounds. Given such realities, to violate that arrangement in the interest of somewhat improved efficiency and income is to underscore the moribund economy of small-scale agriculture in the Basque Country.

Still, the benefits derived from cooperation can easily be recognized and include less subjection to the working schedule of a baserria, which otherwise never allows for a holiday; considerable increase in the borrowing potential to expand the level of productivity; and new possibilities of specialization and distribution of responsibilities. One might have thought that the strong tradition of hauzolan would help to obviate the difficulty in getting along. But again, the real issue is not one of working either collectively or individually. In both systems, work is performed basically in a corporate manner. The issue is the degree of organization supposed by each kind of labor. Thus, the cooperative requires that the labor of several baserriak be integrated into a single schedule and strategy. This implies a different level of organization from the traditional communal collaboration.

The baserri farmer's shrewdness does not save him from being ignorant of the required new methods of production, finance, and commercialization. The problems of a baserritarra in getting information to combat changes in crop diseases and pests, trying new techniques, or simply putting his money in a bank are enormous. He is unable to carry out bookkeeping or make a rational plan according to market opportunities. The sources of his problems are his lack of formal education, the scarcity of information available, and the orally based educational tradition, which ignores any literature on agriculture.

Associated with his individualistic character and the cultural distance that the expert or the middleman present for him is the baserritarra's mistrust. A history of middlemen deceiving farmers is sometimes deemed partly responsible for this. In peasant mentality, knowledge springs from a practical experience on which authority rests. Acceptance of an outsider's more qualified information is tantamount to admitting ignorance in running one's own business. In the baserritarra's view, it is work, the weather, and the power of land that produce, not books or nice talk.

The farmer is used to basing his economic calculations on the seasonal biological cycles themselves; an element of natural arbitrariness and risk is essential to the enterprise. He is not accustomed to monetized rational accounting or to long-term economic planning. Land is the capital upon which his production primarily rests. In the farmer's opinion his goods possess a quality that no other exchange value can surpass. They are food, and nothing is more necessary than his products for the maintenance of life. Monetization and market value are seen as secondary to the real value of nourishment.

For the baserritarra, work is not merely an economic issue or a compulsory occupational time bracketed by rest, leisure, or family life. Unless eating or sleeping, all moments are potentially working time. Baserri time, like baserri space, is not divisible into its components. Farming work in the baserria is the activity that punctuates social organization, authority patterns, daily schedules. It is, simultaneously, the baserritarra's task, skill, family interaction, entertainment, knowledge, and life-style. Granted luck with the weather, hard work is the only perceived condition for food production. "To eat you first have to work" is a daily axiom for the farmer. And the great distinction among men is between "those of us who work" and "those who live off our work." Furthermore, human labor is basically a mechanical activity integrated with animals, land, and climate into the productive cycle. There is hardly any sense of specialization. The baserritarra is at the same time a cultivator, a stockman, a carpenter, an engineer, and a manager. For him such notions as world agriculture being plagued with a too-large labor force do not make sense. Quantitative work as such should signal a proportionate harvest. If one sows, one receives back.

We must ask ourselves what has been the effect of this steady economic erosion on the communal practices discussed above. In a discussion of the dynamics of the interplay between tradition and renovation of the baserri life-style, Joxe Landa, one of the four members of the baserri cooperative and the manager of the fodder cooperative, offered these comments in 1985:

> There has been a big change. It appears that in former times there was much more hauzolan and mutual assistance, and the farmer's way of life was more communitarian. Later on he became more enclosed, an individualistic reaction, so to speak.

> And I believe that this is the result of trying to preserve that way of life that is now seen as disappearing. This [protective attitude] will have economic consequences as well, but probably it is much more significant at the psychological level. This is quite a noticeable phenomenon. There have been attempts here to create associations and so on to solve the economic problem, but they have not succeeded. The ancient tradition of hauzolan should have favored those attempts, but it seems that they were presented at the wrong time. Institutions have been established [such as the baserria, feed, and consumer cooperatives in Itziar], but what has happened a lot is the increase in individualism, the struggle to preserve that primary nucleus.

Women's participation suffered a substantive change in the transition from the baserri life-style to the new cooperative organization. In the opinion of Joxe Landa, "The most disturbing change has to do with the participation of women." In the family economy of the baserria, women traditionally operated as co-managers, sharing the work with the men. With the division of labor deriving from an organically structured cooperative, women's role in the decision-making process and actual work participation diminishes drastically. This has turned into a major source of conflict.

Representation of authority is another key dimension in distinguishing the two systems of communal integration. Needless to say, the management, bookkeeping, commercialization, and planning in a cooperative enterprise require the introduction of formal authority in modes altogether unknown in the acephalous communal association of neighbors. A cooperative model forces the farmer to surrender not just the duty to be responsible for his family but also the right to make decisions for them. He must give up his authority as head of the baserria, which is a direct challenge to the traditional autonomy of each farmstead. Greenwood refers to this as "qualitative changes for the family farmer's role" (1976b: 40).

Such is the enormity of the difficulties that a baserritarra encounters if he is to work efficiently in the new cooperative system. We can begin to understand why so few have joined agrarian cooperatives. The baserritarra's sense of self-sufficiency has relied on his controlling the limits imposed on production by family labor, cultivable land, and the number of cattle. In a cooperative venture all the organizational characteristics having to do with this sense of self-sufficiency are perceived as being fatally threatened. The new cooperative model presents unbearable risks to the farmer who regards himself as solely responsible for his family's maintenance. This is definitely a different system, and he feels he cannot master its rules and organizing notions.

Conclusion: The Incompatibility of the Traditional and Modern Forms of Cooperativism

Contrasting the former communal spirit and the recent agrarian cooperative movement, the following contradiction emerges: it is the persistence of the traditional communal forms, with their specific baserri characteristics sketched earlier, that prevents the farmers from participating in newer and more complex forms of cooperation. Yet in view of the successful industrial cooperative movement in Mondragon, originally devised and implemented by a priest born and raised on a baserria and with many of its initial members coming from baserriak, the opposite argument could be made as well; namely, that the baserria provides an appropriate institutional education for new cooperative enterprises.[7] More to the point of our discussion, in Itziar the feed and the consumer cooperatives are a big success, whereas the baserri cooperative never managed to get off the ground. So how can the same traditional order be made to account for such disparate results?

A partial response is that industrial or commercial cooperatives do not pose a threat to the autonomy of the primary family institution once it is transposed to an urban apartment. In contrast, in the rural society the same baserria serves as both residence and workplace. Consequently, surrendering the autonomy of the individual baserria as a unit of production to a larger system amounts to compromising the autonomy of the primary domestic group as such. The baserritarra can engage himself successfully in secondary or external activities, such as factory work, or even have his own "industry" (pig farms, greenhouses) as long as the basic baserri complex remains. As Joxe Landa put it, the farmer has "to preserve that primary nucleus" that is the ultimate refuge left to him. Besides, the baserri-born urbanite working in a factory or cooperative does not have to face the prospect of his family line and tradition coming to an end as long as he can refer back to the natal farm, whereas the baserritarra has to himself shoulder the final burden and contradiction (should he join a cooperative) of dismantling his baserri heritage in order to revive it.

It is an anthropological task to examine the embedded cultural premises and regulating principles of social systems. The degree of adaptability between two systems is shown by demonstrating their underlying continuities and contradictions. In the case of Itziar, it is misleading to view former communal practices and the modern cooperative movement as two aspects of a single system of collective sentiment and behavior. Rather, participation in hauzolan as representative of an individual baserria is poles apart from disassembling the very institutional bases of the baserria in order to effect a collective response to the twentieth-century crisis of the peasant agricultural system.

A final comment is in order. The sad fact is that in 1975, after nine years of existence during which the baserri cooperative of Itziar was considered a model by many, it was dissolved when the members sold the land to an industrial developer. Larrabiel had already withdrawn in 1973. Despite the enormous initiative and dedication displayed by its members, upon its dissolution the baserri cooperative barely returned the initial investment. The Itziar example is only one case of a deeper structural problem plaguing the agrarian sector within the regional and national economy. The cooperative had not been a failure, yet it had to be sacrificed to the new industrial imperatives.

The Amabirjina of Itziar.

General view of Itziar.

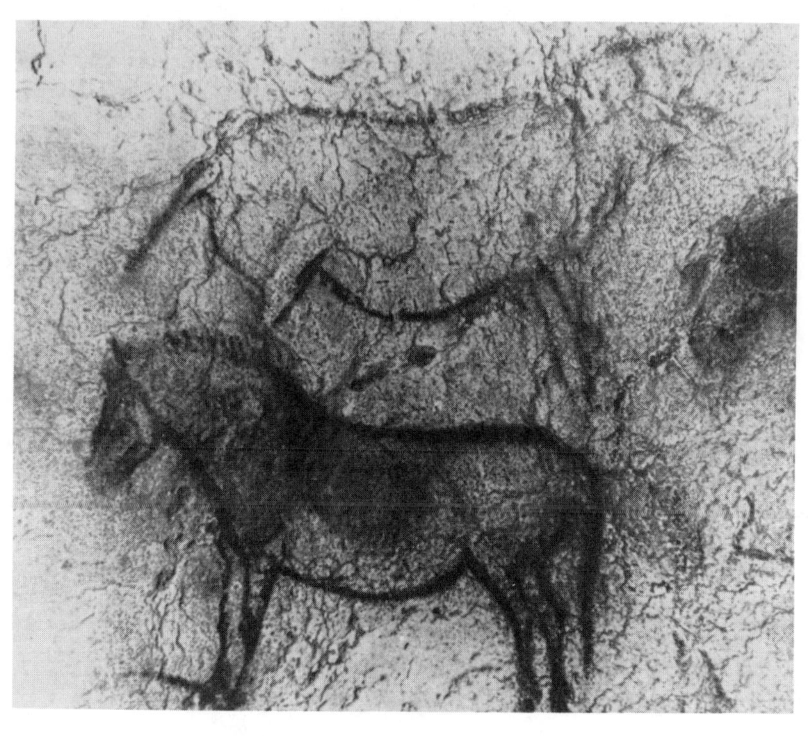

Horses painted at the cave of Ekain.
(Courtesy of Sociedad de Ciencias Aranzadi)

Three generations of the Isasi family during the 1920s. The five boys actively took part in the civil war. (Courtesy of the Isasi family)

A group of Itziar's youth in the early 1930s, with the ikurrina *(the Basque nationalist flag).*
(Courtesy of Pilar Aginagalde)

In a humorous pose: Martin in the center with the flowers; Carlos behind with the beret; José Mari to the left of Martin. (Courtesy of the Andutzene family)

Staging Eun Dukat *in December 1959. Martin, as the good old blind Basque uncle, is counseling Carlos, who represents the villainous urban nephew who is going to steal his money kept under a fig tree. From August 1960 on, Martin and Carlos will play in real life, in the eyes of many villagers, the roles of hero and traitor.*
(Courtesy of the Isasi family)

José Ignacio (on the left) and Iñaki, two ETA activists from Itziar in the mid 1970s.
(Courtesy of José Ignacio)

A multitudinary reception in San Sebastián in July of 1977 for the ETA heroes returning from prison and exile. Flanked by well-known figures, who were to become the main leaders of Euskadiko Ezkerra and Herri Batasuna are Juan Mari (first on the left), Atxega (seventh from the left), and José Ignacio (far right). Iñaki, who had not been arrested and had joined the military branch of ETA, is missing.

Ziaran Zar stone lifting.
(Courtesy of Ziaran Zar)

Typical graffiti framed by ez *(no) against American military bases and Spain's integration into NATO.*
(Photo by Txema)

The bertsolaria *Manuel Olaizola (Uztapide) singing. (Photo by Charola)*

Part 3

Performances in Culture

Introduction

Basque political violence is punctuated and energized by concrete ekintza. This kind of violence is couched in a mentality in which performance itself is the "real thing." It is constantly pointed out that there is an abysmal gulf between speaking, promising, wishing, imagining, and the concrete deed. Real events require action. The rest is only a preparation, rehearsal, or pretense of the thing itself. A mythical identity anchored in a timeless past, a linguistic-ethnic inheritance defined through exclusion of all others, a society in critical transformation having to project its own ideal images in order to recognize itself—these are crucial factors leading toward both cultural confusion and affirmation. In themselves they provide basic frames for understanding the violent reaction. The struggle as such, however, requires concrete modes of fighting, and these vary from one historical case to another. In the Basque situation, an ethnographic research must explore the extent to which the activist mentality of ekintza derives from specific models of performance embedded in the traditional culture. Instead of viewing politics as an autonomous domain with its own norms and rationality, such investigation describes cultural processes in which various spheres of behavior, the political included, share a common grounding.

A word is in order on the use of the notion of "cultural model" throughout the chapters of part 3. Games, hunting, the art of the bertsolari singer are basic performances in the culture; as such they can be taken to expose processes that analogously reproduce in a different domain the structure of the violence. The "reality" of the violence is purported to be represented by the paradigmatic relevance that these other performances acquire in the culture. Obviously no causal relationship is postulated between these performances and the violence itself, for their theoretical status is akin to Weber's "ideal types" by which "in order to penetrate to the real causal interrelationships, *we construct unreal ones*" (1949: 185–86; his emphasis). They are offered primarily as heuristic devices of hypothetical nature, which, nevertheless, are expected to show significant cultural isomorphism with the violent processes by being grounded on ethnographic evidence. Independent confirmation of the validity of these structural comparisons between cultural performances and political violence should rest partly on the recognition of such analogies by the natives themselves. In the descriptions that follow, the actors and spectators of the violence provide to a certain extent such ethnographic confirmation. Still, what needs to be stressed is that the arguments developed in these chapters are based on simile and analogy—they are situations of an *as if* kind that are ethnographically of primary interest and heuristically applicable to the altogether different domain of political violence.[1]

As with any model-building in science, cultural performative models are also descriptions of processes belonging to a more familiar domain in order to talk of what is not yet understood. To the suggestion that recourse to models and metaphors smacks too much of literary allegory, I would respond with Black that models are not epiphenomena, but an irreplaceable part of scientific research, for "metaphor and model-building reveal new relationships; both are attempts to pour new content into old bottles" (1962: 238–39). In this sense, games, hunting, and troubadourial improvisation are not only fictional constructions to talk about violence; they are also, so to speak, descriptions of violence "as it is" among Basques. They are explanations not only "by analogy, but *through* and by means of an underlying analogy" (ibid.; his emphasis).

The notion of cultural model being used here takes into account Geertz's distinction between its "of" sense and "for" sense. Cultural models have a double aspect by which "they give meaning . . . to social and psychological reality both by shaping themselves to it and by shaping it to themselves" (1973:93). Both intrinsic aspects are made into transpositions of one another in performance. From an ethnographic perspective of violent behavior, the assumption is that the basic culture of the actors and spectators decisively determines the selection and perception of these performatives. Cultures are not only repositories of key organizing images but also mobilizers of those images by means of strategic performances. It is primarily from their basic culture that Basques learn how to perform efficiently. When periods of critical transformation force upon a society new acts of creation and violence, the return to the original roots gets partly expressed in tacitly assuming modes of performance long sanctioned by cultural tradition. A truly innovative process in creating a different political culture on the part of the Basques requires that they become cognizant of the extent to which their performances are subservient to these models so that they may be faced with the challenge of transforming them into new modes of thinking and acting.

CHAPTER EIGHT

Joko, Jolas, Burruka

Antagonistic Performances in Culture

This chapter analyzes specifically antagonistic contexts of performance. The *burruka* (fight) and *joko* (game) are polarized competitive frames in Basque traditional culture; *jolas* (play) neutralizes competition. Polarization, as performed in such culturally controlled contexts, is a basic component in Itziar's daily life. These are taken to be the contexts in which villagers from Itziar learn competitive behavior.

As illustrated by the recent history of Itziar, polarization is crucially relevant for understanding people's political outlook and for describing the generation of the ongoing violence at a local level. The tragedy of Carlos is only the most dramatic case. ETA has tried to impose on Basque society a war situation through violent acts, which, although insignificant in warfare terms, have implied a total rejection of the existing order. In such a situation, the bipolar frames to be examined in this chapter provide the required cultural models, strategies, and persuasions for the combatant behavior. This discussion of polarized contexts will be completed in chapter 13 when we examine the opposition between the affirmative and the negative.

Polarization is typically presented in an either/or scheme of mutual exclusion. The syntactical disjunctive *ala* expresses such an either/or frame, as in the slogans "Euskadi ala Lemoiz" (Either Euskadi or Lemoiz)[1] and "Iraultza ala Hil" (Revolution or Death).[2]

The *ala* frame achieves the following: both terms of the disjunctive are at the same level; and both terms are logically exclusive, so that the affirmation of one implies the denial of the other. This is simply the basic logical operation of disjunction by which $A \vee B$ implies $A \wedge \sim B$ and $\sim A \wedge B$; in a subsequent step the single negatives $\sim A$ and $\sim B$ can be deduced. This elemental scheme of thought that interchanges the disjunctive and the negative frames in situations of antagonism may arise as a cultural fetish apparently capable of accomplishing anything.

A burruka and a joko create fields of either/or disjunction. Winning and losing are defined in mutual exclusion. Typically, in a burruka and a joko there are no plural arrangements and no mediating elements. They represent competitive polarization in the culture, the logic of which helps explain certain uncompromising positions. The generalization that "politics is a joko" is often heard. Political behavior, to the extent that it is modeled after bipolar joko, would not allow for mediation or gradual results. Jolas is noncompetitive performance and is reduced to the children's domain. Joko stresses a single linear scale of value and reduces the complex set of results into unambiguous victory or defeat; jolas, by contrast, is of a metaphoric kind, and there is no reduction of values to a win or lose alternative. The interplay of burruka, joko, and jolas in the overall culture presents a performative structure basic for the description of violent processes.

The Burruka Model

A culturally standardized application of the *ala* scheme is the burruka. Burruka is typically a fight or wrestling match between two males, a hand-to-hand combat admitting no weapons. The use of a stick, stone, or knife runs directly counter to the physical wrestling of a burruka and implies the end of it. An equal basis of one to one, whether of persons or groups, is also essential to a burruka.

Burruka characterized Itziar throughout all of my childhood and still is a culturally sanctioned institution. No implications of brutality or arbitrariness are attached to burruka. As children we would arrange burruka, sometimes days in advance, as a game to show off physical and psychological strength. During my fieldwork I saw two children of eight and ten years arrive home heated up and matter-of-factly explain to their parents that they had been in a burruka with someone. The parents did not object. The father, in fact, reacted to what he assumed would be my likely surprise and, without any comment on my part, said, "That's normal."

The male character of burruka is associated with other male domains, such as tavern life and competition in the plaza. After a few drinks, for the youth particularly, forms of competitive behavior include betting, singing bertso, showing off physical strength in athletic competition, and burruka. There is no cultural sanction for two women fighting a burruka. Females fight, but when they do it is said they are *tximetatik tiraka* (pulling their hair). Men do not get into burruka with women.

Situations in which burrukak used to take place were mostly open-air dances and village festivities, the major occasions for drinking and fun. While I was in the field, during the yearly fiestas of Itziar, a serious burruka took place between youths of Itziar and a group that came from a nearby town. Nothing like it had occurred for many years and people were very upset about it. The incident that led to the row was a blow delivered by a half-drunk young outsider to an elder from Itziar who had rebuked him for driving too fast in the village street. The elder's son responded by knocking the youth down, friends of the outsider came to protect him, and the fight expanded to a few people defending each side. As people from Itziar would describe it, "All they wanted was burruka, to make a hell of a row, and any incident was good enough to start it." The five or six people from Itziar who participated in it were not from among the younger generations but in their thirties, and therefore more familiarized with burruka incidents.

Although legitimate in traditional culture, I should hasten to add that during all my years in Itziar I hardly ever heard of and never saw a burruka between Itziar adults. Among married men, particularly, a burruka is extremely rare. While it may be a point of honor to engage in a burruka, someone prone to create unnecessary quarrels is disliked. While I was in the field there were several occasions in which a mild verbal confrontation arose in a tavern but was soon dissipated by the intense expressions of disapproval on the faces of those present. Similar cases pointing to the acute dislike of public expressions of violent behavior have been observed by other ethnographers.

Presently burruka is largely confined to rural areas, and even here participation by adults is now considered out-of-date. Increasingly, such a display of force is perceived as needlessly arbitrary and scarcely enjoys cultural approbation. Yet people are aware of the cultural legitimacy of burruka. The comment of a middle-aged man from Itziar on the *burrukalaria* who tried to disrupt the village fiestas demonstrates this awareness: "It is not that they are bad people, they are just wild. If you know how to treat them, they are not dangerous. They simply need to show off their force; they cannot keep it within themselves. They just feel good after doing something crazy; they need burruka for that." Taking out a knife is never considered justified. A youth from Itziar was associated with an outsider friend who threatened to take out a knife in a quarrel in Deba. Once this incident became known in the area, his reputation was seriously hurt. Using a knife is an abrogation of burruka rules. Shooting someone with a gun is even more so; it is altogether unrelated to burruka. The concept of burruka is not associated with homicide.

In traditional Basque society the notion of violence itself is largely translated into and controlled through the burruka cultural institution. Involvement in a burruka does not necessarily imply a violent character. Since burruka is closely linked to the use of bodily force, the notion of violence that derives from it is one of unduly using personal force. Apart from burruka situations, no abstract notion of violence is employed in Itziar's everyday speech. Presently, its paramount expression is ETA's *burruka harmatua* (armed burruka).

The Joko Model

Joko is a bipolar competitive game that produces a winner and a loser and is almost exclusively the men's affair. Gaming, betting, playing, singing verses, and working can all easily become joko. A pelota game, a race, and playing the card game mus are examples of joko. In another sense, joko is people gambling or betting on the performance of a staged joko or event. Thus, one may *jokatu* money as a wager. It almost does not make sense to compete without betting something on the outcome; the two meanings of joko thus tend to become confused.

The language of joko is pervasive in everyday conversations. When a difference of opinion arises, even if no gaming or betting is remotely involved, the divergence may lead as a matter of course to the expression "Jokatzeit nai dekena . . ." (I bet you whatever you want that . . .). At home it was through joko that my mother would force her nieces to eat or do something. She would say to Aintzane, "Shall we bet Amaia [her older sister] who will finish eating first?" Or she would say, "Let us see whether you finish eating before daddy comes. *Ezetz* [I bet you don't]." Often she would simply announce "*Ezetz* [I bet you don't] do that." Yet she was not fond of joko. "There is nothing as miserable as joko," she often complained. And the lullaby she always sang was an invective against joko:

Aurtxo txikia negarrez	The little baby
dago.	is crying.
Ama, emaiozu titia.	Mom, give him the breast.
Aita gaiztoa tabernan	Bad daddy is in the
dago,	tavern,
pikaro jokalaria.	crooked, given to joko.

When asked about the most memorable happenings in their youth, older generations are likely to point first (besides the civil war) to intervillage joko. Among Itziar's past famous athletes the stone lifters Arteondo,[3] Ziaran Zar, Soarte, and Endañeta stand out. A runner or a stone lifter of one hauzo would compete against another of the contending hauzo. The people of each hauzo would bet in favor of their athlete, sometimes quite heavily. Even today such joko remain.[4]

These joko are considered "really fine." No fraud was supposed to take place in them, a condition that was, of course, difficult to uphold, even in the best times, by those who lost joko. Any loss has tended to be interpreted as *tongo,* or fixing.

The typical way a joko starts is illustrated by the following one that took place at the beginning of March 1980. A bachelor in his late thirties threw down a challenge in one of the village taverns. He was prepared to bet twenty-five thousand pesetas to anyone from Lastur who dared accept it. The conditions were as follows: he himself would cover the distance between two given points on foot, whereas the opponent from Lastur would cover it by bicycle. The bet was that the bicycle would not outdo him by more than ten minutes. People from Lastur took up the challenge and commissioned their best racing cyclist. The day of the race arrived. Dozens of us followed the cyclist by car, and some accompanied the runner on foot through the hilly shortcuts. The cyclist won. Every Sunday in the plaza of Azpeitia, twenty kilometers from Itziar, traditional joko such as ram fights or tests of strength between oxen or donkeys, wood choppers, or stone lifters take place. A group of bachelors from Itziar regularly attends and bets on these joko.

Other forms of joko take place as well. During the first week of January 1980, thirty-four pairs of oxen participated in a yearly competition in Deba in which awards were given to the first eight or ten contenders. The money collected with the tickets was for the Basque schools. The games themselves are called *idi-probak* (oxen trials). Despite Deba being an urban center, many people attend this peasant competition of pairs of oxen dragging a big rectangular stone through the plaza to an uproar of shouts, bets, blows, and sheer pandemonium. The oxen in each *proba,* encircled by about thirty men, including oxen handlers, judges, and oddsmakers, first go swiftly and then falter. At the end they can hardly advance and become painfully engulfed in the deafening shouts of the audience, which tries to urge the teams onward using movements and gestures from a safe distance. All kinds of people are present in these idi-probak, and most bet a hundred duros (five hundred pesetas).

From a purely formal viewpoint, a crucial change has occurred from the above-mentioned bipolar joko to this context in which several competitors participate. The binary model has been replaced by a plural one with respect to the participants. A formerly well-known *jokolari* complained to me that instead of the old idi-joko between two pairs of oxen there are now idi-probak between many pairs. He said, "This is not real joko." The profound difference is that in the binary model the meaning of winning and losing is clearly defined by mutual exclusion. Winning means not losing, and losing means not winning. In the plural model the meanings of victory and defeat get blurred because there are many winners and many losers.

Betting on staged joko remains the same regardless of whether the events are binary or plural. Nevertheless, in *apostuak* (wagers) there is a crucial modification: the introduction of mediating brokers whose role it is to match two people who disagree over an anticipated outcome. These brokers are nowadays a fundamental component in joko contexts such as the oxen championship or the pelota matches (known in the United States as jai alai). No such mediator was present in joko in the past. People of the older generations are fond of recalling in jest that then "people would jokatu everything they had, houses included, and even their wife if you didn't keep watch." In the inter-hauzoa joko I witnessed during my fieldwork there were no brokers. Contemplating these fundamental changes in the joko context, such as from dual to multiple participation, from binary to plural arrangements, from direct to mediated polarity, one begins to understand why the traditional joko in its pure form is becoming marginal. This progression of joko frames into more complex forms can be taken as a major indicator of cultural change.

Joko interaction obviously plays an important role in social functions. During my own field stay I got in contact with many people only through joko. On some occasions it was very significant to me that I was denied joko. In my understanding of the situation, playing together would presumably have meant a sign of comradeship that some people felt reticent about. José Mari refused to engage in joko with Carlos. Best friends play mus or pelota mostly among themselves. A distinction needs to be drawn here, as a youth pointed out to me, between these intimate jokoak and the public joko of the plaza.

The dysfunctional aspects of joko are suggested by the Basque lullaby cited above. One hears of cases of young women who stopped going out with an excessive jokolari. There are printed bertso against joko. No joko is permitted in prisons. As one of the young people from Itziar who had been in prison pointed out to me, even soccer, which was permitted, became in prison life such a source of conflict among friends that they decided on their own not to play it. In a totally closed institution such as a prison, in which the social flexibility needed to escape from each other's interaction was practically nonexistent, the potentially disruptive effects of joko were magnified.

There is, then, an important element of social ambiguity in joko. On the one hand, it is a basic mechanism that triggers social interaction. Within certain contexts, the extent of two people's companionship can be measured by the degree to which they successfully permit themselves to test each other in competitive behavior without risking their basic friendship. On the other hand, particularly in public joko and betting, joko behavior risks a runaway disruption and can be most dangerous. Hence the incompatibility between the roles of good father and staunch jokolari, or between the plaza tavern and the home.

Although the traditional types of joko are sporadically set as events, even in rural Basque society the sports in which most people get involved are soccer and bicycling. Polarized schemes can be detected in these competitive games as well, but they nevertheless depart from the traditional joko in that the strictly bipolar frame is definitely abandoned. In a marathon or bicycle race there is a winner, but it becomes pointless to determine the loser. Presumably the "loser" is the multitude that did not win. That is to say, the two opposing poles do not belong to the same logical type. The condition of bipolar schemes, which is that the two contending poles belong to the same level, breaks down. Similarly, in soccer the winner and loser are teams, not individuals. In the major national soccer competition (*liga*) single victories or defeats are framed within a larger context.

The cultural emphasis on joko behavior is responsible for activities that in themselves are not competitive yet are performed as joko. The bertsolariak singers to be studied in chapter 10 are a case in point. A *bertso* song is an improvised poetical creation in which the argument is developed by metaphorically linking various images. Yet there is a widespread perception that bertso singing is fundamentally a joko; thus, a performance that is intrinsically sustained by the ambiguities of allegory and irony is framed within the joko literalness of competitive winning or losing. This joko definition of bertso singing arose because the singers are usually set one against another in a verbal duel. The bertsolariak themselves find it easier to sing in this antagonistic mode. On many occasions, however, they sing on their own or in circumstances that are not polarized. The recent proliferation of bertso championships reflects the same distorted tendency to view troubadour singing as a competitive performance that can be graded numerically by a jury by setting up rules of technical accuracy regardless of its intrinsically metaphoric nature.[5]

It should be pointed out as well that different kinds of joko present significant variations. The previously mentioned card game mus shows a particularly relevant model of cultural performance. Mus is almost the only card game played in Itziar as well as elsewhere in Basque traditional society, and it is almost exclusively a man's card game; few women know how to play it. Men, taverns, betting, and mus playing are intimately associated. On any public occasion or fiesta, after lunch or dinner, men of all ages play and bet on mus. Nothing can replace mus playing as a means of indoor entertainment. As in poker, bluffing is part of the game. Simple points are scored for holding the highest hand, the lowest hand, best pairs, and best game point. Each outcome is treated in turn as the players calculate their chances and take the measure of their opponents. If a player is confident of winning the high hand, for example, he can "push" his opponents, raising the stakes by, say, three points. If the challenge is accepted the outcome is deferred until everyone's cards are exposed at the end of the round. If, however, it is rejected, the player raising the stakes is allowed to score the simple point irrespective of cards held.

What makes mus the card game par excellence? *Hordago* is what distinguishes mus from any other game. There are two ways of winning, one by summing up points in a cumulative progression until the necessary total has been achieved, the other by means of an *hordago* point, which overrules the progressive accounting, converting the next outcome into a game point. *Hor dago* literally means "there it is" or "this is it." The hordago point has to be accepted by both sides in order to become an all-or-nothing result. The losing side can interrupt the quantitative progression of points at any time by calling for an hordago. If, for example, the hordago is given and accepted with respect to the highest hand held, the cards are exposed and the player (or team) holding the highest hand wins the entire game (not just the round). If it is refused, the player issuing the challenge scores the simple point for highest hand. Thus, the rules provide an hordago alternative to the continuous process of numerical point-by-point computation. The point of an hordago and a point in the ordinary addition are of a different order. Whereas the ordinary point (*enbido*) is inserted in a continuum process, adding toward the total needed for the game point, the hordago point is altogether discontinuous and outside of any ordered pattern. In the continuous process each point is contiguous and equal to the other. There can be no two hordago final solutions in a game—each is unique and rules out any alternative. An hordago solution creates an on/off or either/or digitalization of a ritual kind (see chapter 13). The interplay between the two contexts, the continuous numerical progression and the discontinuous all-or-nothing hordago, characterizes mus.

And it must characterize the men who prefer it to any other game. The cultural connotations of hordago winning are most significant. What mus teaches Basque men for hours on end is the premise that marking as the result of a gradual process can always be offset by the economy of an hordago. By allowing hordago solutions, mus assumes that sudden, partial, arbitrary acts are more decisive than the progressive summation of a process. Since the hordago creates a game point, the losing party is likely to resort to it as a scare tactic and, if used excessively, it even vitiates the game. In daily speech and confrontational political rhetoric there is constant metaphorical use of hordago. The hordago complex offers a key model for describing the ekintza mentality that sustains Basque political violence. (This will be examined in chapter 13.)

The Jolas Model

Jolas neutralizes the competitive frames of burruka and joko. In this regard, the roles assigned by the culture to jolas become decisive in delimiting the meaning of competition. The social significance of either competitive or playful behavior is given by the culturally sanctioned definitions and uses of the joko and jolas models. This social structuring of competition and play is in itself a major cultural proposition of significant implications. As examples, the distinction between the literal and the metaphoric, or between "truth" and "lying," is expressed in performance by the opposition between joko and jolas, game and play.

Jolas belongs to the children's domain. For an adult to engage in jolas is improperly childish. I frequently heard this reproach to grown persons behaving childishly, "Are we going to turn now into children or what? Shall we keep behaving like children always?" Culturally, joko and jolas are mutually exclusive in the same manner that adulthood and childhood are. It is improper for Basque adults to be jolasean (playing), which is children's type of performance, but since children are always around at home one has easy access to jolas anyway. Men are particularly fond of jolas activity with children when they are home from work. Thus, although defined by the culture as belonging to the children's world, jolas actually is a frame of action very accessible to any adult in the privacy of family life.

As I remember from my childhood, a characteristic of these jolasak was their change according to the seasons.[6] In springtime long hours were spent searching for crickets and bird nests; summer was the time to steal cherries or pears; in the fall going out with the hunters was popular; and winter was the best time to be at home and play *izkutuka* (hide-and-seek). Before Saint John's Day on June 24 we used to spend two or three weeks gathering brambles and dry grass for a bonfire. During the corn season, pumpkins were used to represent human faces. During the school period the most practiced games were pelota, running races, and races with tops from soft-drink bottles, snails, or metal rings steered with a stick. Everyone had an irreplaceable weapon as well: the slingshot. In the playing habits of present-day children, war games are also popular. One frequently observes groups of ten or twelve children displaying full-range military strategies through the streets of the village. One group-army challenges the other and gives the opposition half an hour to decide if they dare to accept. After establishing strict rules and conditions of behavior, they engage in total "war." Sex roles are obviously present; girls will never engage in war or burruka and dolls constitute their basic toys.

The jolas frame may encompass a variety of activities. For instance, a burruka for children is mostly jolas. Two children engaged in a burruka may be asked whether they are really fighting or simply jolasean. The jolas frame neutralizes the competitive element of the joko or the aggressive purpose of the burruka by introducing a message of the sort "all behavior here is untrue" (Bateson 1972:184). Significantly, burruka, joko, war games, sports, as well as the simple breaking of social rules or the representation of church ceremonies, can turn into jolas behavior for children. In general, any occupation or activity, animal as well as human, is susceptible to the playful dramatization of jolas in the children's world. Because of the cultural identification of jolas as child behavior and joko as adult behavior, a child can engage in a joko context only fictionally by turning it into jolas, and adults can participate in jolas only on a pretence or as a result of their interaction with children.

In what sense could one say that the "winning" of the child and the "winning" of the youth are not the same? The same arbitrary rules are followed in both situations. In the joko context, however, ordinarily with bets at stake, winning in the game becomes invested with a personal and social significance that is missing in jolas. At the level of personal identity, becoming the "best," the "strongest," the "cleverest" by winning a particular joko results in positioning the entire self on the positive side of the polarity. In this perspective, the adult self itself *is* a joko; that is, the cultural definition of becoming an adult is precisely the capacity to internalize the joko scheme and operate within it. Moreover, the social recognition of personal worth relies fundamentally on the success or failure of such joko competitive performances.

The child is also a "winner" in a jolas. The child is being educated by the culture for joko behavior through jolas, but until he or she reaches adolescence the actual win-or-lose results of jolas are not constitutive of the personal self. The jolas context is not essentially dependent on the final win-or-lose situation resulting from the rules of the game. In fact, many jolasak will improvise rules or even consist of breaking the rules of the game, which is in clear contrast to joko rule following geared to an end result. In jolas, children create personal and social roles in a manner defined by the culture as unreal. In joko, adults establish personal and group identities in a manner defined by the culture as being the real self.

How do women relate to this jolas/joko continuum? Sexual roles are defined in close connection with these performances. In general, joko pertains to the male public domain of plaza and tavern. Women also do competitive things such as playing cards at home. However, women's card games, besides being in the private domain of the home, are not the real joko card game, which is mus. Women do bet symbolic amounts of money while they are playing their card games, either among themselves or with men, but competition in games by women is an oddity. I do not know nor have I heard of any woman in Itziar being considered a jokolari. This would make her conspicuously abnormal, an evidently mannish woman, in the community. In Basque society, women's proper domain is the kitchen. Male definitions of work usually exclude housework. In the male view, what is opposed to *lana* (work) is jolas. The implication is that male adults tend not to treat women as equal social beings. Since the culture does not endorse joko performances for women, males in their interaction with women are pushed to resort to the infantile frame of jolas.

The notion of "truth" gets its meaning in the culture partly from the joko/jolas interplay. Jolas is a context in which everything is acted out *gezurretan* (in a lie). Acting out *egitan* (in truth) is a sine qua non condition of joko competition. The joko frame is a device to remove all ambiguities regarding plus or minus, right or wrong, truth or falsity by a final outcome in a context of polarization. Therefore, when the truth has to be uncovered, the cultural strategy is to resort to joko performance. By contrast, nothing is really serious in jolas; that is the whole point. As a consequence, it is only to be expected that in situations of great personal or social stress the banalities and "lies" of playful behavior will appear to be censurable idleness or confusing immorality.

Conclusion: the Joko and Jolas of Political Burruka

The paramount definition of the Basque political activist is one of burruka. The goal of the fight is, of course, *irabazi* (to win), where victory has been termed as Euskadi's *askatasuna* (freedom) and implies the defeat of Madrid's domination. To call this political activism a jolas would be offensive to the actors' perception of their actions. The saying that "politics is a game" can be acceptable to Basque politicians, but only under the conditions that the game is joko, never jolas. The same cultural logic that defines ETA's violent struggle as *burruka harmatua* (armed burruka) and characterizes the political antagonism with Madrid as joko or *sokatira* (tug-of-war, another popular form of joko) completely excludes jolas as an appropriate context for violent action. During the years 1975 and 1976, at the height of political polarization, the youth in Itziar went as far as boycotting the annual village fiestas, by centuries of tradition the major religious and communal experience of village solidarity. A popular song at the time went, "No feasting, no dancing—the country is in mourning." At a time when the political situation was perceived to be one of dramatic burruka, taking part in the village fiestas amounted to indulging in jolas.

Sometimes the youth of those joining ETA, adolescents of sixteen and seventeen, leads people to question whether they are jolasean. On the other hand, after some particularly strong action by ETA, people have praised the young men by saying, "They are not jolasean." Furthermore, in people's minds there was a competition for toughness between the two ETA branches during the late seventies, which was clearly damaging to the more flexible politico-military branch. This group's actions were sometimes labeled jolasa by staunch supporters of the military branch.

The cultural premise that situates burruka and joko in the male public domain is correlated with the relative absence of women from ETA's ranks. Many young women have, in fact, collaborated closely in the organization with their male counterparts, but, as I have heard some of them complain, when an important action was under way women were left aside. "We were only to do errands and pass messages" is a common perception. A young woman who belonged to ETA's top leadership until 1977 told me, however, that women themselves were to blame for their lack of participation at higher levels of ETA. She had known only two women in the two branches of ETA who were members of the governing body of the organization. Despite substantial female collaboration and despite many women being arrested as ETA activists, no woman has enjoyed the aura of hero and martyr for the Basque cause, unlike quite a few men. Women being burrukalari and jokolari does not fit with the cultural premise of their character. Were women to be heroes, heroism would be close to the jolas frame.

For Basques committed to political radicalism the very idea of presenting a model of heroism based on jolas sounds derogatory. The immediate cultural suggestion is that *bizitza jolastu* (to live to play) is only a childish stage before growing up. Despite the existence of important artists among the Basques, a model of heroism based on playful performance or artistic creativity is altogether missing. Singers, poets, or sculptors may indirectly share the mystique of heroism by celebrating the fallen heroes but will hardly be perceived as such on the merits of their own creation. Playful aspects are latent in the admiration shown for sports players; however, these sports games are competitive joko, never jolas.[7]

In the recent nationalist resurgence the burruka concept has been applied to all efforts to revitalize the culture. Any demand for political rights has been synonymous with struggle. Anyone actively engaged in Basque culture and politics could not receive a more honorable entitlement than being a burrukalari. More specifically, ETA's violent strategy is also a burruka harmatua. Even the politicians of the moderate PNV consider their task a burruka, as is clear from their political rhetoric. A statement that was repeatedly made by those who favored the Statute of Autonomy was that what matters was "to make burruka in Madrid." This was certainly not an opinion shared by the antiparliamentarian group Herri Batasuna. One of its leaders contended in a meeting in Deba, "When we were little we used to prefer to fight the burruka on our own home's porch and not on the opponent's porch. Likewise, we would rather make burruka here in Euskadi than in Madrid on the enemy's porch."

As the burruka context is employed to refer to the confrontational aspect of the political struggle, the model of joko is constantly and explicitly invoked for any ordinary political strategy. The generalization that "politics is a joko" is consciously admitted in everyday speech. The competitors are engaged in such a manner that the notion of pride or honor applies.[8] Compared with that involvement of personal worth, the political game is seen as grudge bearing between the proponents of differing ideologies. There is an important observation about joko in this. The antagonistic performance creates an ethos in which the main personal values are similarly structured; with the winner-loser dichotomy goes the superior-inferior and the best-worst ones as well. Pride stands for the positive side, humiliation for the negative one. Once a worldview is split into positive and negative, sticking stubbornly to the positive side becomes imperative.

But there are, of course, politics and politics. As there are different framings of the same joko context, so there are different models being applied to politics. A distinction can be made between models that are directly bipolar, mediated, or plurally framed. According to the model applied, the corresponding politics are altogether different. If we take the model of the mus game, behavior governed by the hordago premise lends itself to a ritual conception of political process (see chapter 13). In a strictly joko bipolar mentality, what is unacceptable about negotiated politics is its contractual nature.

Right and wrong, truth and falsity, victory and defeat are never a matter of negotiated consensus. Rather, in a joko they are the end result. If contractual negotiation becomes the definition of politics, then in a parliamentary situation of ethnic minorities politics itself is the principle enemy of truth telling. Antipolitics then becomes a necessity in order to preserve minority rights. This is a well-known strategy of recent Basque nationalism.

Without elements of rejection and antagonism Basque politics in recent times would not make any sense. A fundamental perspective of ETA is one of denial of the military-political status quo of Franco's era. Tragic cases, such as that of Carlos of Itziar, need to be viewed from this perspective of military polarization. Among the new parties, Herri Batasuna is the best example of rejection of parliamentary politics. The other major political group on the Basque Left, Euskadiko Ezkerra, although committed to negotiated politics, occasionally used to spread rumors that it might abandon political plays and instead rejoin ETA politico-military. Even the moderate and majority nationalist party, the PNV, has absented itself from the Spanish parliament for long periods as a sign of protest. In a manner similar to the traditional joko being modified into more complex patterns, the political joko may show a spectrum of development toward the acceptance of politically mediating devices.

Yet these varying modes of joko easily find themselves in mutually irreconcilable positions. Formally speaking, introduction of mediation or imbalance of opposing poles breaks down direct polarity and shifts frames to another level. Similarly, the models underlying different political attitudes may exclude each other. One important indication of this incompatibility is the constant ideological battle by parties on the radical Left against the concept of negotiation. From a strictly bipolar strategy, negotiation sweeps away the ground rules. In the context of contending strategies, the election of the model itself becomes the prime struggle for political power.

In its initial pamphlets ETA was most explicit as to the nonpolitical nature of the patriotic task facing the Basques (Hordago 1979). It was a matter of survival to recover freedom for the country, not an issue of political pluralism and party strategy that was to be left for a subsequent phase. ETA's entire course might be seen as an enactment of the narrow bipolar joko strategy, with several critical and always unsuccessful attempts to open up such an elementary scheme of national antagonism. The dichotomy between ETA politico-military and ETA military[9] was only the latest in a series of struggles between a polarized scheme that aimed at politically mediating devices and one that does not. The strategy of ETA has classically been action-repression-action, a clearly schismogenic process, as defined by Bateson (1958), in which ETA seeks the repressive response of the "forces of order" against Basques as a stimulus for further involving the Basques against the oppressive powers.

At the level of personal self, a parallel shift from ordinary to ultimate commitment takes place when a martyrdom ethics of complete life surrender to the cause is embraced in clandestine activism. This attitude is indicated in everyday conversation by the expression *bizitza jokatu* (to bet one's life). Life itself can be put into joko with the final result becoming a life-or-death matter. The type of heroism promoted by clandestine mortal risk taking can be said to be modeled after a joko. It is also an hordago, another basic game strategy, which holds the key to understanding the ekintza's performative dimension as described in Itziar's history.

José Ignacio conveyed to me the strong conviction that political activism is a joko. He was also the one who pointed out to me its jolas dimension: "That wasn't a sacrifice for us. That was our duty, and that's all. It was a *juerga* (good time), a continuous juerga. We were always laughing. Right after we had kidnapped someone we were singing songs and bertso." For him and others, political activism was a burruka duty that, although heroic to those who were hearing about it in the media, for the actors themselves, as if unwittingly, had become jolas.

In the political attitudes of Itziar as a community I never observed the hold of the bipolar antagonistic scheme on my closest friends and relatives as dramatically as during the summer of 1977. The occasion was the first democratic election in Spain after forty years of Franco's dictatorship. During the sixties and first half of the seventies, the politically active forces of Itziar had easily operated within the Madrid versus Basques framework. A real threat to this scheme was perceptible in the elections of 1977, when the political coalition Euskadiko Ezkerra decided to participate in the electoral process. Euskadiko Ezkerra was the first attempt to politically channel the public support given to ETA by people who originally had been or still were active in the organization. Its decision placed it in sharp disagreement with other political groups of the Basque radical Left. Along with certain other political groups, ETA military was totally opposed to such electoral participation. At that time Itziar's young ETA cell was at the peak of its fame. The three who had been arrested and finally released favored the option of taking part in the elections. The fourth member, who had not been arrested and had continued his underground activities, was then a member of ETA military. Therefore, a dramatic split occurred within the pronationalistic group between those favoring and those rejecting the elections. Even close family members who had intensely supported the three young men during their imprisonment and done all they could for their release were forced into the painful situation of having to fundamentally disagree with their political position. The comments of one of the most active nationalists in Itziar are revealing: "Before, it was clear what we had to do. It was Madrid versus the Basque Country. Now nothing is clear any longer." Years of political indoctrination within the strictly dual joko scheme of antagonism to Madrid could not be easily shed when a more elaborate context, with different options on the Basque side, emerged.

CHAPTER NINE

Ehiza

The Hunting Model of Performance

In this chapter the relevance of the hunting model to our understanding of activist violence will be explored. Although not mutually exclusive, the performative model of *ehiza* (hunt) presents a distinct alternative to the static, game-centered bipolar models of joko discussed in the previous chapter.

All prehistoric reconstructions point to the unique occupational centrality of hunting in Basque culture from the Paleolithic era down to the Christian Era (Barandiaran 1953; Caro Baroja 1971). A good part of the folklore imagery that has persisted until the present is staged in a hunting milieu. Devoid of its past economic significance, ehiza is nowadays in Itziar-Lastur, as elsewhere,[1] a favorite hobby of adult males; a house without a shotgun is a rare exception.

Hunting will be taken to provide a fundamental context of performance that illuminates suggestively the strategies and mentality of such violence. The clandestine persecutory nature of the violent methods used in the exchange between the police and ETA is particularly reminiscent of the hunting scenario. Sometimes the comparison may be consciously invoked. Key hunting words such as *bota* (throw down, such as a bird or hunting prey) and *garbitu* (clean up, meaning to kill) are applied in everyday speech to ETA's killing of the forces of order.

This chapter is ultimately about the decisive significance of preverbal primordial experience in political violence.[2] The discussion on hunting condenses a major argument underlying this book;

namely, that under a given situation defined politically as being one of ultimate consequence, primary experience subverts modes of behavior that are arbitrated by linguistic or negotiated forms. As in other human situations of ultimate consequence, in the context of radical underground activism, secondary experience is overpowered by primordial dimensions that are sometimes translated in ordinary speech into arguments of "survival value" and "instinctual reaction." From a perspective that defines politics exclusively in terms of a secondary elaboration of possible alternatives, political behavior relying on primary experience rightly appears as prepolitical or "irrational." Hobsbawm so characterized the situation of the bandit (1959:23). This chapter points in the same direction, but the argument has a different basis: Basque political violence is prepolitical because it relies decisively on primordial attachments.

Ortega y Gasset has meditated on the ethics of hunting. To the fact of natural death and the act of killing, the hunter's "*having* to kill" (1972:57; his emphasis) adds a new dimension of unintelligibility. War is a peculiarly human institution that reproduces the hunter's "having to kill," with the quarry being human in a war setting. Head-hunting, a relevant topic in anthropological literature, strikingly brings into light these similarities. In head-hunting societies, ritual killing becomes a central institution on which the entire cultural system hinges (Rosaldo 1978). Men's social status and personal maturation are dependent on this ritual. In recent years membership in ETA seems to have constituted a parallel ritual of manhood for Basque youth. In both situations killing becomes a ritual necessity imposed by the culture under the pretenses of group defense and heroic manliness. In hunting a categorical distinction is made between killer and victim; police and ETA members similarly attribute the qualities of beast to the other and guardian to themselves. At the sensorial level, in hunting a regression to smell and touch takes place. A parallel return from secondary and public to primary and private experience appears as inevitable in clandestine political violence. In a hunting morality there is no repugnance at killing. The necessity to kill, in both hunting and political violence, emerges as a strategic requirement premised on assumptions of hierarchical difference between actor and victim. From the hunter's compulsion to kill we may gain significant insights into the military compulsion to destroy the enemy target.

The Social Reality of Ehiza

The two men of Itziar's older generation who have written their memoirs in an eminently oral style, Arbalitz and Uztapide, devoted special attention to ehiza. Their descriptions presented hunting as a highly pleasurable activity. The impression of ehiza as leisure performance was confirmed by conversations with Itziar and Lastur hunters. In the baserritarra's experience, hunting and farming are opposed as leisure and work. Work is tied to duty, whereas hunting is not.

Hunters see themselves as "cleaning up" (garbitu) the forests of beastly enemies. Each sign that brings them closer to the hidden wild animal arouses a sense of alertness and emotional intensity that is reflected in a defiant mood or readiness to face the enemy and pursue him to the end. But no matter how fierce the pursuit and how necessary the cleaning up of the environment, nothing is further from the hunters' thoughts than complete extermination of the wild quarry. I heard one of the older hunters complain, after a hunt in which no boars were caught, "They say that there are many around, but there are not that many." There is a tension intrinsic to hunting. The "dirty" enemy has to be "cleaned up," but only to a certain point. It is desirable that the beast propagate as well, so that the territory can be redeemed by the cleansing performance itself.

People of all generations in Itziar go hunting, but the meaning of hunting is changing from generation to generation. For the older generations, hunting was practically the only alternate leisure activity to work. It was practiced in their own habitat; the hunt was close to the baserri house or in forests within a few hours' walk. Dogs who shared daily life with the people were in the closest association with the hunters. Hunting was exclusively a male activity. *Ehizera jun* (going hunting) was in the baserri life-style a daily, normal "leisure" activity. With the change in social organization and life-style from the baserria to factory work and semiurban life-style, the role and nature of hunting is also changing. In contrast with baserri hunting, in the new milieu hunting is not a potentially daily leisure activity but is reduced to a weekend pastime. For the semiurban factory worker hunting is rather an entertainment consisting basically of shooting at the prey.

Among the younger generations hunting again differs. Within

Itziar's male youth, two broad groups can be distinguished with regard to the practice of hunting and traditional joko. One group is associated with the youth center and organizes cultural and entertainment activities, is politically minded, and follows the musical and social fashions. It is extremely rare for people from this group to go hunting or go to joko in traditional settings. When I went boar hunting with my uncles, it appeared so odd to them that I was the butt of jokes for a week.

The other major group of Itziar's youth is not generally involved in any of the social, entertainment, or political activities that characterize the first group. In Itziar it is easily noticeable that this is also the group that will go hunting or to traditional joko. In the same family one brother may be politically involved, and he will never be expected to go hunting. At the same time, his brother who is not involved in any activity of that sort will be expected to go hunting regularly.

A Boar-Hunting Sunday

In Itziar-Lastur I have always been in a milieu in which hunting is an activity of everyday life. Yet I had never realized the actual type of performance entailed by ehiza until I went boar hunting in the autumn of 1980 with my own uncles and cousins. It was set that we were to meet in Ansorregi, the baserria that was taken as the center of operations, by 7:30 in the morning. The people from Ansorregi participating in the hunt included four married brothers of the first generation, who ranged in age from their late fifties to their seventies; three members of the second generation, myself included, between thirty and fifty; and three members of the third generation, between fifteen and twenty-five. There were also three dogs. About a dozen other people from the surrounding baserriak, with several dogs of their own, reached Ansorregi in their cars by 7:30. Batista, the younger husband at Ansorregi, acted as the leader of the expedition. My presence did not please Batista, who asked me in an annoyed tone whether I had ever shot a cartridge. I replied that I never had but would learn. To my complete embarrassment, when they supplied me with a few cartridges I was found to have my cartridge belt, which I had borrowed from my father, on upside down.

At 7:30, on schedule, after Batista described the course that we were to follow, we got into our cars and approached the starting point just two or three kilometers into the mountains. As we were walking in smaller groups toward the exact spot from where the expedition was to commence, the first thing that caught my attention was the collusion of men and dogs. There were about ten dogs surrounding the leaders of the group, alertly walking and running ahead and behind them. I had gone on the hunt mostly to have a chance to talk with my uncles, but I soon realized how wrong my anticipation had been, for any attempts on my part to talk would fall on deaf ears. The communication between dogs and men became the most fundamental one. The leaders hardly spoke except to give orders to the excited dogs.

A dog named Ley was the center of all our expectations. Ley had been the subject of the conversation one Sunday afternoon a few weeks earlier in the bar of Lastur's plaza. Ley, the boar dog par excellence, was praised for his *buru ona* (good mind). The opening day of the season he had been attacked by a boar, which had cut off his penis. Subsequently Ley had been operated on in Bilbao twice. After three months of convalescence he was again taken on a boar hunt. Without Ley the hunters hadn't been able to catch a single animal. His first Sunday back he had found two boars, which were then caught and shot. Ley was an extraordinary animal, a natural wonder that only chance could produce. "If he would live another twenty years . . ." one of the hunters wishfully exclaimed while granting that he would endure only a couple of years. There was complete uncertainty as to how he would be replaced. There was no market where such a dog could be purchased. As those who had been talking of Ley left the bar, a man from Lastur commented: "It's sure that they appreciate the dog more than they do the best cow of the farm." The day of the hunt, attention was again focused on Ley.

We were on the mountain that Sunday morning. My three eldest uncles and myself were instructed to guard a certain path. Others, also in groups of four or five, each with their dogs, dispersed in different directions. The overall plan was to block off a certain area where it was suspected that "they" might be because of reports that boars had been seen or had left some tracks there in recent days. The dogs were initially led to the spots or paths where the boars were likely to have been, but then were released to roam about at will searching for scent.

Usaina (smell) was a key word. Men and dogs were in the mountains among trees, bracken, and bushes but the actual hunting space was an invisible stage traversed by paths of scent. Dogs had a direct instinctual access to the real scenario. Men only had an indirect access to it through communicating with the dogs, first training and ordering them where to start *usaina hartzen* (taking the smell) and then following them once they were on the track. Hunters gather initial information as to the whereabouts of the boars by hearsay from people who have seen them. They guess likely locations from where the pursuit left off the previous hunting day. Hunters also make inferences on the proximity or recent passage of boars by observing the *arrastoak* (tracks). This is always information "distant" from where the action actually is. The sight of the tracks may lead the hunter in the right direction and his sense of hearing may help him to locate the boar, but it is only the dog's sense of smell that can lead the hunter to where the boar is hidden and "pull" the boar out or "move" it.

More symbolically, catching the prey is a ritual purification of the territory. The recent reappearance of the wild boars is a result of the process of arable lands reverting into forest. As a consequence, the mountains and forests are becoming "dirty" with bushes and deadwood. In one of the farms of the area where we were hunting, the boars had damaged the crops the previous week. Still, the boars presented no real danger to the baserriak, at least not to Ansorregi, where no boar damage was apparent.

When my three uncles and I began heading toward our positions across a path that traversed the forest from the top of the hill to the stream at the bottom I still hadn't thought about putting cartridges inside the shotgun. When one uncle ordered me to get ready by loading it, there was a tone of reproach and urgency in his voice. I should have been aware that we were in the middle of the action. In my total ignorance about hunting I was still expecting to have a good chat with my uncles while watching the possible approach of the boar. While inspecting some old boar tracks on dried-up mud, I kept talking despite their unwillingness to engage in conversation. I was to be blamed later because of this breach.

Soon we heard the barking of a dog sounding in our direction. We had dispersed into the forest and bushes not yet twenty minutes before the barking became the center of our attention. When the dog "takes the smell" and is close to the boar he is supposed to start barking. The mark of a good dog is that he should not bark too soon and thereby drive the boar away. Ley was careful to observe this rule, but the other dogs, new to the expedition, were not. The early bark was a good signal, although my uncles dismissed it as being too soon yet to be a real one; that is, a bark that indicated that the boar had been "moved."

It is wrong to assume that the boar, followed by a dog, will come straight to the hunter. Boars also have an acute sense of smell and can easily detect the presence of a person. The wind disperses the smell. Thus, the hunter has to take into account the direction of the wind. Later on, at midday, we learned that the dog had indeed "pulled out" the boar in our proximity earlier but that the trail had been lost after a short pursuit. One of my uncles blamed the prey's not running into us on smell and to our not having been completely silent during the initial minutes. Concentration had to be accompanied by total silence. Although the lead group, which knew the dog had "moved" the boar, was less than five minutes' walk from us at the time of the barking, we did not know about it until three hours later. There had not been a single shout or cry of warning to us. Only the dog's barking could pierce the hunting silence.

Soon I was ordered to move off and watch over a position of my own farther down the mountain. The hunters were divided between those who had gone ahead with the dogs, whose duty it was to pull out the prey, and those of us who had stayed behind, watching over positions lined up in a continuous front. The term *pasatu* (to pass through) has a particular significance. The aim of the hunters waiting for the boar is to create an imaginary wall that will not let the boar through.[3] Passing through can occur within the geographical unit in which the boar normally runs, or the boar may pass through to an entirely different area after crossing the natural boundaries within which it would normally remain if not pursued. Boars may traverse distances that make it impossible to catch them and imperil the return of the dogs that get lost in the pursuit. Both kinds of passing through occurred on that Sunday.

This hunting space can be imagined as a surface hidden under the forests and bushes and crisscrossed by pathways of pursuit and escape. It is an invisible space with hidden nests, cavernous dwellings, and silent tracks in the dark. The beast pierces through, traverses, and escapes because of its sense of smell, sheer physical strength, and luck.

Sounds and sights are only part of the reward when the beast has been killed and you can finally contemplate it. Its silence permits speaking again. The invisible is rendered visible, escape finally stopped, smell turned into meat, silence into celebration. There is a banquet of all the senses with the enemy now turned into a trophy. The territory has been garbitua.

Ultimately, the key to a good hunter is the ability to perform a totemistic kind of identification with the prey. The hunter has to get inside the prey's instinctual psychology and anticipate his own moves were he that animal in that situation. Any trace of tracks or broken bushes is paramount information about the animal's actual moves and intentions. Only this internal identification and concentration on reading vestigial signals guarantees that the hunter will be able to frame the hunting space adequately and proceed in it according to the hunt's proper movement.

The homecoming from ehiza had a peculiar pattern. We had been in the hunting area since 8 A.M. At 4 P.M. we started walking back the approximately one hour's distance that separated us from Ansorregi. Once at home, while we were eating, there was no news of those who had gone ahead after the boars. Ours had been a defensive strategy of staying behind and creating the wall. Theirs was the much harder task of keeping up with the dogs in moving and then pursuing the prey. Days later I learned from one of them that the boars had passed through toward another distant area; the hunters chased after them unsuccessfully until late evening. Each one returned home on his own exhausted. The erratic hunting movement had dispersed us all throughout the day.

Controlling the Animal's Instinctual Patterns

Luxio is an exceptionally good hunter from Itziar. A middle-aged married man living in an apartment in Itziar's center, he belongs to a baserria whose members are well known for hunting abilities. He is Itziar's shoemaker and barber. Despite his urban job and his many administrative responsibilities, hunting has been and still is his favorite recreation. When I asked Luxio what makes a good hunter, he pointed out that aiming (*puntería*) is essential. Yet he immediately added:

> But besides that what counts is ideas; ideas is what hunting is all about. My late father was phenomenal at that. [You have to take into account] also that he had been fond of hunting since his early childhood. The hunters of former times were not like today's; then they had that natural *jokera* [inclination]. They used to know the hunt's peculiar moves. Furthermore, as you participate more in different kinds of hunting, you know more about hunting, and that's what it is about, ideas.

The hunter as a man of "ideas" violates our basic understanding of hunting. These are not, however, abstract ideas removed from the performative context. Luxio himself explained what these ideas are. Recounting highly successful hunting expeditions to Burgos[4] and Castile with his father and brothers, he details the secret of their good fortune:

> We brothers all shoot very well. And besides aiming, we had that something; that is the secret, the mystery, to know how to take a mountain, for example, how to take the hunt, how to treat the hunt, how to gather, how to proceed. Some go each one on their own. We never would do that: we would all take the mountain together, I knew how he would take it, and he knew how I would, we all knew about each other. And thus we used to catch a lot. That is all there is to hunting. Hunting is ideas. That is why nowadays there are no hunters.

These ideas are the discoverable and predictable patterns of animal behavior. In this regard they are intrinsically performative. Animal behavior is difficult to predict. The secret of the good hunter is to be able to discover the possible patterns by which instinctive animal behavior can be organized. Terrain, climate, and season are important sources of auxiliary information. Yet one has to start off with the assumption that the hunt is utterly unpredictable—a mystery. Luxio stressed the point:

> Hunting is a lot of story [*kontua*]. But while hunting, unbelievable cases occur. Jesus! Unbelievably rare cases . . .

> strange cases that never end. . . . Some people make them up. . . . But no, in reality, too [they occur]. Hunting is most mysterious.

The relationship between this unpredictability and the ideal control mechanisms that the hunter has to imagine is explicitly drawn by Luxio when he says, "The harder the hunt and the more uncontrollable, the greater the pleasure." The pleasure derives from the sense of controlling an environment in which the behavior of the animals can be detected, predicted, and reduced to a pattern.[5]

The actual course of the hunt, the real pattern, is determined by the animal's *sena* (instinct). For example, migratory birds take a coastal course when the weather is bad in the interior; they are said to *sendu* (find the instinct, orientation) at the seaside. The sense that is supreme in communicating animal sena is, of course, smell. Typically the hunter makes use of his dog's sense of smell to detect animals hidden in a given area. His strategic ideas are ultimately subservient to the dog's instinct. Luxio made it clear that there is no real ehiza without this interdependence between dog and hunter: "The real hunt is making the dog work, tracing the tracks, and so on. The dog is a wonderful thing; you would never believe the things a dog can do." The dog has to undergo a training process. It is important that the good hunter train his dog in order to refine its instinctual knowledge. There are no specific rules for this. It is mostly a matter of preverbal communication between dog and hunter. As Luxio explains, "For the dog to be well trained you first need a good hunter. If he is not a real hunter he cannot train the dog." By using the dog's animal smell the hunter achieves control of the prey. The ideas of the hunter cannot be reduced to deductions from past experience and are not simply the result of cumulative information. Intrinsic to his ideas is the discovery of unpredictable and yet intuitively controllable patterns of animal behavior.

The Instinctual Freedom of the Beast and the Hunter

Pedro is an extraordinary hunter who lives by himself in a baserria and delights in talking of animal habitats. Between

1975 and 1981 alone he caught thirty-one foxes by means of a trap and only one with the shotgun. As he remarked, "Earlier man had not the shotgun; what he used then was the rope, the trap, holes, caves, and so on." Foxes and wild cats are still hunted by driving them into mountain cavities where they can be enclosed and a trap placed in the entrance to catch them. The pursued animal is betrayed by his own habit of defensive self-enclosure.

Pedro insisted to me that in hunting the animal enjoys a fundamental precondition—freedom. Both Pedro and Luxio emphasized that "in hunting the animal is free." Talking with them it was obvious that this idea of the animal's "freedom" provides the basic justification of the arbitrary killing of the prey. This freedom of the wild animal is directly opposed to the domesticated animal's lack of it. The idea that the animal is "free" creates for the hunter a frame of competition within which he perceives some sort of equal opportunity between the prey and himself. For the hunter this "freedom" of the animal is strategically and psychologically most significant. A key point is that the killing of an animal by a hunter and by a cattle dealer or sheepherder are altogether different. Luxio confessed to me that he is entirely incapable of killing a chicken. Pedro likewise remarked how disagreeable it is for him to slaughter an animal:

> I don't like it at all. I have slaughtered a lamb many times, and with great sorrow. It never did anything wrong. I raised it at home with fodder and milk. I myself raised it, and held it, and caressed it as well—it is so pretty. And then somebody tells you, "Bring me the lamb dead." And I know that if I sell you the lamb you will slaughter it, so I do it myself. But with great sorrow. I'd rather not see it. And on the other hand, take a woodcock in the mountain, which has no fault either (it never did anything wrong), but, because at that moment I enjoy the shot or the skill, I kill it. Think about the different instincts we people have and what we are. Our nature is like that.

A major aspect of a wild animal's freedom is that the animal does not belong to a private owner. Commenting on this, Pedro noted:

> Besides, the animal that lives in the mountain has no owner; it doesn't belong to anybody. Imagine that there are partridges in

> Burgos: they do not belong to the mayor of Burgos, nor to the minister, nor to the Jesuits, nor to anybody. As grass comes spontaneously, so they are born there naturally from their fathers and mothers, and there they live.

But some form of possession is obviously essential to that most "free" context of hunting. Like the act of killing itself, the act of possessing is nevertheless quite different for a hunter than for an agriculturalist-pastoralist. The hunter "owns" his prey only as a final lucky result of his strategy. Catching the prey implies the skillful mastery of the animal's instinctual reactions. The wild nature of the hunted animal can only be controlled by killing it. Possession of the quarry presupposes the destruction of its freedom, which is equivalent to its life. The hunter's act of possession is momentary and random as a result of the hunting strategy. His is a process of elimination rather than accumulation. Once the quarry has been caught, the lifeless object signals the end of an action and the way is cleared for the next action.

Catching the prey requires holding it. It is not enough to merely kill it; the chased object has to be grasped with one's own hands. As explained by Pedro, "If you don't hold it with your own hands you get angry. If you have shot it down from the tree to the bushes or to a bad place and you haven't found it you come home with a bad taste. . . . The thing is you have to bring it in, you have to get it." Pedro noted the case of my grandfather, who used to catch wild cats with his bare hands. On one occasion the wild cat bit and gashed his finger from one side to the other, but he wouldn't let it go: "You can guess from that how much he wanted to catch it. Bear that in mind. Even if his finger was going to be bitten off he would still prefer to hang on."

Therefore, the primordial tools for the capture of the beast's wild freedom are hands and fingers. A common term for "getting hold of" is *eskuratu,* a compound of *esku* (hand) and *-ratu* (to bring something somewhere). Hands are the best gripping implements of capture. More specifically, fingers are the seizing instruments of the chased prey: my father describes grandfather's capturing of the wild cats with the expression *bere atzaparrekin* (with his fingers); he himself displays this finger dexterity by easily catching trout with his bare hands. The hunter has to stop the runaway situation of the fugitive wild game; for this he has to locate and surround it first within some strategic boundaries and then capture it with the power of his shotgun and hands. In his action he is driven by the erratic image of the animal. Initially being himself possessed by the overpowering image of the hidden beast, the hunter's obsession is satiated only by possessing his desired object with his own hands.

The supreme moment of the catch was described by Pedro with these words:

> There at that moment, in that very moment, you don't remember money, or women, or anything. All you remember is to get hold of the prey; that moment arrives when all one's attention is concentrated there, when that is everything, nothing else is in your mind. For us that moment is more thrilling than *anything;* that is the greatest. You don't remember whether you are going to shoot a 25-peseta cartridge or a 100-peseta cartridge. All you are interested in is shooting it, at that very moment, to hit it right there.

Hunters stress the deep psychic gratification involved in killing the prey, which results in "internal heat," heart pounding, discharge of adrenaline, and so on; the experience I have been told is comparable, and which is meant quite literally, is lovemaking.

Two Types of Performative Space and Two Personality Models: Ehiztari and Jokolari

The hunter's mode of thinking and proceeding is different from that of joko. Although there is a significant element of joko in the hunter's pursuit of the prey, the two performative strategies of joko and ehiza can be presented as two personality models and two perspectives of public performance that can be observed in the domain of recent politics.

Associated with their different use of space, the joko and ehiza contexts create two distinct types of personality. As described in the previous chapter, the space in a competitive joko serves only to create a context of discrimination that will result in a winner and a loser. The space of the plaza or the mountain in which the joko is taking place becomes a measuring distance or a bounding frame for the real action. The space as such is static and serves as a staging ground for the competitive performance.

In sharp contrast, the ehiza hunting space is fundamentally an erratic, moving one. Instead of being fixed in advance, the space of ehiza is the unbounded geography of any terrain where the hunt may go. Action is never measured against a concrete static spot. In ehiza the performance is determined by the hunting process itself, which dictates the concrete sequence of actions and moves. Luxio likened this to the moves of policemen.

In hunting, two kinds of space can be distinguished. First, there is the concrete territory, which is only a variable of the performative context. Second, there is the wider space, which is present to the hunter only as a mental map. The secret of the good hunter consists in adequately shifting these two spaces. As Luxio said, "We knew how to take the mountain, how to take the hunt, how to treat it, how to bring it together, how to play with it." In this hunting process the actual territory "slips" constantly into the wider map, nor is this wider context a closed or bounded one. There is a hierarchy of inclusion between the concrete hunting spot, the wider geography of that animal's habitual route, and the unforeseen space to which that animal might escape. Each spatial unit is at a different logical level. Space here is never bounded, static, experimentally preestablished. As the action moves erratically, pursuing the hunt, so moves the space—from one unit to the next, from one spot to the wider geography, from the territory to the map.

The joko space is a significantly different one. In Basque culture the joko is the context of the public man, more recently of the political man. This space lacks the "movement" between map and territory. Space in the joko is simply a signaling frame. Contrary to ehiza, where the space in which action is taking place is essential to the performative strategy, space in a joko is but a previously fixed and taken-for-granted factor. Closely connected with this is the experimental character of the joko space. In Basque culture the joko space defines competition.

Observing the personality traits of the best-known hunting families in Itziar, one contradictory feature caught my attention. They are men of remarkable social standing but noticeably lack the qualities of the *plaza-gizon* (plaza man, or public man). A member of one of those families, a man in his late sixties and a good hunter himself in the past, once confessed to me:

> We are not plaza-gizon. For instance, when my brother made a joko, he performed in the plaza beneath his ability. He used to do better in training. Some grow up in the plaza. Others aren't meant for it. I don't know why. Your insides don't help you, your breath gets *estu* [tight], and you don't give all that you can.

Another of his brothers competed in woodcutting contests twice and won. Significantly, in his opinion, what was remarkable about the two victories was that his brother did not prepare for them. They were sudden, unprepared joko.

When I pushed Luxio into describing the personality differences between the jokolari and the *ehiztari* (hunter), he came out with his personal case. Luxio, who has been a very efficient and respected mayor of Itziar for seven years, told me:

> Ehiza is a sport, a vice. . . . It doesn't have that ambition of the joko. The jokolari and the ehiztari are completely different. I am very good for the mountain, and I am of no value whatsoever for the plaza. I go to see a joko and cannot stay. I get nervous. I will get all wet with sweat. That is what joko does to me. I cannot stand it. It makes me nervous, and that is so despite its being something that does not interest me at all. When I was participating here in the trapshooting championship [Luxio won it] I would have to piss between each round. And I was without appetite for about eight days earlier. Others, on the contrary, get better in public, they get filled with pride. If I participate in a joko without knowing in advance about it, I do much better. That is temperament.

Nobody is more sensitive to the "experimental neurosis" of the discrimination frame of the competitive joko than the ehiztari. His hunting space is the antithesis of the space in the joko, which is fixed by static boundaries—hence the distress and the sweat of my two informants, both men of social standing in Itziar. Connected with this experimental nature of joko, the two of them also mentioned the clear advantages of improvising a joko. Hunting territory is not marked off by boundary signals that decide the course and result of the performance, as in a joko context. Therefore, the space of hunting is always improvised by the hunter according to the course of things and his own ideas.

The hunter experiences stage fright in a public situation because the meaning and context of his own hunting space are not compatible with the nature of the joko space. For the hunter the joko space confuses, so to speak, map and territory. By depriving space of its internal movement and strategic value, the same improvised territory that in ehiza was only a momentary stage in a larger context, dependent on the ongoing process itself, in a joko becomes a fixed signaling frame. From being an essential collaborator in the complete performance, space suddenly becomes a mere spectator and judge of it. Messages such as "being ahead" or "staying behind" that in hunting are altogether relative to the situation in joko get translated into "winning" and "losing." The hunter has been caught in a frame that is not his own. His breathing is *estututa* (constricted); he is already sweating.

Conclusion: The Ehiza of Political Violence

After I suggested in a talk at the Basque University that games and hunting provide cultural models for the ongoing violence, an ex-girlfriend of a well-known ETA figure came to me and said:

> You really hit the mark with [the comparison between ETA and] ehiza. He [his war name] is a true ehiztari. He used to go hunting boars himself. . . . On one occasion, in which he was told something because ETA had killed somebody, he replied: "You know, I am a hunter."

Both in ehiza and in clandestine political activism there is a sort of regression to a preverbal type of communication. Easy talk is a most dangerous personal quality for the underground activist. An ETA member is "really bad" when "he talks too much," as I have heard several times. The refusal to talk is essential to the rebel's personality. Confession runs directly against the ideal revolutionary personality. In the Sunday boar-hunting expedition, too, my talking was utterly disruptive of ehiza.

Commentators and journalists have remarked about ETA members' lack of verbal skills. Personal friends of ETA members have also spoken to me about the activists' difficulties in articulating their thoughts. The truth of things has nothing much to do with verbal skills. Regarding this, a woman well acquainted with ETA refugees in southern France made a distinction between the two branches of the organization: "I prefer an ETA politico-military for talking, they are better politicians, if you wish, but the ETA military are more truthful, more efficient. I don't know how to explain it."

An important source of information at this preverbal stage was pointed out to me by "Wilson," one of the "historic" leaders of ETA. When I asked him how one copes with danger and anxiety in such a strenuous occupation, he responded, "You either learn to smell the danger, or you don't." The figurative use of "smell" could not be more revealing of a hunting scenario.[6] As in ehiza, in underground political activity hunter and beast of prey communicate with each other through scent.

In the communication between the underground activists and those emotionally closest to them, nonverbal means play a significant role. Several women intimately related to ETA members spoke to me on the importance of premonitions and paranormal information. The wife of one ETA member was categorical: "I always knew when he was in danger." She backed her statement with concrete examples.

Correlated with the regression from speech to smell is a sensory shift from sight to touch. As in ehiza, in clandestine activism the eye communication between the pursuer and pursued is only at the final act of chasing and destroying the enemy. In the meantime they are hidden and invisible to each other. Sight is at most used to read vestigial signs. The real action is guided by other means.

In the dark night of action, the underground man needs to feel the protective touch of the weapon that gives him superiority over the prey ahead of him. While alone in his hiding place or walking through the treacherous street, to frighten away his inner fear he caresses its handle. This is a description of the relationship of an ETA activist to his pistols by a friend of his who visited him in his hideout:

> He took two small *pipas* [pipes, that is, pistols] of 6.30 mm. and one of 7.30 mm. that he wanted to try out. So we went to the beach and he shot. The pipas were very small; you could hold them within the palm of your hand. He would treat them very specially, as if with affection, tenderly, the same as a child treats a doll.

It is a doll that gave power to the enemy as well. The access to power and protection is mediated by the secret touch.

This shift from speech to smell and from sight to touch can be considered a regression from secondary to primary experience. In substitution for the secondary life of the self in the external social world of verbal and public communication, in primary experience the private corporeal life of smells and touch prevails. Internal sensations of texture and a private language acquire strategic predominance over the visible common world of experience and public language.

The privatization of communication is correlated with the privatization of performance. The joko requires a rival and an audience to judge the contest—it involves public interaction of people. Not so ehiza, which despite the group expedition of the boar hunt is performed mostly on an individual basis. Both the hunter and the beast are engaged in a strategy of mutual pursuit and escape, but from the hunter's perspective the other is only a target geared to avoid him. If the politician is performing in a joko public milieu, the underground activist's experience is more akin to the ehiza scenario.

Hunting is, of course, a goal-oriented activity: there is no hunting without a target. This creates an interdependence between the hunter and the beast. As in ehiza, not all is hatred between the pursuer and the pursued in the police-activist mutual chase either. "Wilson" was made into a hero by the media during the police search for him. He was finally captured in the summer of 1975 in Barcelona. He recalled for me:

> You know, after years a real bond is created between the pursuer and the pursued. They do not only hate you; they also know you quite personally, and a certain relationship exists. Besides when they catch you they feel very happy. They treated me as an equal. They would engage me in political arguments.

The pursuit of ehiza is carried out individually in relation to the hunt, and the performative frame itself is largely improvised by the hunter in the course of action. No conventional strategy can take into account all the unpredictable behavior of animal instincts. The meaning of "instinctual behavior" in this context is precisely behavior that is not fully controllable. Nor does it make any sense to establish rules of behavior when the other side, the beast of prey, will not conform to them. The outlawed political activist is also beset by unpredictability. The hunting context is here a paradigm for the underground pursuit-guided performance of outlawed political activism. This is again nearly exclusively a male-dominated activity. As in ehiza, there is a fundamental privatization of what constitutes commanding behavior. The rebel cannot rely on any conventional rule. He himself assumes new norms on a personal basis and generalizes them to the rest of the society. His justification is that society actually wants or ideally should want the norms he is espousing individually.

Ortega pointed out the hunter's predicament of "*having* to kill." The compulsive nature of the hunter's obsession has given way to the widespread story of Mateo Txistu. During sleepless nights, my own grandfather, a staunch hunter, used to hear the mythical figure Mateo Txistu whistling and his dogs barking. He is the legendary hunter who in punishment for his excessive fondness for hunting wanders around the world without respite in the company of his dogs. Haunted by his own hunting unconscious, grandfather did not hear spoken words, or see sensible images, or conceive of infernal ideas of eternity. His moments of hunting obsession were punctuated by preverbal whistling and barking; erratic wandering and endless duration framed his hunting activities. The killer for political reasons is also vulnerable to such haunting stories and endless moves. Perhaps this is what was meant by those who told me, "Once you kill, you cannot stop until the end."

Another human institution that reproduces the hunter's "*having* to kill" is war. Although conceived and played out on a bipolarized scheme of the joko type, in its final goal of killing a debased enemy it copies hunting. As Leach puts it, "Within the domain of law, homicide is a crime; within the domain of war, homicide is a duty" (1977 : 25). Even in stateless societies with no regular army, a small group may feel called upon to assume responsibility for the country and declare war against the dominant establishment. Since the early sixties, ETA has been such a warring organization at the heart of Basque society.

The hunter is put off by the killing of innocent domesticated animals for mere economic needs. His own killing implies a symbolic cleansing of the territory; the wild beast is categorized as dangerous, disorderly "dirt." Since the animal's untamed freedom is in defiance of the hunter, its capture is a restoration of man's control. Killing by the police and the military and killing by the underground activist are likewise perceived by Basque nationalists as being of a different order. The former is a mercenary kind of killing performed as a duty for money. The rebel's battleground, like the hunter's, is one of liberty and ultimate control of the community's environment. The enemy can also make use of its natural freedom, but, since it is viewed as being of an instinctual kind and not amenable to cultural integration, it becomes an intrinsic threat that deserves extinction. As a hunter, the political activist may easily find himself in a survival situation in which there is no mediation between the freedom of the enemy and his own freedom.

Pedro remarked above on the sorrow of a hunter who is asked to slaughter a lamb. Killing a domesticated or captured animal is the antithesis of the hunter's context of free, instinctual competition. The political activist, too, may find himself violating implicit premises of his own strategy of hunting for freedom. This was the case when Itziar's cell killed the kidnapped Berazadi. In a hunting strategy he was, like Pedro's lamb, not the savage enemy beast but a leashed animal—innocent, even a friend of his own slayers for whom he had been cooking during the days of captivity. For his killers, who were ordered to sacrifice him, Berazadi's friendship and lack of guilt were the hardest things to swallow. They were hunters slaughtering a lamb.

For the Spanish army and forces of control the harsh repression of such "terrorist" outbreaks is nothing more than the logical defense of "national unity." For Basque separatists, who see such order merely as the result of military conquest, the rebellion against it becomes the ultimate revolutionary necessity. The actual strategy and presuppositions of performance between ETA and the police forces can be seen as one of a mutual hunt. Both the underground rebel and the defender of order basically view the other as an anonymous target for killing. The target in the hunt is only a beast, never an equal person. Within this hunting morality, in which the prey is by definition in a subhuman category, there is no ethical repugnance to killing. A dissolving of categories has to precede the killing. As in the hunt, there is a strategic necessity and personal compulsion to destroy the target.

CHAPTER TEN

The Bertsolariak as a Cultural Model of Performance

The previous chapter argued for the overpowering presence of primordial experience over verbal or secondary communication in hunting and political violence. This chapter discusses the prevalence of oral elements in Basque culture. Most especially, the outstanding cultural institution of *bertsolaritza* (the art of singing *bertso* [verse]) and its unique role in nonwritten textual creation are examined. The *bertsolariak,* or *bertso* singers, provide an irreplaceable model of cultural performance. There are hardly any Basque public events without their participation. The ideology of *hitza* (word) and its definitional import for the notion of *gizona* (man) are also considered.

The study of the oral aspects of culture is crucial to appreciating the nature of violence in Itziar's rural society. The restrictions imposed by oral communication, the contractual nature of the word, the literalness of speech messages, the notion of person required in this type of communication, and the improvised creation of nonfixed texts are characteristics that have a significant bearing on the performance and meaning of the ongoing political violence.

Confronted with the phenomenon of political violence, one common intellectual strategy is to concentrate upon the search for its "causes." The bertsolariak can be taken to provide a revelatory example of the way causal links are perceived in Basque expressive culture; namely, by their elliptical absence. An argument of images needs no consecutive connectors. Ellipsis is a condition for expressiveness and grammar becomes redundant. Instead of a "because" a bertso simply has a next line with the same rhythm and rhyme. "Why" they are related is "because" they are part of the same strophe. This chapter suggests that in political violence as well the argument may rest basically on a juxtaposition of images selected from territory, history, culture, and language. It makes little sense to ask "why" one supports the cause of one's own country, language, or political sovereignty. The basic argument does not rest on ideas or logical inferences, on political treatises or historical legitimations, but on elementary images associated with one's personal and collective identity. In the way a bertsolaria forms his arguments we may learn more about the syntax of violence—that is, the kind of connections that are "causal" in sustaining support for Basque political violence—than in the purely ideological or political arguments.

The Event

It is Sunday afternoon during the 1980 Kopraixak, or yearly fiesta, in Itziar. The plaza and the benches set for the fiesta events are filled with people eager to enjoy the afternoon. The event includes popular games, folk singers, bertso singers, dancers, and bulls. Two extraordinarily gifted bertsolariak have been invited this year—Lasarte and Lopategi. There is complete silence in the audience when they come out on a balcony and sing salutation strophes adjusted to the occasion. The first *gaia* (theme) of the afternoon, about which they will sing improvised rhymed verses according to the rhythmic pattern of a known melody, has been set by me:

> The theme we are going to ask the bertsolariak to sing about is the following: bertsolaritza itself. Some say that a bertsolaria has to be primarily a revolutionary. Others say that the bertsolaria is first of all simply a singer of bertso. How do you view yourselves in the role of the bertsolariak?

They alternate their bertso, each followed by applause:

Lopategi:

Euskaldun denoi ezaguna da gure egoera mingotsa.	All Basques well know our painful place in things.

Kantatzeko ere sarri ditugu	Even to sing we often are
guk bildurra eta lotsa.	taken by fear and shame.
Noiznai baidatoz amenazua	Threats come by the moment,
egunero tiro otsa.	sounds of bullets daily.
Esperantza bat sortu nai luke	The bertso singer's voice
bertsolarien abotsak.	wants to bring forth hope.

Lasarte:

Gaur egunean agertzen dira	So many bertso singers, sirs,
jaunak ainbat bertsolari.	appear in our days.
Len bezelaxe nai genduke guk	We would want to work
oraindik lanean ari.	as we always have.
Al baldin bada erri batean	If it is in our power
umore pixka bat jarri.	to bring a touch of humor to this land.

Bertsolaritza izan daiteke	The bertsolaritza can serve
euskeraren bizigarri.	to bring new life to Euskera.

Lopategi:

Askoren ustez bertsolaria	A bertsolaria who can sing
da gauza arrigarria.	is for many an amazing thing.
Nai genduke ongi asetu	We long to truly fill
anai denen egarria.	our brother's thirst.
Sentimenduen negarra edo	Whether it be the cry of full feeling
umore onez irria.	or good humor's laughter.
Bertsolaria zutik dan arte	As long as the bertsolaria stands up
bizi da Euskal Erria.	the Basque Country lives again.

Lasarte:

Nai den guzia ala ere guk	We wouldn't bring out, though,
ez genduen azalduko.	as much as is wanted.
Ai! Jaungoikoak argitasuna	Ai! If God would not
ez baluke itzalduko.	turn out the light.
Berak ez badigu aldegiten	Should it not escape us

guk ez degu bialduko.	we won't send it away.
Bertsolariak izan artean	As long as the bertsolaria sings
euskarik ez da galduko.	the Euskera won't be lost.

Lopategi:

Baina burrukan sartuak dabilz	Our boys and girls, however,
gure mutil eta neska.	are involved in the burruka.
Oiena degu arriskua ta	The danger is theirs
oien gurasoak kezka.	and their parents' is anguish.
Bere lekura eldutzen bada	If the protest of that youth
gaztedi orren protesta,	achieves what is its due,
garai orretan izango degu	then we shall have
benetako bertso festa.	the true feast of bertso.

Lasarte:

Gu emen gabiltz gaztetxoeri	Here we are trying to teach
zerbait erakutsi asmoz.	something to the youth.
Beste lan danak baino ere au	Far more do we love
maiteago degu askoz.	this job than any other.
Nere biotzak bere iritziz	Deep inside, my heart
beti sentitutzen du poz.	is always happy.
Bertsolaritza ez da galduko	The bertsolaritza won't be lost
gazte berriak badatoz.	if new youth arise.

Lopategi:

Oien barruak jaso ditzala	Let their minds receive
guraso zarren dotrinak.	the doctrines of the forefathers.
Alde batera utzi bitzate	Let them leave aside
kanpotik datozen grinak.	the vices coming from the outside.
Nunnai ditugu diskurso ederrak	Anywhere we have nice speeches,
nunnai ditugu mitinak.	anywhere we have meetings.
Biotza baino ez lezake eman	Nothing but his heart can he offer,
bertsolari ezjakinak.	the illiterate bertsolaria.

Lasarte:

Ustegabean sarri etortzen	Unexpectedly so often
zaizkigu egun tristeak	sad days turn up
ta minberatzen gaitu sarritan	and it grieves us frequently
gu ontara iristeak.	to reach this stage.
Baina kantari sentitzen dira	But singers they feel
Euskal Erriko gazteak.	the youth of the Basque Country.
Guretzako re poz aundia du	Great joy is for us also
ondorengoak uzteak.	to leave offspring behind.

These are professional bertsolariak singing on a theme improvised for the occasion by request in a public plaza. Most singers are illiterate. The verbal skills required for improvising, within strict formal measurements, a sustained thematic development that frequently strikes true poetical or ironic chords amaze and delight the audience.

Yet, at the local level, as significant as these occasional performances of the masters, who are called upon to stage a patron saint's *jaia* (fiesta) or to liven up a special dinner, is the singing of bertso by villagers in Itziar's taverns. Adult males or the youth groups on their weekend outings regularly engage in such bertso improvisation. As an example, during *sanjuanak* (Saint John's fiestas) of 1979 a youth group from Itziar decided to make *gaupasa* (spend the night having a good time) in Hernani, fifty kilometers away. I went with them. Once there, we started going from bar to bar. At one point, Fausto put me in an awkward situation while introducing me to a group of girlfriends. He perceived my embarrassment and commented that I was funny. Shortly afterward he began singing a bertso to me on friendship and demanded that I answer. Somehow I responded by singing back another bertso on the same theme. Alzibar and Galtxagorri realized that we were singing bertso and joined us, each adding a bertso of his own. The four of us alternated singing bertso for about half an hour on various themes. The quality of our tavern bertso was very poor compared with those of the plaza bertsolariak. Some of the rhymes were not consonantal, as they should have been; the measurement and the rhythm were rarely correct. We even sometimes made *poto* (used the same word for rhyming) or left a bertso unfinished. And yet, not infrequently, between drinks we would be surprised by how good a certain bertso was, as well as how much we were "unloading"—"Ori dek esan, ori!" (That is *saying* things!).

The Social Contexts

The contextual differences between the plaza performance and our tavern singing are obvious. The two situations are similar, however, in that in both cases making bertso creates a frame in which communication other than ordinary conversation is permitted. Since Fausto did not want to become estranged from me after he had provoked my embarrassment, singing bertso provided an adequate frame in which he could phrase the message "We are good friends." The same message offered conversationally would have appeared phony and was unlikely to establish the friendly rapport he sought. Likewise, in public plaza performances, it is the role of the bertsolaria to make statements about the nature of the community ties that hold together a village or a group. Statements such as "We are Basques," "We all belong to the samc country," "Let us stay together," and so on are typical of the bertsolaria.

The death of Iñaki in a street confrontation with the civil guards, described in chapter 4, was one such event that called for the redefinition of community ties and restatement of solidarity. It occurred three weeks before the 1980 fiestas in Itziar. He was a local ETA youth, and it was clear that his death should become a theme for the bertsolaria. Upon request, Lopategi sang these three bertso in the plaza:

Gazte jator bat aipatu nairik	I was eager to evoke
ni gogo bizian nengon.	a brave young man.
Bada merezi duen batentzat	For I wanted to honor
ondra nai banuen emon.	someone who merits it.
Gabirondoren gaztetasuna	The youth of Gabirondo
erori zaigu Orion	has fallen in Orio
noizbait Euskadik aurkitu dezan	so that Euskadi should reach
merezi ainbat zorion.	all the happiness it deserves.
Mutil erritar, gudari jator	People's young man, great soldier

denentzako begikua.	appreciated by everybody.
Bere bizia eman zuela	It is sufficient to say
esatea da naikua.	that he offered his own life.
Bere erriak astutzen ez badu	If his village does not forget
Gabirondon meritua	Gabirondo's merit
etsaiek ez du itoko inoiz	the enemy will never suffocate
euskaldun espiritua.	the Basque spirit.
Sustrai oneko landara zan da	He was a plant of good roots,
aren jokoa zuzena.	his joko was just.
Sekula etzun inon ukatu	Nowhere ever did he deny
bere abertzale sena.	his patriotic nature.
Plaza oneri emaiozue	Give to this plaza
Gabirondoren izena	the name of Gabirondo,
Euskadigatik ta euskaldun denen	who died for the benefit of Euskadi
mesederako il zena.	and all the Basques.

The bertsolaria has provided the words by which the community redefines itself in relation to a local son killed in the armed struggle for Euskadi's freedom. Only one other forum in Itziar allows for statements about the community as such—the church. However, the priest's discourse is in prose, conversational, within a dogmatic religious rhetoric, and in a shrine sacralized by the presence of religious icons. The bertsolaria's right to address the entire community and to make statements on the identity of the group and the bonds that hold it together is legitimated solely by his verbal skills. As Uztapide told me, for the bertsolaria the language is the only sacred house and his only "power" is the artful use of *euskeraren indarra* (the force of Euskera). The bertsolaria's images are taken from natural and social life. His only claim to their significance relies entirely on the skillful associations of images within the formal constraints of a bertso.

The bertsolariak have played an important role in expressing and creating the Basque nationalist revival of the sixties and seventies. Heavily politicized themes have been decisive in this regard. As a consequence, the bertsolariak have been beset with censorship problems. Since the end of the seventies, however, disenchantment with things political provoked in the bertsolariak a crisis of adjustment. A politicized theme as such no longer made a bertso "good." The quality of a bertso has to be validated primarily on formal grounds.

It is the bertso as an artistic frame of linguistic play that makes it suitable for socially significant modes of communication. Singing bertso is invested with social significance to the extent that it is an artful performance. Its privileged role in defining sociocultural situations stems from the literary meaning emerging from the formal mastery of a linguistic game. The formal framework of bertso needs to be examined.

Technical Features of the Bertso

Lekuona's early work contains the best analytic study of bertsolaritza. He observes that there are two features essential to the construction of a bertso: "One element is the rhythmic process internal to the verse; and the second, the final rhyme, the four consonances in which the even verses of a strophe have to finish" (1935 : 53). The rhythmic sequence is resolved for the bertsolaria by the given melody in which the entire strophe is sung. As to the rhyme element, Lekuona echoes the popular view, which appreciates the improvisation of consonantal words arranged at the end of even verses. The last verse is "as if it were the bomb of the piece, the most opportune, the sharpest, the one that has to pull out of the audience roaring laughter or enthusiastic applause" (ibid. : 54).

There are four well-known types of metrical measurements for bertso. *Zortziko nagusia* are composed of eight verses, the first, third, fifth, and seventh having ten syllables and the second, fourth, sixth, and eighth having eight syllables. *Zortziko txikia* are also composed of eight verses, which have seven or six syllables according to their being odd or even in the sequence. These two formulae, when two more verses with the same pattern of syllables are added to them, give rise to *hamarreko nagusia* and *hamarreko txikia*.[1]

Bertso rhyme has to be consonantal. Furthermore, frequently it is not sufficient that only the final syllables rhyme. The penultimate syllables, or at least the penultimate vowels, should rhyme as well. This rhyme rule can be observed in Lopategi's and Lasarte's bertso cited above. The accomplishment of this rhyme pattern is usually considered by laymen to be an extraordinary feat. This opinion needs to be qualified by the observation that "to improvise verses in Basque is something relatively speaking not very difficult, since the language—suffix-based for the fundamental—offers in some endings an unlimited series of consonants and assonants" (Michelena 1960:241).

Etena (splitting) is a third technical requirement of bertso. A rhyming verse is called *puntua* (point), and it usually goes in pairs, as in the bertso by Lopategi and Lasarte, or in any of the metrical measurements mentioned above; that is, verses two, four, six, and eight rhyme but not one, three, five, and seven. In other patterns the puntua verses may not be alternated with nonrhyming ones. The *etena* rule means that there should be a verbal termination at the end of each verse as a requirement of "metrical smoothness," so that one word cannot be split between two verses. Furthermore, each verse should be split in two hemistichs. In zortziko nagusia the split is 5/5; in other cases, 3/3/4 is called for by the melody. In zortziko txikia this is not a requirement.[2]

The Movement of Images

Lekuona pointed out that the bertso relationship is "not one of idea to idea, but rather one of image to image" (1935:82). He wrote of the technical devices that create the movement of images in the bertso:

> This rapid movement [of images] is manifested principally in four features:
>
> a) In a relative abundance of elisions and "pregnant" constructions.
> b) In an exceptional absence of rhetorical-grammatical means for linkage.
> c) In a somewhat careless logical-chronological order in the succession and disposition of the narrative elements.
> d) In a somewhat apparent lack of relation or logical cohesion between the images and the theme of the song. (1935:23)

These bertso features can be well illustrated by examining the procedure of a *kopla* (couplet), which is the most elemental form of bertso arrangement. The kopla has its own melodies and is typically sung by groups of serenaders on the eve of special festivities such as Christmas and Saint Agatha's Day as well as in tambourine dances. Lekuona synthesizes the technique of the kopla by saying that the first two verses typically depict "a poetic idea, a picturesque fiction, a stroke of imagination" whereas the last two contain "a more poetic idea . . . although also a more intentioned one" (ibid.: 79). Zubeltzu was frequently the *koplari* in the Itziar group of young males on such occasions. The entire group would repeat the kopla improvised by the koplari. This kopla was sung by Zubeltzu when the voices of the chorus were faltering:

Altuan dago Errenteriya,	Renteria is high up
altuaguan Oiartzun.	and Oiartzun[3] even higher.
Ia ba, nere mutil maitiak,	Come on, my dear boys,
altu ta berdin erantzun.	high and alike respond.

Zubeltzu's kopla is a good example of the technique Lekuona underscores. Zubeltzu first takes the images of two towns situated geographically on a height. In the second part, he applies the relationship of altitude to the repetition of his kopla by the group of serenaders.

The koplak are aimed at the dwellers of the houses visited by the serenading group. This means that the koplari has to know the houses and the people; he himself must live in the vicinity. Zubeltzu sang this one to a young woman:

Mendi ganian pareta onduan	On top of the mountain near the wall
aiziak dabil almitza,	the wind moves to the amaranth,
ingurutako maiorazkuak	the neighborhood heirs
zure ondoren dabiltza.	are pursuing you.

The strategy is obvious: the first two lines stage an imaginary vista; the other two juxtapose a social situation. The mere juxtaposition predicates the initial image on the subsequent one.

What kind of metaphorization takes place here? The two *punto* (points) of the strophe, the two images they contain, are trapped within a single kopla; that is, they are parts of the same rhythmic melody and tied by the rhyme (*almitza, dabiltza*). It is the formal frame of the kopla—melody and rhyme—that binds together otherwise unrelated images. Their juxtaposition within a formula creates the trope. The trope emerging from the juxtaposition can actually be metaphor, metonymy, synecdoche, or irony. The bertso arrangement articulates images and by virtue of the formal frame creates a unified field of meaning for them that is different from the individual images themselves.

Formal arrangement, not grammar, provides the syntactical links between the images. Grammar becomes redundant in the connection of images. Ellipsis is an expressive condition for rendering an otherwise prosaic text into a formulaic category. For this purpose the ordinary flow of discourse needs to be dissected into discontinuous units that then can be classified within a formula. Ellipsis (grammatical, chronological, logical, rhetorical) serves to create such discontinuity.

This elliptical syntax within a formal frame is responsible for a narrative that is basically a succession of images. Ideational elements are notably absent. In general, the discourse is never carried by abstractions. What a bertso aims at achieving is the building of an *arrazoia* (argument, reason). This emerges, as has been illustrated by the kopla technique, through a juxtapositioning of natural and social images. The bertsolariak do not like to be assigned a theme that is in itself an argument. As Amuriza, the winner of the 1980 and 1983 bertsolari championships, said in Itziar at a dinner organized to listen to two bertsolariak and discuss their techniques of bertso construction, "If you are given a big arrazoia as a theme, then it is difficult to exceed that with a greater arrazoia."

The final "reason" of a bertso comes out of a progressive succession of images. Each single image must therefore be visual and concrete. As an example of inadequate theme, in Itziar's 1980 fiestas I gave Lasarte the text of a well-known folk song, "The sea is cloudy / up to Bayonne's dock. / I love you more / than the bird its nest." Contrary to my expectations, Lasarte, an outstanding lyric bertsolaria, did not seem to enjoy the theme. Most of his three bertso dealt with the first image of the cloudy sea, not with the relationship between the two couplets. I had given him a "big reason," an accomplished match of two images, a relationship instead of one image. The only way he could make a successful bertso was by excelling it into a higher-order relationship, which is particularly difficult for a bertso improviser. It is not relationships or ideas but images that are juxtaposed in a bertso to generate metaphoric or ideational relationships. As Lekuona observed, the bertso relationships are not those "of idea to idea, but rather of image to image."

In this succession of images a syntax of causals and conditionals is unwanted. The expressive power lies precisely in the discontinuity of the images, in their not being linked in a causal process, in the elliptical yet metaphorically successful connection of images belonging to different domains of experience. Causality here is ellipsis. A bertso is not composed of "because" propositional connectives but simply has a next line with the same rhythm and rhyme. "Why" they are connected is "because" they are part of the same bertso. A further aspect of the bertsolari style of succession of images is that the images are visualized in themselves without being subordinated to a linear temporal sequence; chronological progression is unnecessary.

The Meaning of Improvisation: Nonfixed Texts

Since Lekuona, improvisation has been considered the outstanding characteristic of Basque troubadours by students of bertsolaritza. Lekuona wrote that improvisation is in Basque oral literature "what attracts the attention most powerfully" (ibid. : 16). Likewise, Michelena stated,

> It is not easy to define a bertsolaria. In one of its forms, perhaps the purest, it is a matter of the witty and direct improviser . . . the skill shown by some bertsolariak . . . is really marvellous. The tradition is ancient and it goes back at least to the verse improvising ladies of the fifteenth century reported by Garibay. (1960 : 24–25)

As an instance of this improvisational facility, during the bertsolari competition that took place in San Sebastián in January 1980, approximately 2,000 new verses were improvised before a large audience by the eight participants upon the assignment of previously undisclosed themes.

Azurmendi has warned against a subjective definition of the

bertsolaria: "At most, improvisation will be a general condition, not the defining element of the bertsolaritza" (1980 : 161). He backs up his position with Hauser's remark that "improvisation is one of the characters of the romantic concept of folk art [representing] a feature of the instinctive essence of the artistic creation" (quoted in ibid. : 163). The most significant point for us is that in people's eyes improvisation is the outstanding quality of the bertsolaria. The same stanzas, or even better ones, have a qualitatively different value when written on paper than they do when improvised before an audience. The bertso as such is primarily an oral product, and writing it down is, from the hearer's perspective, merely a redundant and partial transcription. The bertso words and melody are to be heard as they come out from the bertsolaria for the first and last time. Reading bertsolariak implies dissociating the words from the melody, the text from its oral utterance, the eyes from the ear. It implies also that the original stage situation of actor/audience is lost in the private reading. It is true that in the past there has been an important tradition of *bertso-paperak*; that is, bertso written on paper regarding some eventful theme and sold in the marketplaces. However, these "writers" were, for the most part, bertsolariak trying to popularize their bertsoak. Putting the bertso in print was a partial solution to the severe restrictions imposed on the performer by the lack of transportation, which limited his personal attendance to places within walking distance. Important bertso writers are not considered genuine bertsolariak unless they also improvise in front of an audience (see Dorronsoro 1981 : 145).

Frequently the bertsolariak were asked to make *bertso berriak* (new bertso) for print by a private person in order to publicize some event. Zubeltzu, the bertsolaria from Itziar, was asked for such new bertso by a rejected boyfriend who wanted to air his ex-fiancée's deceit. On such an occasion, as in other bertso he wrote for publication, Zubeltzu dictated his bertso (Zabala 1970). The "written" element in this type of dictated bertso-paperak is redundant and perfunctory to the oral process in the bertsolaria's mind. Lord makes this point clear for the Yugoslav epics:

> It is vastly important that we do not make the unthinking mistake of believing that the process of dictation frees the singer to manipulate words in accordance with an entirely new system of poetics. Clearly he has time to plan his line in advance, but this

> is more of a hindrance than a help to a singer who is accustomed to rapid-fire association and composition. . . . When an oral singer is through with a song, it is finished. His whole habit of thinking is forward, never back and then forth! It takes a vast cultural change to develop a new kind of poetic. The opportunity offered in dictating is not sufficient. (1960:128)

During this century the bertsolaria's mobility has increased radically with the train and the automobile and as a consequence his public performances have multiplied. Associated with this increase in bertso singing, the earlier tradition of bertso paperak has been neglected by all major bertsolariak, with the exceptions of Basarri and Enbeita. Uztapide is one of the bertsolariak who never wrote bertso until he was incapacitated and unable to sing in public.[4] Uztapide's arguments against writing bertso are significant:

> But I couldn't come to terms with this [writing bertso]. . . . Do you know why I say this? The bertso once you write it down on paper is not yours. Everybody will learn that bertso by heart and they will even sing it to you. . . . And because of that, you cannot sing it again in a plaza. . . . Furthermore the bertso put on paper ordinarily are sold. That's why they are not yours. You have no right to earn money with them any longer.
>
> Then, I had no hope that I would write very good bertso, and how do you start off? Even if one gets along improvising bertso, the writing down on paper has problems of its own. That remains there forever. The bertso sung in the plaza, on the other hand, the wind takes them away.
>
> For that reason, I have always been less scared of singing in a plaza, than of putting the bertso down on paper. (Olaizola 1976:19–20)

With rare exceptions, the bertsolariak have been illiterate in the past (Onaindia 1964). Even now the formal education of most bertsolariak does not extend beyond primary school. The advantages literate bertsolariak have over the illiterate is a frequent source of commentary among bertso followers. Recently, bertsolariak have been facing the problems presented by the passing of baserri culture. Traditionally they have operated in a peasant milieu, with peasant vocabulary and metaphors. Nowadays, a large proportion of Basque speakers lives in urban centers, and the baserri worldview and expressive language are losing their former power. In the past, bertsolariak performed in front of very local audiences and with markedly dialectal speech. In situations such as the competitive championships, the bertsolariak have to face audiences of several thousand people coming from all the Basque provinces as well as extensive diffusion of each bertso by the media. In order to be understood the bertsolariak have to overcome localism. The "schooled" bertsolaria has considerable advantages in such a setting. The art itself of singing bertso, however, does not depend primarily on written texts or on holding up-to-date information about things; it has to do with the mastery of Euskera—verbal paradigms, suffixation, rhymes, vocabulary—and the mental ability to combine images meaningfully. Such command of everyday language and images does not derive from schooling.

Although oral bertso are considered to be made permanent upon being recorded, the fixing of texts is alien to the bertsolaria. Lord considers oral and written techniques "contradictory and mutually exclusive. Once the oral technique is lost, it is never regained" (1960 : 129). To become a "literary" poet one has to "leave the oral tradition and learn a technique of composition that is impossible without writing, or that is developed because of writing" (ibid. : 130).

Yet Lord's stand that "formula analysis should be able to indicate whether any given text is oral or literary" does not apply to bertsolaritza in the same manner as it does to Yugoslav epics.[5] It must be pointed out that bertsoak are not composed of formulaic expressions; it is a mark of poor singing to insert *bete lana* (filler work), by which is meant anything repetitive or not strictly necessary to the bertso. However, a bertso is a formal armature by definition; the consonanted rhyming, the musical rhythm, and the internal splitting of verses are highly formal requirements. Still, there is nothing distinctly "oral" as opposed to "written" in this formal frame as such. A "literary" creation may fulfill the very same conditions of the bertso.[6]

The Pressure and the Pleasure of Time

If we do not employ formula analysis, what can help us to distinguish the "contradictory and mutually exclusive" oral and written techniques? The public's evaluation is clear: improvisation, that is, unredundant time. The themes are given to the bertsolaria for immediate elaboration; he has to subject himself to creating a text within the rhythmic time of a melody. In the typical versifying context, one bertsolaria has to respond to what the other has just said. A significant element of chance is involved. The public nature of the performance ensures that the bertsolaria is proceeding without pause to prepare his bertso. The absence of redundant time makes bertso singing a fortuitous performance *bat batekoa* (of the moment).

Many of the bertso improvised in public by the bertsolariak are now being collected in anthologies. What makes them artistic and memorable is that there was no trial-and-error process, no redundant time. Had the same bertso been created in the "unlimited" time of trial and error, their value would be of a different nature. Here is the first bertso sung by Uztapide upon request in a competition in front of several thousand people on the theme *Ama* (Mother):

Auxen da gai polita	What a beautiful theme for singing
orain neregana	is given to me
alboko lagunandik	by the friend
etorri zaidana.	at my side.
Bertsoak bota bear	Each one is asked here
emen iru bana.	to sing three bertso.
Ortan esango nuke	In this fashion I will express
nik naitasun dana.	all I wish to say.
Beste ze-esanik ez da	There is nothing to be added
esanikan: "Ama."	after saying: "Ama."

Later on, in his second book, Uztapide "wrote" sixteen bertsoak dedicated to Ama. No matter how good the written bertsoak are, they do not add anything new to the three he improvised in the plaza, which are known by heart to many. This is the first of the written bertsoak:

Esan nai nizuteke	I would like to tell you
zein zan gure ama,	who our mother was,
amaika aldiz guri	who so many times
bularra emana,	gave us her breast,
ezin asperturikan	never was she tired

ematen laztana;	of giving tenderness;
bizi naizen artian	who will never be forgotten
aztuko ez dana;	as long as I live;
une guzitan neri	who all the time keeps
oroitzen zaidana.	returning to my mind.

(1976:32)

This bertso written at home is something Uztapide could ordinarily produce in an improvised manner in a plaza. Thus, nothing new is added to the original bertso technique in terms of enhanced perfection or expression and much is lost by not being the result of a "timeless" first flash of inspiration.

The time limit of a bertso is therefore strictly determined by a given musical rhythm. No other time for consideration is allowed to the bertsolaria. The time limits are strictly bounded. To each temporal unit corresponds a verse; as moments of time are not repeatable, neither are the verses. Spontaneity imposes a heavy temporal constraint on the bertsolaria—it deprives him of anticipated or repetitive time. What at first sight appears to be a temporal "limit"—a real "fixing" of temporal units—is in fact the surrender to the momentary nonrecurrence of chronological time. It is this equivalence between time sequence and textual creation that makes a bertso unfixed; that is, made in and for a certain concrete public moment. In contrast with the time of the bertsolaria, the contemplative work of the writer is not subject to the enslavement of spontaneous, instantaneous creation, but neither is the writer rewarded by the expressive power arising from such equivalence.

The kinds of problems a bertsolaria is faced with when he becomes a writer are predictable. As Uztapide complained above, "How do you start off?" The writer's time is not marked by a chronometer. Once you are given redundant time you have to start by patterning time itself, and you are supposed to put down on paper the pattern-text that is best after all possibilities are exhausted. There is another difficulty on which Uztapide has commented: the selection of themes on which to compose bertso. He said, "I had to invent them myself, and that isn't as easy a job as one might think. Many times it is more difficult than making a bertso" (1976:22). Thinking up a theme contrasts with the instantaneous verse making where it is the moment's reality that is celebrated. Bertsoak have no titles that are a significant part of the text itself. One essential task of the writer is to provide those patterning frames that become constitutive of the text itself. In a written poem the author has to provide title, theme, and text. The title and the theme operate as metaframes for the text. The bertsolaria does not have to metacommunicate at temporal and thematic levels of patterning. The oral text typically does not allow for fixed metaframes. The theme itself comes from "outside" to the bertsolaria.

As Lopategi observed, in the bertsolari performances the applause of the public is an essential element. A concrete bertso does not stand as an autonomous text but as part of the entire performance, which includes singer and public. The bertso, as any other oral performance, is typically a spontaneous response to a situation, a theme, a problem, a pun, a puzzling proposition. It is a response to the public and to the bertso challenge of another bertsolaria.[7] It is a response that makes sense only within the questioning context that frames it. The public's admiration focuses on the entire performative process rather than on concrete textual bertsoak. As a result, it is the bertsolaria as the carrier of such spontaneous inventive process who becomes the object of admiration; the bertsoak are taken as evidence of his natural "genius" rather than end products in themselves.

"The End Is the Beginning"

There is a penetrating slogan that sums up the bertsolaria's mental procedure in the making of the bertso: "Amaia da asiera" (The end is the beginning). Another version of it is "Atzekoz aurrera" (Reversed).[8] These slogans describe the creative process of the bertsolaria. Upon being given a theme or listening to a rival's bertso, the bertsolaria has to figure out the rhymed endings of his verses so that he can proceed to pay attention to rhythmic splits and to the textual content of his words. Thus, the ending words that support the rhymed structure come to mind first. Furthermore, it is the final rhyme that determines the rest. That is, the last punto rounds off the entire bertso, completes the argument of the stanza, or makes the pun. As such, the arrazoia that will be completed in the final rhyme has to be decided in the bertsolaria's mind before he begins the bertso. Uztapide's bertso on Ama is a good example of a stanza that merely prepares for the final punto.

The musical space of the melody provides a time frame for the bertsolaria. And yet, because of this reversal of time by which the end and the beginning are the same, in the bertsolaria's mind the creation of the entire bertso must be instantaneous.

Lord observes that the Yugoslav troubadours can remember thousands of verses. This capacity of the troubadours to recite verses for hours "does not involve memorizing a text, but practicing until he can compose it, or recompose it, himself" (1960 : 25). Significantly, when young Yugoslavs began to memorize songs from books,

> they were moving away from the tradition by memorizing some of their repertory from the song books. The memorization from a fixed text influenced their other songs as well, because they now felt they should memorize even the oral versions. The set, "correct" text had arrived, and the death knell of the oral process had been sounded. (1960 : 137)

Lord's remarks can be applied to the bertsolaria, whose process is not one of memorizing. A bertsolaria never sings the same bertso twice. The audience does sometimes memorize bertsoak for private recollection, but never to sing them again in public as a new performance. Nor has the bertsolaria a "song" or written text that he is supposed to recreate in his singing. His story is as changing as daily events, and his public varies significantly from place to place and from year to year.

The memory of the bertsolaria embraces the entire language. For each bertsoa he has to hold in mind all the possibilities of the language simultaneously. His memory has to hold together vocabulary classified by rhymes, so that he will be able to choose the necessary endings for a bertsoa with no time for consideration. He has to be skilled in all the grammatical devices available to facilitate the correctness of his verses, yet his memory has to be musical. He must have a precise sense of the measurements of the words chosen for a given bertso, and must be able to adjust his words to fit each situation. His memory is a global one. The mind has to be "filled" with language, but "empty" of actual forms. What are fixed are the grammar, suffixation, and rhyme endings. Actual sentences are never fixed; beginning and end are simultaneous.

The Subject in the Oral Performance

Subject and audience are different in nature according to whether the text is oral or written. There is a personal interaction in oral exchange that is absent in the text-reader relationship. I learned this best at home from my father. He is of the same generation as Arbalitz and Uztapide and like them was born and raised in a baserria. He reads the newspaper—mostly in Spanish—every day. For this he prepares himself by putting on his glasses, finishing the meal if he is at the table, or putting aside whatever else he is doing. Soon after he plunges into the first page in the corner of the kitchen he is likely to raise his head and have something to say. He might have read about the political murder of the day, and with worry on his face he will say, "Somebody has been killed." Details will follow: where the victim died, his presumed political affiliation, if he was married or not, how many children he had, and so on. After he has made sure that everybody has heard the news (it does not matter to him whether anyone cares to comment), he returns to the silence of his reading. His main reading consists of collections of bertsoak. Since the time of his childhood and youth, in my father's baserria, as in most others, the people have bought bertso paperak during the occasional market days, later to be sung and learned by heart at home. During my own upbringing, my father's singing in his kitchen corner from some book of verses, in a low voice so as not to bother anyone but high enough to let everybody know that he was singing bertsoak, has been a familiar sound. Frequently, after he had finished singing a bertsoa he found funny, he would start laughing. Raising his head from the book, he would tell the pun to everybody as a story and then sing it again. Despite nobody paying any attention to him, he would continue singing bertsoak and accompanying them with laughter or explanation.

A printed newspaper, much less a bertsoa, is never primarily a written object for my father. Therefore, he needs to relate to them orally. After a first translation from Spanish to Basque, the second translation is from written to oral speech. For him news that is not voiced is not truly news. He knows we all read the newspaper in turns. Were my father not to be allowed to comment orally on what he reads, he would be uncertain about its reality. The activity of reading is primarily a technique of voicing what his eyes see, and when nobody is around it is not uncommon for him to read in a loud voice.

Baserri culture is preeminently an oral culture. It was not until the Second World War that radios and newspapers were introduced into Itziar. Prior to this media revolution, people depended exclusively on *hitza* (word). Even today in church one can observe individuals moving their lips while praying or murmuring in a low voice.

One immediate quality of oral communication is that it must be personal. It travels from mouth to mouth. Therefore, the truthfulness of the spoken word is an essential premise in this communicative process. Validation of the veracity of what has been said rests ultimately on personal knowledge. There is a marked distinction between the *omen* (they say) hearsay story and the account of something personally observed. The speaker is not responsible for omen hearsay news. By contrast, all other speech is assumed to be personally verified.

The mastery of the word becomes an essential skill in this type of culture. People with sayings and humorous parlance become central figures in social life. "As so and so used to say . . ." is a major ingredient in defining concrete social situations. Ingenuity in making a pun, puzzlement by contrast, the skillfully precise description, the quintessential word are means by which the verbal universe is enriched and social standing acquired. As a priest of Itziar, inarticulate in Basque, knew through painful personal experience, "The baserritarra pays much more attention to *how* something is said than *what* is said."

In a culture in which transmission of knowledge is oral, cultural creation lies more in restating the received cultural heritage than in questioning its contents. As transmitter of past knowledge and cultural forms, the word is conservative. Ultimately, the word is not merely a medium but the message itself. This also holds for the speaker of the word, the person. Hitza becomes a fundamental factor in defining the value of the person. Thus, the notion of ideal person in baserri culture is closely linked to the ideology of hitza. When I asked Joxe, a bachelor in his fifties, to describe the ideal person, his first remark was, "Among the characteristics that a man needs to have, one at least is proper hitza; great importance is given to that."

There is an essential quality of unambiguity to hitza. Economy of expression and literalness are basic to this oral communication. Double-dealing and a word with two meanings are abhorred; the term *tratante* (dealer) is considered most pejorative.[9] Talkativeness equals "story" equals sham. Hitza is the self-evident statement of fact; verbosity is an attempt to convince and hence to deceive. The insistence on literalness in speech means that even fabulation tends to be perceived in literal terms and that village people may afford representations of imaginary personages (see Zulaika 1982).

Joxe insisted on the centrality of *gizona* (man) himself as the subject and locus of this oral universe. As he put it, "In that society the man himself was the institution." There is a significant essentialist element to this notion of gizona that evokes the image of an interior "substance" compared with which all external appearances are believed to be superficial and deceptive. The primary means by which this essential man is turned into an observable and describable pattern is the word, which then becomes totally identified with the man himself. What is formally required from both word and man is, in Joxe's account, to be well singled out, concrete. "The word has to be sharp but also distinguished and profound, always a word with meaning, the filler word was never approved. Tratanteak and so on, that's what they have, wordiness." Formalism becomes basic to this patterning of the word. Meaning appears to emerge more from the patterning of words within a sequence than from the intrinsic independent significance of the words themselves.

Rhythmical marking thus acquires a decisive role in structuring a speech act, as the bertsolariak and their work exemplify. The function of such marking is clearly one of providing pattern and fixity to the oral meaning. It is as if verbalization generates such a fragile text that it needs support from a code of bodily gestures, marking of the speech sequence, musical components, and the formalized structure of the utterance itself. A sequence needs to be well bounded, never too long. Not only do oral utterances need to be formally well structured but, furthermore, the meaning of the words, so we are told by Joxe, is not primarily "wordiness" but "commitment" or "contract." The man who speaks this word is bound to it personally in a total manner. The speaker of the hitza has no fixed texts but those provided by his memory. In a larger sense, the oral person has no other text but himself or herself, which in each case can only mark the meaning of words and actions by the ostensive reference of the total person.

Conclusion: The Political Activist as a Bertsolaria

The bertsolaria constantly surprises the audience with how he can improvise in public within the strict formal restrictions of versifying. What he is saying amazes and pleases because of how he is saying it. This impromptu quality of the bertsolaria is well mastered in politics by ETA strategy, in which unpredictability and improvisation in the course of action is essential. Some of the general features attributed to Basque oral culture, such as insistence on literalness, the word as commitment, and economy of expression, provide significant insights into the nature of violent political action. The intellectual skills fostered by this oral culture, as formidable as they prove to be in the bertsolaria, for example, are not of a critical nature. The mind must operate in a manner that precludes further elaboration or framing of the sudden performance. The ETA type of political activism is also based on the same sort of spontaneous intelligence stemming from the urgency of the situation.

The mentality of action is in itself indirectly but intimately related to the ideology of hitza and the meaning of acts of speech. Verbosity and double-talk irreparably devalue the worth of hitza, which has to fulfill a fundamental contractual function. Words "do" things for people who "do" them not only in speech but also in their lives. The insistence on verbal economy turns into a one-sided appreciation of *ekintza* (action). The implication, a dramatic one in the history of ETA, is that no intellectual elaboration per se has the power to modify the course of action, for it is basically *hitzak*—fleeting words. As an intellectual once actively involved in ETA's leadership told me, "In ETA you get power to the extent that you are an *ekintzaile* (activist) and risk your life." He acknowledged to me that his status as a political scientist with publications had no influence whatsoever on the course of ETA. The meanings of "doing" and "saying" in this activist mentality are of course very different from the rhetoric of mass media politics; that is, "when saying is doing" (Paine 1981). One thing is hitza; a very different one is ekintza. It is part of ETA's doctrine that a good ekintza should speak for itself with no need for further explanations.

In the recent political struggle the bertsolaria has been the unchallenged troubadour, the singer of the desires of rebellious youth. As a poet, he is the hero's memory; as a singer, he is the community's political voice. No other men are able to appreciate the value of Euskera as profoundly and as vitally as the bertsolariak. They have identified, with good reason, the cause of Euskera with the cause of ETA. A significant change has occurred, however, in the bertsolari endorsement of ETA. Some bertsolariak have affiliated themselves with the PNV, which has opposed ETA's violent course. The public itself, tired of the political saturation of the middle seventies, has demanded a less politicized verse.

My interest here with the bertsolaria is primarily at the level of cultural models of performance and textual creation. In terms of moral influence he has been eclipsed and left aside by Catholic priests. However, the native model of speech and of a performer is still the bertsolaria. He is the genuine generator of expressive culture. He is rendering into speech collective sentiments of solidarity and proposing solutions to conflictive aspects of social life. The validation of the bertsolaria's performance rests on his individual skills and personal involvement. The solitary underground fighter draws from this model. He, too, has to show the truth of his cause through a strictly personal commitment and has to create a text that is reminiscent of the bertsolaria. A literary critic may rightly consider the art of improvisation to be one of the characteristics of the romantic notion of folk art. Yet, for the audience, ETA's capacity to outmaneuver the police, recover from its mistakes, and keep in sheer suspense foes and partisans alike also relies on this art.

Were ETA to achieve its political goals by means of a legally constituted party and in obeisance to a constitutional charter, it is likely that this would be perceived by the public to be the same as Uztapide writing his bertso. The "rapid-fire association and composition" of the epic singer described by Lord would be missing altogether. Literacy and schooling have been and still are pointless to the bertso singer in the majority of cases. The phenomenon of the schooled bertsolaria is new. Although it is recognized that schooling and literacy do contribute to the overcoming of localism, no follower of the bertsolaria would argue that the essence of his art has much to do with formal education. The art is ultimately impervious to writing or textual learning. Much the same has happened with the art of underground activism. Theories, programs, political texts are decorative additions to the "real" thing. As Uztapide put it, in irreconcilable contrast to the frightful fixation of the written text, the fate of the words of the bertsolaria is that "the wind takes them away." So, too, did Txiki commend his spirit a few hours before his execution when he admonished everyone not to cry over his death, for he was to become a "wind of freedom."

The versifying dictum "Amaia da asiera" (The end is the beginning) has a counterpart in the way the political activist projects his course of action. The revolutionary morale never tires of beginning once again by drawing energy from anticipation of the end. Bertso texts get expressive power from ellipsis and from disrupting normal causal links. Ellipsis is also a rhetorical device well exploited by ETA. The saying "If they did it there must have been some reason" epitomizes how well the public attunes to the internal logic of the performance. If ETA does not give explanations of its actions it is because this is essential to the art. Explanations are as uncalled for as the establishment of causal links within a formulaic frame. Power lies in imposing a sequence of images without rhetorical connections. What frames them is the mode of performance.

The strategy of the bertsolaria is typically to create an arrazoia that is marked by rhymed endings. The final rhyme carries the weight of the argument by concluding it in a stroke. As Lekuona put it, it is "as if it were the bomb of the piece." The "bombarding" strategy of the bertso applies more than in analogy to the politics of the ongoing violence.

More significantly, the bertsolaria makes his arrazoia in a succession of images. He dislikes being given an arrazoia to sing about, for this means having to develop a "bigger" arrazoia, which is a difficult task of improvisation. An argument over an argument cannot purely rely on a succession of images, for a relationship of images is already given. The abstract relationship of an arrazoia can only be the concluding result of a juxtapositioning of images, never a starting point. The building of the argument would have to develop a higher degree of abstraction, for which the bertsolaria could not rely on images.

The arrazoia of the political activist also is primarily based on a juxtapositioning of images, not of ideas. Euskadi Ta Askatasuna (ETA), "Euskadi and Freedom," is, as if in a kopla, the juxtaposition of a concrete image of Basque land with a fictional image of unbound freedom—Txiki's "wind of freedom." Images of national freedom are contrasted to images of foreign domination of the native land. Politically, the big arrazoiak have this type of structure:

> This land is ours.
> (because)
> We were born here.
> These caves and rupestral paintings are ours.
> (because)
> They are situated in our land.
> This is our language.
> (because)
> Our forefathers always spoke it.
> This is our culture and history.
> (because)
> It is tied to our land and language.
> This is our country and nation.
> (because)
> We are not Spanish and French.

The "because" does not connect two propositions in a linearly causal chain. They could be inverted and the "because" would create much the same argument. The "because" creates the fiction of a causal link between propositions, as the succession of various punto in a bertso frame creates an interconnectedness of an arrazoia. By the same strategy of juxtaposing images, Basque land is "not" French or Spanish, Basque language is "not" Romance or Indo-European, Basque culture or country is "not" any surrounding culture or country. As if it were a bertso frame, the political "because" creates a territorial, linguistic, and historical boundary. By the inclusive limits of this frame, the juxtaposed images are arranged into a political argument. It makes no sense to ask "why," although the "because" comes as if it were the response to some question. Why is one born Basque? Why does one speak Basque? Why does one support one's own country? The argument is not one of ideas or logical inferences, of political treatises or historical legitimations, although these are welcome.

The argument is built like a stratigraphic superimposition of layers or the succession of images in a bertso: you have a territory, you have the land and its wealth, you have certain socioeconomic institutions, you have history and mythology, you have a language and culture, you have a sense of collective identity and will, therefore, you are a country and a nation. The bertso can close up the series at any given point and the concluding punto will evoke the "bombarding" arrazoia: Euskadi Ta Askatasuna. "Why?" . . . *because*. Yet, rather than causal explanation, this bertsolaria type of argument comes closer to what Wittgenstein regarded as "aesthetic explanation."[10]

The bertsolaria appeals to his own verbal skills to legitimize his performance. He points to himself as a person and to his art as a bertsolaria to support the validity of his arrazoia. The ETA activist seeks legitimation in the personal arrazoia that he gave his life for his country. Both the bertsolaria and the underground militant's performances are validated by the claims that they are founded on a personal image of total surrender to the exigencies of the urgent present.

A seeming contradiction emerges between the bertsolaria's text being only part of a wider performative context and the difficulties inherent in framing his text. Contrasting oral with written texts, it was pointed out that what differentiates the one from the other is the kind of frame they employ. Whereas the oral text is part of a wider performative context, the written one is defined by a larger literary frame. Thus, in an oral performance the text per se can have no claims to an autonomous status; this rests only with the entire performance. What is autonomous is not hitza but ekintza. ETA's history illustrates this point over and over.

The cultural premises underlying an over-evaluation of unfixed improvised oral texts, argument by images, and iconic personal communication are extended in the political domain to immediacy of unplanned activism and identification with actors. Because of their complete immersion in the present to the point that time is ruled out, the bertsolaria and political activist have real difficulties in framing their performances—in picking a title, choosing a theme, delimiting a cause, or being able to see and use the redundancy of literary-political realities. This inability to create a metastatement ("this is a text," "this is a political program") links both to other modes of communication in between primary and secondary processes. Myth and dream are typically such modes in which metastatements are not possible. In the absence of a textual metastatement the wider frame can be provided only by action. In parts 4 and 5 we consider how mythical metaphors and ritual action necessitate each other.

Part 4

The Cultural Metaphors of the Beast and the Beauty

Introduction

In the chapters on cultural models of performance, comparison and analogy were used to illuminate the main arguments—they are *as if* descriptions of Basque political violence. The chapters in the present section are grounded in metaphor and sacrament—they are descriptions of the violence as experienced symbolically by actors and audience. These are persuasions addressed to "The Beast in Every Body . . . and the Metaphors of Everyman" (Fernandez 1972). Therefore, metaphoric identification plays a key role throughout these two chapters. Existential statements of a sacramental nature provide ultimate justifications. Ritual action, to be studied in part 5, becomes a necessary vehicle for expressing the truth of things contained in these symbolic frames.

In Catholic belief mere metaphor and sacrament are emphatically different. There is a literalness and affecting participation in sacrament that metaphor does not capture. Metaphor abounds in loose "sort of" relationships, whereas in sacrament a strict identity between the sign and its referent holds.

We found cultural insistence on manly literalness in the ideology of univocal hitza and the single-valued joko to the exclusion of ambiguous speech, double-dealing, and childish jolas. At the level of symbol a parallel distinction emerges between metaphor and sacrament. As a performance has markedly different connotations according to whether it is situated in a jolas or joko frame, likewise politics is different in kind depending on its being experienced in a metaphoric or sacramental context.

Models are icons in Peirce's terms. Thus, in the bertsolaria's model of performance there was a crucial aspect of iconic communication between singer and audience; in the domains of the farmer and the hunter, face-to-face interaction with animals is iconic; a dual joko is a structural icon of a polarized scheme. Yet the iconism of the chapters that follow is of a different order. They explore cultural contents that are symbolic in the Sperber sense that they afford "a second representation" after "conceptual representation fails" (1975: 118). Primordial identities typically resort to these symbolic compensations for conceptual failure. One line of inquiry looks at the subjects rooted in animal images (chapter 11). A different analysis places them in religious iconism wherein they find transcendence (chapter 12).

The reader might be misled into thinking that we are presenting these chapters on cultural metaphors as factual evidence to support some speculative assertions about the cultural roots of Basque violence. If we write on the metaphors of the beast and their application to men, it is not to invoke some profound Basque cultural trait by which such identifications and differences between humans and animals hold the key for understanding the political violence. Or if we employ the relationships between two kinds of killing in a legendary text as an analogy for the kinds of killing involved in the ongoing violence, this is not offered as an excuse or justification. The evidence offered by these materials is only metaphoric. Their inclusion here obeys not only the assumption that the search for explanatory models and metaphors is an essential part of an intellectual inquiry, but also that they are a relevant ingredient for an ethnographic contextualization, or "thick description," of the phenomenon under study. Any discourse on political violence is likely to be confronted with the preconception that its explication must depend on tracing the historical roots, political antecedents, or sociological causes of the same. Thus, an attempt at placing the phenomenon purely in the realm of the imagination might appear at first blush almost frivolous.

Furthermore, no account of the phenomenon seems to deserve the status of an explanation unless it is presented along the traditionally established categories of understanding. Cultural anthropology is increasingly sensitive to the various kinds of explanatory logics offered by culture (Dougherty and Fernandez 1982). Metaphor is one such device to organize thought, and the metaphors brought about in this part are introduced as core manifestations of the local cultural imagination. Like Needham's "primary factors," it is assumed that they "may play in imaginative consciousness a part similar to that of ultimate predicates in epistemology" (1978 : 21).[1] These metaphors, in a manner similar to Needham's "synthetic images," suffer a process of synthesis by which primary factors accrete into the complex image, and "we cannot give this a causal explanation" (ibid. : 43). The metaphors investigated in these chapters are taken to set limits on the culture's capacities for representation. These root metaphors can be likened best to Vico's "imaginative universals." A fundamental aspect of these metaphors, or ideal portraits, in the form of fables, is that they have "univocal, not analogical, meaning" (Vico 1968 : 210); that is, the poetic or ideal character is the cultural reality and the individual derives his or her reality from identifying with it.

Basque nationalism and political violence are viewed in these chapters strictly as products of the imagination in Vico's sense of the term. We are thus far from the bias of the political scientist that would grant decisive priority to party organizations and ideological debates in the constitution of such political phenomena. Needless to say, the placing of these phenomena in the soil of the imaginary does not imply a negative predisposition toward them but is only an analytical requirement for the adequate study of collective representations. The assumption is that political mythology shares with other cultural creations, such as art and fiction, the evasion of rational constraints that is intrinsic to human imagination. The intellectualist search for conceptual cogency is abandoned for the proposition that "every people gets the politics it imagines" (Geertz 1973 : 313). These primordial metaphors, which operate as determinants of the cultural unconscious, are thus presumed to be inescapable guides for studying the symbolic complexes generated by the political imagination.

CHAPTER ELEVEN

Beasts and Men

Primordial Metaphors of Savagery, Enclosure, and Ascent

You must know, then, that there are two methods of fighting, the one by law, the other by force: the first method is that of men, the second of beasts; but as the first method is often insufficient, one must have recourse to the second. It is therefore necessary for a prince to know well how to use both the beast and the man. Machiavelli, The Prince

"Animals and persons are the same" is a deep-rooted axiom in baserri mentality, which I have heard repeatedly in Itziar, and elaborate descriptions comparing people's and animals' habitual behavior may follow. Yet it is the implicit and unquestionable assumption of the categorical distinction between men and beasts that gives to this literal identification such a metaphoric force. Thus, other times an axis of continuity is postulated between animals and persons in which individuals or groups move up and down, and one hears that a certain person or village is "more burros than ourselves." I once witnessed a bar argument among several people who were comparing Basques and northern Africans. One side contended that they are more religious than we are; the other side countered that they could kill people more readily. The final argument made by a man in his sixties, one that ended all discussion, was that "they are more animal than we are."

In baserri society, animals traditionally have provided traction force, companionship, protection, and joko partnership. Furthermore, as we shall see, animals serve as the basic source of similes and metaphors appropriated by people when formulating personal identities. An initial fundamental distinction separates animals into wild and domesticated. In pastoral societies, such as the former Basque one, this prime division of animals can afford a basic paradigm for the step from nature to culture. People and societies as well may position themselves in the wild/domesticated continuum.

The idea of closure is essential for creating a frame of domestication for animals and of enculturation for people; wildness implies liberation. Different degrees of cultural enclosure may either generate a process of adaptive learning or lead to labyrinthine confusion. In the latter case, in order to regain the original freedom one has to symbolically "raise up"; images of verticality such as mountains and trees serve for metaphorically performing this ascension. "Up there" the untamed original society and ascendant freedom reign.

The metaphor of savagery revisits the argument developed in the chapter on hunting; namely, the primordial significance of preverbal experience in Basque political violence. In local explanations of violence, allusions to "instinct"[1] play a crucial role (Genovés 1986: 52). Animals provide identities (Fernandez 1974) and behavioral patterns that are most expressive of this survival-oriented resistance.[2] Furthermore, as a prelude to those more religious and ritual aspects of political violence, to which the following two chapters are devoted, the present one introduces the basic sacrificial element of animal substitution (Robertson Smith 1901). Girard makes it most explicit: "Strictly speaking, there is no essential difference between animal sacrifice and human sacrifice, and in many cases one is substituted for the other" (1977: 10). What happens to beasts happens to men.

The Call of the Basoa

The autobiographical account by Arbalitz, introduced in chapter 6, is a narrative in which ecology, social organization, and personal identity are articulated around a mountain. The image of Mount Andutz served to sketch a cultural map of baserri imagination. Andutz is a mountain, yet it is not wild forest but a territory belonging to Itziar's baserri society and an irreplaceable anchor in the village's spatial configuration. The image of Itziar being "under Andutz" is constantly invoked in the church and bertso songs. "Andutz" is also a proper name and, as a compound, forms part of several baserri names.

A mountain that is beyond agrarian appropriation is *baso* (forest). *Basoa* is the wilderness to which untamed life belongs. The adjective for this wild state is *basati*. In the baserri way of life many animal and plant species are present in both wild and domesticated forms; when this is the case the wild species' name is preceded by *basa* (wild).[3] Arbalitz's book is entitled, significantly, *Baso-Mutillak* (Forest Boys). The title refers to the groups of youths who were hired by timber merchants to cut trees in the mountain forests for long periods. My father's favorite memories are of those years in his youth when he was a *baso-mutilla*. A member of my father's woodcutting group was Uztapide, the bertsolaria and author of an autobiography in which he describes at length the life of the woodcutters. The important place that the image of baso plays in the memory of these men is associated with the "liminal" features (Turner 1969) inherent in that mode of life. The baso-mutillak were away seasonally from home and lived with a group of peers under hard climatic and working conditions from dawn to dusk. They constantly competed and engaged in the comradeship of singing bertsoak and playing mus. Occasionally, even deviant behavior such as not going to Mass was permitted because of distance imposed by their special occupational status.

The baso-mutillak were tree cutters. The image of the tree is inseparable from the idea of basoa. Large portions of the Basque Country are forest land, and trees abound. Most baserriak have a protective tree by the house. In the traditional mythology one of the forms adopted by the flying Mari in her aerial trips is a tree. An Itziar custom, practiced until the 1970s, consisted in placing a tree in the plaza on the first Sunday of July, the occasion of a special festival of the Virgin; gifts and a flag hung on top of the tree as prizes for the climbers. In one of Itziar's annual bailara fiestas, in Salbatore, this custom is still in force.

In Basque mythology the figures of a superman and a superwoman called *basajaun* and *basandere* stand out (Barandiaran 1972:57–59)—compounds of *basa* plus *jaun* (lord) and *andere* (lady). They live deep in the forest and are endowed with portentous powers. When men from Arbalitz's generation search in their autobiography for the most significant events it is not surprising that the baso looms as an almost ritually secluded space that they in their youth visited and experienced. They do not encounter any more mythically self-defining designation than baso-mutillak. Likewise, a hunter from Lastur summed up a conversation on hunting with the words, "I am a *basa-kristaua* (basa-Christian)." *Tasio,* a film that portrays the forest life of a Basque charcoal-burner and hunter, became popular in the early 1980s.

The very term for the farmstead, baserria, the basic rural socioeconomic institution studied in part 2, is a compound of *baso* and *herria* (people, community). Particularly when viewed from the valley's urban settings, the baserri society is imagined up in the mountain in close proximity to the wilderness. As suggested by the name itself, it tends to occupy an ambiguous position between the domains of the baso, or wilderness, and the erria, or civilized society. In the ideological projections of the baserri way of life there is an attempt to recapture the original experience that existed prior to the perceived ills of the present civilization. As animals and plants may present themselves alternatively in the form of a cultural (domesticated, grafted) state as well as in their *basa* (natural) state, so, too, can persons undergo ritual transformation into baso-mutillak through the temporary social segregation of the woodcutters or by turning into basa-kristauak by virtue of a "wild" occupation such as hunting. The erria society realizes its "natural" state in the baserria.

Wild and Domesticated Creatures

As Pedro the hunter described for me, there is a world of difference between the untamed behavior of a hare and the domesticated behavior of a rabbit. He has tried on four occasions to tame hares he trapped alive, but to no avail. A simple touch will always provoke the hare's frightened jump; it will never be in the open; it eats only at night; it will not make any sound or movement during the day. Pedro marvels at such radically different behavior from a rabbit.

A basic definition of domestication is given in the culture in relation to enclosure: a domesticated animal tolerates being enclosed, whereas a wild animal does not. Enquiring about the relationship of animals to enclosure, I was told of cases such as that of the cat that will not tolerate total enclosure within a room: "When you close the door the cat will start jumping here and there, and finally it will jump on you. The cat does not get completely domesticated. . . . You can't teach him. The dog, yes. The dog gets domesticated. The cat doesn't. That's it."

I was given a psychological explanation of the wild animal's fear of enclosures: "That is because of fright; it sees itself imprisoned and it gets upset; it protests. That happens to any untamed animal when enclosed." The Basque term for getting anxious is *estutu*, which derives from *ertsi* (to close up). The wild animal cannot remain inside an enclosure without internalizing the exterior cage and reacting aggressively. Contrary to the tamed animal, which puts up with external enclosure without psychologically being bothered by it, the wild animal reacts as if such enclosure is affecting all of its inner senses. The "closed up" wild animal is thus incapable of interaction with humans. Pedro offered a good example of the effects of closure on a wild animal: when a fox attacks chickens in an open field, it will get just one and leave; but when it attacks them inside a shack it will kill all of them first and then leave with just one. Pedro observes that this must be because in an enclosed place it feels threatened in a way it does not in an open area. He concludes that animal behavior is determined completely by enclosure.

Yet, as we know from the chapter on hunting, wild animals, too, make use of self-enclosures for protective purposes. Undomesticated learning, however, is guided solely by instinctual drives for acquiring survival techniques, whereas domestication implies the animal's recognition of boundaries and adaptation to various degrees of interaction with humans. Fences are the most common means of enclosures. Unlike the wild animal, the domesticated one is capable of experimental learning and sensory control, an adaptive capacity exploited by humans.

Individual names are given to domestic animals but never to wild animals. Dogs in particular are culturalized by proper naming—

the names are usually Spanish or English (such as "Pastor" and "Blacky"), numerals (such as *Bat* [One] and *Bi* [Two]), or adjectives (such as *Txiki* [Small]). The cows and oxen of the stable are named with some adjective that indicates their color or dimension, such as *Gorrixa* (Red), *Pintua* (Spotted), or *Motza* (Short). Cats usually are not given proper names.

A crucial difference between the wild and domesticated animal has to do with response to human touch: the domesticated ones accept caresses, the wild one's reaction to touch is to escape or bite. Since the wild animal never accepts a caress, the hunter's touch can only be deadly. With the pastoralist the hand ceases to be an instrument of capture to become the tool for domestication; activities such as milking and shearing provide situations of extended and intimate bodily contact between human and animal. The hunter's final handclasp turns into the master's discipline and right.

The Fiesta of the Enclosed Bull

In Basque traditional culture the bull stands somewhere between the wild and the domesticated. In Itziar, as elsewhere in rural society, the bulls afford the paramount entertainment during the four days of yearly fiestas. Contrary to the Spanish *corridas,* in which a few professional matadors sacrifice the beast after virtuoso bullfighting performances, this is popular "playing" with the bulls. The plaza is closed, the bull is taken from the stable, and anybody from the audience is allowed to jump into the arena to provoke and escape from the beast's blind charges. Playing with the bull is playing with the culturally crucial step from the wild to the domesticated. The aggressivity of the animal turned wild in the enclosure of the plaza becomes a never-ending source of danger and entertainment.

Itziar-Lastur is recognized as the breeding home of a particular breed of bulls. *Lasturko zezenak* (the bulls from Lastur) are well known in most Basque towns during the yearly fiestas. The plaza of Lastur is a *probadero,* its purpose being to "prove" the quality of the bulls before taking them to other plazas. Nowadays a baserria from Itziar, Saka, raises most of the Lastur bulls.

Agustín, one of the members of Saka, the baserria that raises most of the bulls, described them as being "the liveliest, the most twisting, those with sharpest instinct, with greatest genius." The pure Lastur race is becoming lost, though. Castilian bull breeds are bigger and stronger, but calmer, Agustín contends. They don't serve for the local *sokamuturra*[4] or the popular fiestas in which dozens of youths may "get out" in the plaza to run around them. Agustín told me, "Those big bulls from outside are calmer than oxen; they go straight to the cape, they have no malice at all." Malice is what is needed from a bull in the village fiestas surrounded by dozens of people he has to catch in order to create drama and entertain the audience.

In former times every baserria in Lastur had bulls. My mother's natal baserria still keeps some, although its head, José Mari, complains that with pine trees there is no sense in preserving them any longer. In the past the bulls were left in the mountains throughout the year, except for the period of snow in the winter and during the summer season of plaza performances when the bulls were captured in the mountains and brought home. This expectably provided some of the most enjoyable moments of the year for men who had to spend entire days chasing after them. One can still hear of a certain bull who escaped from the rest and required three days to catch. Bulls and cows roam in groups in Lastur's and Itziar's mountains.

The bull's psychology is much admired. That the bull "knows" its owner is a very graphically depicted quality. "The owner can do a lot to help the bull when he is going to the plaza," Agustín told me. My mother commented many times how tame the bulls are at the stable, "just like any other animal." As soon as a stranger visits, the bulls in the stable will start bellowing. "They know perfectly well who is from the etxea and who is not." She described them as much less dangerous than rams, who may attack you in an open field upon realizing that you are the owner of their opponents.

The bull is most illustrative of the different types of enclosure to which animals might be subject in baserri society and of the animal's reactions depending on the context of enclosure. The bull stays most of the year in the open mountains, but it is also kept inside the baserri stable during winter or during the period in which it will be taken to plazas. Contrary to oxen and cows, which will spend all their time stabled or within a nearby fenced field, heifers and bulls are in their most proper habitat when free in the mountains. Yet theirs is not the freedom of the wild boar or fox, which can only be controlled by hunting them down. Although staying in the mountain without the baserritarra's immediate care, their space is still loosely bounded and has to be controlled by periodic visits to their sites. Normally, bulls respect the boundaries, but transgression of them is also to be expected.

The bull behaves thus as if it were a domesticated animal for most of the time. Yet, as I was told by a farmer, "it has wildness. It gets used to staying inside a stable, but there, too, it gets wretched. You can stroke a bull and feed him fodder, and he remains quiet. But tie him with a rope and start pulling him and goading him, and he starts striking back; at the end he will even butt the owner." The bull-raiser Saka is credited with having a bull so tame that he used to put him to work in a yoke with an ox, "but even those working in a yoke all start hitting back when they get mad."

A rare event occurred in Itziar in 1980: a bull attacked a hunter on the open mountain. It was a matter of conversation why the bull should have acted contrary to its habitual behavior. The hunter himself explained to me that dogs had been barking at the bull earlier, and that this had probably *estutu* (distressed) the bull, which then became aggressive. The incident illustrates how the bull's delicate balance changes from an open context, in which no aggressivity is triggered, and a closed one, in which it loses all control. Being in a narrow path can be sufficient signal of enclosure for the bull. Another situation of danger is when cows have calves to protect and to which they are "tied."

There is a place, of course, where the bull is all defiance and danger—the plaza. This is his paramount context of enclosure. The plaza is the only place where the bull does not recognize his owner. The bull trapped in the plaza is the paradigm of the wild animal captured by humans, of the mountain wilderness encircled by street civilization, of the open space turned into an enclosure. There, in front of an audience, the "free" animal is forced into an experimentally aggressive context, and everybody can watch the effects of the beast's natural goodness being turned into deadly fury.

The bull is fatefully trapped in the plaza among strangers who from all sides instigate, confuse, and then escape his aggressivity.

Relentlessly harassed and pursued by people inside the plaza and by the eyes and shouts of the audience watching the action, the infuriated animal blindly assails anything or anybody that moves or stands in its way. In the plaza the bull is imprisoned by the walls or fences, by the watching audience, and by its adversaries on foot. The trapped bull can only remove the visual and olfactory walls of the people inside the plaza by frantically pursuing them.

Were the bull to have a way out from the plaza it would instantly escape, leaving behind the assault of its tormentors. During my youth, in both Itziar and Lastur's plazas a bull escaped from the plaza after a formidable jump over the fences and public viewers. During the village bullfights it is normal to see a bull trying to find a way out by pushing against the fences or against the door that gives way to the bull's stable. On other occasions, when the time has arrived for a given bull to leave the plaza and the exit door is opened, the fiery bull refuses to turn his back upon the harassers and thereby makes it impossible to force him out.

In the plaza the bull is, as Luxio said, in an *itxixa* (closed) context. But enclosure penetrates the bull's psyche far deeper than the restraint of fences and walls. He gets psychologically and, according to some accounts I was given, even visually "closed" to the point that he gets blind and loses his normal sense of recognition. Agustín told me of cases in which a bull came out into the plaza so "completely blind" that he attacked his own mother. The summer of 1982 a much-commented-upon event occurred in Azpeitia during the plaza rehearsal that precedes the bullfight. Two of the bulls, still "blind" from having been enclosed in the stable, charged each other frontally and cracked heads as if in a ram fight. Both died on the spot. Martin, who saw the bulls' fatal blow, commented to me on the bulls' blindness when they come out to the plaza and compared it to the blindness of a person arising from a siesta. Agustín explained: "They hit each other wherever they can, they go one against the other blindly; until they return to their right minds, until they start recognizing each other again, they don't see anything." When they are taken to the plaza for the first time they are particularly susceptible to such blindness; later they get used to it, "they learn tricks as people do." In brief, the spatial closure of the plaza provokes the psychological closure and even the visual closure of the bull. This results in his loss of any control; abandoned to his wild condition, the bull can only respond to the danger by resorting to innate aggressivity.

In rural Basque society such as Itziar it is obviously not incidental that bulls provide the greatest entertainment during the annual fiestas. The animal turned wild within the hostile plaza—responding to imaginary threats of people as if they were real, unable to distinguish between a piece of cloth and real people and thereby bringing "real" danger into the arena by its aggressively conditioned reflexes—becomes for the audience an endless source of "deep play." This popular entertainment with the bull in a plaza is not categorized in Basque culture as a burruka nor even properly as a competitive joko but as jolas. As Pedro said after contrasting the Spanish bullfighting style, which concludes with the sacrifice of the animal, with the popular diversion with the bull in Basque traditional society, "What we do here is *jolasa* (play) with the bull." The play is situated in the interaction between wild behavior and the artful mastery of the instinctive responses through a higher level of control. The bull's harassers do not really plan to chase or hurt the bull, but this is known only to the people, never to the trapped animal; the bull's aggressive attacks are intended to really hurt people. Mastery of the bull's wild behavior is deeply gratifying, but it is so only after its actual risks have been assumed and resolved in the bull's own context of aggressive enclosure. It is all a jolas in which players make a fool of the wild beast, if only they dare to face the actual risks and not be intimidated by its frightening blind attacks.

Cultural Metaphors of Enclosure

As adaptation to enclosures defines an animal's domesticated state, likewise, internalization of cultural norms characterizes a social person. Yet persons, like animals, may show differences in tolerance for cultural enclosures and, like bulls, may travel back and forth from the domesticated to the wild. Thus, it is common to say that so and so is *basati* (wild), or that in a moment of rage someone turned into a *fiera* (wild beast). In these untamed situations the ordinary social conventions no longer rule. For the ever-present state of savagery to be kept under control, rules or enclosures must be applied to animals and people alike. Thus, systematic fencing is assumed as the key organizational principle, and the idea of closure becomes a central hypothesis to the cultural order. As in a fenced territorial distribution, an architectural construction, a kinship organization, or a belief system, the internal arrangement of a cultural pattern implies some general notion of closure. In Basque culture and language, as shown below, the hypothesis of closure appears to be a definitional predicate in these cultural systems.

Basic aspects of language, cognition, performance, and space organization are culturally anchored in the idea of ertsi (Zulaika 1987a). Boundary marking and fencing, which provide the primary mapping of rural territory, are elementary instances of controlling enclosures. "Fence" is *esi*, which derives from ertsi, ersi; "fence, enclosure" is also *itxitura*, from *itxi* (to close up). Houses and buildings (*itxeak*) are likewise enclosures; this identification is used by historians such as Iturriza y Zabala (1967 : 1 : 87). In addition to discussing its architectural enclosure, in chapter 5 we stressed the institutional enclosure inherent to the etxe of the baserria. *Etxe* means both "construction, system, ensemble" (Lhande 1926) and "frame" (Múgica Berrondo 1965); "window frame," for instance, is *leio-etxe*, and "doorframe" is *ate-etxe*. Thus, language clearly associates closing and framing, enclosure and system, and advances the cultural premise that systemic arrangements require the notion of ertsi/itxi.

Associated with the enclosures of territorial organization, house building, and domestication of animals, the sense of possession and ownership arises as well. The wild animal does not belong to anybody; the domesticated animal, on the contrary, belongs to whoever sets it within an enclosure. Not only is the basa animal not privately owned, but in former times the baso of the sheepmen was likewise communal. Communal lands were not permitted to be enclosed, nor could the cabins in those lands be locked up or permanently roofed—enclosure was by definition private ownership. The new system of land organization was grounded on a new exercise of enclosures.

The idea that enclosure is possession is derived from another primordial function: clutching and seizing is also *ertsi* (to enclose, to grip, to handclasp). From being an instrument of deadly capture for the hunter, *esku* (hand) turns into an instrument of control and training, even of intimate contact, as in milking and shearing, for the pastoralist-agriculturalist. The hunter's right to the wild animal is a "natural" one in that the animal belongs only to nature unless captured; the sense of right changes with the possession of domesticated livestock, which must be legitimized by social convention. Now *esku* also means "right, faculty." The basic normative notions of "jurisdiction" and "legal right" are *eskualde* and *eskubide*. Through the esku metaphor the ertsi idea of enclosure-seizure is extended to the domain of normative law. In the prime social system of kinship, *ezkondu* (to get married) can also be related to ertsi.[5]

In another relevant domain, psychological notions hinge on the idea of closure. Linguistically and kinesically, distress in Basque culture is a narrowing of the body's internal space. *Ertsigo, erstura, estuasun*, all compounds of ertsi, are the common terms for "distress." Either material or psychological lack of space is *estu* (narrow, tight). Other expressions of psychological closure are phrased in terms of the inability to find a way out. The kinesic movement that accompanies being estututa is the shrinking of shoulders and the tightening of the body. Likewise, the key psychological term *etsi* (to give up, to get adapted), which will be reviewed in the next chapter, is a close variant of ertsi.

Domestication is described primarily as adaptation to enclosures. Yet the conformity of the domesticated animal to the imposed boundaries should not be overstressed. As Pedro remarked, "That is because we have them tied up, otherwise they all leave. There isn't one that doesn't leave." Thus, to the notion of itxitura is added here the one of *lotura* (tie, leash). A wild animal does not submit to being caressed or touched. Consequently it will never endure being leashed or yoked, domesticated situations. There is no individuation of wild animals; they are named and categorized only as species, contrary to domesticated animals, which may have proper names. Being *lotuta* (leashed) implies an individuation of the general frame of enclosure.

The idea of ertsi derives in the psychological domain from picturing anxiety as closure. A parallel derivation of the idea of *lotu* (to tie) can be observed in *lotsa* (shame), a compound of the same root, *lot*, and presumably *atsa* (breath). The relevance of the lotsa complex in the traditional ethos as a positively valued mechanism of social control was pointed out in chapter 6. The individual self's subjection to social norms is expressed by internalizing the bonds of lotsa. Thus, as domestication is forced on individual animals by means of a lotura, so is social control imposed on personal selves by psychologically tying them up with the metaphor of lotsa.

To the extent that domestication and enculturation are defined by the notion of systemic enclosure, both are viewed in the culture as similar processes. The initial notion of boundary marking becomes subsequently a root metaphor in the global cultural order, as evidenced by its presence in the various domains described above. Enclosed animals must either adapt themselves through domestication or else try to jump over the fences. Individuals or societies afflicted by excessive psychological or political enclosures are also compelled into higher degrees of integration by means of cultural transcendence (to be discussed in the next chapter) or else the situation turns into a labyrinthine maze. In the latter case the desperate attempt to find a way out is conducive to embracing the assumption that freedom requires the return to an original savagelike state unaffected by the paradoxes of cultural enclosures.

The metaphor of cornered animals is commonly applied to ETA members. People very close to the organization repeatedly asserted for me the "instinctual" nature of their actions. The following exchange with an ETA sympathizer is typical:

> ETA's ekintzak are not politics.
>
> So what are they?
>
> They are survival. ETA guys are like animals
> who have to count basically on their instinct.
> They are like cornered animals holding to their
> instinct for survival.

The image that comes to mind is the bull trapped in the plaza. Bulls capture the utmost attention and provide the highest entertainment by dramatizing in front of an audience the blinding effects of enclosure; in the national arena the entire society watches in suspense the charges of violent activism provoked by political enclosure. The analogy of the cornered bull applied to ETA suggests that the perception of a survival threat in a situation of political blockage is a major factor in generating Basque support for the violence. The systemic enclosures are sustained by ideological premises and private sensorial experiences. The drama and the fiesta that the bull and the audience impose on each other serve as a metaphor for a cornered country, enraged by centuries of political enclosure and hardly able to learn how to distinguish legitimate self-defense from blind aggressivity. The only way out seems to be to jump over the fences and run up the mountain with the beast and the metaphor.

Gora, or the Ascent of the Beast and the Metaphor

It's so beautiful and deep-rooted,
as ancient as time the suffering of that people.
It's so beautiful and deep-rooted
as all the colors of green
in that month of May.

All the colors of green
Gora Euskadi! *fiercely cry—*
the people, the land, and the sea,
there in the País Basc.[6]

Raimon, "El País Basc"

During the village fiestas of Itziar and Lastur it occasionally happens that a bull being played at the plaza will jump over the fence and the spectators and frantically escape *mendian gora* (up the mountain). While groups of youths run to the mountain after the bull, the plaza is left empty. The incredible jump is the ultimate feat that an entrapped bull in desperation can make, and the audience finds great entertainment in the discovery that the bull can conquer the plaza enclosures. The surprising escape is only the natural victory of the mountain's wild freedom over the plaza's unbearable subjection. The latest case happened in 1983 when the bulls that were to run the *encierro* (penning) through Itziar's streets all ran away to Mount Andutz. Once again it was going to be the ceremony of the mountain forced to travel nervously through the street, of the foolish beast caught up by civilization; yet this time the paved enclosures could not contain the wild impulse—the natural savage had been saved by the *gora* (upward) ascension to the mountain.

The bull escapes up the mountain. Also up there, deep in the forest, dwell the mythical *Jentillak* (Pagans) and the wild portentous hero, Basajaun, who is uncontaminated by civilization. To the mountain of mythical power and ritual seclusion ascends also the lonely poet: "A palace of closed windows seems the forest. . . . Shadow!, most beautiful daughter of the Forest. . . . Temple of repose, filled with columns, / the firmament formed with a multitude of leaves and feigned stars" (Lizardi 1970: 152). Up the mountain to the Amabirjina's shrine of mercy and grace ascends likewise the pilgrim. Hermitages and churches that have left a lasting imprint on Basque folklore, such as the one devoted to Saint Michael in Aralar and to Saint Anthony in Urkiola, are built on high mountain elevations. The most venerated sanctuaries of the Amabirjina, such as Aranzazu, Begoña, Arrate, Juncal, or Itziar, are also on top of hills; a visit to them requires climbing.

During the 1960s the ascents to Aranzazu became focal points for Basque youth's pilgrimage devotion as well as political activism. During a spectacular Saturday-night pilgrimage of singing, praying, and fiery preaching by the priests, over ten thousand boys, many with torches, barefoot, or carrying crosses on their shoulders, would go up the steep ten kilometers that separate the town of Oñate from Aranzazu. The night ascents by the boys became an exceptional occasion for ETA's propagandizing ekintza. On a different Sunday as many or more girls ascended to the sanctuary, disappointed that the political rhetoric was reserved for the boys. In 1968, under pressure from the governor, both pilgrimages were suspended. The first political arrest in Itziar in 1960, that of José Mari from Andutzene, was provoked by one such pilgrimage ekintza in which he planned to help distribute the priests' letter protesting the suppression of the Basque language and culture. Ascending in religious devotional zeal to Aranzazu, Itziar's youth experienced political activism and police repression simultaneously.

A preference for the gora posture and movement can be observed in the traditional culture. The onomatopoeic term *eup!* is one expression of it.[7] Among baserritarrak a characteristic way of walking is called *jaikixan* (rising up), which consists of buoyantly straightening up the body on the toes at each step. Basque popular dances, performed with the body in erect position and with hands raised over the head, clearly show such preference for gora posture.[8] The call for ascending has its prime arena in the climbing of mountains, which still is a favorite weekend pastime for many people.[9] The valley has been left below and the mountaineer finds satisfaction in the height conquered with effort and spirit. The constraints of the narrow valley turn into open vistas at the peak. Up there the air is pure, space is unlimited, the self is free.

Mountaineering and political activism have been close allies in the history of Basque nationalism. The political significance of groups of mountaineers can be traced back to 1904 when three *mendigoizale* (mountaineer) organizations were founded in Bilbao. In 1912 eight groups formed a federation and soon they were expanded into other Basque areas. By 1921 the Basque Federation of Mountaineers included sixteen groups from Vizcaya, ten groups from Guipúzcoa, and one from Alava. These mountain excursions had ideological objectives, as clearly stated by the PNV's periodical *Euzkadi;* cultural activities were part of their agenda. These groups numbered the activist minority within the nationalist youth (Elorza 1978:389–90). During the 1930s the federation of mountaineers gained importance as the bastion of uncompromising nationalism by providing organizational support to the weekly periodical *Jagi-Jagi* (Get up–Get up). After 1935 the radicalization of nationalism forced the Federation of Mendigoizaleak to practically break away from the PNV. In chapter 1 we met these mendigoizaleak when in August of 1931 their federation from Guipúzcoa came to Itziar to proclaim the Amabirjina their patron saint. Zebain, the chronicler from Itziar, had written in *Argia:* "We were seeing from all over large groups of the Mother country's robust soldiers filled with love for her, shouting Gora Euskadi! 'Up with Euskadi.'"

"Gora Euskadi Askatuta!" (Long live free Euskadi!) is the forcefully shouted slogan that epitomizes the ultimate aspiration of recent Basque nationalism. In multitudinous demonstrations, political ceremonies, or meetings of any kind the cry of "Gora Euskadi Askatuta!" will be answered with a resounding "Gora!" The official hymn of the Basque Nationalist party begins with the words "Gora ta gora Euskadi" (Up and up with Euskadi). A most popular song starts likewise with a solemn call: "Get up, get up Basques, dawn has broken." With the morning light will irresistibly rise the ETA activist's final cry before execution: "Gora Euskadi Askatuta!"

"Gora!" is the ascensional command that metaphorically lifts persons and situations toward their optimum position. Physical potency, for instance, is tested by the capacity for upward movement, as in stone lifting, one of the favorite Basque popular games. Moral rectitude adopts an ascending direction; we children used to try to visualize the saved souls of the dead ascending straight to heaven from the cemetery. The standard expression to wish a deceased person eternal peace is "Goian bego" (Let him/her be above). Political strength is expressed by the posture of standing up—ETA's main periodical has been *Zutik!* (Stand up!).

The tree provides another ascensional image. Tree-climbing has always been a favorite pastime of children and youths. The tree placed at Itziar's plaza during the annual festivity of the Virgin was the public occasion when climbing skills were tested. The political and juridical symbolism of the tree among Basques is a rich topic on which much literature can be found (Caro Baroja 1974b). The most famous of these symbolic trees is the oak of Guernica under which since time immemorial the general meetings of Vizcaya took place. Within an oral framework, these meetings had a legislative character that was granted by the formula of swearing "under the tree." Castillian kings since Alfonso XI in 1334 came to Guernica to take under the tree the oath of observing the ancient traditions and fueros. General Franco aimed at the heart of Basque historical consciousness when he bombarded Guernica with Hitler's aircraft on a market day of April 1937.

The last Spanish king to pay such a ceremonial visit to Guernica was the presently reigning monarch, Juan Carlos, in 1981. For Basque nationalists the foreign domination symbolized by the Spanish king could not go uncontested; during his speech the representatives of Herri Batasuna rose up to sing, their voices trembling, the Basque soldiers' song: "We are Basque soldiers in order to free Euskadi; our blood is ready to be poured out for her. Having heard an *irrintzi* [cry] at the top of the mountain, let all the soldiers go after the *ikurrina* [flag]." Antagonistic as a war cry, timeless as a mountain peak, the rebellious tune could not be extinguished until the singers were forced out violently. It was Unamuno who in his exalted nationalist youth wrote that the "blessed tree" of Guernica is telling the Basques: "Gora, always gora!" (Aranzadi 1981 : 346).

The war cry calls from the mountaintop. The mountain metaphor is a close associate of military situations. *Echarse al monte* (to rush to the mountain) is a common expression for rising up in arms. Particularly in the tradition of guerrilla warfare, which characterized last century's Carlist wars and of which ETA's tactics are partly a continuation, the mountain setting plays a decisive role. The mountain symbolizes the place where the ordinary social conventions have been left behind; a war situation cancels out the civic society and calls for a redefinition of the moral order. For this the warrior has to return to the state of savagery and innocence kept intact at the mountain and from there start all over again. It is a common opinion that many ETA activists have been recruited among mountaineers. As an instance, the ETA members tried at Burgos have insisted on the prime importance of their mountain outings for their activism (Morán 1982 : 73, 95). Clandestine activism is underground in the street milieu, but it no longer has to be secretive on the mountain. Here one can talk freely without the presence of potential informers. The mountain is a sanctuary of many sorts—for planning, for training with arms, for escape. Still, it is not accidental that these activists find themselves most at home in the mountain landscape. The Itziar cell of the middle 1970s was a typical case of such fondness for mountain life. They worked or studied in urban centers and even rented an apartment in Bilbao; yet it was in the mountains where they felt safe and where they spent most of their free time. Not only did they tour mountains, but they were thoroughly familiar with all the many caves of Itziar and Lastur. In one of the caves they kept captive an industrialist while waiting for ransom money. Likewise, the following generation of activists, some of whom were arrested by the police in 1983, formed a speleology group.[10]

In describing the identification with the land characteristic of a rural culture, we made use of Arbalitz's territorial image of Mount Andutz in chapter 6; it offered him local identity. He grew up in the mountain and, we could add, the mountain grew up in him. This is at least the way Arantxa Arruti, one of the "historical" members of ETA tried in Burgos, expressed herself when she replied to a journalist: "Rather than an ideology [what we had] was an instinct for fighting. . . . We were all life . . . we gave everything . . . because we were born here, because that mountain was born in me and I from that mountain, simply because of that . . ." (Morán 1982 : 40). The mountain is again a primordial source of identity. Many ETA cells are named for physical features, especially mountains. One of Itziar's ex-ETA members told me that his having joined the organization was intimately related to a mountain experience he had during the fiestas of the Guipuzcoan town of Ataun. At daybreak he had heard the echoes of the *txalaparta*[11] being played from various mountain peaks and in a state of emotional intensity decided to join ETA. It was, we might add, a primordial experience motivated by the combination of primary factors of experience such as sound, mountain air, and liminal comradeship in the basoa. Once again the call for the heroic was mediated symbolically by the uplifting imagery of the mountain.

Animal Impersonations, Witchcraft, and Taboo

"An animal is exactly like a person. You look at its eyes and you know how the animal is. You know if it is tired or hungry or sick by looking at the eyes. That is the whole secret with animals: to know them." I have frequently heard statements such as this when talking with the baserritarrak. For them there seems to be no qualitative difference between the psychology of persons and animals. The person and the animal can *ezagutu* (know) each other and develop a communication that is perceived as complete. "You have to know how to treat the animal to make him work." Another frequent statement is: "Except for talking, animals can do everything a person does." Eye communication with animals epitomizes this psychological closeness. Through the eyes the animals speak in every way except in words.

Animals constitute the peasant's wealth. But animals are also guardians, co-workers, and friends, and accordingly the peasant's experience of living with them is not colored solely by economic interests. A real emotional bond may develop. This was most obvious one day when I was talking to Itsaiz during the fiestas of Lastur. We sat beside each other during lunch and his conversation was solely about his ox who had died by accidentally falling down a cliff in Andutz two days earlier. Itsaiz was at home at the time of the accident when another ox came home roaring and took him to where the dead ox lay. He repeated several times, "It has given me such grief that I haven't eaten for these two days." He kept on repeating "how good" his ox was for both work and joko. The suggestion that his grief was primarily motivated by economic loss would have offended Itsaiz.

Animals are, of course, widely used to characterize persons: he is a donkey, he is a bull, she is a cow, and so on. Not only does one frequently hear expressions such as "she is a cow," but also, as Cátedra (1981) found among the Vaqueiros, detailed comparisons between a woman and a cow in reference to childbirth. For instance, I was told that "it is the same as with a cow; if the woman is herself in good health and strong her child will be likewise." This example suggests that metaphors might be intended as actual descriptions. Animals are used as signs that in an axis of nature/culture or reality/representation would stand closer to the nature and reality pole than to the metaphorical representation one.

Religious rhetoric has made constant use of animal metaphors. In my childhood the imagery that sins were like repugnant animals (toads, serpents, and so on) filled our consciousness. The most vivid description of confession was always throwing up those animals through the mouth while telling one's sins. The annual church obligation of confessing and taking Communion by Easter was popularly called *txala saltzea* (to sell the calf). *Txala botatzia* (to throw up the calf) is the popular expression for vomiting when drunk.

The closeness of the animal persona to the individual self is symptomatically hinted at by the following event that took place in Lastur some years ago. A peasant from another town who was married to the daughter of a baserria in Lastur was visiting his wife's home during Lastur's festivities. In the usual after-meal drinking he began to imitate a ram. Ram fights are among the most enjoyed games. However, he got so carried away in his impersonation that "he got out of himself" and started hitting objects with his head. At one point he hit one of the members of the baserria for no reason and threw him down while boasting that none among all his wife's family could bring him under control. He "went mad" in his ram impersonation. It seems that in the structurally weak situation of being outside his own town and with his wife's domestic group, in this case considered to be a particularly wild one, this insecure husband was driven to assert himself by impersonating animal powers.[12]

Consideration of animal impersonations immediately invokes the still-recent memory of witchcraft metamorphoses mentioned in chapter 1. The very same animals of domestic protection—dogs, cats, donkeys, goats, cows, oxen—are turned projectively into beasts of mythical aggression. The traditional mythology gathered by Barandiaran is filled with such animal imagery.[13] In my childhood I repeatedly heard stories of encounters with priests who suddenly changed into dogs and of injured cats that next morning in ordinary life happened to be the neighbor woman with a broken leg. In the religious domain the offering of animals for ritual purposes survived almost until this century (Urquijo 1923:350–51; Arrinda Albisu 1965:254–55).

The witchcraft complex revealed the phenomenon that the struggle between the non-Christian and Christian worldviews was fought significantly over the acceptance or nonacceptance of displaying a cultural unconscious pictured in animal imagery. The image of the flying Mari and the weird animal metamorphoses of the witches were salient expressions of this cultural configuration (Caro Baroja 1966b). These were, in Vico's sense, fables of univocal meaning that were the perceived reality and from which individuals derived their identities. Presently, ETA activists can be seen as the carriers of the Basque witchcraft complex. They, too, embody the resistance to the extinction of cultural and political forms and carry it to its ultimate consequence. By being in possession of either magical or diabolical powers, like witches in earlier periods, ETA men, too, are purported to be capable of turning into either dragon slayers or becoming repugnant beasts that "produce nausea." With ETA the struggle is over the permissiveness of returning to a political unconscious that expresses itself primarily as wild "instinctual" behavior. By assuming the defense of the Basque Country, at home ETA has been perceived to be the domestic guardian of its historical identity. Just beyond the home borders, however, they are seen as the practitioners of intolerable aggression. For the outsiders they soon become abominable beasts deserving nothing but extermination, as the following quote from the March 23, 1981, editorial of a Madrid newspaper, *Diario 16*, makes plain:

> The activists of ETA, who are not men, who are beasts. To what degree do beasts deserve human rights? . . . Beasts are enclosed behind the heaviest bars that there are in the village; first they are hunted by all kinds of tricks. And if in the venture someone is killed, bad luck, or good luck. . . . No human rights come into play when a tiger must be hunted. The tiger is searched after, is hounded, is captured, and if necessary is killed. Fifty ETA members might die in combat and the hands of Spain will continue to be clean of human blood. The policemen who will shoot against will be received as brave men. (Quoted in Castells Arteche 1982 : 143)

As shown by this quote, ETA can turn into a collective representation for the Spanish media, much like the institution of witchcraft for the Spanish Inquisition. The dramatic power of these metaphors of beastly hunt reveals to what extent the inquisitorial idea of witch-hunt is still in force. All that is asked from the public is to confirm the collective representation. The state will do the rest by providing the police and whatever means are needed to annihilate the repugnant beast. It has been said of the Catholic church that by creating and sustaining the witchcraft institution it was part of it; likewise it can be said of the Spanish state that by turning ETA into a collective representation and perpetuating it with repressive means, it has become its satellite.

In the end ETA becomes fully vested with the danger and power of taboo. The approximation between the notions of "taboo" and "sacred" has been long recognized. Thus, while for its supporters ETA assumes the form of sacred protection, for its foes it acquires the dimension of uncleanliness and ultimate danger, and both perceptions complement each other in the creation of the taboo representation. Steiner (1967) concluded that two separate social functions of taboo are the classification and identification of transgressions and the institutional localization of danger, both by the separation of the dangerous and by the protection of society from it. ETA fulfills these two functions, which explains the political convenience of "terrorism" as a collective representation and the force it obtains in the imagination of the general public. With pollution and taboo we are in the realm of terror; with "terrorism" we are at the center of political taboo, its true value residing more on ritual and magical powers than on military ones. Anthropologists have remarked that pollution ideas work at two levels, one largely instrumental, the other expressive, and that some pollutions are used as analogies for expressing a general view of the social order. This insight invites us to consider "terrorism" accordingly as characterizing the relationship between parts of a national or international territory.

A Tale of Beasts and Archangels

> First Murderer. *We are men, my liege.*
> Macbeth. *Ay, in the catalogue ye go for men;*
> *As hounds and greyhounds, mongrels, spaniels, curs,*
> *Shoughs, water-rugs and demi-wolves are clept*
> *All by the name of dogs.*
>
> *Shakespeare,* Macbeth

"You are a dog!" the two ETA men shouted at Carlos before they shot him to death in his bus in front of several Itziar women. Soon afterward I was faced with the women's horrified eyes. Their question "But how can that be?" left me speechless. Since the women who assaulted me with their question were in their fifties and sixties, I could perhaps have answered them with a tale of their generation. It is a tale of beasts and archangels that my father, for one, tells as if it were true. This story of Saint Michael, which is also the Basque version of the Oedipus myth, is probably the most popular heroic tale in Basque oral tradition. The story shows the fluid relationship of human individuals vis-à-vis their superhuman and subhuman counterparts. As pointed out in the quote from *Macbeth,* on close inspection the boundaries of categories as basic as "dog" and "man" may become blurred or, as evidenced by the ETA killers' indictment of Carlos, such dissolution of ordinary categories might become imperative for deciding that certain kinds of murder are necessary.

During my field stay I asked my father to repeat Saint Michael's story for me. He replied to my query with a shortened version:

> A man, whose name was Goñi, thinking that his wife was in bed with another man, killed his father and mother by mistake. Then, as a penance, he had to wander through mountains and forests until the chains hanging from his feet wore away. At that time a monster-serpent used to come out from the cave of Aralar [the mountain where there is a shrine to Saint Michael, most famous for the cult that shepherds have devoted to him since the earliest Middle Ages] and descend to the nearby towns such as Lecunberri. After drawing lots, once each week they had to offer him a Christian, for otherwise he would create terrible havoc. On one occasion, on which the lot had fallen to a girl, when she was by the cave waiting for the monster to come, the penitent man Goñi appeared and told the girl to kill his lice. By that time his hair must have surely reached his feet. He said that nothing would happen to her, for he would kill the monster. When the monster showed up, Goñi called Saint Michael, who came down with his sword and cut the monster-serpent's neck and the penitent's chains.

There are two kinds of killings in the story of Goñi. At the outset he is portrayed as a criminal murderer for killing his father and mother for no other reason than a misperceived violation of a marital rule. Then Goñi is made a heroic killer with the help of Saint Michael. The second type of killing, requested by the penitent man fated to wander through the wilderness until the chains of sin he is trailing along wear out, is of a different nature, for it is in response to the arbitrary murders of the monstrous serpent who since time immemorial had been razing the innocent land.

The second type of killing clearly surpasses human individuality—the killer levitates upward into an archangel and the victim descends downward into a monster. None of the confusion and guilt generated by the killing between kinsmen, who are in the same category of beings, applies to the second killing, in which killer and victim belong to different categories. There is no murder or guilt in Saint Michael's sword slashing the monster's head.

What characterizes mythic or primordial thought is, according to Vico, the power to assert identities rather than similarities. The individual does not have a reality apart from the generic character. This identification relieves personal responsibility and guilt. About some acts of political violence, such as the killing of innocent victims, I have heard comments such as, "How must the killer be feeling at this moment?" as if a sense of moral reproach should burden his conscience. From all I know, guilt is absent from their inner experience. The young cell from Itziar was driven to such nonsensical killing in the case of Berazadi, the Basque industrialist whom they had kidnapped. After the engineer Ryan, employed in the nuclear power plant of Iberduero in Lemoiz, was kidnapped and killed by ETA's military wing in the winter of 1981 (an act that was protested on the streets by multitudes of Basque demonstrators), I had the following conversation with two of Itziar's ex-ETA activists who participated in Berazadi's killing.

J. Z.: I heard someone saying that the killers will necessarily have to have some moral conscience problem, or something of that sort, after Ryan's death.

A.: They will never have any burden of conscience. As an example, the other day there were in San Sebastián forty thousand people demonstrating against them; well, they would say to that: "Forty thousand sons of bitches deceived by their political parties." You just accept the decision taken by the organization without question.

J. Z.: You might think that killing someone in a certain situation is wrong, and yet what matters is the decision made by the organization.

B.: Of course, your opinion does not count. That is so in any organization.

J. Z.: But isn't there something else? It is all right to follow what the organization orders you to do in a concrete action. But isn't taking the life of someone a kind of action that is logically and ethically at another level?

A.: There it happens that one ideology kills another one. The whole thing is very impersonal. You kidnap a man and you don't even know him. You have no personal interest either to kill him or not. It is always a political act. What is at stake are the political interests.

J. Z.: Would you be capable nowadays of establishing such an identification between yourself and the organization?

B.: Of course, or else I would never rejoin the organization. A program is always what kills. That's why it is political.

J. Z.: What would be a criminal act then? Would it be a personal one?

A.: It would rather be a personal one. It is always a plan [a project, a program] that kills, it is never [in the ETA type of performance] a person killing another person. This holds the same for you and for him [the political opponent]. What matters is what ideology you represent and which one he represents. I don't think that normally there is any hate or anything like that. If in former times I had killed ten or fifteen civil guards I would never have had the slightest hatred. It is their symbolism, what they represent, period.

When in the tale Goñi brings about the death of the serpent, it is not himself but Saint Michael who slays the monster. The necessary link between the human and superhuman hero is faith. Faith caused the guilt-ridden penitent's metamorphosis into a glorious partner in heroic killing. Goñi believed in the archangel's powers and prayed to him at the decisive moment. When the ETA activist kills somebody, as with Goñi's divine help, "the whole thing is very impersonal"—the victim is a "dog" or a "pig" and the killer is a "plan," "an ideology," the organization ETA. Faith turns primal guilt into a revolutionary act. Yet, faced with guiltless homicide, the paradoxical question, But how can that be? keeps returning. Not even conscious guilt can rule it.

In the baserri society of Itziar, dogs are the domestic guardians and companions. In hunting, the dog provides the indispensable link between prey and hunter. The delicate link between man and beast is achieved by the dog's sense of smell. Yet the txakurra's metaphoric gift is no less significant. As in the Homeric world of the *Iliad*, the suggested proportion is that "man is to god as dog is to man" (Redfield 1975: 194). The most terrifying of witch metamorphoses encountered by Maria from Errementeri (see chapter 1) was the turning of a priest into a dog. In the class of dogs, scavengers, too, are included, and thus civil guards, police, informers, and military people are txakurra. Analogy gives way to identity, fable becomes reality, man *is* dog.

In the myth of Saint Michael, Goñi's killing of his parents out of jealousy leads to guilt and punishment, whereas the killing of the dragon by Saint Michael is a heroic feat. In the killing of Carlos, the archangel and the beast are categorically paralleled by ETA and the txakurra. If not for the infernal dragon, Saint Michael could not have exercised his divine powers. If Carlos were not a txakurra, ETA could not have engaged in heroic killing. The txakurra turned the fateful event into an act of revolutionary justice. The beast's wild nature forces the hunter's intervention.

For human killing to be a "normal" affair it must be preceded by a redefinition of categorical distinction. It is all right for an archangel to murder a beast. It is all right for an army to destroy an enemy target, or for a community to extirpate an adverse member—the higher whole and the lower part are categorically distanced. In these situations humanity is no longer a strict categorical marker; it is rather a loose "catalog." Thus, as Carlos became for ETA killers "sort of" a txakurra, so is Macbeth telling the murderers who claim to be men that they are "sort of" men. For men to manipulate these categorical distinctions and act out this ordinary tale of beasts and archangels, all that is needed is the power of ritual metaphor.

CHAPTER TWELVE

The Amabirjina

Icon and Sacrament

In Itziar, religion is focused upon the figure of the Amabirjina, to which the local sanctuary is dedicated. This religious image of the Virgin Mary is an exquisite work of art around which the ideas of beauty and grace have centered for the last eight centuries. She is always proclaimed to be *ederra* (beautiful) and *graziaz betea* (filled with grace). For the believer she is an image beyond image that is experienced in a religiously iconic context, never as a mere object of artistic contemplation. By becoming a transcendent icon in which the distinction between reality and its representational form vanishes, she invites person-to-person communication, by which means the entire process of salvation is mediated. It can be said of her, too, that she is "an intuitive apprehension, something experienced in response to certain situations but known directly only to the imagination and not to the senses" (Evans-Pritchard 1956:321).

Mythical images from the traditional cosmology have persisted in the popular imagination and were still viable during the active years of the older generations. Yet images fixed in actual carvings and paintings are the work of the Catholic church, and religious instruction has shaped in Itziar the basic education for perceiving images that transcend natural objects. This religious context is therefore essential for assessing the relationship of Itziar people to images. To the extent that political violence is also an attempt at creating a new nationalist imagery, this local interaction with images becomes crucial for our understanding of the meanings of such violence.

As we know from part 1, the recent political involvement in Itziar is intimately tied to the institution of the Catholic church. Intense religious devotion has been considered a salient characteristic of the Basques (Linz 1966). The social and political movement of the 1950s was initiated in Itziar by an earlier religious conversion. As is well known, priests and seminarians played a key role in ETA during the 1960s. Later on the activist youth broke with the institution of the church, yet the self-transcending experience required by membership in ETA was truly of a sacramental kind. Inevitably, the nationalist audience perceived the total patriotism of its ETA martyrs in a context of transcendence that was learnt primarily in the church.

Girard has argued forcefully that "violence and the sacred are inseparable" (1977 : 19). Religion thus humanizes violence, religion being understood in a sense deeper than its theological trappings. In the Basque case, Aranzadi was the first to call attention to "the unequivocal religious subsoil of the problem" (1981 : 24), which he reduces to an ideological skeleton that is "nothing but the Judeo-Christian millenarianism" (ibid. : 29). The present chapter addresses the religious dimension by providing an ethnographic description of the phenomenon in a concrete community and by sorting out the kinds of sacramental symbolism present in such localized context.

I will proceed by examining the Amabirjina's popular cult and exegesis and by describing the image and its metaphoric extensions. An exploration into the nature of the icon reveals that radically different perceptions of the same image obtain depending on whether the context is artistic or iconic. On the basis of this distinction, the notion of "iconic politics" emerges. The sacramental aspects of the Catholic religion as experienced in Itziar and their crucial import in understanding Basque political violence are examined in the final sections. Ultimate concerns having to do with human existence, such as readiness to sacrifice one's own life for one's own country, take the form of a sacrament. As in religion, in politics "the thing" itself of a sacrament is beyond image and speech. The loose metaphoric images of the beast, which in the previous chapter submerged the subjects into primordial identities of immanent immediacy, are dissolved here into imageless ideas such as grace and freedom. In connection with the Amabirjina's image, this chapter underscores the sacramental context of Itziar's local religion and its presence in political activism as a sanctioned frame of meaning available through the religious experience.

Image, Cult, and Grace

In his comprehensive two-volume study of Basque madonnas, Lizarralde describes about two hundred icons situated in Guipúzcoa and Vizcaya. He writes of the Amabirjina of Itziar,

> One does not know how to explicate the perfection with which this gracious effigy is carved, the most beautiful, surely, of our iconography. The graceful immobility of the body is remarkable, with a discreetly wise adaptation of the clothes; the anatomical proportion of different members, with the exception of the excessively lengthened bust of the Child, and, above all these perfections, the ineffable smile, of both the Mother and the Son. (1926:39)

Viewing the Amabirjina from the main nave of the church, one notes the following qualities of the icon: (1) There is the figure of a mother holding her son in her hands. The son, in turn, has in his hands the figure of the world. A relationship of inclusion structures these three figures, wherein the mother contains on her lap the son, and the son contains the world. (2) The composition in its totality is named Amabirjina, which expresses the unity of the three images to the beholder. The overall image is perceived as a single female person. (3) Her position is elevated. The shrine is on a hill, and within the sanctuary she is elevated in the apse. (4) Surrounded by lights, she is perceived as an altogether different kind of image from the other carved wooden ones of the altarpiece. (5) She is dressed in white clothes, which change according to the degree of solemnity and the liturgical cycle as if she were a living person. Underneath her cloth dress she also has "natural" carved clothes, which have suffered alterations in different historical periods. A crescent moon under her feet serves as adornment.

The legendary apparition of the Amabirjina and her subsequent historical centrality in shaping Itziar's Marian personality were introduced in chapter 1. It is not the legend, however, but the intensity of the cult devoted to her that is outstanding in the daily religious experience of Itziar. I asked a middle-aged man about the kind of religion that is practiced in the village. His response was direct:

> Amabirjina is all that religion is here. Each time you need something, each time you have a problem, are suffering, or anything, the first thing always is the Amabirjina. Have you ever heard of someone making a promise to Jesus Christ? Jesus Christ comes much later compared with the Amabirjina. I would even say that Jesus Christ comes in the third position after the Amabirjina and some peculiarly peasant saint such as Saint Anthony, Saint Isidro, or Saint Nicholas. Peasants when they have problems with their animals believe a lot in these saints. For me, Jesus Christ is tied up with the Lenten period. But here the Amabirjina is everything; even Jesus Christ is seen as her son. She is her son and much more.

The most elaborate occasion for worshipping the Amabirjina of Itziar takes place during the novena that precedes her yearly festival on the first Sunday of August. For nine days villagers from Itziar and devout persons from nearby towns join every evening in the Amabirjina's sanctuary for prayers and worship. The prayers that Pedro Joseph de Aldazabal wrote in 1768 for this *bederatziurrena* (novena) have been said ever since.[1]

In traditional Catholicism the rosary has been the habitual prayer. In its standard form it has five sequences, each composed of an Our Father, ten Hail Marys and a Glory in remembrance of a Christian mystery. In most houses of Itziar we grew up with nightly praying of the rosary at home. Sunday afternoons the rosary said in church was well attended.

The Hail Mary has been for centuries a most intimately savored prayer. No other religious text seems comparable to this ever-present prayer for handling everyday emotional and practical situations. One could say that the Marian ethos is basically the creation of this infinitely repeated prayer.[2] The Hail Mary's dual expression of her excellence on the one hand and of the supplicant's need for forgiveness on the other marks the fundamental attitude toward the Amabirjina that is expressed in the prayers, songs, and pilgrimage practices of Itziar.

There is a popular exegesis of the Amabirjina that is constantly reflected in the rhetoric of the local church. While attending the sanctuary of Itziar during my childhood, I heard the following maxim often: "Since nobody knows the Son better than the Mother and since the Son can never refuse what his mother asks, there is no safer way of achieving anything from our Lord than addressing his mother with a request." The Mother's mediation is seen as omnipotent. The central mediation in this religious experience is not, therefore, through the Son to the Father. In the Marian translation of Christianity, as it obtains in Itziar, mediation is performed by the Mother in relation to the Son.

There is also a significant sacramental aspect to the cult of the Virgin. The book of baptisms of Itziar is witness to the many children brought to the sanctuary from nearby towns to be baptized.[3] Some devotees of the Amabirjina have chosen likewise to be buried in Itziar. The sacramental appeal of the sanctuary has its highest expression today in Itziar being a very popular place for weddings in the area.

Pilgrimages afford the most dramatic enactments of Marian religion. The pilgrim of the Virgin is a penitent. Only through sacrifice and freedom from sin can the pilgrim merit the reward of her vision and grace. The call comes from her. Nevertheless, the object of religious identification is the Son. Through identification with her son the devotee can become one more child in the Mother's family. She is the persuasive factor that promises grace. He is the "fruit" of the grace.

What is the meaning of "grace" in this religious experience? The soul must confront the dilemma of either sin or grace. Being in a state of grace implies freedom from sin and its terrible consequences in the afterlife. The mediating purgatory between heaven and hell can be anticipated and purged in present life through penance. The suffering figure with whom one identifies during this redemptive pain is Christ the Crucified, whose great mission was to give up his life on the cross and thus "open up the door to heaven." In this experience the drama of Christ is his passion and death, compared with which his resurrection is seen as a mere aftermath. In fact, it appears as if resurrection belongs more properly to Mary in this kind of religious experience. After the painful *via crucis*, the pilgrim, frequently barefooted or carrying a cross, finally reaches the sanctuary at the top of the hill where Mary shines in compassion and splendor. The torment of a guilty conscience is here replaced by the blessing of being in the Amabirjina's realm. Hers is not a suffering grace, the purgatory of the *via crucis,* but the final blessing after the hardships of the soul's pilgrimage are completed. Unlike the incarnated mediation of Christ, hers is a fleshless immaculate state of being in which the soul finds ultimate solace. She is the port of salvation, the protective refuge, the always accessible solution. Resurrection and grace reside primarily in her.

The Projected Image of Ama

In the 1930s, the first appearance of the PNV's nationalist movement was accompanied in Itziar by significant cultural events; best remembered among these are the staging of plays and the publishing in the weekly *Argia* by half a dozen amateur local writers. The temples of the new political universe were the batzokiak, the PNV's meeting centers, a combination of cultural centers and dining clubs. In the weekly chronicles from Itziar, written before the outbreak of the civil war in 1936, a constant feature is the use of *ama* (mother) in the new nationalist rhetoric. By a process of visual-conceptual concretization, the ama root image was extended to other domains. Basque nationalism in Itziar insisted upon love for the Ama Aberria (Mother Country). The language, Euskera, the native country, *aberria,* and the land, *lurra,* the political name for the country, Euzkadi, the church, *eleiza,* and the Virgin, *Birjina,* are all constantly preceded by ama.[4]

Tene, the playwright we met in chapter 1, spoke to me about the significance of the mother figure.[5] When I asked her to compare it with the father figure, she said:

> The Amabirjina is more than Saint Joseph. How can it be that the woman is less, and that in religion and similar things ama is the main relationship? It might be that there she is more important. Always, "O my mother!" The man, too, says ama and ama and ama. There is always more pity for the mother, more love. Look, nowadays when you can hear so many terrible things, they have killed so and so, I never feel pity for the dead,

> for I think, the dead is dead; a shot, and the pain must have been momentary. But his mother, what suffering his mother must experience.

The father figure also has its political projections. It is a common expression to say that "the father" lost the civil war against Franco. Historians of ETA emphasize a critical point in its self-affirmation: the rupture with the PNV. The resistance kept alive by the PNV was revived by ETA, but ETA's initial stance toward the "paternal" party was one of rejection. The PNV was seen as a cowardly, conforming father that had done nothing during the twenty years since losing the war. That the father's generation was the one that lost the war was a belief also held by the Catholic Baserri Gaztedi movement of the late 1950s. Several times while talking to its leaders I heard the expression, "Our fathers are a nonexistent generation." They insisted that, compared with their fathers' lives, theirs had been a much more fulfilling generation.[6]

All known political insurgency in Itziar has been carried out by unmarried people. The image of the adolescent in ETA may be exemplified by the sixteen- and seventeen-year-old boys from Itziar. Seminarians and Catholic priests have been crucial in Itziar's political activism. It is striking that the father figure is totally absent within the ranks of ETA operatives. The very idea of an active ETA member with children sounds curiously odd, destroying with a stroke the entire revolutionary model. Nothing seems further from a photograph of a lone ETA man in the media than his being seen holding hands with his children. Fatherhood seems to clash directly with the charismatic image of the revolutionary who has given up everything for the country.

The overpowering influence of the mother on ETA's young men becomes most apparent when they are arrested and incarcerated. A common perception is that mothers play a far more active role than fathers in such situations. Once when I was visiting the family of an ETA member after the police had searched their house at night, the mother complained that she had had to face the police forces and treat them disdainfully while her husband was incapable of getting out of bed. In a commentary that is reminiscent of Tene, for whom the mother's suffering was more dramatic than the son's death that caused it, an ETA member spoke to me once angrily about his brother's suicide, adding that if he were alive he deserved to be killed again, "not for himself but for the pain he caused our mother." The close affective bonds between mothers and ETA sons, as well as the potential for conflict between the sons and their fathers, has been an issue of public discussion in Itziar. The activists themselves have confirmed for me such unequal significance of mothers and fathers in their lives. Particularly during the period of prison or exile, when the state of personal dejection requires most urgently the assistance of such projections, the mother provides the protective figure.

Icon versus Art in Religion and Politics

Allegory and Vision ought to be known as Two Distinct Things. Blake, A Vision of the Last Judgment

I borrow from Redfield the icon/art distinction, which I find helpful in understanding the Amabirjina's distinct level of signification as compared with the rest of the religious imagery of Itziar's church. Speaking of a Dogon carving, Redfield wrote, "The wooden object that is our central text may be seen as art or as icon according to the kind of meaning that is attributed to or connected with it" (1971 : 42–43). He characterized their difference as follows:

> For him who experiences an object only as art its meanings are immanent in the object [whereas] to him for whom the object is a stimulus for associations it has with something other than the object, its meanings are transcendent: they go beyond or outside of it. The icon is only one kind of object with both immanent and transcendent meanings. (Ibid.:63)

Redfield argues that, although the two efforts toward understanding art and icon are parallel, "the aesthetic and the iconic are two worlds of thought. . . . Between the two, as systems of thought and feeling, of meaning and value, there are only slight direct connections" (ibid.:63).

This icon/art distinction implies, therefore, a difference of context depending on the recognition of either representationally immediate meanings in an art object or transcendent meanings in an icon. This is obvious from the two descriptions of the same Dogon wooden sculpture: whereas an artistic framework indicates aesthetic qualities, in Ogotemmêli's iconic framework (Griaule 1965) what are denoted are cosmological relations. The personal identifications required by the aesthetic and the iconic forms of interpretation are of a different nature. In aesthetic contemplation the viewer enjoys the achievements of a given artist or historical period, which are compared with similar features in other works of art. In iconic contemplation that information is insignificant and the viewer relates to the icon only through a total personal involvement by which the icon itself is perceived as a living representation of an entire cosmology.

This same qualitative difference in the interpretation of images can be applied to the imagery of Itziar's church. According to critics, Itziar's altarpiece, which is believed to be a creation of the sculptor Araoz in the early sixteenth century, is perhaps the best example of Basque plateresque art. It has twenty-nine niches distributed on six superposed panels, which narrate the life of the Virgin Mary. What is most significant about this altarpiece in Itziar's religious experience is precisely its irrelevance. This I know from personal experience, for I never paid any attention to it nor did I ever hear of its possessing any value. As I thought about it I was puzzled by the altarpiece's nearly total lack of religious import. When I asked other people of Itziar about the altarpiece images, I was relieved to hear from them statements such as this one:

> When I go to the church of Itziar the only image I see there is the Amabirjina. Those in the altarpiece? I don't even know what they represent. They must be the life of Christ, ending in a cross at the top. They don't exist for me.

Side by side with the Amabirjina, these altarpiece images are altogether of a different nature; they are so decorative that their very capacity of being perceived is in jeopardy, so irrelevant that they remain largely unnoticed. The icon of the Amabirjina creates a field of exclusion, which, so to speak, empties the church of any unessential image.

The Amabirjina has several statues in the church besides the "real" one. There is a portable copy of the Amabirjina,[7] one dedicated to the Virgin of Sorrows, the "blue" Virgin of Conception, and the Amabirjina of Elorriaga (a fourteenth- or fifteenth-century sculpture). Many other images of her are also carved on the altarpiece. Despite this diversity of icons, the Amabirjina is obviously experienced as a single person. Her icon par excellence, of which all others are derivative copies, is the one at the center of the altarpiece.[8]

According to Redfield's basic distinction between icon and art, in the experience of the Itziar parishioner the Amabirjina is a different sort of image from those of the artistic altarpiece. An important difference is that the altarpiece images are ordered in a narrative sequence in which each image is situated within the scenic representation of a niche, each niche within the body of niches at the same level, and each body within the total story of the altarpiece. Images and scenes are articulated in time and space sequences. In contrast with this multiplicity of altarpiece images, the Amabirjina's icon is contemplated as a particular and unique one. There is, moreover, a sense of participation in the liturgy of the Amabirjina that the altarpiece images do not have. The former practice of priests exposing the Amabirjina to the public only during religious ceremonies is a clear statement of such personal participation.

There is another, deeper sense of participation of the Amabirjina in the experience of the believer. In the inner dialogue with the image the devout are continuously speaking, listening, praying to the Amabirjina. The liturgical expressions and gestures reinforce this sense of direct communication with her. Her presence is truly the presence of a living person. Personal qualities of speech, hearing, sight, and smiling are literally attributed to her. It is in constant interaction with this personage that the believer's self plays out the entire drama of personal salvation. In the presence of this "live" effigy the rest of the religious images become redundant and perfunctory.

Basque violence can be seen as an attempt to create a new political imagery. The youth of Itziar, directly or indirectly involved in the violence, as well as the Itziar spectators of such violence, have all been schooled in reading visual images basically in the iconic mode of their church's religious imagery. A striking insight into the nature of the ongoing violence is gained when the distinction of the two modes of interpreting the Amabirjina and altarpiece images is applied to the political arena. The politics of ETA could be labeled "iconic politics." As the same wooden carving, when contemplated as art or icon, may invoke such radically different worlds of thought and meaning, likewise there is a world of difference between the image of a politician considered as "merely" doing politics and the iconic image of a militant patriot demanding life-or-death personal involvement. The initial pamphlets of ETA insisted that their activism should not be regarded as "doing politics." This would come later, they argued; what must be done immediately was to insure the very survival of the mother country by achieving its freedom. What art is to icon, "politics" is to this survival-oriented single vision of patriotic affirmation. "Political" acts—a current definition of politics being "the art of what is possible"—deal with fragmented views, diverse styles and options, negotiable qualities and goals. Iconic acts, on the contrary, create or relate to images as parts of a transcendent single whole of ultimate irreducible value.

Believing Is Closing

As Redfield stated, in the iconic experience "meanings are transcendent." That is, meaning does not reside in the object per se but in the other-worldly or other-than-the-object associations it calls for. A map, a model, a portrait may be icons when what they denote is entirely beyond themselves. In a religious domain, the element of transcendence, or other-worldliness, becomes essential to iconic communication.

As advanced in the previous chapter, ideas of adaptation and transcendence can be achieved in the culture through the key notion of closure. An iconic frame could be described as one of self-enclosure. Depending on context, the notion of ertsi acquires different meanings. In this section we are interested in the cultural semantics by which ertsi informs a hierarchical process of self-transcendence at the level of psychology and belief.

The psychological edifice hinges on the notion of closure—in a variety of forms, "distress" is simply "closure." A close variant of ertsi and a key psychological term is *etsi*.[9] Depending on context, *etsi* may mean either giving up and despairing or adjustment and forbearance. Closure may be conducive to adaptive or nonadaptive mechanisms. Two contexts in which etsi acquires paradigmatic value are the following. In a joko competitive situation, etsi is the prime case of negative psychological closure, which amounts to giving up or despairing. At the opposite end, in a hierarchical context, such as succession of life stages or changing conditions demanded by new life situations, etsi is the required psychological acceptance that implies adjustment and adaptation.

The hierarchical use of etsi—a self-reflexive concept that permits the relationship of inclusion—implies that the notion itself of transcendence is inseparable from acts of enclosure. The etsi that is obtained, for instance, from the sequence of rites of passage is merely one of hierarchical juxtaposition—the newly married have to *etsi* (adjust) to their new condition or the terminally ill have to *etsi* (accept) the prospect of impending death. Each stage of the sequence is closed up and transcended by the subsequent one. The psychological response elicited by the act of closure may vary from despair to acceptance to pleasure. The Christian notions of belief and hope require the idea of etsi closure. The etymologies of the terms bear witness to this connection, for to believe in the Christian sense is *sinetsi,* a compound of *zin* (oath) and *etsi.* Religious belief entails, therefore, being enclosed by an oath of faith. The ordinary notion of belief, in the sense of opinion or idea, is *uste,* which Michelena (1976:281) considers to be a verbal substantive derived from *etsi.* Likewise, hope is *itxaro,* which is a compound of *itxi* (to close up) and *aro* (period, time). Although there is a semantic continuity of self-reflexivity between *etsi* and *sinetsi,* there is also a transformation of symbolism between the native and the Christian uses. This change could be described as the replacement of a more indexical symbolism, based on etsi relationships of contiguity, with a more canonical symbolism, based on sinetsi conventions of historical belief.

A distinction between a "natural" kind of transcendence and Christian religion was explicitly pointed out to me by Joxe Landa. He observed:

> You can see that difference at the levels of religion and transcendence. It is as if the Basque traditional man had faith [other than Christianity] from earlier times—the afterlife and so on. I think that for judging man and his behavior, they used to ground themselves on *transcendence* rather than on religion. For I think that *gizatasuna* [manliness] was sufficient to judge man's be-

havior. I think that the religious projection was not needed, that gizatasuna was enough to decide whether a man did right or wrong.

Joxe insisted there was an excessive elaboration of Christian belief, as if, like the altarpiece imagery, it were all superficially decorative and unnecessarily theological. He is basically saying that the etsi type of transcendence is sufficient. His notion of man is well fitted to the iconic type of politics mentioned earlier. The symbolic center of political violence is the life giving and life taking of the participants in it. This violence has unquestionably been the recognized preeminent mode of personal transcendence in Basque society since ETA was formed. Although participation in political violence has implied rejection of the belief system imposed by the Catholic church, such rejection is seen as perfectly logical when the locus of personal transcendence is situated in the human condition itself.

Beyond Metaphor

Comparing medieval and modern understandings of symbolism, Ladner rightly labels the medieval one as "sacramental symbolism." Ladner characterizes it as being "not so much a metaphorical as a metonymical symbolism, for sacramental symbolism is not merely one of similarity, but rather one of contact, or participation of man with Christ, in Christ. The sacrament is altogether a very different kind of symbol: it not only signifies, but also effects what it signifies" (1979:240).

Features of the sacraments as administered by Catholic priests include the following: they are defined as visible signs of invisible grace; grace unfolds in various actions; the notion of the sacrament participates in the special character of that of life; an exchange between God and the believer takes place by means of the sacraments; the Christ-event is the foundation of all strictly sacramental modes of communication; for the sacraments as for the church, Jesus Christ is the mediator who fulfills the will of the Father; sacraments are the salvation of Christ in action; their efficacy is *ex opere operato;* sacraments have an essentially eschatological character.

A middle-aged man from Itziar commented to me: "In earlier times, when there was greater devotion for the Amabirjina, the sacraments were less important than now. The practice was to fulfill the Easter obligations [yearly confession and Communion], and that was it. Now you have less devotion to the Amabirjina and more insistence on the sacraments." This quote points to a tension between a mariocentric devotional cult and christocentric sacramental ritual. Contrary to the christocentric outlook, in Itziar's preaching the ordinary analogy of the Marian scheme is the Mother's domestically central role. The maxim that the Son cannot resist his mother's requests implies that the notion of mediation is primarily associated with the role of the Mother. Some features of this mediation are conceptualized as follows: (1) she is a mother who intercedes vis-à-vis the divinity; (2) she is a person whose grace is the result of her providential association with God's plans; (3) she relates to God as to her actual son by the rights of physiological motherhood; (4) she is at the same time a mother and a virgin whose divine maternity overcomes the natural order of kinship. In this scheme of mediation, God is conceptualized basically as a son. In the Marian perspective he is a son, not primarily of God the Father but of Mary the Amabirjina.

There is a sacramental aspect to Mary's mediation in which two steps can be distinguished. First, she becomes the Mother of God by being the mother of Christ. Mary thus mediates between divinity and humanity. Second, she mediates between her son's divinity and the collective filiation of humankind. She is a common mother to both Christ-God and humanity. The sacramental identity is here one of filiation of the same mother shared by God and humankind. Christ the man is God through Mary's motherhood. Anyone who partakes of Mary's collective filiation is Christ's brother or sister and therefore shares his divinity. The sacramental "is" of the identity is granted by Mary herself as the necessary condition for a common filiation.[10]

Ultimately, the image of the Amabirjina is the basic expression and actual center of this sacramental exchange. Above all other symbolic elements, such as water, bread, or the absolution formula, the fundamental matrix where grace resides is in the sacramental icon of the Amabirjina with whom the devotee deals personally in all matters concerning salvation. This Marian type of grace resides, so to speak, at the level of experience that is prior to its expression in churchly sacramental signs. It is the general state of grace, the return to the Mother's protection, that the Amabirjina is capable of realizing.

Analytically, the Amabirjina's iconic world can be characterized as a context in which "the distinction of the real and the copy vanishes, and is for a moment a pure dream. . . . At that moment we are contemplating an icon" (Peirce 1885: 181). In the local religion of Itziar, that which is sacramentally identical to what it represents is primordially the icon of the Virgin. As the pilgrimage ethos of these Marian shrines shows, church sacraments such as confession and Communion are experienced as requirements conducive to the religious experience with the Virgin, or as postconversion expressions in allegiance to the Mother. The goal is communion with the Amabirjina herself.

In the end, the image itself vanishes in such iconic contemplation. The Amabirjina is conceived of as an imageless vessel of grace. Grace is an idea with no image or form. Like air it can only be given imaginary form by an act of containment. In traditional mythology, supernatural power was captured by many footprints and vestigial signs of mythical beings that populate Basque geography. These mythical containers are called *aska,* which in daily life is the prime "container," for it means trough, manger, furrow, ditch, trace, cup; it is also part of compounds such as *seaska* (cradle), *arraska* (sink), and *aberaska* (honeycomb). In her function of divine containment the Amabirjina is also called *aska,* a faceless empty vessel.[11]

A term with the same root as aska is *aske* (free). In folk medicine, curing is imagined as a process of freeing or emptying the body; *askatu* (to free, to untie) can be made to share the root image of aska in the sense that a body that is "released" from an illness or internal substance is turned into an empty aska.[12] In Basque modern art the sculptor Oteiza (1963) developed influential theories concerning the "disoccupation of space" and "aesthetic curing." The folk healer and the artist share the same cultural premise that emptying is curing. Faced with the problem of abstract imageless ideas, such as cure, grace, freedom, and beauty, Basque traditional culture resolves it by applying to them the idea of a container—since they cannot be imagined, they can at least be formally contained. The predicative notion *uts* (void, empty), essential to this discussion, will be examined in the next chapter.

The key term that has summed up the political aspirations of Basque nationalism since its founding by Sabino Arana is *askatasuna* (freedom). In the new nationalist symbolism, askatasuna is the concept that substitutes for grace in the religious domain. The root image for askatasuna is the open container, aska. ETA is an acronym for Euskadi Ta Askatasuna (Euskadi and Freedom). The image of the native country as a land of askatasuna, which the nationalism of the ETA years has inherited from its founders at the turn of the century, inevitably draws from that aska imagery. How does one imagine askatasuna? An important metaphor is "wind," as in Txiki's words written the night before his execution in Barcelona. The phrase *askatasun haizea* (the wind of freedom) has become popular in songs. As the wind, freedom is high, immaterial, colorless, a total atmosphere that encompasses everything, a pure element one breathes and lives in. Another major metaphor is unchained—freedom is the opposite state to that of being constrained.

Ultimately, askatasuna transcends any image. Conforming with the negative image of aska as a mere container, Burke remarks, after listing dictionary definitions of "freedom," that the "list clearly reveals the 'unnish' or 'nonnic' nature of the concept" (1966:439). Askatasuna is the ideological basis for the photographic negative from which the image of the new order may be produced.

The iconic "dream" of an unmediated vision mentioned above by Peirce requires refusal of metaphor. The dreamer is awake when realizing that the dream is nothing but image and metaphor. Thus, metaphor implies awareness of absence, of something being "only" metaphor. Sacrament implies manifestation of presence, the experience of something being fully what it is. In sacrament, meaning is superseded by being. Grace, cure, freedom must be.

Conclusion: Politics as Sacrament

I am filled with awe, with a profound, mystic, silence-enjoining awe, in the presence of the religious greatness of the damned . . . of the type of the afflicted and the possessed, in whom saint and criminal are one. Thomas Mann, "Dostoevsky—in Moderation"

The intimate connection in Itziar between religious experience and political commitment leading to the recent violence was emphasized in chapters 3 and 4. The religious conversion of a small group of male youth played a crucial role in the village's awareness of social and political realities. The two youths who for the first time in Itziar got involved in a clandestine nationalist organization later absorbed by ETA were exemplars of intense religious practice. They excelled in sacramental life and puritanical mores. The authenticity of the religious conviction of these men has never been questioned in Itziar. This is what marks the beginning of ETA in the village.

During the sixties the Catholic movement Herri Gaztedi provided pedagogical instruction and the organizational background for the political involvement of youth. In the midst of political polarization and police repression, Herri Gaztedi dissolved itself in 1973. In Itziar this was followed by affiliation with ETA on the part of the four adolescents who had started their social and political indoctrination in Herri Gaztedi. The four organized a commando group that made front-page news throughout 1975 and the spring of 1976 until they were arrested. In historical and sociological terms, Catholic organizations and ETA in Itziar are either indistinguishable, as for the first generation of activists in the late fifties, or occur serially, as after the collapse of Herri Gaztedi.

As discussed in chapter 3, under the guidance of the priest Urkola a very significant change regarding the attitudes toward the sacraments took place in Itziar throughout the sixties. New experiments such as private conversations with a priest on a person-to-person basis outside the confessional were felt to be a substitute for the sacrament of confession. Villagers were involved with priests in public discussions regarding the centrality of sacraments. Some priests abandoned the priesthood and thus showed by their own example that sacramental bonds were not absolute. The lessons in desacramentalization that Itziar went through dissociated the religious dimension from its more sacramental and magical aspects. Nevertheless, concurrently with this desacralization of religious symbols and rituals there was an emphasis on the resacramentalization of life experience as a whole. Urkola's teachings and those of others, as well as *Gazte*, the periodical of Herri Gaztedi, extolled this with wearisome insistence. For instance, priests should be secularized, but the other side of the argument was that everybody shares in the priesthood, which ultimately resides in the community of believers. The fulfillment of this sacramental commitment in the political domain was illustrated unequivocally by the sacrifices of ETA operatives.

No other subgroup in Basque life has carried the acceptance of political violence into a religious dimension as strongly as local Basque priests and seminarians. It is well known that in the initial stages of ETA these churchmen played a crucial role. Having talked for many hours with some of these key figures, now living normal lives in the vicinity of Itziar-Deba, I have been impressed by their human qualities. Although "experiencing in my own life the tragedy of ETA," as one put it, and understanding its deep motivations, most of them now disagree with ETA's recent course. There is no questioning the validity of their claims that it was a strictly moral matter for them to protect and help those engaged in the defense of Basque cultural and political identity. Involvement in the national revitalization movement was for them a conscious obligation of their religious faith. Later, however, particularly when ETA engaged in killings of the forces of order, no such collusion of orthodox faith and activist participation could be easily legitimized. This presented, in some cases, dramatic moral dilemmas.

Once the established faith had lost its meaning for the activists, ethical justification was guaranteed by the natural transcendence of a life-sacrificing attitude. In a later phase, at the turn of the sixties, when the justification of political violence gained consensus among politically motivated people, participation in it did not present such moral dilemmas. The identification with one's own country to the point of being willing to give one's life for it marks, in substance, the sacramental commitment to a higher cause that transcends one's own identity. In Camus's words, "As a last resort he is willing to accept the final defeat, which is death, rather than be deprived of the last sacrament which he will call, for example, freedom" (1954:21). In Itziar, as elsewhere in the Basque Country, membership in ETA more than any other commitment has been the key decision signaling such complete identification with Basque collective identity. Fanon made this same point in his book *The Wretched of the Earth*, which became a textbook for ETA leaders during the sixties.

Needless to say, the patriotic injunction for surrendering one's own life has to be understood in most literal terms. There is a literalness to sacrament that is lacking in mere metaphor. The politics of life giving and life taking aim at being nontranslatable to other, politically conventional languages, as if such translation would imply the deceits of arbitrary language. This text is not to be read metaphorically. The only nonfallacious political language is assumed to be premised on the literalness of life and death.

As with the iconic totality of the Amabirjina and the sacramental identification with the Son requested by her, the image projected by an ETA member during the early seventies was unmistakably one of surrender to the transcendental cause of saving the Basque country. The general strikes and massive demonstrations in favor of ETA members sentenced to death in the Burgos trial of December 1970 provided the clearest occasion at the regional and national levels for ETA's political and moral legitimation. Frequently, at moments when a critique or a question mark as to the moral or political validity of ETA's actions seemed to be emerging, I heard a statement that seemed to utterly dispel any possible objection: "They give their lives for the country." They act out with their lives the negation of a political domination imposed from the outside. The expression "He gave his own life for us" is learned in the church and applies to Christ. No matter how different the sacrifice of Christ and that of a terrorist may appear from the outside, in the internal context of the violence of Itziar such approximation is indeed unconsciously and consciously very intense. During my fieldwork I heard a bertsolaria sing, "If Christ were to be born nowadays in Euskadi, he would be of ETA." I have been told of local priests giving the following religious justification to devout mothers when their ETA sons died: As Christ gave his life for the world, so your son gave his life for what he believed to be the right thing for the Basque Country. In a most conscious manner, both are sacramental figures for the mother and for the supporters of ETA. In situations in which the very survival of the historical and cultural frames of reference are at stake (and this is how most Basques perceive their fate), the defense of that identity may present itself as the ultimate sacrament.

Sacramentally, violence and the sacred are equivalent (Girard 1977). In the Christian scheme the immolation of the Son is the sacrificial requirement. At the same time, in the iconic representation of the Amabirjina, the Son is the infant in the mother's lap. The sacrificial son is represented in the icon as a child. Her image, from the perspective of the iconic child, cannot be perceived with the immanent qualities of art but must be perceived as the transcendent whole of an Amabirjina (Zulaika 1984). The identification with the icon is expressed in the Son's sacrificial offering. The disturbance of categorical differences between man and beast, which was observed in the previous chapter at the origin of violence, here comes full circle with the sacramental lack of difference between man and God.

Images have been transcended. Only ritual action can express the conversion to the supersensory idea of total askatasuna. In part 5 we will examine the ritualization of action in Basque traditional culture and the ongoing political violence.

Part 5

Ekintza: Ritual Action

Introduction

In the following chapter I propose a shift from functional to ritual kinds of causation in the study of political violence. Consequently, I examine the preeminence of ritual practice in Basque traditional culture and contemporary politics. Materials from traditional folklore and mythology are presented to explore ritualized modes of causation, in which formal and contextual elements take precedence over immediate or final explanations. Ritual is here taken as a basic social act necessary to obtain and express a sense of reality. It is not final cause in the ordinary sense of the term *function,* but formal cause, implied by the structural characteristics of cultures as adaptive systems, which I intend to analyze. These ritualized models are applied ethnographically to argue for the priority of ritual elements in the ongoing political violence.

Anthropologists have found it necessary to distinguish between the following three types of behavior: (1) rational behavior aiming at specific ends in a strictly mechanical way; (2) communicative behavior, in which there is no mechanical link between means and ends but only culturally defined connections; (3) magical behavior, which is efficient in terms of the cultural conventions of the actors but not in a rational-technical sense (Leach 1966). The proposition guiding this research is that Basque political violence cannot be properly understood as a rational type of behavior alone, but rather that communicative and magical behavior, which we would define as "ritual" behavior, are essential components of it. The cultural models studied in part 3 are, in general, communicative behavior and, as such, an element of ritualization is intrinsic to them. The ritual models of this final part belong to the third type behavior, in which magical kinds of efficacy play the key role.

Confronted with issues of political violence, one common intellectual strategy is to concentrate upon the search for its "causes." These causal links are not understood as ritually "communicative" or "magical" in the above sense, but rather as a mechanical chain in an action-reaction response. There is a large body of literature on the "causes" of war and political terrorism.[1] An example of the causal approach to Basque political violence is Goñi and Rodríguez (1979), an enquiry in which one hundred intellectuals from the Basque Country and Spain "analyze the causes of the violence and present solutions."[2]

A critical reexamination of this causal type of thinking is presented in this chapter. Caro Baroja has recently pointed out the dangers in this etiological search, for this habit of thinking "leads us frequently to be mistaken or to establish connections, cause and effect relations that are problematic" (1984 : 86). As Wittgenstein pointed out, "The insidious thing about the causal point of view is that it leads us to say: 'Of course, it had to happen like that.' Whereas we ought to think: it may have happened *like that*—and also in many other ways." (1980 : 37e). In the chapter on the bertsolariak an initial critique of these linear explanations of Basque political violence was sketched. Indeed, the search for "causes" rather than pointing to the solution can well be part of the problem by reproducing the thinking behind the political violence. Military thinking is conspicuously causal as necessary or sufficient causes are adduced to justify going to war, and final causes are elaborated by politicians to create an ends-means perspective on the ongoing bloodletting. The encounter between the contending parties is a one-way, functional, nonprobabilistic, causal relationship.

Devoid of feedback and different orders of prediction, in this type of thinking all creativity is reduced to the purposive means-ends syndrome. The fundamental issues derived from learning and classifying behavior at different levels are precluded. It is thinking anchored in the misleading energetic metaphor of "force" rather than on information or form. The prevailing theories of war, from

Clausewitz to the debates over the armament race, are based on elementary "physical" causes, action-reaction, purposefulness, ascension to the extremes, perfect oppositions. The shift from the physical event to the idea of the physical event, from function to meaning, has yet to take place.

On the basis of an ethnographic analysis of a Basque rural community I propose to rethink, then, the cause-and-effect approach to political violence by situating it in ritualized contexts in which social interaction and textual creation do not rely on simple rational-instrumental links. Such ritualized situations may rely significantly on what Weber termed "chance causality" (1949:182). An investigation that is uncritically based on the idea of "cause" tends to ignore categorical differences in various kinds of causation. Thus, Bateson stresses the difference, crucial to this discussion, between "causal explanation" and "cybernetic explanation" on the grounds that the former "is usually positive" and the latter "is always negative" (1972:399). Cybernetically what matter are the alternative possibilities, which could have occurred but did *not* occur because there were restraints. This is akin to the reductionist argument by which all but one of the possible propositions are invalid. In the following chapter, ritualized examples of negative explanation are drawn from traditional mythology and folk practices in a deliberate attempt to remove the billiard-ball model of cause-and-effect relationships. Our line of argumentation regarding causation is also based on the Aristotelian distinction between "final cause" and "formal cause," as discussed by Rappaport (1979:75ff.). We disregard final causal explanations, which explore the contribution that some component makes to the system of which it is part, in favor of formal causal explanations, which aim "to elucidate what is entailed by, follows from or is intrinsic to a particular form or structure" (ibid.:76). Ritual situations are typically not governed by intrinsic or instrumental means-ends connections. The study of such rituals taken from Basque culture will provide, then, the most adequate models for getting at the kinds of causation occurring in the ongoing violence. The constitutive power of culture as representational and emergent binds together these various ritualized frames and provides the appropriate context in which the discourse of Basque political violence needs to be situated.

In a broad sense, ritualization denotes "the adaptive formalization and canalization of motivated human activities so as to secure more effective communicatory ('signalling') function, reduction of intra-group damage, or better intra-group bonding" (Huxley 1966:258). Ethologists have reached the conclusion that most animal behavior patterns entail a process of ritualization. However, there is a radical difference in the ritual behavior of animals and humans. The former is derived from genetically determined instinct, while the latter is transmitted in nongenetically based symbolic codes, that is, culture.

Rituals and ceremonies are basically magico-religious in origin. "Military rituals" are among the classical ones. For want of better military means, the Basque nationalist resistance has even resorted to terrorist actions.[3] It is only to be expected that premises of a magical kind and ritualized behavior should become constitutive of such performances. As anthropologists well know, no strict separation holds between things "sacred" and things "profane." The study of ritual behavior has been a classic case in which rational-nonrational, instrumental-expressive, or sacred-profane dichotomies collapse. This is an ethnography of Basque political violence, and at first blush to view such secular violence through a prism that is more commonly applied to the religious domain might be regarded as undue analogizing. What in this discussion ties together politics and ritual is their common grounding in a specifically Basque culture.

The underground activist is repudiated by the media as a murderous terrorist and becomes the object of relentless repression by the establishment. Consequently, his signalling actions become more and more stereotyped and repetitious. Soon, as with many of those with so-called psychotic traits, conventionally noncommunicative behavior is used to communicate. The investigation should not be directed toward the "criminal acts" themselves, but rather toward the presuppositions on which they are premised. Silence and opposition to any mediating device or political negotiation may become a program in itself. As with that of the psychotic, "This type of communication has its own rules: it is highly formalized; it is limited in temporal sequence; it is resistant to change; it is cryptic" (Laing 1966:334). These abnormalities of behavior can be seen as "meta-rituals," in which "deritualization of normal human rituals" occurs, and, by their becoming more and more rigid, constitute "an aberration of an aberration" (ibid.:335). This process of ritual deterioration deserves particular attention.

In stress situations, rigidification and nonambiguity of form become essential for animal communication (Morris 1966:329). As Erikson pointed out, "We suspect that in man the *overcoming of ambivalence* as well as of ambiguity is one of the prime functions of ritualization" (1966:339; his emphasis). Politics thrives in ambiguity. The military feels compelled to rescue political discourse by forcing the unambiguous logic of warfare. Only disjunctive signals of an either/or kind are considered valid in such situations.

The distinction between verbal and nonverbal communication is not relevant from the perspective of ritual performance. Verbal communication is, in fact, plagued with problems of deceit and lying deriving from the arbitrariness of the word-sign. Ritual, which mobilizes nonverbal elements, is a partial solution to this problem. In the realm of politics this leads to a deep-seated mistrust of the politician's "mere" talk. Something more is needed, and that is readiness to die for one's own political ideals. Sacramental surrender is what the political activist claims for himself, and words alone cannot express that surrender. Only action of a ritual kind can communicate such total behavior. The study of ritual aspects is the appropriate way of getting at those nonverbal components in political violence.

Rather than describing the "reality" itself of the ongoing violence, in this chapter we shall attempt to formulate explanatory devices inspired by ritualized materials offered by the traditional culture. Since they are no longer part of the behavioral reality of the Basques, the validity of taking ritual forms encoded in traditional mythology and folklore and applying them to present realities may be questioned. The permanence of that mythology centered in Mari's aerial flights and witchcraft events during the early life of Itziar's older generations was discussed in chapter 1. Witchcraft and related superstitions were the basic source of storytelling during my childhood in Itziar. Nevertheless, for the youth involved in political violence these myths and rituals are at best an ethnographic curiosity. Yet, in accordance with previous chapters, in which the argument that violence draws from cultural models of thought and performance has been maintained, we want to examine in the present discussion the extent to which the traditional forms of ritual performance are reenacted in the ongoing violence. We are contemplating political violence as the paramount context of ritual performance produced by Basque society during the ETA years. By situating the political violence in the context of the culture's semantic space, it will be seen as constituting one form of ritualized behavior within the traditional cultural system.

At a conscious level, these forms of traditional culture per se tell us nothing about the ongoing violence except in the vague sense that they are thought of as part of the native culture that must be preserved and revived in new forms. Although irrelevant as conscious guides, the sign categories and ritual forms expressed by those cultural codes can be recognized in the practice of violence. In the previous chapter we discerned a consciously motivated historical and psychological continuity between religious experience and the commitment to political activism in Itziar; in this one we shall suggest a link with those more latent cultural elements that integrate conscious and unconscious processes. Still, we are not interested primarily in the symbolic multireferentiality of those partly unconscious constructs, but rather in showing how the depths of ritual behavior are manifested in surface forms that guide actual performances. The discussion follows Rappaport (1979) in stressing that formality and performance are the two necessary elements in ritual and there are two broad classes of messages being transmitted therein: those concerned with the here and now and those concerned with the enduring. Ritual performances will be explored as emerging from invariant formal sequences of cultural signs and actions. The traditional forms are postulated as models from which newer myths and rituals evolve.

The discussion is guided by the following theoretical frames: cybernetic theory as applied by Bateson (1972) to the human sciences in general and by Rappaport (1968, 1979) to the study of ritual in particular; Peirce's semiotic theory and its use by Silverstein (1976) in the analysis of a double type of reference (symbolic and indexical) in language; and Burke's dramatistic approach (1945, 1966) to symbolic action.[4]

CHAPTER THIRTEEN

Ritual Forms and Performances in Basque Mythology and Political Violence

Ez (No), Bai (Yes)

An examination of Basque mythology confronts the reader with a most cryptic conceptual sustenance: the flying witch Mari as well as the mythical *lamiak* (sirens) are nourished by *eza* (negation, or, literally, the no). To the question "What is your subsistence?" mythology reports that Mari's flat and repeated response has been "eza." In one tale, for instance, she offered a shepherd excellent cider. He asked, "What kind of apples did you use to make this cider?" Her reply was, "With those given to eza by the Lord of Monte de Ikaztegieta." In another tale, when asked about her friends' whereabouts, Mari replied crisply, "They are in Elgoibar searching for eza." Although there is never a narrative in which she lives on affirmation alone, in a report from Kortezubi she is said to have been fed *ezagaz eta baiagaz* (with the no and the yes). In six out of seven tales recorded by Arrinda Albisu (1965: 191–93), Mari subsists on negation alone. Barandiaran remarks, "It is common to say that Mari supplies her food store both at the expense of those who *deny* what is and those who *affirm* what is not" (1972: 166). In either denying what is or affirming what is not, the end result is a statement of the negative eza.

The polar opposite of *ez* (no) is *bai* (yes). As a variant of *bae, bai* also means "sieve,"[1] and again, under the image of the sieve, bai is a conspicuous theme in Basque mythology. On various occasions the Devil punishes his unfortunate captives by ordering them to perform "interminable tasks" with a sieve, such as carrying water with a bucket whose bottom is a sieve or separating white flour from bran flour by sifting them—sheer impossibilities. These endless tasks attached to bai clearly speak of a threshold that fails to sort out two different kinds of things or of a container that lacks the compactness (form) needed to hold water (substance) within. Bai depicts an indeterminate series with no possibility of classification and order. Paradox is inevitable with bai, much the same as with a logical series in which no discontinuity between member and class can be demarcated.

If bai is lacking in the notion of definite limit and therefore results in caverns of indeterminacy and paradox, its logical opposite ez provides in culture the fundamental concept of limit, either material, psychological, or logical. No wonder that the cultural hero Mari is nourished by eza. How else could she protect the culture from the chaotic effects deriving from affirmation? Through Mari's story we are presented in mythology with the question of how the affirmative can be separated from the negative, what is from what is not, the continuous from the discontinuous. A basic paradigm of order is thus established by the opposition between the affirmative and the negative.

The Subordinating Syntax of the Negotiating Bai

The mythical elaboration of the affirmative/negative polarity reflects a tension that is present in other areas of the culture as well. There is, for instance, a most significant syntactical use of the affirmative bai. In Basque syntax, causals and conditionals, and classically all sorts of subordinate clauses, are formed with bai or its derivatives *bait-, ba-*. The linguist Lafon has made this point most explicit when he writes in a summarizing statement: "Thus, the two verbal prefixes of syntactic value in Basque, *ba-* 'yes' and *bait-,* mark of dependency, repose on two affirmative particles of which the second derives from the first" (1966:224). Schuchardt had made the same point earlier: "*Bai* and *ba* are in any case a single word; *ba* is an alternated form of the former. The Basque we are studying here does not have a *ba* with the sense of 'yes'; it only appears in connection with verbal forms, and then with double use" (1947:72). Of *bait-* Villasante states: "It appears, however, that its basic function or typically specific value is its *relative* character in a general sense, namely, that it is relational and an index or marker of subordination. In itself it does not have a definite sense, and may adopt the most various ones depending on each concrete case" (1976:209; his emphasis).[2]

From this sameness of bai and *ba-/bait-* it follows that bai statements can be both assertive and hypothetical for the Basque speaker. When they are part of a longer sequence, bai statements are syntactically subordinate and never complete in themselves. The syntactical meaning of affirmation is therefore one of asserting hypotheses, conditionals, causals—all of them subordinate and indeterminate clauses. Adversive relationship is produced with *baina* (but), which is "the adversive conjunction par excellence in Basque" (Villasante 1976:29). The kinship between baina and bai is recognized by Schuchardt. Although not subordinated by the preceding one, the sense of the baina clause arises in opposition to it, whereas the sense of the initial clause does not depend in itself upon being followed by a baina one. Thus, the baina particle is also perceived as expressing derivative and dependent clauses in consistency with bai's syntactical meanings. As the mythical bai (sieve) cannot distinguish white flour from bran flour, neither does the syntactical bai differentiate categorical from hypothetical affirmations. The mythical bai generates indeterminate series that can never be completed; the syntactical bai marks incomplete subordinate clauses.

From a logical standpoint there is nothing surprising about the double nature of bai as assertive and hypothetical particle, for conditionals and causals are, in a sense, affirmative sentences. "In using 'if-then' sentences and in using 'because' sentences we are stating or asserting" (Ryle 1971:235). How then are bai hypothetical and bai assertoric propositions distinguished? Besides difference in intonation, hypotheticals are part of a longer sentence, whereas assertoric ones are not. "Gizona badator" (The man is coming) is assertoric; but if it is made part of a larger sentence it then becomes hypothetical: "Gizona badator, gelditu egingo naiz" (If the man comes, I shall stay). As Geach puts it, "The assertoric force of a sentence is thus shown by its *not* being enclosed in the context of a longer sentence" (1965:456; his emphasis). On the other hand, by merely changing intonation it turns into the interrogative "Is the man coming?" In all three cases (interrogative, hypothetical, affirmative) it is the same *ba-* that is asserting, not the truth value of the thought of the sentence but only the (interrogative, hypothetical, affirmative) sense of it. As Frege pointed out, "A false thought must be admitted, not indeed as true, but as sometimes indispensable; first, as the sense of an interrogative sentence; secondly, as part of a hypothetical thought-complex; thirdly, in negation" (1977:37). It is the sense of an interrogative or the possibility of a hypothetical or the affirmative response to an implicit or explicit question that is asserted by *ba-*. In brief, the subordinating bai asserts but does not determine the sense of hypothetical-causal sentences; for this the complete sentence is needed. By bringing in indeterminacy, syntax rules out the assertoric force of individual sentences. The mythical bai's inability to dissociate white flour from bran flour is a metaphor for the syntactical bai's inability to determine the sense of an interrogative, hypothetical, or categorical statement.

The indeterminate nature of the affirmative is mythically elaborated not only by showing its results in conceptual paradoxes, but also by enmeshing action in the antithetical predicament of moving and not moving at the same time. While given to the endless task of sifting with the bai, the mythical hero Atarrabi is constrained to respond "Emen nago" (Here I am) to the Devil's persistent question "Where are you?" So the devilish impossibility of dissociating bran flour from white flour is expressed in action by the contradictory results of an activity that is both continuous and nonprogressive. Atarrabi moves his sieve, yet he does not advance; he is being active, yet he remains in the same place—"Here I am." He can escape the situation only by the magical act of teaching the bai (sieve) to respond "Here I am." It is only when the bai is able to stop its endless course by making a statement of definite position that Atarrabi can leave the labyrinthine cave.

In political discourse the concept of negotiation entails an indeterminacy comparable to the syntactical use of bai, for the process of negotiation can be described as a strategy of "getting to yes" (Fisher and Ury 1981). As observed by Taylor (1971), a contractual notion of negotiation, based on the assumption of autonomous parties in voluntary relationship, is not true of every society. Other cultures may lack a vocabulary to describe negotiation and insist, for instance, on unanimous decision—"bargaining" would have there a different social reality. To the extent that negotiation is obtaining a "yes," which in the semantics of the culture creates a syntax of subordination and a mythology of labyrinthine paradoxes, the indeterminacy associated with bai should work against such a risky process. Particularly in times of politico-military struggle, when an aggrieved party aims at ridding itself of the ills of subordination, the negotiating bai may become an anathema. It is therefore not surprising that at times in recent Basque political attitudes the very concept of negotiation has been branded downright treason. Among the slogans chanted in political demonstrations there is the salient one that certain issues, such as amnesty for political prisoners or the Basque status of the province of Navarre, "are nonnegotiable." The risks involved in political flexibility are no less threatening for the other side, and the slogan that the sovereign state will never negotiate with terrorism is displayed as a hallmark of commitment to democracy.

Labyrinthine trapping is mythically represented by Atarrabi's response to the Devil; escape from the cave requires a magical feat. In political geography Basque perception of closure is one of being contained in Spain while being denied a politically autonomous status. Basques feel trapped and uncertain of their chances of preserving their historical and cultural heritage because they have to comply with the militarily stronger enemy yet resist the bai affirmative requests of political agreement. It is the drama of a double-binding closure in which giving in entails political and cultural extinction while resistance implies military defeat and harsh repression. This is the political equivalent of Atarrabi's "Here I am," which, in response to Madrid's inescapable control, breeds contradiction and stirs up the desire for evasion. Only by mythically teaching the bai to stop its endless running can Atarrabi move from subservience to freedom. ETA's radical denial of the Spanish status quo is also a ritualized "Here I am," which promises the escape from the cave. As

Atarrabi's paradoxical predicament leads to magical solutions, so does Basque violence attempt an ultimate solution to a political paradox.

Although valid to generate a syntax of hypotheticals and causals, bai lacks the definiteness of sense essential for the ritual marking of transitional states. For this all syntax must be reduced to an either/or. What is wanted from ritual is precisely a clear sense-demarcation of interrogative, hypothetical, and categorical propositions, so that a transformation from one to the other might be achieved through ritual performance. The devilish syntax of bai acquiescence has to be dissolved into the ostensive "Here I am."

By establishing a polarity between bai and ez, mythology presents its own theory of order.[3] The contradictory results of hypothetical affirmation and nonprogressive movement must be avoided in ritual. In contrast to the affirmative's disqualification as a device for creating unambiguous statements, the negative stands out as the marker of discontinuity essential for ritual. Since the syntactical bai achieves only hypothetical marking, ritual order needs to rely on the clear demarcation of the negative.

The Flow of Eza (Negation)

> *What is a rebel? A man who says no: but whose refusal does not imply a renunciation. He is also a man who says yes as soon as he begins to think for himself. Camus,* The Rebel

Nourishment by the negative is what we find in the mythical paradigm of eza. The repercussions of bai's indeterminacy are far-reaching in Basque culture. The notion of person is a case in point. The "yes-man," who has not mastered ez, is not trustworthy. A too-frequent use of baina reveals a man's inability to take a stand. Among people of the older generations, a frequently used expression to charge the youth with being too permissive is "These days the youth say bai to everything." *Baia* (affirmation) takes the meaning of "defect" as well. *Baiago* (a compound of *bai* and *ago* [stand up] is the term mothers use when their children tenuously stand up for the first time—affirmation and indeterminacy once again.

The clearest definition I heard in Itziar of what it is to be a person is the following: "To be a man is to be able to say ez." This centrality of eza as a fundamental cultural premise was pointed out in its simplest form by a man of seventy-five, who in a criticism of young people lamented, "Gaurko gazteak ezik ez" (Today's youth does not have a no). On another occasion I was told, "It is totally necessary to have to say ez to certain things to give meaning to life. That's all, for me that's all that makes life meaningful and nothing else." These quotes are indicative of the extent to which the culture's ideal persona is grounded in mastering the negative. Normativeness is here defined in negative terms, and the person required to fulfill such norms has to be intimately acquainted with ez. It is within the logic of the culture that the notion of the person also should be founded on ez as the bearer of the idea of limit essential to personal autonomy. Becoming a person is accepting the differences that circumscribe the self in relation to the rest of society.

When I asked about ez I was told that "you say ez to the children." During fieldwork, my niece Aintzane was able to say ez when she was twelve months old and did not learn to say bai until she was nineteen months.[4] This became a source of amusement because at times she would understand questions that required bai (such as after dinner, "Have you had dinner?") and, being unable to say bai, she would smile and lift up her shoulders, meaning "I don't know." When Aintzane was twenty-three months old, her cousin Mikel from Bilbao stayed at her home for a few days. What really caught Aintzane's attention about Mikel was that he, instead of saying the Basque negative ez, would say no in Spanish. This was so significant to Aintzane that she nicknamed him "No" and would refer to him by that name. On one occasion, Mikel's mother wrote from Bilbao, and Aintzane remembered Mikel with the two Spanish words *mio* (mine) and *no,* thus linking in her perception of him the two primary ideas of identity (mine) and negation (no).

Achieving manhood is a particularly critical issue for the youth, and the conversation below illustrates well the pervasiveness of ez in daily attitudes. In one of our meetings at the youth center of Itziar we were talking about authority with particular reference to its place in Basque traditional society when suddenly Zuriko, an avowed antiauthoritarian, introduced into the conversation as a matter of course the theme of eza. Zuriko, José Ignacio, and Juan Mari, all in their early twenties, and myself were the main speakers in this exchange, in which other young people participated as well.

Z.: One thing I see among Basques is [the insistence on] opposing what someone else has said.

J.Z.: To what extent do you think that going against somebody is taken as a sign of *indarra* [force]?

Z.: Many times, even if you don't want to, you say ez without realizing it yourself.

J. I.: You can see a lot of that among bachelors in Itziar. Tell them anything and, just to oppose you, they will say ez!

J. M.: Zuriko has a tremendous power to say ez, even knowing that it is a stupidity. I remember when he was a kid, and Guillermo [a school friend] would hit him on the head and ask, "Does it hurt you?" The response was, "Ez!" And a harder blow, and again, "Does it hurt you?" "Ez!" And that was the response, even knowing in advance that a harder one would follow. And like that in a thousand things. I instead would tell him that it was hurting me, I would cry, "And go fuck yourself." On the one hand I would be weak, but on the other a little intelligent.

Z.: Instead of saying ez, nowadays it is more impressive if you "pass by" everything and do whatever you like.

J. M.: Many people consider it a sign of inferiority to do anything you are asked to do. And perhaps they are right.

Z.: In my opinion the best way to show your indarra is not by saying ez. That has been all that there was in the Basque Country, and I myself have had that, of course. But for me nowadays the greatest strength lies in "passing by." Let him do whatever he wants to do, and you do whatever you want yourself. The damn thing is that I don't know anyone here who has reached such a point. Ez will come out of him all the time. Then, what is best? that in-between or . . . ?

J. M.: The best thing is the in-between. You have to jokatu a bit. Neither ez nor bai. You have a thousand things there. Sometimes you will say yes as best as you can, and then do whatever you like.

J. I.: I realize also many times that although you are saying ez the other is playing the fool, and in the end you do whatever he wants you to do.

Z.: This is what Andres [a bachelor in his early forties] does: You ask him to play mus, and many times, even if he would like to play, he will say ez out of sheer habit.

J. Z.: Quite a few girls have told me as well that, when they are asked to dance, for instance, they will automatically say ez at first, and then they are sorry that they have said it.

J. I.: That is quite common.

J. M.: It has happened to me many times, "Do you want a *porro* [joint]?" And I respond ez because I damn well feel like it, when in fact I was depriving myself, wanted to smoke it, and should have said bai.

J. I.: Suppose that Andres would tell you bai; what a blow that would be to you! So you are asking him to play mus partly because you want to hear his ez.

J. Z.: Bai means, therefore, to accept someone else's authority.

J.I.: In our own opinion we are so progressive today that, in the same manner as everything before was saying ez, now it is to "pass by." All that is mere fashion. Before it was fashionable to receive a blow in front of people and to say ez. Now it is to "pass by."

Z.: For me that is not fashion.

This conversation underscores the behavioral meanings of ez and bai in relation to personal identity. It reminds me of a revelatory ritualized practice during my own primary school days in Itziar that consisted of younger brothers being tested by their older ones for their endurance of physical abuse. The torture would continue as long as the young brother kept answering ez to the question of whether he was feeling pain. Finally, incapable of further resistance, he would burst into tears with a bai. Thus, the older brother asserted his dominance over the younger by extracting bai from him.

But it is the performance of ez in political attitudes that is presently most significant among the youth. Just as the personal self is nourished by the performance of eza, so is the collective one; thus, one frequently hears that "being Basque" is "*not* being Spanish" or "*not* being French." As we wondered previously at the cryptic eza of mythical food, we might be puzzled as well by such linkage in the graffiti of the last underground years of activism, in which the one word that looms noticeably large for its profusion and size is EZ. During my fieldwork the majority of the youth sympathized with and voted for Herri Batasuna, a self-proclaimed "no-saying" coalition of radical opposition to Madrid's post-Francoist political reform (Letamendia 1979). Basque political forces have had much to be antagonistic about during the last decade: dictatorship, death penalties, hundreds of prisoners and exiles, a Spanish constitution rejected by all Basque political parties, the risks of nuclear power. These have been and some still are the issues of contention. Terms such as *Konstituzioa* (the Spanish constitution) and Lemoiz (the town site of a nuclear power plant) have become so inextricably united in political rhetoric with EZ that they have come to be treated as if they were a single compound word. EZ not only points out the rejection associated with those terms but also marks a context of combative antagonism. More significant than the given concrete item that is negated, the central message about EZ is that it marks a context of rejection and readiness to fight.

Ez becomes a kind of verbal amulet, indispensable for personal endurance in extreme situations such as torture when all other language and resistance has been destroyed. This is certainly the case in the cryptic description given to me by José Ignacio when he recalled the days of torture in the police station: "To be tortured, and ez and ez and ez." The act of negating becomes a means of survival by preserving the most intimate identity in the everlasting no. Discussing torture, Scarry writes: "Intense pain is also language-destroying: as the content of one's world disintegrates, so the content of one's language disintegrates; as the self disintegrates, so that which would express and project the self is robbed of its source and its subject" (1985:35). When extreme repression or pain obliterates all language, the ultimate self-assertion is an ez. The alternation ez/bai frames the self not only in its everyday presentation but particularly in ritualized practices such as the children's endurance test described above or in a torture chamber. As Foucalt remarks, "Torture forms part of a ritual" (1977:34), for there is "an element of duel" over truth and power between torturer and victim. Inflicting intolerable pain is the torturer's form of asserting power; the only power left to the prisoner is the truth of the cause, integrity in self-perseverance, persistence in the ez. The duel for truth and power is fought in the duel between bai and ez.

Psychoanalysts have long recognized that "in analysis we never discover a 'No' in the unconscious, and that a recognition of the unconscious on the part of the ego is expressed in a negative formula" (Freud 1925: 185). What negation accomplishes in this perspective was stressed by Freud: "The subject-matter of a repressed image or thought can make its way into consciousness on condition that it is *denied*" (ibid.: 182; his emphasis). The young man Luther in Erikson's study offers a historically consequential performance of negation. Erikson devotes an initial chapter to Luther's fit in the choir. He considers the incident decisive in determining Luther's career. In his fit, Luther is reported to have roared in German or Latin, "It isn't me!" or "I am *not!*" Erikson views the fit as part of a severe identity crisis "in which the young monk felt obliged to protest what he was *not* (possessed, sick, sinful), perhaps in order to break through to what he was or was to be" (1958: 36; his emphasis). Compelled by the need to negate, Luther's

> fit in the Choir presents only the symptomatic, the more pathological and defensive, aspects of a total revelation: partial loss of consciousness, loss of motor coordination, and automatic exclamations which the afflicted does not know he utters. . . . In Luther's fit, his words obviously expressed an overwhelming inner need to deny an accusation. (Ibid.: 37–38)

This can be compared with José Ignacio's responding to torture with "ez and ez and ez." A first meaning here is that he should resist disclosing information that would be damaging to his ETA companions. At a deeper level, to persevere in negating is tantamount to preserving inner integrity and holding on to the center of identity. For this, the pain and humiliation of torture have to be denied. By so doing, the devastating accusations of terrorist murder or unmanly weakness are rejected.

Luther's no during his fit in the choir was accompanied by partial loss of consciousness. There is not a no in the unconscious, but, in Freud's words, a recognition of the unconscious is expressed in a negative formula. In the logic of Basque myths as well the cultural unconscious is recognized as eza. The uncontainable flow of eza reaches unconscious levels. From a logical viewpoint, Frege (1977) remarked that negation must not be regarded as a content of consciousness. The mechanical use of the cultural negative in everyday affairs is illustrated by the no-saying definitions of the person. It is only to be expected that the political unconscious of a people whose culture hinges so openly on the negative should be manifested in negative forms and performances.

The Negative Character of Ritual Form

Eza nourishes the mythical sirens and Mari; in the image of the bai as sieve the affirmative works as the Devil's instrument in breaking down all sense of orderly progression. As a mechanism for bringing about a transition between two states, ritual presupposes a boundary or discontinuity between them. For this a clear notion of limit is required. In the paradigm of order examined in the first section of this chapter, mythology opposes the negative as a sign of definite limit to the affirmative's sign of indeterminate sense. Thus, the negative form in mythology is the model of ritual's function of demarcating discontinuous states. The key notion of limit being recognized in culture as eza, ritual is formally negative in that its intrinsic function of establishing and crossing boundaries is founded on such a notion of negative limit.

The negative character of ritual needs to be understood in formal terms. In this regard it is comparable to the formally negative sign of a cybernetic system: "Causal explanation is usually positive," whereas "cybernetic explanation is always negative" (Bateson 1972: 399). Negative explanation considers alternative possibilities that did not occur; the inequality of probability is due to restraints in the course of events. The mythical explanation of Mari's universe being energized by eza is also of a negative kind. Like probability, eza is of zero dimensions; like the concept of information in cybernetics, eza quantifies in negative terms. A means/ends explanation is positive—a causal link is inherent to it. Negative explanation operates in exclusions—all alternatives but one are impossible. Ritual is not premised in a means/ends causal linkage. Its form is negative.

In daily speech the negative is digitalized into the ez/bai opposition. Rappaport has argued that "ritual occurrence resembles digital computing systems" (1979: 186).[5] Processes whose values change by discontinuous leaps are "digital." Digitalization reduces complex "analogic" processes (instances of which are maturation, prestige, mood, temperature) into the binary "on/off." The ambiguity of the "more-or-less" fluctuating information is eliminated by the ez/bai binary system, which creates discontinuous states and thus increases clarity. According to this view, a ritual frame likewise dissolves the ambiguities of possible states and conditional implications by reducing them to a digital on/off step. Since contradiction and deceit abide in such a world of logic and verbal syntax, ritual is a mechanism for ruling them out.

A peculiarly verbal phenomenon that multiplies the possibilities of deceit is lying (Rappaport 1979: 223–43). Similarly, the fictional truth of an *alegia* (tale)[6] is not intended in a literal sense. A Basque tale ends typically with the maxim "Oi ala bazan sar dedilla kalabazan" (If that happened so, let it get into a calabash)—this formula displays the *ba* (if-then) mode of implication in *bazan* (if it happened), which is again reiterated phonetically in the second half of the final word *kalabazan* (in the calabash). Another formulaic tale ending is a strophe whose last line is "And our entire tale is a lie" (Barandiaran 1960–62: 3: 80), which connects the "lying" of storytelling with the ba hypothetical implication. This fictional truth, much the same as merely syntactical assertion, is of a ba kind. To the extent that ritual is a device to restore truth, it cannot rely on ba modal or fictional propositions. In the bai/ez digital mechanism, ritual literalness and discontinuous marking must depend on the negative ez.

In relation to the performative aspects of ritual to be expounded in the following sections, a point of particular significance is its nonverbal nature. Bateson has speculated insightfully on the step from animal to human communication as a shift from iconic to verbal signalling (1972: 411–25). In his analysis the key factor for such a primary step is the formation of the simple negative. An animal can communicate the message "don't" only if the other animal can iconically propose the pattern of action that is not to be followed. But there still remains a great step from "don't" to the simple negative "not," which is essential in human language because it creates the separateness between signal and referent necessary for naming. The mythical component of such a crucial step from animal to cultural communication is the ez that nourishes Mari. Iconic communication is characterized by the absence of modal markers and the negative. In Basque culture this amounts to saying that it lacks the negative ez as well as the affirmative bai. Since bai operates the "if-then" logical implication required for grammatical syntax, the affirmative has to do with designating modality. The negative, on the other hand, designates in nonmodal or deictic terms. The "if-then" of implication produces logical paradoxes and ambiguous verbal duplicity. No such unwanted results derive from the negative syntax of ez, which, unconcerned with modality, designates the verbal or the iconic deictically. Ez provides the appropriate syntax of discontinuity and mode of reference for the negative form of ritual.

Picturing the Negative: Imageless Ideas and Action

The ability to master the negative, that "marvel of language," is also where Burke discerns the specific nature of human language. A central remark of his is that "the negative is not picturable, though it can be *indicated*—as by a headshake, or the mathematical mark for minus, or the word *no*. It is properly shown by a *sign*, not by an *image*." (1966:430; his emphasis). In the mythical stories mentioned earlier, the affirmative bai found its image in the metaphor of the bai (sieve). The negative, even if functioning as food of mythical beings, could only be hinted at by the word eza—the final *-a* is the determinate article "the," thus turning the imageless negative into a discrete unit by its functioning as a substantive. More significantly, in culture the negative can be pictured by transforming the verbal-logical ez into its analogue *uts* (void). Not only is Mari nourished by eza, but her underground caves are filled with *uts*—empty golden containers such as cups, canteens, and candlesticks. The digital negative ez is one of mere contiguity. The spatial negative uts is based on similarity as well, for it provides the imagery of containers. Yet there is clearly an imageless quality to this uts imagery as well, for what it depicts is not an individualized and separate image but the relationship of containment or inclusion.

If in the origin of language the step from iconic to verbal communication is crucially related to mastering ez, in the origin of pictorial language an equivalent step must be achieved by the visual negative uts. The key role uts plays in Basque cultural semantics suggests that the visual negative is in fact the more relevant.[7] We must elaborate on the notion of uts as it best demonstrates the interdependence between cultural premises and ritual action.

One only has to enunciate the meanings of uts to realize that it is a superconcept in which diverse and even contradictory referents are brought together into the semantic field of a single term. Azkue gives this list for uts: (1) void; (2) mere, pure, simple; (3) absence; (4) vain, item without value; (5) mistake, blunder; (6) fault, flaw; (7) bad result; and (8) barren, unproductive (1969:2:386–87). Furthermore, uts can be used in compound words indicating a total or partial nakedness. Despite the diversity of meanings, for the Basque speaker uts is a single term and concept. What is its overall meaning? It is an order of possibilities and as such is prior to image and experience.

The full significance of the notion of uts can only be appreciated in the predicative functions it fulfills in the culture's semantic space. Uts changes its meaning according to its grammatical function—it can be a noun, adjective, adverb, or verb. Considerations of logical typing have a decisive bearing as well on the various meanings of uts, for its predicative function varies according to the level of abstraction at which it is applied. With a quality such as *gorri* (red), *gorri utsa* means "completely red"; applied to an object or structure such as *etxe* (house), *etxe utsa* means "empty house"; with an abstract idea such as *on* (good), *on utsa* means "absolutely good." Furthermore, the lexical function or logical type of uts is context-dependent in its use meaning. Thus, for instance, an ordinary construction such as *gizon utsa* might, depending on the context, mean "a real man," "only a man," "an empty man," "a vain man," and so on.

Yet, despite all this semantic and contextual ambiguity, uts is for the speaker a single term that produces unambiguous sentences. The question arises as to how a single term can present such a contradictory polysemy and be understood by the speaker as a single concept whose various meanings have an obvious semantic coherence. What the speaker grasps is the second-order predicative function of the word prior to its diverse particular meanings, and thus the apparent contradictions resulting from its diverse senses do not affect that predicative function. What does this predicative function of uts do? It creates a field of exclusion, a frame of "nothing but"—this is equivalent to the above-mentioned negative form of cybernetic explanation. When applied to primary or secondary qualities, exclusion means that they are "only, completely" that quality; if applied to objects such as containers or bodies, exclusion means "absence, emptiness" of material elements; and the field of exclusion turns concepts of higher order into "simply, absolutely" those abstractions.[8]

The dialectics of container/content relationship is a prime means of visualizing the formal notion of uts. In this regard a container is a perfect icon of uts. It is in relation to a container that the predicate uts acquires the meaning of "empty." The identification of the predicate with the icon is so close that it creates a tendency to reduce the meaning of uts to the container/content dialectics and mistakenly to think of uts as the digital opposite of *bete* (full).[9] The "emptiness" of uts is pictured by a container. The characterizing properties of the iconic sign are thus based on the uts predicate. It follows that the sign displays as well different orders of uts meaning depending on ritual context.

With qualities or bodies the uts field of exclusion creates the formal separation needed for image-formation. Yet, at the level of pure abstraction, uts discontinuity transcends any image—it is simple negative form. The formal necessity for simplicity, essential to any conceptual system, is thus linguistically resolved by the uts field of exclusion, which determines noncomposite states. Wittgenstein observes that the question "Is this object composite?" does not make sense outside of a particular language-game (1968:47). In the case of Basque language-culture the problem of determining whether an object, quality, or concept is simple is resolved by the language-game of uts, which excludes any compositeness.

The transition from the iconic to the verbal was identified by Bateson as the great step from "don't" to the simple negative "not," which is essential for human language. "This step would immediately endow the signals—be they verbal or iconic—with a degree of separateness from their referents, which would justify us in referring to the signals as 'names'" (1972:425). In the paradigm of order drawn from mythology, the eza that nourishes Mari and its transformation of uts containers that abound in her dwellings are the mythical proponents of such a crucial step at both verbal and iconic levels.

My niece Amaia showed me a drawing of a house, and when I asked her whether it was real, she responded, "Marrazki utsa da" (It is *only* a drawing)—the partial negative "only" (*utsa*) marked the difference between the picture and what it represented. Uts functions as the negative, which, by predicating a field of exclusion or discontinuity, achieves a definiteness of sense. The primary-process thinking of dreams or myths is characterized by the absence of a metacommunicative frame that states, "This is *only* a dream" or "This is *only* a myth"—in Basque, uts provides that partial negative. The iconic communication of animals and primary process turns into cultural communication when the notion of uts can be separated from the qualities or containers in order to form a name or separate image of them. By creating a field of discontinuity or exclusion a definiteness of sense essential for naming and imaging is thus achieved by ez and uts.[10]

Ez and uts are the digital and the iconic versions of the negative: the ez/bai opposition indicates the here and now, the ritual step from one state to the other, whereas uts provides the enduring representation and the invariant aspect of the ritual form.[11] The icon of the Amabirjina studied in the previous chapter illustrates the tension concentrated in the uts idea.

In daily life and mythology, *aska* (trough) was considered in the previous chapter the prototype of container. As with uts, aska is formally negative in that it becomes a container by a process of exclusion of matter. The digital negative resembles number, whereas the analogic negative resembles quantity. The quantitative resemblance of analogic negative is displayed by containers such as aska, which establish a continuum of being "more or less" uts; this is suggested in etymology by quantitative notions such as *asko* (a lot) and *aski* (enough) sharing the root *ask-*. From the viewpoint of ritual image, there is a common denominator of uts exclusion to the mythical aska, the golden cups of Mari's dwellings, the cured body after expulsion of sickly substances, the depiction of the Amabirjina as container of her son's grace, and the *aberria* (native land) being an *ama* (mother) demanding a state of *askatasun* (freedom). A general quality of uts formal emptiness and passivity is manifested by this iconic imagery. The negative character of ritual form is digitally indicated by the imageless negative ez and iconically shown by the negative image of uts.

A fundamental consequence derives from this imagelessness of the negative. Since it cannot be imagined, it can only be acted out. Burke made this transition masterfully when he wrote:

> Yet this Tribal No resides basically in the realm not of sensory image, but of supersensory idea. If sensation is the realm of

> motion, idea is the realm of action. And action is possible only insofar as the rational agent transcends the realm of sheer motion—sensory image. He does so, however, by forming adequate ideas of the limitations defining this sensory realm. And insofar as his understanding of the world's necessities approaches perfection, he is correspondingly free; he can *act*, rather than merely being *moved*, or "affected." (1966:430; his emphasis)

The mythical Mari, who lives from eza, is the perfect cosmologizer of the Tribal No. Historically the Amabirjina herself was a denial of the flying Mari's legitimacy. If Mari was nourished by negation, the Amabirjina proclaims herself to side with affirmation. And the Amabirjina's pilgrim troubadours, in the popular collection of ballads dedicated to her, pray and sing, "The bai will win out over the ez" (Mitxelena 1949:130). Yet, defying all prayers and political persuasions, the everlasting tribal ez resists being engulfed by a higher, domineering force (church, state), which demands submission through a subordinating bai.

In the end the eza "of the rational-tribal idea" gets confused with "the essential nolessness of image" (Burke 1966:430). In the absence of the image of one's own identity or in the absence of an image of the other, the imageless idea forces action. Since eza cannot be imagined, it can only be acted out in ekintza.

What Can Only Be Shown

In previous chapters it has been emphasized that the notion of the ideal person, the ideology of word and action, and performative models such as that of the bertsolaria are based on iconic modes of meaning in the culture. For its followers the unique validity of ETA's performance rests as well on iconically showing personal and political self-transcendence. This incarnation of political belief is what makes an ETA member's truth unquestionable. The iconic sign is multireferential; when ritually acted out it condenses various domains of meaning. This blending together of disparate messages is likely to appear illegitimate to those not participating in the ritual, yet "that which is noise in ordinary language is meaning in liturgy" (Rappaport 1979:204).

Iconic coding is nonverbal and has no negatives or modal markers. Hence, like an artist or a dancer, the iconic political activist engages the audience in a communication that is partly conscious but is also partly unconscious. This iconic advantage of the ETA kind of politics makes parliamentary politicians appear hopelessly superficial and flawed, for theirs is the communication of merely conscious talk, which inevitably leads to lying—they attempt to define Truth only verbally or consciously. In several Basque folktales, to the question What is Truth? the response is *kaka zarra* (old shit). This folk definition points to the presence of a cultural premise according to which truth cannot be apprehended only verbally; truth, like morality, should rather emerge from ritual performance and be shown by the total person. The obvious disadvantages of iconic politics are, on the other hand, that, communicating partly on an unconscious level, its practitioners cannot be fully aware of their way of acting and of the aberrant messages they produce for those not sharing the premises of their political unconscious. What is meaning in liturgy is confusion in ordinary language.

Iconic signalling appears to take precedence in survival situations. Because it places the signaller in a position of readiness to attack, an iconic sign of aggression "probably has more survival value than would a more arbitrary signal" (Bateson 1972:418). The survival mentality in ETA's attitudes, summarized in the often-heard expression "they are like cornered animals," was emphasized in the chapters on the beast and hunting, in which the preverbal and sensorially primary experience was seen as subverting the verbal and socially secondary experience.

Survival situations are also paramount occasions for ritualization. Rites of passage, rites of curing, defense from witchcraft, rituals of collective supplication, and warfare are situations in which personal or group survival is at stake. Strong emotional responses are likely to be triggered by ritual performances concerned with survival situations. The effectiveness of ritual symbols may in fact reach unconscious and organic levels, as in the experience of healing. A performance such as hunting, in which the requirement for killing the prey likens it to ritual action, produces as well intense physiological effects. The development of a new kind of perception ("you learn how to smell the danger") among ETA people, pointed out in the chapter on hunting, could be viewed as an equivalent organic effect derived from the ritualistic nature of their survival-oriented performance. Massive political demonstrations may also reach a climax in which the participants are "transformed" into a different psychic state as manifested in singing, shouting, or facial expressions—these, too, are ritual occasions on which the purely conventional is surpassed by the actual embodiment of emotional and psychological states.

Wittgenstein's distinction between what can be said and what can only be shown is relevant to this discussion, for ritual performance is a necessary means for ostensively manifesting cultural sense. Pseudopropositions are mistaken attempts to say what can only be shown. His insistence on the insignificance of what can be said finds a cultural equivalent in the primary relevance of ritual as performative and factitive demonstration. Ritual evidences the necessity for performatively acting out the structural relations in the culture. In this regard, ritual is "*the* basic social act," which includes "social contract, morality, and even the concept of the sacred" (Rappaport 1979: 174; his emphasis). Thus, ritual becomes invested with logical necessity to express otherwise unsayable things.

It has been said that Basques are sparing in words. Nowadays this tradition of silence finds its most accomplished exponent in those who practice or support political violence. It is easy to express violence with gestures, bodies, actions. Yet, when the time comes to speak up, to make it understandable to others and oneself, the only worthy argument seems to be silence—words cannot capture its intensity. Nobody expects that a bullfighter, a hunter, or a gambler can reveal in a conversation the secret of his art; we know in advance that his explanations will be distorted translations of what he experiences at a preverbal level. Yet, outraged by the senselessness of political violence or the arms race, we never tire of asking for the "reasons," as if they could be arbitrated by a logic of syllogisms. It is hard to forgo the illusion that rational discourse could "show" where the violent logic went wrong, or that profound enough introspection into the conscious motivations would adequately "interpret" the meaning of the violent action. One must learn to listen to that silence first.

A Case of Iconic Reading: Independentzia

To the extent that ETA has succeeded in defining political discourse in iconic and sacramental terms, an element of self-enclosure becomes essential to all political signs. A good illustration of this occurred in Itziar in the summer of 1982 when the word *independentzia* (independence), written by a radical nationalist group on the village bulletin board, was ordered erased by Itziar's PNV mayor during the yearly fiestas. On a previous occasion, when the PNV was going to open its batzoki center, the mayor had done the same thing with the same word, which had been displayed on the board for months (the PNV is not now pro-independence). His repeated action elicited from those who had written *independentzia* a leaflet accusing him of being an *alcahuete* (pimp), which has clear overtones of police informer, and *herri-saltzaile* (seller of the country). During the seventies being a chivato marked one for death; the killing of Itziar's chivato in 1975 was generally approved of by pro-ETA Basques; and throughout the eighties alleged chivatos are still being killed by ETA. Thus, the simple erasing of a graffiti word by the mayor, an otherwise amiable man and well liked by most villagers, brought him dangerously close to becoming a direct enemy condemned to death for his treachery to the Basque cause. I was one of the many who were incensed by the leaflet being distributed during Itziar's fiestas, the yearly occasion for village solidarity. I might have expected that this leaflet would be disapproved of even by sympathizers of Basque separatist parties. However, this was not the case when I vented my anger at home.

In the course of the acrimonious argument that ensued I realized that two quite different readings were given to the mayor's act by some members of my family and by myself. For me there was not anything particularly offensive to the Basque cause or any intolerable abuse of power in the behavior of the mayor when he erased a coarsely written graffiti from the village bulletin board. The word had stayed there for months. The village is regularly spruced up for the fiestas; house facades and walls are painted. That summer various houses were deplorably defaced with crudely painted Basque nationalist slogans containing elemental spelling errors. If anything was abusive, I argued, it was the intolerable writing of such graffiti on someone else's walls, some of which had been recently painted at considerable cost. Furthermore, hardly anything could be more offensive than the appalling illiteracy of radical revolutionaries who did not even know how to spell ez (they wrote it es). There was, however, a very different reading of the event on the part of my critics. They agreed with some aspects of my argument—they, too, found the graffiti coarse and shameful, they did not like the direct attack on the mayor by inclusion of his personal name in the leaflet, and so on. Yet they strongly rejected my acquiescent attitude toward the mayor's action and found that ultimately he deserved the attack for his abuse of authority. One of my opponents insisted on two reasons: the suffering experienced by those who wrote the leaflet during years of imprisonment or exile, and the *bai ala ez* (either yes or no) context in which Basque politics has to be situated. This was not scholarly musing but an intimately painful argument at the core of my family life.

One way of explaining their reading of the erasure of *independentzia* is in terms of iconicity. The political aspirations of the last thirty years of activist struggle spurred by ETA could be summarized in that single word, *In-de-pen-den-tzi-a!* chanted as a slogan in large nationalist demonstrations. The word can be made to stand for the hundreds of activists who in this last struggle have been tortured, imprisoned, exiled, or killed. In a political confrontation with Madrid, perceived in a context of Basque historical survival, words such as Euskadi, freedom, and independence can be experienced with a sacramental type of identification. Totality and closure characterize these messages. Nor is their iconic nature recognized solely by the Basques, for under Franco's long dictatorship they provoked brutal police repression. The very utterance or writing of the word Euskadi, to say nothing of holding the Basque *ikurrina* (flag), has amounted to total insubordination until very recently. Several deaths of nationalists and civil guards were caused by the display and repression of the ikurrina. The mayor's erasure of *independentzia* was one more event in that odious chain of repression. Furthermore, support for the Basque Country's independence is a political option embraced by the second and third major nationalist parties, Herri Batasuna and Euskadiko Ezkerra. The majority nationalist party, the PNV, was also historically pro-independence. Repressing the concept of independence amounts to obliterating this political goal, still ardently pursued by a substantial number of Basques. This is perceived characteristically as a bai ala ez antagonistic context in which each alternative excludes the other completely. For them, erasure of the independence option was tantamount to the suppression of Basque inalienable political aspirations.

Iconism and Deixis: Ritual Centering

Iconic mode of meaning is typically multireferential; that is, it is extended to new referents on the basis of iconic equivalence.[12] The example of aska illustrates this point well. An economy of expression is thus achieved because, as Munn observed of the schemata of primitive pictorial systems, "a single element can stand for a variety of different meaning items" (1971 : 344). This implies that, although the icon offers a characterizing sign, the actual signification that obtains in each case depends on concrete acts of ostension.[13] This leads us to the issue of the deictic orientation in culture.

When Mari, the queen of Basque mythology, is visited in her underground dwelling, there is a set of rules that the visitor must observe: (1) she must be addressed as *hika,* namely, in the direct familiar *hi* (thou) form and not in the respectful *zu* (you);[14] (2) one must leave the cave in the same manner in which one entered it, that is, one never turns one's back to Mari; (3) one never sits down when in Mari's caves (Barandiaran 1972 : 166). As a native Basque, I have always been puzzled by these rules. Addressing the queen of witches with *hika* sounds disrespectful. The image of a visitor backing out of her cave seems ridiculous. Not being allowed to sit down during a visit is odd. Yet mythical injunctions could not be entirely devoid of logic. Formality and performance are the two defining features of ritual. By imposing this stylized behavior, mythology is determining models of ritual form in the traditional culture.

One issue that emerges at once from this set of rules is the presence of a controlling center. Confronted with Mari, the visitor loses freedom of orientation and movement. Mari is the only center of orientation, and only radial movement is allowed in her presence. Were the visitor to turn around, in formal terms a new center would be formed in the peripheral area, and Mari's single irradiating centrality would be violated. A similar rule of facing the center applies when a supernatural being, such as a soul or spirit, appears.

A fundamental model of Basque cultural space is a centered one. Such centered space can be observed in hundreds of cromlechs of the Bronze and Iron ages (Barandiaran 1972), primitive round buildings (Caro Baroja 1943), the organization of territory in strictly circular *sel* arrangements from which in many cases the present baserriak originated (Iturriza y Zabala 1967), the baserri and village organization with a nucleated center (Douglass 1975), the circular systems of exchange still ethnographically describable (Ott 1981), as well as in many aesthetic expressions in dance, funerary stelae, decorative motifs, and modern sculpture. In such a model of centered space, internal organization hinges at the central point, which formally irradiates a peripheral circle.[15] The funerary stelae are the best aesthetic expression of the phenomenon of central irradiation.[16]

This centering of a given orientational field in ritual attitude is analogous to deixis in language. Deixis "indicates the spatio-temporal relations of some presupposed referent in the speech event to speaker, hearer, or other referent" (Silverstein 1976: 25). Reference is achieved not by naming something but by locating it in relation to the source—"to the left of him," "now," "over here," "that one." Thus, a deictic anchor functions as the controlling center of an orientational field. Based on differences regarding object-centeredness or ego-centeredness, the field being closed or open, deictic centering varies significantly from culture to culture (Hill n.d.).

Feet positioning signals culturally relevant centers of deictic orientation. Thus, in former times, people slept with their feet oriented toward the central fire; the burial position in the cemeteries is, even at present in Itziar, with the feet toward the east; likewise, deceased people must be carried inside the church with their feet forward; in one tale a woman cannot turn her back on her house (Azkue 1939–47: 2: 393). Funerary stelae express this orientational command of the disc's center when sometimes the name of the person for which the stela has been erected is written from bottom to top of the socle.[17] The sun, the village church, the altar in the church, the house for the woman in the tale, the disc's center for the stela still function, in folklore and habitual practice, as deictic anchors providing a centered order and commanding ritual orientation. The dynamism associated with such centers (burning, irradiating, splitting, orienting) is achieved by ostensive acts or indexical signs.

Peirce characterized indexicals by the following marks: they have no significant resemblance to their objects; they refer to single units or collections of units; they direct attention to their objects by blind compulsion. Psychologically, the indexical association is by contiguity. Without resembling their objects and by blind compulsion, indices are pointers or indicators of individualized events. The connection between the senses of the observer and the object is a dynamic one.

Candidates for such pointing functions are sharp objects. In this regard it is noteworthy that Basque folklore is replete with such pointed objects as thorns, needles, thistles, teeth, fingernails, goads, scissors, combs, axes, teasels, and so on. One of the names of the mythical Mari is Orratz (Needle). These pointed objects, which are frequently interchangeable in their functions,[18] are responsible for all sorts of magical feats. Pointing a goad at somebody who harbors the evil eye can neutralize it; a thistle on the door protects the house; a thorn or an ax pointing at the sky eliminates the dangers of storms. A cursory look at Basque folklore reveals the pervasively prominent role of these pointers. What makes them such powerful signs in traditional belief? They are, in Peirce's sign categories, indexicals.

Demonstratives are a case of genuine indices. In Basque there is a progression of three in adverb and pronoun demonstratives: *hemen* (here), *hor* (there proximate), *han* (there distant); *hau* (this), *hori* (that proximate), *hura* (that distant). The "secondness" that characterizes Peircean indices[19] is best conveyed by hor and hori.

Deictic aspects of language refer to "lexical items and grammatical forms which can be interpreted only when the sentences in which they occur are understood as being anchored in some social context" (Filmore 1975:38). These formal properties include the place and time as well as the identity of the interlocutors in the communication act. In Mari's mythical situation, the rules imposing an orientational center convey place-deixis in culture.[20] And there is person-deixis as well, indicated by the injunction to use the pronoun *hi* (thou) in mythical and supernatural encounters. Among the personal pronouns the strongly indexical one is the second person singular *hi*, which is gradually being replaced by the more respectful *zu*. *Zu*, like the French *vous*, is grammatically plural. There is an obvious reason for preferring hi to zu in a ritually indexical context: the plurality of zu violates the referential singularity of indexicals, which is, according to Peirce, one of their three distinguishing marks. Even the third person *berori* (himself) treatment used to be employed to address priests; the Spanish respectful *usted* (you) is also a third person. These plural or third-person forms express degrees of deference but miss the direct immediacy of a pointedly singular and deictically frontal relationship.[21] Thus, as the place-deixis commanded by Mari's mythical center is expressed by body position and the reduction of movement to a single direction, likewise person-deixis is indicated by the signalling directness and singularity of hi.

The Reductive Process in Ritual Performance

The negative character of ritual form is a kind of reductionist argument in which all other alternatives are eliminated. A performative equivalent of such reduction of alternatives is given by cultural deixis, as when in Mari's presence the visitor cannot turn around or sit down, reference being reduced to a single point or direction that is ritually controlled. Traditional folk medicine, in which curing is hypothesized as an emptying process, provides a primordial model in which the negative is obtained as a final result of ritual performance. I was given a good illustration of this in Mendata when I was introduced to a woman well known in the area for her powers of extinguishing warts; her formula was: "13, 12, 11, 10, 9, 8, 7, 6, 5, 4, 3, 2, 1, 0: here in this place, warts no more."[22] As recorded by Barandiaran, a decreasing numerical series beginning with the number 9 was a sorcerer's formula for curing ganglia as well.[23] With verbal and gestural acts a reduction of all other alternatives is progressively carried out until the final smashing into zero or nothingness is ritually achieved. *Leertu* (to explode) is a favorite evil invoked in cursing. Reduction to *auts* (ash) is a typical wish against the enemy, which calls for the same nothingness achieved by ritual. A clearly digital version of the formula against warts can be found in Azkue (1939–47:4:243): a cross is made with reeds and applied, alternating both sides, to each wart while saying, "This one, this nothing; this one, this nothing."

As shown by these examples, ritual process, like ritual form, is of a negative character. This formal perspective derives logically from Frege's dismissal of the commonsense view that affirmative and negative judgments are polar opposites.[24] Digital computer systems are based on discrete transitions between binary poles. The act of judging needs the psychical process of a subject, whereas "negation on the other hand is part of a thought, and as such, like the thought itself, it needs no owner, must not be regarded as a content of consciousness." Thus, the act of negating is perhaps "a chimerical construction, formed by a fusion of the act of judging with the negation that I have acknowledged as a possible component of a thought" (Frege 1977:44). This chimerical construction of negating has a parallel in the ritual, which, having reduced a complex state of affairs to a digital frame, combines an act of performance with the formal "passing" from one state to another. Ritual enactment is not concerned with truth per se but with achieving such mechanical transition.

By examining the ritual aspects of the ongoing violence, this chapter argues against a final causal view of the phenomenon. The negative explanation drawn from traditional mythology and curing is a deliberate attempt to remove the positive billiard-ball model of cause and effect. The difference can be illustrated with concrete killings from Itziar. Berazadi's murder is a chilling case; in the usual final-cause terms the rationales for the killing were the need to get money and need to show determination to Madrid and to other potential victims. A different picture emerges if we think of the killing in formal terms. In negative explanation a kind of reductionist argument by which alternatives are eliminated takes place. Killing Berazadi was not going to result in ransom money, yet it was seen by ETA as the only alternative after money from his family and possibilities of negotiation with the government were removed. What in fact precipitated the event was the discovery of the kidnapping by the kidnappers' family members, which eliminated all free movement in the village. When I asked one of the participants in the killing about it, nothing like an act positively aimed at provoking a final result was revealed in his response: "Isn't it terrible? It was the only thing left to do." On the basis of the premises of an armed struggle and by a logic of exclusion, killing was chosen as the only way out. There is obviously a causal interconnection in the series of events leading to the fateful ending. The existence of a closed circuit in which a solution had to be given forced the killing—letting the hostage go free without getting the ransom was tantamount to denying any feedback in the system. Yet what made the chain of causation adopt that concrete outcome was the presence of random events: being discovered by family members and the Madrid government's alleged blocking of the negotiations were unexpected events. In what is typical of a closed causal circuit, the random event provoked a nonrandom response. Rather than the results in randomly caused concrete acts, what must be examined are the systemic presuppositions that inform the given pattern of behavior. Truth and error apply to the ideas upon which particular actions are premised.

Bai Ala Ez (Yes or No)

A salient form of reductionism adopts the *ala* (either/or) scheme. When ritual marking is needed in culture to establish a discontinuity between two distinct states, the negative strategy of exclusion and reduction applies. The ritual form eliminates all other alternatives by reducing the complex and the ambiguous into a bai/ez digital mechanism. Thus, the negative character of ritual form entails logically the on/off of the ala scheme.

The political violence of ETA is also experienced by Basques largely as a mechanism that creates an either/or—an ala frame of disjunction that mutually excludes the political aims of Madrid and Euskadi. A frontal antagonism to Madrid's military domination dispels once and for all any political ambiguity. ETA's violence can be seen as an attempt to sustain such military confrontation between Spain and the Basques, and ETA is still widely regarded as the major threat to Spanish democracy. The art by which ETA has maintained for decades a bellicose situation between Madrid and the Basques without an actual war is equivalent to the finding by students of animal aggression that ritualization of hostile behavior reduces actual combat. In fact, many Basques view ETA's fighting as a very economical way of sustaining war. For this the economy of ritualization is necessary.

A definition of total either/or exclusion between Basque and Spanish political goals was easier for ETA to sustain under Franco's rule than under the new forms of democracy. With the advent of democracy, when even a pro-independence party such as Euskadiko Ezkerra decided to participate in the Spanish political process, I repeatedly heard complaints in Itziar that "before, we knew clearly where to stand, it was Madrid versus Euskadi; now everything is confused." It is the other radical independentist party, Herri Batasuna, that has mostly taken advantage of the Basques' political adherence to the total either/or antagonism during Franco's dictatorship. Herri Batasuna carries over into the political arena ETA's military refusal of any compromise with the constitutional order established by Madrid. A platform that inflexibly demands Basque independence risks everything on one hand—it is reductionism of all political alternatives.

Ritual imposes a new order by reducing an ambiguous state of affairs to the clarity of an either/or. A confrontation of order and disorder is staged. The radical denials of Basque political activism, no matter how terroristic and unruly with respect to the established order, are in a ritual sense attempts to escape the maddening contradictions imposed on the Basques by Madrid's politico-military domination. By transcending time and proclaiming a new political foundation, radical violence aims at ritually founding a new order.

At a political level all ambiguity is removed by a complete separation of Euskadi from Spain. Yet the ritual discontinuity of the violence could be staged at the level of self as well. The very act of joining ETA implies such a radical personal decision of a yes-or-no kind. The self is faced with an all-or-nothing alternative, which does not allow for any middle ground. In such a situation of polar opposites, the meanings of yes and no consist in denying the other alternative. This is well illustrated by the way Marije (a friend of Itziar's politicized youth from a nearby town) made her choice. She was seventeen and very involved in a social youth organization when she was asked by a male friend whether she wanted to join ETA. She recalled for me,

> I said bai instantly. It was automatic, without thinking a minute about it, something immediately required by my whole way of being. Had I said ez to that proposal, it would have meant the

> total end of the course on which I was engaged. There was no middle ground between the bai and the ez. It was all or nothing.

Marije, who as so many others ended up in prison, exemplifies the context of ETA affiliation. For Marije, who was educated by nuns during her adolescent years, yes or no to the proposal of a politically radical performance was equal to yes or no to personal realization.

Framed in the ala disjunction, "Askatasuna ala Hil" (Freedom or Death) is the slogan, common to other insurgent groups as well, that encircles the acronym ETA within the logo on its publications. After a major split within ETA in the early 1970s, one group was known by that acronym, whereas the other group adopted "Iraultza ala Hil" (Revolution or Death)—the ultimate goal could be named differently, but the positioning of the self-transcending attitude in an ala frame was the same. It establishes for personal identity the most radical of all discontinuities. This means literally that taking part in ETA entails the ritual attitude of accepting personal death as an intrinsic component of the political commitment. The implication of death as a ritual sacrifice applies both to one's own self and to the enemy. As in hunting, killing becomes the final reduction of life by which a radically new stage is brought about; by the extinction of the beast or the enemy, the hunter or warrior recreates a new self out of an either/or context of deadly antagonism. The acceptance of the life-or-death attitude does not imply immediate ritual combat; yet the readiness to engage oneself in total risk signals an anticipation of a qualitative change in the self of the neophyte: it is equivalent to a rite of initiation marking a leap from ordinary to self-transcending identity. In traditional cultures the transition from boyhood to manhood requires some puberty rite in which personal endurance is tested to the extreme. When in my conversations with the youths of Itziar who either had joined or attempted to join ETA in the middle seventies I suggested that a similar ritual of manhood was implicit in the commitment to ETA's armed struggle, they agreed. Becoming one of the chosen by militating in ETA implied the profoundest transformation of personal identity—the local villager had changed into a guardian of the country, the adolescent boy into an armed man, the ordinary citizen into a national warrior.

Hordago Politics

A game that expresses the performative reduction of alternatives and serves as a perfect model of ritual mechanism is mus (described in chapter 8). The *hordago* of the mus game presents in particular a performative all-or-nothing reduction formally comparable to the ritual process. The deictic *hor!* (there!) marks in *hordago* a ritual context. An hordago is reminiscent of the defiant behavior of swearing and cursing, both forms of ritual. By having access to the hordago alternative, the steady linear process of point summation is interrupted and substituted for a different game frame. By automatically creating a game point, an hordago is of a different order than a regular one. As with indexical signs, an hordago is unique because it refers to a single point, which decides the entire game. In the manner of a cybernetic device, an hordago proposes a reductive situation in which all alternative points are ruled out. It entails the discontinuity of an on/off or either/or digitalization. The hordago challenge, entrenched in the mentality of the culture, can thus be seen as a mode of ritual performance. The relevance granted in the culture to the ritually deictic mode of acting can be identified by inspecting the hordago complex. Ultimately the hordago solution becomes a cultural premise of efficacy based on the ritualization of performance.

In the above curing formulas, as well as in mus, words play a key role. The magical effects obtained in folklore by means of sharp pointers have their linguistic counterpart in the magical power of ritually employed words (Tambiah 1968). Russell's reduction of naming to ostensive pointing, when he asserted that the egocentric particular "this" is the only genuine name, underscores the relevance of deictic reference in language.[25] Silverstein (1976) has made a distinction between two linguistic mechanisms for achieving reference: one based on the symbolic mode of signs, which presupposes grammar; the other achieved by shifters or referential indexicals following the pragmatic rules of use constituted by the speech event itself. By imposing on language the form and functions of pragmatic performance, speech becomes a prime means of ritualization. In such ritualized context, as illustrated by hordago in mus, words are used not to communicate symbolically but as mere referential indexicals.

The metaphor of hordago is constantly applied to the current Basque political process. Thus, it is said that local authorities have presented an hordago challenge to the central government, or that in the political infighting within a given party someone has flung an hordago. Publishing houses, a theater group, a movie, and an activist group have named themselves "Hordago." Yet the paramount situation of hordago politics is offered by the violent ekintza. The view of ritual performance as not only expressing things but also as doing something is well received in the ekintza mentality. An ekintza resembles ritual performance in that it is a discrete unit of action that signals discontinuity in the ordinary flow of events and attempts to make a transition to a different state. If anything, ETA has been a succession of ekintzak; its real power lies in that sudden ekintzak provoke disruptions in the existing order. ETA's ekintzak are the ritual equivalents to the hordago in mus: they attempt to switch the entire game into a different order by arbitrarily postulating its resolution on the basis of a single point. As in ritual, both the hordago and the ekintza mark a context in which the intrinsic means-ends relationship is abandoned and the entire process reduced to a single point or action. Among Basques in recent years, political violence, more than any other cultural manifestation, has imposed ritual elements upon personal and collective performances.

Consubstantial to the hordago premise is the element of chance. The win-or-lose point plays with the logic of random chance in an ala alternative. This is again a key ritual component that breaks down all the cause-and-effect instrumental links. Thus, for example, the institution of drawing lots to choose innocent victims for ritual sacrifices is found in various societies (Girard 1977:312). Election by chance guarantees the innocence of the victim. It is also a salient feature of ritual violence that it strikes against innocent victims. What from a rational perspective is the very essence of terror is from a ritual perspective but the precondition of the perfect victim.

Deictic versus Theatrical Performance

Deictic control calls for the strong indexical *hor*, magically efficacious pointers in folklore, and hordago type of reduction in performance. *Hor* is the proximate adverb "there"; the distant "there" is *han*. While *hor* is best suited to indicate a face-to-face deictic interaction, the distant *han* marks a different kind of spatial discontinuity. The distance spatially marked by *han* seems to be reproduced at the level of sign in the separatedness required to create a relationship of similarity (*antz*) and at the level of performance in the staging of a theater play (*antzerki*). The adverbial distinction between *hor* and *han* illuminates the difference in cultural contexts between a ritual, where direct participation of the congregation is commanded by the ritual center, and a drama, where theatrical distance allows the audience to merely observe the fictional reality.

Theater has an audience that watches; ritual has a congregation that participates. Those who act in a drama are "only acting," the synonym of drama being "play." Ritual, in contrast, is in earnest and performed quite literally. The separation between performers and audience characteristic of theatrical dramas is not permitted in ritual. In the context of militant nationalism, conversion from participant to mere spectator may amount to "treason." Some ex-ETA activists who abandoned the armed struggle to live as civilians suffer such accusations and receive death threats.

The distinction between theatrical and ritual contexts is a useful one to distinguish the politics of organized parties from the politics of ETA. In Itziar, among ETA sympathizers, one can hear constantly that politicians are simply feigning appearances or staging a play—"it is only theater." The obvious implication is that politics are all a lie, like a theatrical representation, unworthy of being believed. They are merely a propaganda ploy used by people who have nothing to offer and thus hide their real, self-interested intentions. None of the deep suspicion and even contempt provoked by representational politics applies, of course, to the veracity of ETA's martyrdom politics for its follower. ETA members, hidden in the occult underground world, never present a facade but only the factual results of their naked action. If politicians are deceitful actors in a play, ETA practitioners are authentic actors in a ritual enactment. And, accordingly, the participation and personal identification required from the audience in each context is also of a different kind. One can be a spectator at an antzerki and be aware that it is only a symbolic representation, but in the ritual performance a deictic facing is required and, abandoning the distance that turns the drama into a mere representation, one must believe and participate. The purely denotative transmissions of ritual are better suited to point to the truth of things and are preferred in a situation in which political theatrics become intolerable.

The ongoing political violence displays an essentially hordago or indexical character in its deeds. In traditional folklore, axes, thorns, needles, and all sorts of pointed objects were used to direct the magical sign into the thing itself. In one tale, regicide was attempted by placing needles in the hat that the king was going to wear. ETA's individualized killings of forces of the established order are also indexical in that they merely point at the unwanted reality of Spanish military domination—one killing at a time is sufficient to indicate the all-out rejection. There is no intrinsic means-ends relationship in ritual, as when in earlier times the blade of an ax was directed toward the stormy sky in ritual protection. A symbolic emblem of ETA is an ax entwined by a snake; the former ritual functions of the ax have been replaced in the hands of ETA by the new indexical symbolism of the arms. The politics of hordago rules out the politics of theatrical performance. It is action for its own sake that becomes an essential aspect of what is expressed and achieved by this type of performance.

Two Kinds of Energy in Culture: Indar and Ahal

The obtention of the reductive processes in ritual requires not only formal arrangements of sign categories and representational devices, but also collateral energy. In a culturally encoded performance the energetics of ritual process is founded on the basic notions of the culture. In what follows we examine *ahal* and *indar* kinds of energy. *Ahal,* or its contracted form *al,* is conceptualized as potential energy, whereas *indar* is actualized energy. In systemic terms, ahal is concerned with the overall closure/disclosure of the system in question, whereas indar is a flowing energy unconcerned with formal boundaries.

The notion of potency associated with al can be gathered from terms such as *ala* (power), *altsu* (powerful), and *almen* (capability).

Al takes several syntactical modes related to potential moods. The meaning of *indar* is "force." A strong man or animal has a lot of indarra.[26] There is an unbound, external, irradiating quality to indar, whereas ahal type of energy is latent and internal. In relation to deictic centeredness, indar and ahal behave respectively in centrifugal and centripetal ways. An indar center extinguishes itself in outward-oriented irradiation, whereas an ahal center is typically one of attraction and is complete when all internal becoming is ended. The two types of energy thus have different senses of motion and dynamism.

Al type of energy lends itself to bounded and discrete units. These could be formally correlated with spatial and temporal intervals such as *aldi* (instance, time) and *alde* (side, turn), as well as with the notion of *aldikatu* (alternation).[27] The exclusive ala (either/or) disjunction partakes of the logical markedness of al/aldi,[28] and the ala model of polarization we observed in games and ritualized politics is thus formally related to alternation and closure.

The male/female axis applies to the indar/ahal difference at the level of basic cultural structure. Males are expected to show indar. Basque popular games are a celebration of such physical strength. Females are not associated with manifestations of physical force. The al type of energy is better suited to the female domain. In kinship terminology, Bähr finds that there is a high probability that ala and the female sex are related on the basis of *alaba* (daughter) and *alargun* (widow) (1935 : 11). Other terms of female connotation are *alu* (female genitalia) and *altzo, magal* (bosom, lap).

The mechanical dynamics of indar, as when two bodies come into contact by pounding, grinding, hitting, playing, and so on, is subsumed under the notion of *jo*. In a fight two people are *elkar jotzen* (beating each other); making love is *narrua jo* (to pound the skin); falling to the ground is *lurra jo;* knocking on a door is *atea jo;* even a perceptual contact such as a look or a smell is *jo;* playing an instrument is *jo*. The mechanical model of jo hitting applies to competitive sports and betting—the winner in any sport has to *jo ta irabazi* (hit and win). What kind of energy is used in jo interaction? It is obviously the indar type of quantitative energy. Jo as such does not create a fixed pattern, except its own repetition, in order to perpetuate the action. As long as there is indar, the mechanical jo can continue. In Basque culture, jo stands for what Bateson calls "the old syntax" of ball A hitting ball B, where the metaphor has it that A gives energy to B, which responds by using it (1979: 101). An obvious connection is made in the culture between jo and atomization, as expressed in sayings such as *jo ta apurtu* (hit and turn it to bits), *jo ta txikitu* (hit and turn it to small pieces), *jo ta autsi* (hit and turn it to ashes). These common expressions are used in a variety of situations, from threatening a child to cheering a jokolaria. Forceful jo dynamics results thus in smashing objects and reducing them to *auts* (dust), as will be examined in the following section. The jo action is likened as well to fire, which reduces objects to ashes by burning.

Yet, to the positive jo hitting of actualized indar, culture opposes the negative energy of potential ahal. The mechanical pounding of indar substance is counterbalanced by the nonmechanical attraction of ahal's domain of mere possibility. At the level of sign, some sort of iconic container is necessary for the indexical jo acting to take place. As the jo context of hitting presents the cultural hypothesis for mechanical causality, so the ahal type of potential energy advances in culture the understanding of dynamic processes in formally negative terms. In the culture-language ahal and indar operate as interdependent kinds of energy. The ahal potential energy becomes actualized into indar in ritual action and vice versa.

The elementary reading of political violence by Basque nationalists is one of a display of indarra. The greater the violence, the greater the indarra. Nevertheless, if ritual is understood in formal terms as generating discontinuity and thus increasing clarity, ahal takes precedence as the type of energy that establishes qualitative difference. While indarra is a continuous flow, incapable of form or pattern, ahal creates the digital discontinuity of an either/or, inside/outside, closed/open. Hence, ritual energy is best understood as the turning of quantitative indarra into qualitative ahal. The vitality of ritual emanates from the systemic exchange between the two types of interdependent energy. A political mode of action that relies solely on an indar type of efficiency, reduced as it is to one-dimensional mechanical energy, has the weakness that the political or military enemy may win by sheer quantitative means. A one-sided insistence on indarra assumes that the flexibility provided by ahal in closing and opening the energy system is unnecessary, as if it were taken for granted that the circuit should always be closed. Yet in cybernetic terms such systems are always open in the sense that the circuit is energized from the exterior and events within the circuit may influence outside events. Basque sculptors are well aware of this when they attempt to create open fields by breaking apart aesthetically closed spaces. The political or military activist tends to operate in a hermetically closed system, in which all energy is of the quantitative indar type, never one that shifts closure upward and downward in a potential ahal hierarchy. In so doing, the activist is mistakenly identifying inflexibility with strength by assuming the cultural premise that one-dimensional closure and mechanical energy show the greater power.

The Autsak (Ashes) Fallout

A salient expression of the energetic dimension is the reduction of matter into its smallest ultimate constituents, which in folk mentality amounts to *auts* (ash, dust). Ashes perform an important role in connection with ritually centered spaces. Circular irradiation can be illustrated with the sel arrangements, which have at their center a boundary stone named *austarri* (ash stone).[29] Barandiaran (1972:214) makes an explicit link between the sel territorial arrangements with the austarri at their center and the cromlechs in which ashes were located at the center in an urn supposedly for religious purposes. In fact, autsak are placed at the qualitative center of several circular arrangements. Prehistoric fireplaces, primitive circular buildings, the so-called cromlechs, or circles of stones, as well as the sel circular distribution of land all employ at their center the autsak.

Folklore and ethnography abound in ritual uses of auts. Atomistic auts is the ultimate reduction of form, and "formlessness is also credited with powers" (M. Douglas 1966:95) that energize ritual situations. Thus, for example, Christmas-night ash should be kept in a container and scattered on the fields to prevent rust in the potatoes (Azkue 1939–47:2:88). As a remedy against children's pimples, Saint John's herbs are burnt and their ashes carefully kept (ibid.:294). The artful treatment with eggshell auts established a wide reputation for a curer (Barriola 1979:42). Blessed ash is spread on the fields on Holy Saturday; blessed ash is of two kinds: the one received in church on Ash Wednesday, and the other made in the fireplace at home (Azkue 1939–47:1:242). To go to heaven one had to eat, bit by bit, a measure of ash throughout one's life (ibid.:242). Two expressions connecting ashes with unusual skills are "Nire begiak autsak daukaz olangoari igarten" (My eyes have ashes in discerning such things) and "Autsak daukaz onek" (This one has ashes) (ibid.:3:318). One of the ingredients to be included in a *kutun* (amulet) was ash (Barandiaran 1960–62:1:188). Because of its special ritual status, the ash produced by the fireplace was preserved in the *austegia,* or ash chamber, whose facade became a major object of decorative art (Veyrin 1931:115). Archaeologists have found in prehistoric caves ashes spread on ritually significant spots; see, for instance, Freeman and González Echegaray (1981).

Associated with its centrality in ritual form and function, mythical Autsak are "mysterious beings of which men make use to achieve prodigious feats in their enterprises" (Barandiaran 1972:155). They are kept inside a needlecase, and they can be gathered by leaving a needlecase open in a bramble patch—they are thus associated with needles and thorns, natural indices in folklore. Their magical quality shows up as well in their proverbial association with witches. Curative and protective functions are carried out with autsak. In brief, by being situated at the very centers that result from domestic fire, religious incineration, or land distribution—basic occasions for ritualization—autsak are invested with various religious, magical, and protective qualities.

During the winter of 1984 a new ritual development in the politics of ETA took force: on several occasions the body of a political exile assassinated by GAL[30] in southern France was cremated and the remains vented to the air in the presence of family members, political leaders, and ETA sympathizers. The photograph of the mother or wife, holding over her head a crystal box containing her ETA son's or husband's autsak, would make the front page in the newspapers. The commentary of the people in the street stressed the impressive solemnity of the moment. The political ritualization of cremating a body and venting its autsak reproduces the traditional beliefs concerning the ritual uses of ashes. The fallout of the ashes energizes the combat with ritual power.

Ritual Morality

Le sacrifice est immoral, la poésie est immorale.
Bataille, L'experience interieure.

As Rappaport observes, "Morality, like social contract, is implicit in ritual's very structure" (1979:198). As the chapters on Itziar's recent history and local religion made clear, from its inception Basque political violence was substantially nurtured by most morally minded people such as priests, seminarians, and Acción Católica activists. In the Itziar of the late 1950s, when underground resistance to the established order first ignited the Amabirjina's village, the role of heroes was assumed by those rigidly committed to the moralism and liturgy of the Catholic church. During the late 1960s and early 1970s the journal *Gazte* insisted on a new revolutionary ethic, which would supplant the outdated traditional morality. Readiness to give one's own life, as Christ did on the cross, became the mark of true ethical commitment. The new political ritual of life risking and life taking created its own ethical code compared to which ordinary moral rules appeared as contemptible obedience to institutional impositions.

ETA's morality was accepted as valid by the Basque population at large. The massive strikes and demonstrations of solidarity on the occasion of the Burgos trial was the clearest expression of such legitimacy. In the absence of a judicial system constituted with Basque political consent, ETA could be granted legitimacy only by ritual manifestations. When democratic elections for the Basque parliament were held in 1979 the two parties that were viewed as political screens for the two branches of ETA received approximately 20 percent of the entire vote and about 40 percent of the nationalist vote. These percentages are increasing in subsequent elections.

Not only morality but "sanctity itself may emerge out of ritual" (ibid.:197). A sort of martyrology has developed during the 1970s with images, stickers, songs, and anniversaries of those "fallen" invested with the sanctity of sacrificial death. This is consonant with the sacramental aspects of political violence examined in chapter 12. Politics based on ritual sanctity finds inspiration in what Weber called an "ethic of ultimate ends," which disregards rational calculation of means. When both contending parties are guided by this morality of sacred ends, the "reasons" on both sides appear equally valid, and we are led to the distasteful conclusion that "violence operates without reason" (Girard 1977:46). The "religious" nature of this type of conduct springs ultimately from the existence of irreducibly competing ideals that no scientific analysis can arbitrate, for there is an insurmountable logical gulf between factual and ethical truth (Weber 1949). The violence generated by this conflict of ultimate ends can only be expressed and legitimized by ritual action and morality.

The ETA activist displays his truth by "giving up his own life." Any critical assessment on the part of the public of this sacrificial act appears contrived and beside the point—it is simply a verbal commentary on a nonverbal act. As pointed out earlier, this self-transcending act is akin to a ritual of manhood. This crossing into the warrior and hero state by the sacrifice of one's own life if necessary is a ritual act in that only performance can express it: first by the decision to take up arms, then by concrete acts of war, finally by actual martyrdom. A ritual form of action, which combines performance with the formal passage from one state to a subsequent one (from boyhood to manhood, citizen to warrior, life to death) is required to achieve that logically necessary step. No commentary or theory can substitute for this requisite of actual performance, which alone provides a criterion of ritual validity.

Loyola, Sacramental Closure, and Ritual Oversanctification

Certain things fall under the sphere of immutable election. Ignatius of Loyola, Spiritual Exercises

Loyola makes his decision in Basque style and as a soldier. Oteiza, Ejercicios espirituales en un túnel

ETA was constituted on July 31, 1959, the feast of Saint Ignatius of Loyola. The congruence between ETA's birthday and the feast of Saint Ignatius, founder of the Jesuits and prototype of Basque military man, betrays an intimate connection between the militants and the patron saint. In a profound sense, understanding him is understanding ETA men. Recently Ong (1962) and Barthes (1971) have written insightfully about Saint Ignatius; what they write has a special bearing on the arguments of the previous two chapters as they relate to this one.

Ong's perceptive commentary focuses on the puzzling imagery that had extraordinary prominence in Saint Ignatius's mind to the degree of permeating his entire imaginative approach to the invisible world. A passage from his *Spiritual Exercises* synthesizes it: "In meditation of something invisible, as here on sins, the composition will be to see, with the eyes of the imagination, and to consider my soul to be closed up in this corruptible body as in a prison, and the whole composite as in exile among brute animals. I say the whole composite, soul and body" (quoted in Ong 1962:243). The interpretation of Loyola's picture of the soul and the prison-cage of the body thrown together with the brute beasts presents difficulties, and Ong calls for psychological and anthropological analysis. In the two previous chapters we found the primordial relevance of the notion of closure in Basque culture in defining the architectonics of a construction, a body, a psychological or belief system, and we venture to say that the key to Loyola's imagery must partly rely on such cultural unconscious. Ong himself relates the "rudimentary character" of these images to mandala-type constructs such as circular patterns or enclosures such as houses or psychologically "in its way of picturing the self as a kind of enclosure" (ibid. : 225), which is also the case in Basque traditional aesthetics. Moreover, the working together of the interlocking images (soul, prison, beasts) is not surprising in such aesthetics, for the same ambivalent notion of closure defines belief, body constriction or anxiety, and animal domestication. That these imaginative constructs draw upon the Basque culture's unconscious imagery is reflected in another telling instance provided by Saint Ignatius. He had frequent visions of the divinity as an erratic ball of fire, which is exactly the form the flying witch Mari has assumed for Basque farmers. As Ong observes, "The reasons for such facts go deep into the structure of the personal consciousness" (ibid.:254). We are reminded again of Vico's "imaginative universals," the characterizing mark of mythic thought being its power to assert identities; the particulars are directly conceived as universals and not only does the image facilitate the perception of the concept but imagination turns it into the embodiment of reality itself. Knowledge, then, begins directly with the image. The fixing of the partial sensation does not occur by analogy; the *is* is made in such a process by identifying the whole of the flux with the single sensation. The particular and the universal originate simultaneously, not in a relationship of analogy or similarity (Verene 1981). In the argument of this book, sacramental character lies in such imaginative identities of univocal meaning, which are therefore closed to any further interpretation; Loyola's "immutable choice" regarding sacraments is an either/or cast once and for all, thereby precluding any further decision. These ultimate images concern the very constitution of the self. The symbolic closure of Loyola's prison-cage, as well as his championing of the Counter-Reformation's sacramentalism, calls for "spiritual exercises," that is, ritual acting. As ethologists observe, the caged animal reacts by rigidification of behavior and intolerance to ambiguous messages; the economy of ritualization becomes essential in such stress situations.

Ritual discourse, as does any language or social order, produces its own truth or sanctity in terms of that "quality of unquestionableness" imputed by a group to its ultimate postulates. The ritual order rests on these unfalsifiable truths. Political ritual is no exception. Yet although it is a means for reducing the deceits of symbolic codes such as language and law and creating sanctity in response to such threats, ritual is not safe from its own modes of lying and oversanctification.[31] The possibility of idolatry, or absolutization of the relative, is intrinsic to sanctity. Cultural consensus may be sanctified into absolute truth. The ritual achievement of a military goal may be enthroned as the indispensable condition for personal and group existence. The bluffing intrinsic to the mus game illustrates the kind of lying that underlies ritual action. The hordago bet is typically a feedback mechanism for offsetting negative results by deceitfully turning the entire process into a game point. Yet by betting everything in a single all-or-nothing bluff, ritual action is able to suspend ordinary temporal processes.

Saint Ignatius provides a good illustration of ritual oversanctification in his autobiography. Having converted from chivalric fighter into Christ's soldier, on his way to Jerusalem he was angered by a Moorish knight who, although he believed in the Virgin's Immaculate Conception, still thought that she had lost her virginity at the moment of Christ's birth. After they parted company, an infuriated Saint Ignatius was unable to discern God's will as to how he should respond to the knight's disrespect for the Amabirjina (he had paid a special visit to her in Aranzazu as a prelude to his pilgrimage) and opted for the following artifice while approaching a crossroad: if, on its own volition, his mule followed the path of the Moor, Ignatius would pursue and stab him with a dagger; if not, he would leave the Moor alone and continue his pilgrimage to Jerusalem (1947 : 149–49). Saint Ignatius used a crossroad as a ritual device to ascertain God's will. The crossroad reduces the possibilities into an either/or frame, and the function of Saint Ignatius's divinity is to indicate the right alternative.

Saint Ignatius's submission of the right and wrong of assailing the knight to the sign manifested through a mule's choice at a crossroad illustrates the aberrant results of oversanctifying the ritualized form of an either/or. In this frame, truth emerges as an act of mere exclusion, and God's will is the random result of digital marking. Since the choice will be decided by the ritual form itself, which entails a sacralized unquestionable context, no personal responsibility remains. The subject merely puts into operation the decision that has been arrived at on a different plane. In Barthes's words, "As to the ignacian I, at least in the *Exercises*, it has no other value, . . . it is truly the *shifter* ideally described by the linguists" (1971 : 56). Given as he is to a ritually radical either/or frame, the Basque political activist is, like Saint Ignatius, his compatriot and model of complete surrender to an ultimate cause, vulnerable to idolizing the sacred truth of ritual action.

Ritual establishes order in principle. Yet, as Geertz found in Java, in an equivocal cultural setting "the rituals themselves become matters of political conflict" (1973 : 167) and "the religious form which must be employed acts not with but against the grain of social equilibrium" (ibid.: 168). Symbolic consensus and social consensus are of different order (Fernandez 1965). The very same ritual that achieves in the culture logico-meaningful integration may fail to produce in the society functional integration. The revolt that found extensive support when directed against Franco's dictatorship may increasingly appear as a ritual oddity in the context of

Spain's present democracy, denying the very nature of political discourse. Ritual political behavior, at one time sacralized as heroic struggle, generates its own momentum and obstinately resists adaptation to new forms of political ritualization. Although culturally interrelated within a society, ritual structure and political structure are not mirror images of each other, but rather remain independent domains of meaning and function. The ritual thermostat can be equilibrated at a temperature that is so high that it suffocates the entire political environment.

Ritual and Time: The Power to Deny and Change

Freud spoke of dreams as the royal road to the unconscious. This chapter suggests that in the case of the Basques presently involved in political violence such ritual action is the most eloquent manifestation of their personal and collective unconscious; the paradigmatic forms of such ritualized behavior can be drawn from traditional mythology and folklore.

Nourishment by the negative is a salient manifestation of such mythical identity. Recognition of the political unconscious by the collective representation is expressed in a negative formula. Like art, dream, or myth, the political ritual of life giving and life taking lies also in between primary and secondary processes and has a special relationship to negation. On several occasions the comparison with Basque modern art as a parallel expression of cultural semantics has been suggested, for it also hinges on formally negative notions such as void or limit. In conversations with ETA activists the centrality of personal creativity through risk taking, as if in a gambling game or artful performance, becomes apparent. It is inevitable that under such extreme conditions the underground activist is involved with his total being, the conscious mind playing only a part. Where the negative obtains there is a crucial manifestation of cultural creativity. Unable to any longer endure decades of cultural and political repression, Basque youth violently repudiated Spanish dictatorship during the 1960s and 1970s. To do so they had to shed the immobility imposed by fear and an overly rigid morality; the impotence of the merely conscious mind had to be transcended in order for the "total individual" to rebel. Political action could only be of a ritual kind when all other avenues were harshly suppressed. In the late 1970s the Spanish political system changed, permitting legalized parties and democratic elections. Parliamentary politics replaced a military dictatorship. ETA's politico-military rebellion could no longer have the same effect when directed against the new system. Yet, after having experienced for twenty-five years a political education in which ritual performance and martyrdom were essential for patriotic self-defense, a change in attitudes is tantamount to an epistemological change affecting the very premises on which political order and personal identity are founded. This change from a ritual to a parliamentary approach to politics is analogous to a change from sacramental to metaphoric predication.

It is not the content of Basque political violence per se that is so abnormal; rather it is the wider Spanish and European context in which the violence is situated that makes it appear so. The power to deny is thus confronted with the need to adapt to new political realities. The ritual intrinsic to any social-political contract must recreate its forms to give birth to a new order. Despite total self-involvement, the activist's performance is very much guided by ulterior, conscious purpose. The askatasuna of the Basque Country remains the single overpowering goal. Integrity of motivation does not free a course of action from its paradoxical consequences. Purposive systems without self-corrective mechanisms turn into runaway breakdown. The consideration of time is essential to these corrective changes. In Mari's mythical domain, ritualization of form was concerned with space and pronominal relationships, not with time. Contrary to myth, ritual action requires time as well. Yet the negative character of ritual form has a peculiar relation to time: the ritual "not" on the one hand is timeless and lies outside of history, but it also determines the moment of ritual change in history.[32] The hordago switch, which we took to be a paradigm of the ritual reductionist "not," is also timeless; yet, if accepted, it determines the changes in the rules of the game. The ritual mechanism employed by Basque violence demonstrates that, even regarding the very premises of personal identity and political rule, the power to deny is also the power to change.

Conclusion

Now, if merely to be present at a murder fastens on a man the character of an accomplice; if barely to be a spectator involves us in one common guilt with the perpetrator: it follows, of necessity, that, in these murders of the amphitheatre, the hand which inflicts the fatal blow is not more imbrued in blood than his who passively looks on; neither can he be clear of blood who has countenanced its shedding; nor that man seem other than a participator in murder who gives his applause to the murderer and calls for prizes on his behalf.
Lactantius

This book began in Itziar's street when on a Saturday morning in the summer of 1975 I was surrounded by a group of horrified women who had just witnessed the death of Carlos. I could have tried to answer the shock and puzzlement of their "But how can that be?" along the lines of chapter 11 by telling them a tale of their generation in which Saint Michael beheads a terrible dragon. Or, confronted with that primal question, I could have told them that I was going to substitute a new tale for the old one of beasts and archangels; that is, that this book is my answer. I would address their profound concern by proposing, in keeping with the arguments developed herein, that a belief, a song, a dream, a model of heroism, a ritual, an absence of guilt, a history of polarization, and a dance all incorporate the response. Still, although definitely pointing at "the thing" itself, their puzzlement could never be resolved by the explanations offered through such cultural models and metaphors.

Like Rosaldo's "why?" to the headhunters, the "But how can that be?" of Itziar's women is ultimately the recognition of an irresolvable question. One can take as models of writing Evans-Pritchard's (1963) analysis of Shilluk regicide or Dostoevsky's literary treatment of Raskolnikov or Wittgenstein's objections to Frazer and talk about the metaphors of ritualized killing—manhood, terror, self-consciousness, mystical order, sacrifice. The thing itself, the sacramental literalness of the sacrificial act, cries out against any final interpretation. Killing for political, military, juridical, or aesthetic reasons is now, as in ancient barbarous times, the order of the day. Any attempt at finding a "latent meaning" behind the horrible evidence of the act can only be a cowardly retreat, a deceptive alteration of the unspeakable text itself. Still, pointing at the inexpressible in violence does not imply that we take it as an ineffable reality about which we can say or do nothing. Although this book may appear as an attempt to finesse moral judgment by disassembling the violence into Culture and History, that is not my intention. By insisting on cultural forms and representations and by stripping the violence down to its all-too-human faces, this ethnography of Itziar is an attempt to confront the reader with the stark "normalcy" of ritual killing once it is understood in its own terms.

Lactantius's statement on the killings of Christians as sport and entertainment in the Roman amphitheater resonates the arguments of this book concerning the tension between metaphor and sacrament, theatrical drama and ritual sacrifice, the audience that merely observes and the congregation that participates in the violence. The political pathos experienced by most Basques springs precisely from the awareness of being "accomplices" in the violence, the results of which are abhorrent to us. Yet I am afraid that after reading these pages some critics will be quick to accuse me of being just such a passive accomplice. They may wish that I had distanced myself altogether from such moral dilemma. To this I must reply that the reality I am compelled to live in Itziar, and which I want to convey in this ethnography, precludes me from the kind of distancing that would exempt me from the political predicament of my co-villagers. I must share the responsibility for our past actions, the tension of our present dilemmas, and the uncertainty of our future.

Epilogue

Dancing in an Empty Building: The History of a Discotheque

Apur dezagun katea.	Let us break the chain.
Kanta dezagun batea.	Let us together sing.
Hau da fandango.	This is fandango.
Biba Berango.	Long live Berango.[1]
	Aresti, *Harri Eta Herri*

Throughout this work we have examined cultural forms as both metaphors and models with which to analyze Basque political violence in general and particularly its local expression in the village of Itziar. There is a sense, however, in which the argument may be condensed and reduced to a consideration of the history, present circumstances, and future prospects of a single building in the village nucleus of Itziar. Reference is to a discotheque called Mandiope currently housed in a structure built in 1966 by the baserri cooperativists described in chapter 7.

The building, erected with the members' own hands, was the common stable in which four baserriak pooled their livestock. For years the building was the most forceful expression of the innovation and spirit of adventure implicit in farmers' cooperativism in Itziar. A few progressives had dared to break with the centuries-old basic institutional structure of the self-sufficient baserria and merge their individual holdings into a larger cooperative structure with the lofty intention of achieving a better economic return while pursuing a more integrated social life. It was hailed as an exemplary case of successful baserri cooperativism and visited by many farmers from thoughout the province seeking inspiration. Yet the experiment of the communal stable ended when the industrial park of Itziar offered to buy out its lands. After several years of effort the economic returns had been negligible, and in Itziar, as elsewhere in rural Basque society, industry was patently triumphant over baserri agriculture. The cooperative stable stood empty as witness to this humiliation.

The empty edifice soon prompted a second cooperative initiative. By the early 1970s implementation of the ikastolak became the major vehicle for cultural and nationalist vindication in Euskadi. In many towns they were opened privately without any official aid, and Itziar was no exception. In order to ease the financial burden of the private ikastola it was decided to turn the deserted building into a Sunday-evening dance hall run by volunteers. The villagers of Oikia, Arrua Goi, Mendaro, and Itziar agreed to take on the project and offered voluntary labor to remodel the stable. They named it Mandiope, which means "under the attic." Each Sunday volunteers from one of the towns staffed the facility. Still, given expenses such as paying for the music and the initial construction costs, the profits were scanty. After three years of cooperative effort, the four partners decided to close Mandiope.

The building was again empty and available for a new adventure. This third time, in the autumn of 1979, the youth of Itziar decided that Mandiope could work if the cost of hiring bands was eliminated by turning it into a discotheque. The profits were to go into cultural and recreational assistance for Itziar's youth. Furthermore, a few jobs would be created for unemployed people in the community. Once again the youth volunteered labor, initiative, and even personal loans. There was much enthusiasm, and the cooperative stable was outfitted with dancing platforms set at different levels and made of marble donated by Altuna, the owner of a local quarry. The painter Bixente Ameztoy, a long-time friend of Itziar's youth, provided innovative decoration in blues, greens, and yellows. The rock group Orquesta Mondragón, one of the most popular bands in all of Spain, offered free publicity that alluded to Mandiope's origin as a stable. They urged their listeners to come to Mandiope to dance "with horses, cows, pigs, chickens." The presence of Txitxarro, a privately operated, very large, and popular discotheque in Itziar that was well attended by the youth from throughout the region, seemed to guarantee the success of Mandiope. Txitxarro played music drawn from across the broad spectrum of popular rock. By this time there was considerable ambivalence toward it among at least a sector of Basque nationalist youth. On the one hand, the new music seemed to crowd out traditional Basque forms and threaten the very survival of the latter. On the other, while certain Basque groups were performing modern rock music as well, they did not enjoy the same access to the mass media as did trendier groups adulated internationally by youth around the world. Mandiope was to redress the balance at least somewhat, playing recordings of Basque rock bands and dedicating an occasional evening to the live performance of Basque rock and folk musicians alike. As with the agricultural cooperative, there seemed to be tacit recognition that some semblance of Basque traditional cultural forms could only be salvaged if they were modified. The difficulty, indeed, the impossibility of the task was soon apparent when, despite the initial enthusiasm of the organizers, Mandiope was largely ignored by the region's youth.

A contest sponsored by Mandiope called Euskal-Musika 80, in which thirty-five Basque rock and folk groups and individual performers participated, was a disconcerting failure. Held on Saturday nights, publicized widely, and showcasing the music of four or five performers weekly, the contest attracted only a few dozen spectators. Meanwhile, if the disc jockey played Basque rock music on other nights of the week he was likely to be booed. Faced with economic disaster, the organizers began to sponsor concerts in other towns for commercial gain, and Mandiope itself began to play popular rock exclusively, irrespective of its origin.

Ironically, the latter measure killed the intent but saved the business. Mandiope began to prosper and in the process became infamous throughout the region as a center of drug distribution and consumption. Itziar's older generations were deeply perturbed by these developments. It seemed that an enterprise designed to preserve Basque traditions had become a frontal assault upon them. To close the circle of irony, in the summer of 1983 the police arrested a group of Itziar youth accused of ETA involvement. It seems that among their other plans they intended to bomb Mandiope.

Mandiope, then, has served as a kind of echo chamber resonating the logic and contradictions, the triumphs and tragedies of Itziar caught on the horns of twentieth-century social, economic, and political dilemmas. Agricultural cooperativism transformed into industry; ikastola volunteerism transmogrified into disco dancing. The effort to revitalize native music resulted in reinforcement of international popular rock. ETA's selfless heroic demands and warrior ethos resulted in the laxity of an egocentric drug culture. All are examples of cultural initiatives defeating their own purposes and becoming almost their opposites. Yet Mandiope's failures were also resounding victories. Thus, the initial cooperative movement has left the legacy of a thriving livestock feed and consumer's cooperative. The ikastola survived and is now a government-sponsored school. Mandiope the discotheque finally became fashionable and now turns a profit. Mandiope currently awaits its own corrective to become obsolete.

The originators and current owners of Mandiope's building, who in the early sixties combined cooperative ideals with strict moralism, could never have imagined that their edifice would come to such a dubious end. Theirs was the generation that experienced the religious conversion that crystallized in promises such as never indulging in social dancing because of its moral dangers. Now their building has turned into a disco, rumored to be a focus of immorality and drug culture, in which staid social dancing has been eschewed as old fashioned in favor of the frenetic and sexually explicit newer forms. As original builders and owners of the structure they, too, felt implicated in Mandiope's decadence and corruption.

I had to find the contexts of meaning of political violence in Itziar, and at moments Mandiope's dancing became the most revelatory metaphor. When asked about the "meaning" of her dance, Isadora Duncan answered: "If I could tell you what it meant, there would be no point in dancing it." This is the sort of thing one has to keep secret, because "it is something one *cannot* tell" (Bateson 1972:36; his emphasis). Like a sacramental kind of dance, political violence can also be experienced at times as the interface between the conscious and the unconscious, and no amount of words can ever say what it *is*.

On May 3, 1985, three bombs exploded in Mandiope. A few minutes earlier a voice that identified itself as ETA military warned of the explosions. The media pointed out alleged charges of drug trafficking by Mandiope, which were dismissed as unfounded by

Itziar's youth. Actively supported by a section of the youth and repudiated by another segment as a frivolous center of perversion, Mandiope was once again resonating the moral dilemmas within the village.

I drafted a communiqué for the media, which was approved by Mandiope's members. It stated that the youth of Itziar were supporters of Herri Batasuna and Euskadiko Ezkerra and that the village had a tradition of sympathizing with ETA. Therefore, we were dismayed and ashamed that ETA would bomb our discotheque, the only one in the area conceived by young people and operated for social benefits. We were not going to bow to ETA. Besides opening Mandiope to the public the day of the bombing, we defied ETA to produce any proof that there was drug trafficking on the premises. Unexpectedly, Herri Batasuna representatives from Deba came out with a communiqué approving of ETA's action. This outraged Itziar's youth, including those of Herri Batasuna, and prompted a response from us challenging our Deba critics to a public debate. They ignored the challenge. Thanks to Mandiope, ETA was being contested in Itziar, one of its sanctuaries.

An Anniversary and a Town Meeting

Iñaki was killed by a civil guard in Orio on June 13, 1980. Six years later, on the anniversary of his death and within a week of cultural events in his honor, I was asked to give a talk in Itziar on the village's recent political history. No other forum could have been more challenging to me, no other occasion more compelling.

I began by recalling Urkola's return to Itziar in 1968 to explain to his ex-parishioners why he was abandoning the priesthood and I drew a parallel with the changing modes of commitment to the ongoing political struggle. With sociological and theological arguments, Urkola discussed various aspects and historical forms of the priesthood. He said that the priestly office did not derive from personal commitment to a sacramental state, but rather from the community of believers. He no longer agreed with its present Catholic conventions. In leaving the priesthood, Urkola was challenging, in theory as well as in practice, the immutability of a sacramental form such as the Catholic priesthood. I told my audience that certain kinds of political commitment are also of a sacramental nature and that our internal disagreements regarding the future course of Basque politics should cause us to question the changeless model of heroism. A political priesthood, too, can be lived in various manners; the challenge was to understand why some pursue it as a Catholic sacrament while for others it is nothing but myth and theatrics. The very act of reflecting upon and questioning Urkola's former priesthood was at the time something unprecedented in Itziar; that we were now discussing Itziar's political violence by trying to put Iñaki's calling into perspective I found equally revelatory.

Any meditation on heroism and tragedy in Itziar's recent history inevitably has to reflect on the story that typifies it—the milk brothers Carlos and Martin who unwittingly became agents of each other's fate. It was Martin who upon Carlos's death could view the life pattern of his rival as a whole. The tragedy of Carlos was also Martin's. By publicly tracing the roots of their forced enmity and examining its logic we were restoring the intimate relationship of Carlos and Martin. That ceremony of reconciliation on the anniversary of Iñaki's death was confronting us with the paradox Martin faced when he learned that Carlos had been killed by ETA. It was within the boundaries of a single community, our own, that the opposing figures of the hero and the traitor emerged. Indeed, it was the very intimacy of the local context that gave them their epic proportions—the irony of a shared mother and their ultimate reconciliation in eternal repose in the village cemetery. The ethics of unswerving commitment advanced by Martin and carried out to their ultimate consequences by Iñaki posed a challenge for us all.

My audience understood the argument at once. A long and friendly discussion followed in which differing viewpoints were offered by people who variously supported or criticized the ongoing violence. The phenomenon did not present for us a problem of "understanding"; we were faced with a moral dilemma but not an enigma. Even members of the same family took different stances on the violence, and we were all aware that the desired resolution of the conflict did not depend primarily on verbal explanations. Still, only a few years earlier such public discussion would have been unthinkable, almost sacrilegious. It seemed that, by being actors and supporters of the violence, we had all gone through a rite of passage and that our present act of reflection was casting in a new light our individual renewed commitment or detachment.

It was inevitable that we should discuss a recent political development in ETA. In accord with the government's "measures of social reinsertion," since 1982 there have been ETA members who decided to abandon the armed organization, trading amnesty for a formal refutation of the armed struggle. For those opposed to the change, this amounts to "repentance." An ETA activist who decides to leave the armed struggle is not likely to renounce his past, much less repent. Yet for those committed to the violent struggle the change amounts to the profoundest transformation a person can make, the transformation of a hero into a traitor. In a Catholic society, confession is the paramount context for repentance. That a change of political attitudes should be viewed in such terms gives an indication of the extent to which it is perceived as sacramental. Under torture the activist is likely to confess, yet never repent. From the viewpoint of the activist stubbornly holding to uncompromising ideals and ready to undergo any torment for the cause, the prospect of the ex-activist leaving the organization and publicly acknowledging a change of attitude is intolerable. In the end the real dilemma confronting the activist is not one of betrayal of anybody but rather of the kind of politics he wishes to pursue. In a sacramental conception of politics the self must remain unswerving in the defense and preservation of the community's rights and values. When politics is conceived as the domain of relative values and negotiable alternatives, change of options and attitudes while exploring new styles of being a person signals adaptability. For the latter conception, flexibility is the essence in a successful system; for the former, flexibility is tantamount to treason. It amounts to concession and defeat and trivializes the torture and death endured by the martyrs to ETA's cause. Indeed, ETA hardliners have threatened to kill the "repentants," and did so in one instance. Thus, the anniversary of Iñaki's death was inviting us to reflect on the opposing models of heroism being acted out in Basque politics. There is Promethean Man, who heroically denies ambiguity, compromise, and change; there is Protean Man, vacillating and uncommitted, whose heroism admits doubt and experimentation (Peacock 1975). In Itziar's local politics one can find heroes of both kinds, although it is the unyielding figure that is the most intriguing and disturbing.

With no pretensions of resolving the conflict, while honoring Iñaki's memory that night we were exorcizing ourselves of the demons that can turn Itziar once again into a battlefield. Some were holding to the image in which the hero is unchanging if he is to be true to himself; others preferred the heroism of men like Urkola, who are brave enough to change their preconceptions and then act upon their new convictions. This exercise in critical reflection was uniquely rewarding to me, for it meant that my writing had reached the audience I always thought I should address before the academic or general public. I have always conceived this work as located within the historical narrative of the living generations of Itziar sketched in part 1. As such, it is an addition to the chronicles that "Atxurra" and his friends wrote in *Argia* in the 1920s and 1930s. It imitates the work of past and present bertsolariak such as Zubeltzu and Uztapide. It attempts to bring new food for critical thought as did the social-political movement of Herri Gaztedi in Itziar. It is closely linked to Urkola's efforts at "de-sacramentalization" throughout the 1960s. It continues Itziar's young ETA activists' ideal search for askatasuna at levels of experience that go beyond the political-military sphere. The same kind of cultural necessity that forced Maria from Errementeri to relate her own experiences with mythology and sorcery and forces ETA members to embrace the hardships and paradoxes of political violence has compelled me to write this ethnography. In this sense "doing anthropology" is like "doing myth" and "doing politics" (Drummond 1981:647). The anthropologist's task is to reveal and recreate the collective representations and the partly unconscious ritual performances the group is engaged in. Thus, a successful ethnography must itself become a distancing device by pointing out the "otherness" of what people experience, the ethnographer included, within the boundaries of their own cultural constructions. By performing such interpretation the anthropologist is inviting his culture to understand and ultimately question the role of the native. No matter how elementary and indecisive my presentation and our discussion were, they forced us to examine our collective dreams and sacraments. By provoking such dialogue between irreconcilable worldviews I felt I was sharing with my Itziar neighbors and friends anthropology's subversive character of being "a tragic discipline in that it goes far to isolate and alienate its practitioners from full conviction in their own mode of thinking and doing" (Beidelman 1986: 214). That night we were all anthropologists in Itziar.

It was most noticeable, however, that a group of youths was missing from our discussion. This is the group that will never question Iñaki's legacy since they view the Basque Country as dominated militarily by a foreign state and Iñaki as the avenging angel. For them, honoring his memory is not a matter of mere talk and reflection but a matter of battlefield action. Herein lies the dilemma that casts its long shadow over the future of Itziar and the Basque Country.

Notes

PROLOGUE

1. Itziar is fifty-three kilometers away from the provincial capital San Sebastián and sixty from Bilbao and Vitoria. It belongs to the municipality of Deba, which has a population of over 5,000. Leaving aside the 4,000 inhabitants of the urban center of Deba itself, we will be dealing here with the approximately 1,100 people of Deba's rural area, which is mainly that of Itziar and the closely related hamlet of Lastur. Itziar's population, besides its center where the church is located, is scattered in *bailarak* (neighborhoods), which include: Itxaspe, Egia, Arriola, Mardari, and Elorriaga. This total population of 1,089 was distributed as follows in the summer of 1980: Itziar's center, 310; Itziar's bailara, 488; Lastur, 291. The longest distances between the bailarak range from six to ten kilometers. Ecclesiastically this entire area pertains to Itziar; that is, its residents are buried there.

PART I: HISTORICAL REPRESENTATIONS

1. History as Myth, Legend, and Devotion

1. For a description and analysis of Ekain's materials, see Altuna and Apellaniz, 1978.
2. These skulls were decisive for archaeologists in establishing the hypothesis that Basques originated in the present Basque Country through an autochthonous evolution. Altuna has expounded the thesis: "The deposit of Urtiaga is important among other things because in it appeared a series of skulls that illustrate to us the origin of the Basque race. The oldest of them belongs to the end of the Upper Paleolithic and shows great similarity with the Cro-Magnon man, even

if it has initiated already its evolution toward a type of present-day Basque. The Azilian skulls of the same deposit are intermediate between the Cro-Magnon type and the Basque type. Finally, the skulls of the Bronze period of the mountainous part of the country are mostly of the Basque race. This one, therefore, was not formed outside the country, coming subsequently to settle down in it, but originated right here, in the western Pyrenees, through an autochthonous evolution starting from the Cro-Magnon man" (1975:64; my translation). The descriptions of the various digs by Barandiaran and Aranzadi throughout the years 1928–1936 can be found in Barandiaran (1972: 12:169–324).

3. Maria from Errementeri first talked to me about José Miguel de Barandiaran. They were from the same town of Ataun, and she spoke highly of his unusual intelligence. Still productive at ninety-seven, he is a priest who for a period of over seventy years has pursued single-minded dedication to Basque archaeology, prehistory, and folklore. He is respected with almost reverence by scholars and lay people alike. What links Barandiaran's biography to Itziar are the yearly visits he made to the cave of Urtiaga between 1928 and 1936 and then again in the 1950s. In the company of Aranzadi, he made important archaeological finds in Urtiaga; a series of four skulls at different layers of the deposit, from the Upper Paleolithic to the Bronze period, prompted the thesis of Basque autochthonous evolution. In July of 1936 the outbreak of the Spanish civil war caught him digging in Urtiaga (Barandiaran Irizar 1976:164).

   When I first returned from Princeton to the Basque Country to conduct fieldwork for my doctorate, I felt privileged to pay Barandiaran a visit. I told him of my misgivings about working with my own people; at least I was not going to be in my own province, for I had decided to go to Guernica. To my surprise he objected not to my studying my own culture but to my not doing it in my own village of Itziar. "An ethnography of Itziar would reveal for you most interesting results," he insisted several times. After that summer I decided to follow his advice and go home to Itziar. In this manner, in the splendid company of Maria's stories, the skulls of Urtiaga, and the horses of Ekain, I am pleased to bring him back to Itziar, this time not for an archaeological dig or to record verbatim a tale, but to show him the continuation through this ethnography of the myth-making process within the culture.

4. One night, while returning home from an open-air dance, he swears that several times he heard leaves rustling and chains engulfing him as in an avalanche. His brothers, coming from another direction at the

same time, heard him scream, terrified by the witchcraft, and found him deathly pale.

5. See chapter 11 note 13 for more on this topic.
6. A list of some of the most famous linguists includes Humboldt, Linschmann, and Bouda from Germany; Prince Bonaparte, Vinson, Gavel, and Lafon from France; Van Eys and Uhlenbeck from Holland; Schuchardt from Austria; Dodgson from England; Fita, Cejador, Tovar, and Menéndez Pidal from Spain. We could quote the renowned Spanish humanist Menéndez Pidal as an example of the importance granted by these scholars to Euskera: "There is no historical document deserving more veneration than this living document, this language preserved on this territory, since an incalculated period; who knows whether it is earlier than the present climatic and geological period. In her multisecular sediments, she offers us precious remains to illustrate the most obscure problems of our history. You have the fortune that your country is the depository of the most venerable relic of Hispanic antiquity. Others will have a more artistic value, they will be more admired universally and widely sought after, but there is no other one which has the importance of this language, without a profound study of which never will be fully revealed the foundations and the primitive courses of the peninsular civilization, nor will this one be essentially understood" (in Euskaltzaindia 1978:153–54).
7. The connection of Itziar to the Kingdom of Navarre was established through the monastery of Roncesvalles, to whose jurisdiction the village belonged. Two of the most authoritative historians of Guipúzcoa have stressed the historical antiquity and significance of Itziar. Carmelo de Echegaray wrote of the "venerated Sanctuary of Itziar, whose first origin gets lost in the nearly impenetrable obscurity of the Early Middle Ages." Likewise, Gorosabel states: "The existence of Itziar dates from the most ancient and immemorial times. In fact, whether it be taken for the Tricio Tubolico of the time of the Romans, as I believe it is, or whether this conviction is rejected, it cannot be denied that Itziar merits to figure among one of the first villages of Guipúzcoa" (1972:229).
8. Historians confirm that the overriding aim of such founding privileges was socio-political control (García de Cortázar 1973:200; Fernández de Pinedo 1974:13). The 1294 proclamation of villa status did not solve local problems. The seaport, an important center for the export of the wool coming from Castile and a maritime base, was situated in Deba at the mouth of the estuary of the same name. It was five kilometers from Itziar's center. Deba's populace found this distance excessive. A dispute arose, which was ended when King Alfonso XI

granted another founding privilege to Deba in 1342. Ecclesiastically, Itziar's Marian shrine preserved its autonomy and its prominence as the major pilgrimage center in the area. However, administratively it had become a quarter of the villa of Deba.

9. Similar legends are common elsewhere. Carvings of the Virgin Mother are, in fact, numerous in the Basque region. See Lizarralde (1926).
10. The present church has a single nave with a rectangular plan of 29.80 by 15.32 meters and a transept vault. The ribs are formed by four pairs of half columns leaning against the lateral walls and are divided into three sections. The sanctuary contains in its main apse an altarpiece by the sculptor Araoz, believed to have been executed during the early sixteenth century. The statuary of the altarpiece depicts the life of the Virgin Mary in six separate panels.
11. The ship hanging from the ceiling in the middle of the church of Itziar stands for this occupation particularly favored by the Amabirjina. It has been an ancient tradition for fishermen to say the rosary and the *salve* when their boat passed along the coast by Itziar. When the church was spotted from the sea, artillery salutes were given in her honor. Subsidies and alms offered by the faithful have supported her sanctuary, the *cofradías* being the main context for such collections in the past. Furthermore, famous seamen have offered large amounts of money for the cult of the Virgin. As an example, Elcano, who completed Magellan's first circumnavigation of the world, left in his will forty of his fifty-two golden ducats to the Amabirjina of Itziar. In recent times the rowing team from Orio dedicated to her its victory flag won in the national championships.
12. Nowadays the yearly village fiestas in honor of the Virgin are still called *cofradías*.
13. Arpal writes: "Whether they are *anteiglesias* [literally, "porch of a church," referring to the parish church of some Vizcayan towns] 'lands' and universities [i.e., a corporation or community], or villas, the ecclesiastic space appears as a central meeting point for arrangement of communal life" (1979:73–74). He distinguishes three ecclesiastic models of social organization around the sacred space, according to whether we are dealing with a church, monastery, or convent. Itziar in its earliest historical period, the tenth and eleventh centuries, was part of the monastery of Roncesvalles. Since the time it became a center of pilgrimage and yearly *cofradías* in the thirteenth century, Itziar has been a typical parish-church community, described by Arpal in these terms: "*The churches,* understood as parishes, depend directly on episcopal jurisdiction and have the villa as their patron. As a group, a structure of interaction, the church can be defined as the parish-

ioners. As a formal group there is a typical access, baptism, but also a periodical checking of the membership to the parish. [Compliance with] the Easter duty that was—and still is—annually registered in an enrollment [was the] legitimation of the condition of parishioner" (1979:78).

14. The sepulturia has been studied among others by Douglass (1969).
15. In the direction toward Lastur there are three of these *Amabirjina bistak* at approximately one, two, and seven kilometers from the sanctuary, signaled with a cross. Toward Zumaia and Deba there are also two *bistak* at about three kilometers from the sanctuary. When passing through these spots, people used to say the *salve*.
16. As recently as the early fifties, a girl at the age of puberty living in a baserri of Itziar was visited by the soul of her uncle, a *pelota* (handball) player who had died in America. In typical fashion, the repentant soul asked for three masses of atonement, and while attending them the handkerchief of the girl burned in her own hands. "Miracle!" was the congregation's immediate reaction. The official skeptic on these occasions, the village doctor, had to face the burden of his unbelief: "Do you see it?" the parish priest assailed him menacingly with the burned handkerchief, irrefutable proof of divine intervention. The Catholic church's ambivalence on such occasions is well known. The burnt handkerchief was shown to people on the street as a supernatural sign aimed at arousing their belief, but at the same time the priests cautioned, "These things should not be believed too much."
17. See chapter 12 on the historical significance of the Mendigoizaleak.
18. The chroniclers of Itziar writing in *Argia* during the 1920s and 1930s make constant use of *ama* extended rhetorically to other domains. See chapter 12.
19. The *zortziko* is a 5/8 rhythm considered typically Basque.

2. History as War

1. See García Venero (1945) for a discussion of the fueros in Spain.
2. Carr (1966), Garmendia (1976, 1984), and Barahona Arévalo (1979) study the ideological basis of Carlism.
3. For a discussion of the nationalist movement during Arana's period, see Beltza (1976), Solozábal (1975), Larronde (1972), Azurmendi (1979), Elorza (1978), Corcuera Atienza (1979), and Heiberg (1981).
4. The two best known are *La Revista Internacional de Estudios Vascos* (1907) and *Eusko-Folklore* (1921).
5. This was September 1936. The war had begun on July 18, 1936.

6. These conversations were taped in the summer of 1975; he died the following year of a heart attack. An unusually intelligent and graceful man, his memory is precious to me.
7. Picasso's renowned painting *Guernica* was based on this act of war carried out by Hitler's aviation under orders from Franco's quarters.

3. History as Heroism

1. "Interior" refers to the underground members operating inside Spain and is used to differentiate them from those in France and abroad.
2. For information on the origins of ETA, see Clark (1984).
3. The burruka as a cultural model of performance is studied in chapter 8.
4. This custom of "accompanying the girl" consisted of escorting her home at night after the Sunday *romeria* (open-air dance); it was also the occasion for all sorts of sexual advances.
5. For a discussion of the cooperative movement in Itziar, see chapter 7.
6. The first Holy Communion took place at the age of seven; the Big Communion, which was a repetition of that ceremony, used to occur at the age of twelve.
7. The younger generation, by two or three years, who tried unsuccessfully to get into ETA.
8. This term is used by Basque nationalists to negatively categorize people who have taken positions that are deemed to favor Spanish interests to the detriment of the Basques.
9. "Ezkerra" was a well-known leader of the ETA arrested in the summer of 1975; he was released in the spring of 1977.
10. The *joko* model of performance is analyzed in chapter 8.
11. "Ondarru" was an ETA member of the nearby town of Ondarroa who was killed by civil guards in 1980.
12. Berazadi's case is narrated in chapter 4.

4. History as Tragedy

1. Written in 1934 by the Lekuona brothers.
2. For more cases of chivatos, see Heiberg (1981 : 249–55).
3. Although some elements of the Stockholm syndrome could be found in Berazadi's relationship with his captors, we could not say that he totally identified with them since purportedly he once hid a knife, which was discovered and taken from him.
4. According to a letter of December 7, 1980, signed by twenty-seven

lawyers, an average of three hundred people per month were tortured in the Basque Country (which has a population of over two million), the great majority of them being released afterward without charges (Castells Arteche 1982:31).

5. For a description of the types of maltreatment (e.g., mock execution, "the bathtub," "the bar," electric shocks, "the motorcycle," semi-suffocation, mock hanging, "the operating table"), see, for instance, the 1980 report.

PART 2: BASERRI SOCIETY AND CULTURE

Introduction

1. In Basque declension, *-a* marks a determinate article and *-k* is a pluralizer.
2. The notion of "traditional" society and culture is not meant to imply a sharp conceptual break with the "modern" present; the entire ethnography of Itziar is a denial of such assumption.

5. The Baserria: A Social and Economic Institution

1. Besides farming, the occupational distribution of Itziar's and Lastur's populations was the following in the summer of 1980: small workshops and factories, 104, services, 52, construction, 35, transportation, 19, garage repairs, 15, quarries, 10, other, 43. Only about thirty-five females, holding jobs outside their homes, are included in this estimate of the working population; the rest are housewives or single women who work at home for the domestic group. There were several people who had only part-time jobs, and at least six were living on unemployment, but residence in baserri houses makes this figure deceptive since lack of jobs in industry tends to be substituted for by more farming. Several other youths were serving in the military service or were shortly to become unemployed.
2. A liberado is a salaried leader exclusively dedicated to the organization.
3. Clark writes: "No matter how far away from their farm they may travel and how much time they devote to E.T.A., they remain steadfastly bound to the life of the traditional small Basque village. . . . E.T.A. has embedded itself organizationally in the everyday life of the Basque village. This it has done for strategic and tactical reasons, no doubt. Yet there is a personal and psychological dimension to this deci-

sion as well, for it is from small town traditional Basque culture that individual *etarras* [ETA members] derive their emotional strength, the unusual mixture of social, cultural, and psychological force that sustains them in a constantly failing guerrilla war" (1984:161).

4. The architect Baeschlin wrote: "In its general features the *baserria* . . . reveals very few variants" (1930:50).
5. For further information on baserri house types, ethnographic accounts of artifacts, and religious aspects of the fireplace, see, among many others, Agirreazkuenaga (1974) and Caro Baroja (1978).
6. Despite this prevailing dispersion, however, there is an alternative pattern of farmhouses clustered in a village center and surrounded by the farmlands—the *villas*. These are a more recent creation and have been linked to the emergence of urban centers.
7. In Itziar-Lastur in 1980 there were 16 three-generational households, 116 two-generational, and 12 one-generational. These data signal a tendency toward the nuclearization of the family and away from the traditional three-generational stem family model. Cultural and economic factors militate against realization of the traditional extended household model in which unmarried descendants had the right to remain in the residence in their natal etxe in exchange for farm labor. Under the present economic situation, the heir's siblings are expected to find a factory job and/or marry out of the household.
8. These public performances are examined in part 3.
9. According to Etxezarreta (1977:344) the yearly net profits in 1973 of baserriak under five hectares were estimated at 19,000 pesetas. Granted an investment of half a million pesetas in enlarging the stable and with an annual risk of 194,000 pesetas, the net profits of a baserria of ten hectares in 1973 were estimated at 214,000 pesetas—barely sufficient to give a living to an average family.
10. For an opposing argument regarding the baserria's economic feasibility, see Greenwood (1976a).
11. Presently in Itziar the case of a tenant baserria is rare. Out of the 118 operating baserriak about which I obtained information, 23 are not owned by the baserritarrak. There was, in fact, a distinction in the classification of these 23. Only in a few cases are any of these referred to as *errenteroak. Errenteroak* describes instances in which a tenant has recently entered a baserria and might expectably leave in the near future, or when a baserria is leased to a nearby one after abandonment by its former inhabitants. In the other cases the tenants are said to be living on their baserria "since all time." Upon questioning it might be admitted that "the baserria is not theirs." The comment is added, however, "but they live there as if it were theirs." Actually, on

occasion my informants were unsure as to whether a given baserria was owned or rented by its residents, which shows that independent possession is not essential in defining baserri status.

12. Mendata is a rural village of four hundred people situated near Guernica in the province of Vizcaya about thirty kilometers from Bilbao.
13. The provincial differences concerning inheritance legislation result in a diversity of succession practices. An ethnographic comparison of such differences is detailed by Douglass between Murelaga (Vizcaya), where "the cultural norm of preferential male primogeniture crystallized the problem of succession at an early age," and Echalar (Navarra), where "succession to baserria ownership is uncertain until the parents make a decision based upon the relative merits of their offspring" (1975:49).

6. Baserri Culture: Obsolescence and Symbolization

1. In addition to baserri names there are also lineage surnames internal to the households. The dual nature of naming can be seen as a distinction between "external" baserri names, based primarily on a geographical mapping, and "internal" family names, based on continuity of lineage. The clear social predominance of the baserri name over the family name is indicative of the family's dependence on the etxe. In Itziar it is still rare to know people by their surnames.
2. Speaking in general terms of the whole Iberian peninsula, Caro Baroja distinguishes *honor,* "a word possessing poetic and social overtones," from *honra,* "founded on personal virtue, and created by the actions of the individual." He argues that notions of honor and dishonor have changed with historical transformations in Spanish social structure. He notes that the infamies of the early Middle Ages, found in the *Partidas* of King Alfonso X, arose from fact (such as being born out of wedlock or admitting to theft), from law (a woman engaging in adultery or cohabiting with a man less than a year after her widowhood), or from common law (persons living by certain trades, such as panderers, minstrels, and usurers). Subsequently, the opposed concepts of *valer mas* (to be worth more) and *valer menos* (to be worth less) appeared. Caro Baroja points out that this concern continued to the point that "during the latter part of the middle ages (from the thirteenth to the fifteenth centuries) there were many who considered that disputes over 'prestige' and 'disgrace' were, in fact, the mainspring of most human action" (ibid.:88). Significantly, he finds that "'prestige,' in fact, is connected with an idea of honour which [was]

not individual but collective. It was based on a system of patrilineal clans. Being 'worth more' or 'worth less' affected the entire lineage" (ibid.:89).

Caro Baroja sets the next stage in Basque historical sequence with this commentary:

> Between the sixteenth century and the seventeenth, the people of the Basque provinces evidently made the change from a social structure in which factions, lineages, and the honour of blood were dominant to one in which the families best known as heads of factions lost almost all their influence to other, newer ones whose pretensions were rooted only in a sort of collective nobility common to all natives of the provinces and compatible with the exercise of the humblest professions of artisans and laborers, and above all with that of industry and commerce on a large or small scale. (Ibid.:114–15)

3. Arpal (1979) made extensive use of Weber's work on status groups to describe Basque traditional society, which he characterizes as *estamental,* or status grouped. He distinguishes vertically four status classes in the social organization from the sixteenth to nineteenth centuries: (1) elite lineages made up of lords ennobled in foreign ventures or the economically and socially exalted aristocracy; (2) an extensive class of noblemen settled in the lands owned by the family lineage; (3) a peasantry of tenants; and (4) marginal minorities. Itziar had in the past its share of noblemen and landlords. This past nobility can be documented through the church archives and the heraldry on the front of some of the village houses. Speaking of status honor, Weber has asserted that "in contrast to classes, *status groups* are normally communities. They are, however, often of an amorphous kind" (1968:186–87). This is clearly the case with baserri society. Weber has also stated that in a "status situation" people's lives are typically determined "by a specific, positive or negative, social estimation of honor" (ibid.).
4. Ortega y Gasset wrote: "The Basque thinks that the mere fact of having been born and of being a human individual gives him all the value that it is possible for one to have in this world. . . . It is an affirmation exclusively nourished by his individual energy, feeding completely on itself, and it amounts to a bold declaration of metaphysical democracy and transcendental egalitarianism. Who can doubt that there is a kind of rugged greatness in this attitude toward life, satanic though it is!" (1961:115). He went on to praise the Basques, finding that they alone of all peninsular peoples preserve "the inner discipline of an unspent

race" and "a sound and spontaneous ethic." His central proposition is, however, that their pride "is an antisocial force" (1961 : 116). It is not difficult for any observer of the Basques in their recent political struggle to find support for this proposition. Nonetheless, our study of the baserri society reveals that Ortega's picture of Basques as supreme individualists is flawed. Ortega fails to situate the ethos of egalitarianism and negation in a concrete social structure, that is, traditionally in the baserria. Nor is his premise rooted in a given historical perception of antagonism to a centralized military power.

5. Translation by W. Douglass.

7. Baserri Cooperativism: Testing the Limits of Communal Ideas

1. This discussion benefited from a symposium on the place of the commons organized by Professor James Fernandez at the NAAM held at Princeton University in March 1982. I was initially stimulated by Fernandez's essay "The Call of the Commons." The Princeton presentation elicited a detailed response from Professor M. Estellie Smith, which led to some significant changes.
2. Having begun in 1956 with $200,000 capital and twenty-three members, by 1978 the Mondragon industrial cooperatives alone (there are also teaching, housing, agricultural, and service cooperatives) totaled 16,161 members and annual sales of $620 million (Jackobs 1979 : 1). Considered to be the most successful cooperative movement in the world, it has attracted the attention of many social scientists. Basic works on Mondragon include García (1970), *Jakin* (1973), Campbell and Foster (1974), Gorroño (1975), Jackobs (1979), and Servy (1981).
3. See Etxezarreta (1977 : 123), who gives an approximate total amount of 36,232 baserriak for 1973 but qualifies it with two other estimates—there were 17,696 units between four and fifty hectares and 23,921 units if the counting begins at two hectares.
4. As one example, Bidart wrote of the traditional French Basque community: "The life of these communities is articulated essentially around two elements which contribute to the equilibrium and conservation of the social group: the *etxe*, or house, inserted within a system of vicinal relationship; *the communal lands,* support of the economic system. Structuring the social, economic, and political life, the *etxe* and the collective property buttress each other" (1977 : 27, my translation).
5. Unamuno reports on *ordeak,* or labor exchange, and the *lorra* institution, which he considers to be "one of the most important manifesta-

tions of social solidarity in Vizcaya." *Lorra* means "dragging" and by extension, "bringing." There used to be *zimaur lorra* (the bringing of manure), *bildots lorra* (the bringing of lambs), and *zur lorra* (the bringing of timber); these lorrak consisted of gratuitous contributions by the neighbors.

One of the mutual services described by Echegaray is called *etxealdatz,* whereby, on the rare occasion a domestic group changed baserriak, the first neighbors transported the household's furniture and implements. The construction of a new house also presented an occasion for the gratuitous transportation of building materials. Serious fire damage or cattle loss was met with neighborly assistance as well. There were no written rules or statutes; the precepts were consuetudinary. In the baserria Endañeta of Itziar there was one such *terrama* association (1933:32) whose members visited all the stables of the associated baserriak every three months to determine the health of the insured cattle.

6. The policy errors of agrarian credit institutions have been pointed out by Etxezarreta (1977:367). Basically, loans have been given for more fixed assets, such as construction or mechanization, but not for buying cattle or new land.
7. The argument linking Mondragon cooperatives to the traditional cultural forms has, in fact, been made by Jackobs (1979).

PART 3: PERFORMANCES IN CULTURE

Introduction

1. The reader is warned not to misunderstand the explanatory nature of these cultural models. I am not claiming even remotely that there is political violence among Basques because they practice these performances, nor do I assert that the presence of versifiers or hunters "explains" Basque violence in any simplistic way. A different writer could have chosen other themes as cultural models, and that writer's explanation could be equally relevant, which is not to say that every cultural account is equally valid.

8. Joko, Jolas, Burruka: Antagonistic Performances in Culture

1. During my fieldwork (1979–81) the most contested issue in the Basque region was the construction of a nuclear power plant by the

Iberduero Corporation in Lemoiz, near Bilbao. Lemoiz was viewed as the greatest environmental danger; it represented the most unwanted capitalist assault on the region. The slogans of rejection, "Lemoiz Ez," and "Euskadi ala Lemoiz," were visible everywhere, and helped to mobilize an estimated two hundred thousand people in a protest demonstration in March 1978. After many acts of sabotage by ETA against the plant, including the killing of two chief engineers, in 1983 the government decided to stop its construction indefinitely.

2. Another slogan is "Askatasuna ala Hil" (Freedom or Death). See more on this in chapter 13.
3. The stone lifter Victor Zabala, "Arteondo," was born in Itziar in 1886 and since 1910 was for two decades the undisputed champion of his epoch. He gave a new dimension to stone lifting by dismissing irregular stones and fixing their forms and weights. See Aguirre Franco (1978 : 197–246) on the history of Basque stone lifting.
4. During the summer and fall of 1979 alone the following joko of the traditional type were staged in Itziar: twice a runner from Itziar bet against a runner from Lastur; a bachelor from Itziar bet that nobody from the bailara of Itxaspe could climb Mount Andutz within a given time; and another bachelor from Itziar bet that his cow could pull a stone further than another cow from a nearby town.
5. In Zulaika (1985) I argue against such verse championships.
6. Some of the traditional jolas may be described as follows. *Erria katian* consisted of two people catching the rest of the players in a field, who, as they were caught, lined up in a chain. The two catchers had to be on their guard because anyone not already captured could undo the entire chain by touching anybody in it. This same game was called *erre-erreka* when the chain was fixed to a particular spot. *Tximilikorteka* consisted of people hiding and being caught when seen. The one that "stayed" and searched for those hiding had to reach a given spot ahead of one seen and say his/her name plus "tximilakorte." If some of the hidden players reached the spot ahead of the catcher, everybody was freed and the game started anew. When everybody had been discovered, the one that was caught first "stayed" for the new game. *Pañueloka,* in English "steal the bacon," was another favorite game. While someone held a handkerchief at a point equidistant from both sides, one player from each side ran into the center trying to get hold of the handkerchief and get back to the starting point without being caught by the opponent. A side lost when all its players were eliminated in this way. A similar game was *ertenka,* in which there was no middle handkerchief and people *erten* (got out) in turns, advancing toward the other side. Players from both sides came out alternately by pairs, taunted each other, and defended the players of their own side.

Girls played *kozinaketan* (kitchen work), *josten* (sewing up), or *umezaintzen* (baby-sitting). In the fifties and early sixties, *sasikopatzu* was a particularly playful time for children. Sasikopatzu involved going to the mountain in groups and preparing and eating food there, particularly toasted chickpeas. The search for and discovery of good places for playing, kept secret later on, was a significant part of sasikopatzu. These outings afforded occasions to initiate not quite proper activities, such as smoking. Favorite entertainments were doing somersaults down the slopes and searching for crickets and bird nests for entire afternoons.

7. In this type of culture the image of the playful Orpheus cannot be but a child. Liberation is far from being understood as something in which "the expanding realm of freedom becomes truly a realm of play" (Marcuse 1955 : 222).
8. On the theme of honor, see chapter 6.
9. On this point, see Clark (1984:chap. 3).

9. Ehiza: The Hunting Model of Performance

1. In Guipúzcoa alone, with a population of seven hundred seventy thousand, there are thirty-three thousand hunting permits.
2. By "primordial" we do not mean some idiosyncratic construct having to do with the beginnings or origins of Basques. It refers to certain "primordial attachments" by which "is meant one that stems from the 'givens' . . . of social existence: immediate contiguity and kin connection mainly, but beyond them the givenness that stems from being born into a particular religious community, speaking a particular language, or even a dialect of a language, and following particular social practices. These congruities of blood, speech, custom, and so on, are seen to have an ineffable, and at times overpowering, coerciveness in and of themselves" (Geertz 1973 : 259). For a sociological study of these primordial elements in Basque politics, see Linz (1986). Hunting is here taken to be a mode of performance relying on such primary factors that set limits to our powers of action and representation. By leaving aside an intellectualist approach that concedes preponderance to ideological or ethical components, this chapter is an invitation to take into account primordial factors analogous to those of hunting for the comprehension of political violence.
3. The boars themselves are not referred to as "boars" or by a separate pronoun such as "it" or "they" but are unnamed. Verbs such as "to go," "to escape," "to run" are not used in reference to the boars.

4. Burgos is a Castilian province that borders the Basque Country to the south.
5. Compared with the thrill of animal unpredictability, shooting at the small plates (*platillos*) in competitive contexts is "artificial," for "that is always the same thing, automatic, repetitive, nothing but that reflex as to how the small plate comes out."
6. There is an interesting parallel in the novel *Shibumi* in which the assassin/hero has the paranormal ability to "smell" danger. He went to live in retirement in the Basque Country because he thought the Basques possessed *shibumi*, the Japanese word for the ability of a person to transcend his own physical limits via mental control and projection.

10. The Bertsolariak as a Cultural Model of Performance

1. The bertso strophes quoted in the previous pages follow the zortziko nagusia pattern.
2. See Abel Muniategi in Dorronsoro (1981 : 148) and other technical aspects of bertsolaritza by several authors in ibid.:200–202.
3. Errenteri and Oiartzun are two towns in northern Guipúzcoa.
4. The occasion on which this happened is one well remembered by bertso followers. In San Sebastián, in front of a large audience, Uztapide was asked to sing on a very politicized theme. In the middle of the bertso his voice failed him as the result of a ruptured vein in his throat and he was unable to continue singing. The "father" of the bertsolariak at the time, he was never again heard in a plaza. As if his broken throat were not sufficient to still his beautiful voice, he was banned by the governor of the province from singing after that performance. He died in the spring of 1983.
5. He has argued: "An *oral* text will yield a predominance of clearly demonstrable formulas, with the bulk of the remainder 'formulaic', and a small number of nonformulaic expressions. A *literary* text will show a predominance of nonformulaic expressions, with some formulaic expressions, and very few clear formulas. The fact that nonformulaic expressions are already present in an oral text proves that the seeds of the 'literary' style are already present in oral style; and likewise the presence of 'formulas' in 'literary' style indicates its origin in oral style" (ibid.).
6. See, for instance, some of Aresti's poems, which are written in the bertsolari tradition.
7. This is why to make an anthology of a single bertsolaria requires an

anthology of all the bertsolariak who sang with him; see the collection of "Auspoa" bertso books by Zabala.

8. Literally, this means "backside front."
9. The *tratanteak* are men who barter by buying and selling, hence use probing offers without revealing their final one in hopes of gaining advantage.
10. The reader may wonder whether, by applying to political violence the bertsolaria's type of elliptical argument, we are disdaining the search for cause and effect relationships. I know well how scandalous such an admission would be to our social science tradition; I dwell on this issue in the final part of the book devoted to ritual. As to the bertsolaria, since he is producing an argument he needs some kind of syntax for connecting the meaningful images. Although implicit, these linkages could be seen as "causal" in the sense that they establish an interrelatedness of meaning within the bertso frame. Nevertheless, what is of interest in the bertsolaria's argument is the very absence of a rhetorical syntax of causals and consecutives; that is, the form of the argument is not one of positive explanation by explicating cause and effect linkages, but one of discontinuous jumps in formally negative connections. Thus, we are not saying that ETA's violence is related to Basque cultural forms simply because they coexist as two lines in a bertso; what we are arguing is that the proper form of explanation of Basque violence cannot be reduced to positively lineal arguments but must take into account the bertsolaria's kind of elliptical implications in which causation is formally negative and emerges from the overall pattern of performance. This is more akin to what Wittgenstein called an "aesthetic explanation," and it is in this sense that we could say with him, "An aesthetic explanation is not a causal explanation" (1983:18). The bertsolariak provide a supreme example of such an aesthetic form of explanation in the culture.

PART 4: THE CULTURAL METAPHORS OF THE BEAST AND THE BEAUTY

Introduction

1. These "primary factors of experience" are characterized by Needham as "the capacities, proclivities, and constraints that universally make up human nature" (1978:8). In his heterogeneous list of primary factors, Needham includes sensory perceptions of color and sound, numbers, and physical contrasts such as hot and cold, wet and dry, which are employed in making not only physical judgments but moral estima-

tions as well. They are vehicles for significance without conveying explicit universal meanings; "they are phenomena of the same order, and this order is defined by simplicity and immediacy" (ibid.:11). This conceivably very economical range of primordial factors is subject to formal constraints such as opposition, symmetry, transitivity, correlation, and logical possibility. On the other hand, these primary factors "are not consciously selected or fabricated," nor are they related by necessary systematic interconnections, but constitute "symbolic complexes" as exemplified by shamanism or ritual sacrifice.

11. Beasts and Men: Primordial Metaphors of Savagery, Enclosure, and Ascent

1. Despite occasionally mentioning "instinctual" components of violence, we are far from committing ourselves to any instinctivist theory. We are simply recording local explanations. For a criticism of instinctivist theories, see Montagu (1976).
2. Fernandez's discussion of metaphor as "the predication of a sign image upon an inchoate subject" and his argument that animals provide such primordial "predicates by which subjects obtain an identity" (1974:120–21) are guiding propositions throughout this chapter.
3. Thus, *antzar* (goose), *urde* (pig), *behi* (cow), *katu* (cat), *auntz* (she-goat), *aker* (he-goat), *asto* (donkey), *txakur* (dog), *erle* (bee), *oilo* (chicken), *oilar* (cock) all have their *basa* counterparts—*basantzar* (wild goose), *basaurde* (wild boar), etc. The same applies to *gaztaina* (chestnut), *ilarra* (pea), *kipula* (onion), *larrosa* (rose), *lizar* (ash tree), *mahats* (vineyard), *perrezil* (parsley), *porru* (leek), *aran* (plum), and so on, all of which have their *basa* undomesticated counterparts. With other species, such as *azeri* (fox) and *azkonar* (badger), there is no wild/domesticated dichotomy and no *basa-* prefix is needed. With birds no wild/domesticated distinction is made either.
4. *Sokamuturra* consists in the bull being roped by the horns and taken through the streets.
5. In the Vizcayan collection of proverbs of 1596 *eskondu* appears with the meaning of "to get married" (proverb 110) as well as with the meaning of "to catch" (proverb 457), which Michelena (1976:368) relates with a question mark to *erskondu* "to consolidate, to grip tightly." The relationship between the double meaning of *eskondu* as catch and marriage can be found in other cultures as well.
6. This is a fragment of the song "El País Basc" (The Basque Country) by the well-known Catalan poet-singer Raimon. When he used to sing

it in the sixties the slogan "Gora Euskadi!" (Up with Euskadi!) at the end of the song, in Basque in the original, was not permitted, so he sang instead "Gora Gora!" (Upwards upwards!).

7. Frequently, adults lift their children over their heads with a loud eupa!; playing with children is usually accompanied by eupa! People of the older generations like to tell that they used to go to their Sunday open-air dancing amid shouts of jeupa! that could be heard across the valley. Eup! has been a traditional mode for greeting and still is the ordinary salute in Itziar. This festive mood was present when performing communal work as well, for they worked in those occasions *jeupaka ta uxuaka* (with jeups and shouts). The joko context of betting is an occasion for shouting jeup! in support of your favorite competitor—the jeup! are accompanied by raising up the body and sometimes by lifting the arms.
8. In the choreographed dances, a most peculiar movement is the lifting up of one foot above the level of the head, another characteristic is the dancers' constant jumping with their bodies in erect position.
9. Mountains are always close in Basque geography. Its less than twenty thousand square kilometers are traversed by the Cantabrian chain, a continuation of the Pyrenees consisting mainly of the sierras of Andia, Urbasa, Aralar, Aitzgorri, Amboto, and Gorbea. Basque mountaineering reached its peak in 1980 when an expedition climbed Mount Everest; Martin Zabaleta, the Basque mountaineer who implanted at the top an *ikurrina,* or Basque flag, became a national hero. Whether professional mountaineers or not, many Basques enjoy mountain climbing and hiking.
10. During the mid 1980s, however, radical activism is adopting overwhelmingly urban symbols and attitudes. Mountaineering and ruralism are being replaced by a new awareness of ecological issues, more attention to fashion, and, among the youth, other components such as hard rock music.
11. The *txalaparta* is a Basque autochthonous instrument consisting of two boards on which two players improvise a rhythmic dialogue by hitting them with two short sticks; it is thought that originally it attempted to imitate the galloping of horses.
12. I was told of similar bull impersonations as well.
13. In his preliminary remarks Barandiaran writes: "We could say that the background of beliefs and myths of the Basque Country is dominated by genii or divinities having forms of diverse species of animals—horses, bulls, wild boars, she-goats, rams, snakes, vultures. Supposedly they inhabit the interiors of certain caves. There exists, furthermore, a genius or anthropomorphic divinity of female sex, troglodyte

as well, which sometimes takes animal appearances or has some animal part—she-goat's feet, vulture's claws, etc.; her name is *Mari*. This shows that the same artistic-religious representations of the paleolithic Cantabro-Aquitanian people are those mobilized and portrayed by Basque mythology. The same world of images and icons, occupying the same temples or dwellings, repeats itself in both cases. Basque mythology projects shadows and figures akin to those of the paleolithic hunter" (1972:13).

12. The Amabirjina: Icon and Sacrament

1. The daily prayer that initiates the novena is a most expressive synthesis of the attributions, invocations, and entire ethos of this Marian cult. A second, more elaborate part of the daily prayer summarizes the Amabirjina's attributions and virtues. It begins: "O Mary, most saintly, Virgin Mother of God, Queen of Heavens, and of the Earth, our tender and delightful Mother, for our good you wanted to put your beautiful image in the world, choosing for that the blessed village of Itziar." The elements that describe Mary in this salutation are (1) a name—Mary; (2) the simultaneous attribution of virginity and motherhood, thus transcending natural law; (3) the highest political position, queen, but the political domain is surpassed, for she is simultaneously queen of heaven and earth; (4) the domestically most elevated role in Basque society, motherhood, but a motherhood of God and of us universally, thus transcending the kinship system; (5) an image—the Amabirjina; and (6) a concrete spot she chose for her miraculous apparition—Itziar.
2. This is the full text of the prayer: "Hail Mary, full of grace, the Lord is with you. Blessed art thou among women, and blessed is the fruit of thy womb, Jesus. Holy Mary, Mother of God, pray for us sinners, now and at the hour of our death. Amen."
3. Aldazabal wrote at the end of the eighteenth century: "The custom of bringing children for baptism to this miraculous Sanctuary is practiced in our times as well, as in earlier centuries, not only from places of the Province of Guipúzcoa, but also from the Señorio of Vizcaya, and the bishopric of Calahorra" (quoted in Esnaola 1927:80).
4. The intense identification of aberria or Euzkadi with ama can be gathered from this sample written by Atxurra on January 24, 1932, which I translate with deliberate literalness:

   Since you have her [the aberria] as your mother, you are bound to confess that with love she leaves to you for your bread the riches

> that she has earned with her sweat. And will you deny her what she is asking? If you have a heart it really is little and is not something impossible either: love is what the race, the aberria is asking for. Identify yourself and show up at the batzokia; she will welcome you in the kitchens that she has there. And lo! she gives you the bread, and if you don't want to recognize her as your mother I am myself going with her because you don't have anything to do with Euzkadi.

5. Psychologists and psychiatrists writing on Basque character have emphasized the mother complex. See, among others, Crawford Bamber (1982) and Redondo (1983). In this regard there is a major academic controversy about an alleged "Basque matriarchy." Roman geographers reported on female inheritance and matrilocality among the Basques and other peoples of northern Spain; women were also said to be in charge of domestic rituals and agriculture. Both Barandiaran and Caro Baroja have echoed these writers in their work. The mythological materials collected by Barandiaran rely heavily on female images, particularly the flying witch Mari. Based on this kind of data some writers have gone so far as to expound a theory of "Basque matriarchalism" (Ortiz-Osés and Mayr 1980) and "Basque gynecocracy" (Hornilla 1981). They could be viewed as one more aerial projection of ama. For a recent ethnographic description of the changing roles of Basque women, see del Valle et al. (1985). Deep-sea fishermen, away from home for long periods of time, are particularly prone to relate to women through projective images (Zulaika 1981); this explains partly why the Amabirjina of Itziar is the patron saint of fishermen and has enjoyed a special devotion among them (see chapter 1).
6. See similar findings in chapter 6 of Clark (1984).
7. A substitute copy of the image of the Amabirjina is kept at one side of the church and used in the ritual "passing beneath the Amabirjina." After hearing mass, the pilgrims conclude their visit to the sanctuary with this ritual, which consists of passing underneath the portable substitute image held on the shoulders of four men. On many Sundays throughout the year, children are brought to Itziar just to pass beneath the Amabirjina.
8. Itziar villagers identify strongly with the "real" Amabirjina. When in 1960 it was taken to Madrid to rid it of the destructive woodworm attacking it, a general feeling of loss dominated the village for the three months it was absent. On the way back from Madrid it was transported triumphantly from Deba to Itziar in a truck made into the form of a ship, a fitting reminder of her patronage of mariners.

9. *Etsi* has the following meanings: (1) to despair, to give up hope, to distrust; (2) desperate; (3) great effort; (4) to close up; (5) ferment, leaven; (6) to please; (7) light lunch or dinner; (8) to accept; (9) to consent to, to be convinced of; (10) to feel all right, to become adapted to a place, to be acclimatized; (11) to leave; (12) to resign oneself; and (13) to repute, to appreciate (Azkue 1969:1:229). In Itziar's daily use, *etsi* takes all the above meanings, with the exception of numbers 5 and 7.
10. As Mitxelena's Marian poem, based on the collection of popular ballads, underscores, the Amabirjina's request for the building of a hermitage is only the prerequisite and metaphor for the construction of a greater hermitage—the mother's demand for the mystical building of Christ's body (1949:110). This mystical making of Christ's body is expressed preeminently by participation in the church sacraments. Mitxelena was a Franciscan friar living in the sanctuary of Aranzazu. Aranzazu has been the main Basque center in fostering and propagating the Marian version of Christianity expounded here; other centers, such as Itziar, have inevitably been influenced by Aranzazu's teaching. Azurmendi (1984) has sketched the important role of Aranzazu in Basque postwar religiosity and political consciousness.
11. For further elaboration of *aska* and its relationship to the predicate *uts,* see Zulaika (1987a).
12. Empty of pain and sickness, the cured body is *aske*. The metaphoric image of aska seems present in the curing practice of putting over the patient's breast animals that have been slit open in order to open it up and release sickness from it. Barriola (1979:64) relates one such treatment of pulmonary tuberculosis. The aim of the curer appears to be to turn the sick breast into an *aska* (trough); that is, to askatu it, or free it by turning it into an aska.

PART 5: EKINTZA: RITUAL ACTION

Introduction

1. There is a rapidly growing literature devoted to suggesting "hypotheses relating to the causation of civil violence and terrorism" (Wilkinson 1979:46). In this perspective the social scientist "must at the very least ask, For what? By whom? Why?" (ibid.:102). Likewise, Gurr's behavioral approach, and even the title of his classic *Why Men Rebel,* point in the same direction of causal search. Violent action is typically conceived as generating a dialectic of terror versus counterterror.

Even the transnational flow of information is viewed "as a cause of terrorism" (Sands Redlick 1979:73). The stock definition of terrorism becomes "violence for effect" (Jenkins 1975:1), or, in Aron's terms, "when its psychological effects are out of proportion to its purely physical result" (1966:170). As a process, terrorism is characterized by three elements: the decision to use terror as a systematic weapon, threats or acts of violence, and the effects of the violence on the immediate victims. These causes and effects are linked in a rational-instrumental chain; the military action-reaction mentality is echoed by this type of thinking, searching for functional-final causes.

2. They were asked to answer five questions, which included the following: What are the causes of the spiral of violence? Do you believe that in the Basque Country there are three types of violence—institutional, revolutionary, and repressive? What are the chronological, causal, or other kinds of relations among the various types of violence? A fourth question requested solutions, and the fifth asked for an evaluation of the efforts made by Basques in their attempts to win self-determination as a people. In the presentation of their findings, the editors distinguish two classes of responses regarding "the origins of violence." One is historical, tracing the violence to the Franco dictatorship and the succeeding "pseudo-democratic" government. The other is institutional, has a concrete setting in Franco's period, and no longer exists with the coming of democracy. In brief, the endemic climate of violence among Basques was explained either by pointing to its "causes" in the past historical processes or in the present institutional repression.
3. Perceptions of what constitutes a terrorist act vary substantially. After completing a comprehensive study of ETA's patterns of violence, Clark does not consider it to be a terrorist group. He observes that "most of the time ETA was careful to avoid harming civilian bystanders in its attacks but that its record is not flawless in this regard, and several very serious mistakes did result in the killing and wounding of numerous bystanders" (1984:132).
4. In various parts throughout this chapter I make use of linguistic materials to support my arguments. I should hasten to warn the reader that Basque linguists are unlikely to be convinced by some of my linguistic associations. In my treatment of language, different levels of etymological and figurative use can be distinguished. For my discussion the stronger cases rest on ethnographic evidence, such as hordago in the mus game. In a number of cases the etymologies have already been established by the linguists, and the evidence is recorded in the text. In other cases the connections have not been established, but

they are suggestive when predicated upon semantic considerations or prompted by metaphoric extensions. There are other cases, anathema for etymologists, in which my connections rest on plain or partial homonymy, as when I associate *bai* (yes) with *bai* (sieve) in the interpretation of a mythical narrative. In these latter cases I make no etymological claims whatsoever; instead, I look at the relationship as a kind of word association that a dream or pun might unconsciously provoke on the basis of mere phonetic similarity. This is the kind of linguistic connection that psychoanalysis holds as a characteristic of true symbolism (Jones 1967). Translations from Lafon, Michelena, Villasante, and Yrigaray are my own; Schuchardt was accessible to me through Yrigaray's translation.

13. Ritual Forms and Performances in Basque Mythology and Political Violence

1. Etymologically *bai* (sieve) is generally believed to derive from *bane*, whence the Romance *van* and the older Basque *bahe* (Michelena 1976: 143; Agud 1980: 112–15). Lafon (1952: 79) considers it originally Basque.
2. Lafon (1966) lists the following uses of the prefix *bait* in verb forms: (1) In subordinate sentences "it marks a relationship of dependency between the proposition where it figures and another proposition"; (2) clauses with the prefix *bait* are frequently preceded by indefinite interrogatives, such as *nor* (who), *zer* (what), *nola* (how), *zeren* (since), *non* (where); (3) sometimes the proposition containing the prefix *bait* is introduced by the conjunction *eta* (and), which results in establishing a causal relation; and (4) in exclamative propositions initiated with the *ala* interjection. Furthermore, Lafon thinks that in the comparative conditionals of the type *bailu bezela* (as if he had) and the suppositional comparatives of the type *bailitzan* (as if he was), the *bai* is the affirmative (yes). Lafon adduces as well Azkue's distinction between two kinds of causals: the so-called impulsive causal, which is formed with the prefix *bait*, and the conjunctive causal formed with the suffix *-lako*. Indefinite pronouns and adverbs are also formed by adding *-bait*. The common use of *ba-*, *bait-* in Itziar's daily speech are (1) conditionals, as in *Esaiok, ikusten badek* (Tell him, if you see him); (2) subordinate sentences, as in *Etzekiat, ez baidiat ikusi* (I don't know, since I didn't see it); (3) affirmative sentences, as in *Bazekian* (he knew it); (4) indefinite pronouns and adverbs, as in *Nunbait izan dek* (He has been somewhere); (5) causals, as in *Alperrik*

ari haiz, ez baidik emango (It is all in vain, because he will not give it to you).

3. This cultural elaboration of the themes of the affirmative and the negative in order to produce the fundamental paradigm of interpretation—the locus of the true and the false—is not different in orientation from the one adopted by the first hermeneutic treatise, Aristotle's *On Interpretation,* on which Ricoeur comments: "The problem of the opposition between affirmation and negation becomes the central theme of the treatise" (1970 : 22).
4. This is a feature common to children of other cultures as well.
5. See also Turner (1977 : 54): "Implicit in these general notions is an insight of fundamental importance into the structure and function of such rites. This is the notion that the phenomena of the liminal phase constitute, in structural terms, a different (and higher) level of the same system of relations as that represented by the secular order of social relations. The existence of such a hierarchical relationship between the liminal phase of a *rite de passage* and the social relations with which it deals, considered together with the transformational character of this relationship and the regulatory functions it performs within its social setting, strongly suggests that what is at work is an underlying structure of a cybernetic type."
6. *Alegia* is also a quotative evidential meaning "presumably."
7. For a systematic elaboration of this semantics, see Zulaika (1987a). My interest in the idea of *uts* was originally sparked by Oteiza's work.
8. Not surprisingly, uts has given origin to metaphysical interpretations. Goenaga (1975) applies the Heideggerian dialectics between "being" and "nothingness" to uts, which is "the expression of nothingness"; "Every *uts* is transcendental" (ibid.: 137); "The *uts* is the *no,* but the no of a something. The being is the *yes*" (ibid.: 145). This metaphysical dialectics, which demands that uts "will always be void, solution of continuity, sin, error, nothingness" (ibid.), obscures the formal nature of the concept.
9. This is the case with Goenaga, for whom uts and bete are "antithetical" concepts: "*Uts* was the concept of lack of what was needed in one way or another, be it in the realm of value or being. *Bete* is presented to us as the antithesis: the perfect, the adequate in the world of value, performance, being" (1975 : 158). Goenaga himself recognizes that bete deals with "the quantitative plenitude" and that "the concept of plenitude is a concept always, fundamentally, essentially relative" (ibid.). From this quantitative nature of bete, he should have proceeded to realize that uts presents a qualitative space, and that there-

fore bete could never exercise "the same function" as uts to express "the maximum of quality" (ibid.:156).

10. In other terms, uts is a solution in culture to what Goodman calls "the problem of abstraction" (1951:110). The negative form of exclusion, either by the digital-verbal ez or the iconic-visual uts, reveals a primitive relationship in the cultural system. Yet the problem of abstraction is inseparable from the problem of concretion—"The two problems are so closely parallel that to explain one is to explain a good deal about the other" (ibid.). The mythical pattern of transformation is that the uts containers in Mari's dwellings turn into *auts* (ashes) in the outside world. What is uts golden empty form in the mythical-ritual realm in the external world of appearances is compound dusty matter. Thus, we are given by mythology the hypothesis that auts stands for the indivisible constituents of substantive matter. Many data in the traditional culture support this commonsense view. In brief, uts solves the problem of abstraction in negative form by creating a field of exclusion and solves the problem of concretion by operating as a conceptual container, which brings together separable qualities into an indivisible unit of experience, or auts. Since concretion consists in the material determination or inclusion of qualities, abstraction is reached by their uts exclusion. Basque culture creates a paradigm of order by proposing the primitive uts or its logical equivalent ez for mythicoritual form.
11. "In recognition of the regularity, propriety, and apparent durability and immutability of these messages," Rappaport calls these enduring messages "canonical" (1979:179). In our discussion "iconic" messages are defined basically by a relationship of inclusion and are visualized typically by containers.
12. This iconic multireferentiality can be well illustrated with the human body. The body's functioning is imagined in culture as a container in which physiological, medical, and psychological processes are staged. The religious-cosmological projections of the human body are expressed by the funerary stelae, in which the trapezoidal base represents the *bizkar* (shoulder), and the circular disc the *buru* (head) (Barandiaran 1970). The buru defines a symbolic space in which various representations establish an iconic equivalence between human and cosmos. The multireferentiality of buru can be gathered by merely looking at its various lexical meanings (Azkue 1969:1:187). Iconic metaphors derive similarly from bizkar, *esku* (hand), *oin* (foot), and so on. The human body sets a primordial model or analog, which maps the noncorporeal reality.

13. Icons provide image and character to indexical signs. An indexical sign designates what it points to but does not characterize it. The icon offers a characterizing sign, yet the actual signification achieved in each case depends on the indexical acts of ostension framed in a given symbolic context. Thus, icons and indices imply each other. Both classes of signs have their own kind of indeterminacy: indexical signaling does not fix the reference of a text; iconic signaling fixes it multireferentially.
14. The equivalents in Spanish are *tú* and *usted,* and in French, *tu* and *vous*.
15. A crossroads, for instance, provides such formal center, and it is not surprising that crossroads were conspicuous spots where ritual events used to take place, such as witch reunions, apparitions of souls, or the burning of a deceased's objects. Using the Fregean distinction between sense and reference, the center generated by a crossroads presents one point of reference with two different senses. In a circumference the center reduces all the senses of the radii into a single point of reference. Later on we will describe ritual as a reductive mechanism; the imposition of cultural centers brings about such formal reduction.
16. Duvert (1976) has made a formal analysis of the stelae. He specifically addresses the problem of signification posed by the central region.
17. This was brought to my attention by Martzel Etchehandy.
18. Since the indexical sign does not characterize its object, the same function may be performed in folklore by a series of interchangeable indices: eggs intended for incubation, for instance, can be protected by putting beside the nest a piece of iron, an ax, or blessed laurel, or by putting a drop of wax on each egg, making the sign of the cross with charcoal on each egg, arranging each egg with its pointed end upward, and so on (Azkue 1969:1:95–101). Or the same index may perform opposing functions: a needle may be used either for curing or for killing (ibid.:2:290). There is a saying about needles, a typically indexical object: "The needle dresses all the world, and she herself remains naked." An indexical sign lacks reflexivity—it cannot dress itself; like exploded dust or like a thrown arrow, it cannot return to itself. An iconic sign, on the contrary, displays reflexive self-containment.
19. "An *Index* . . . is a Representamen whose Representative character consists in being an individual second. If the Secondness is an existential relation, the Index is *genuine*. If the Secondness is a reference, the Index is *degenerate*" (1955:108; his emphasis).

20. As befits timeless mythology but differentiates it from ritual, which entails a temporal process, there is no time deixis in the formal set of rules with which Mari must be met.
21. If one wants to find proof that *hi* has been the least marked and thus the more general form, Lafon provides it: "In texts of the sixteenth and seventeenth centuries, the marker for 2nd pers. sing. is usually zero; in French-Basque, however, the pronoun is *hi*. New 2nd pers. pl. forms have been created by adding plural suffixes to the old forms, which had become polite singular forms" (1972: 1767). Although in urban centers it is being lost to *zu*, in rural areas such as Itziar *hi* is still the usual mode of speech among equals.
22. In Basque the words are: "Amairu, amabi, amaika, amar, bederatzi, zortzi, zazpi, sei, bost, lau, iru, bi, bat, bapez: emen leku onetan geixo garatxarik ez."
23. In order to cure a ganglion infarct this formula is said by the patient while making a cross over the ganglion with a grain of salt and without breathing: "The ganglia are nine; nine are eight; eight are seven; seven are six; six are five; five are four; four are three; three are two; two are one [*bat*]: let the ganglion be *zirt-zart* [onomatopoeia for something being smashed into pieces]" (Barandiaran 1972: 52).
24. Frege remarked: "If we call such a transition from a thought to its opposite, negating the thought, then negating in this sense is not coordinate with judging; for what matters in judging is always the truth, whereas we may pass from a thought to its opposite without asking which is true" (1977: 44).
25. Russell reduced his "egocentric particulars" to the pronoun "this," which he treated as a logically proper name (Gale 1967: 152). In Basque, *hor* (there) seems to be the best candidate for this function.
26. Douglass and Bilbao (1975) and Ott (ms.) have underscored the ethnographic centrality of the concept of indarra.
27. Ott (1981) provides superb ethnographic evidence of the prime significance of the principle of *aldikatu* in ordering experience in a French-Basque community.
28. Michelena (1976: 585) favors the likelihood of an etymological connection between *ala* and *al* over alternative possibilities.
29. The *sel* is a circular arrangement of territory "formed by placing a central boundary stone which becomes the axis of a circle" (Douglass 1975: 55). The replacement of the external circular boundary by a central boundary stone expresses the formal equivalence between center and peripheral circle.
30. Grupo Anti-ETA de Liberación (Anti-ETA Liberation Group). An orga-

nization of mercenaries dedicated to killing Basque activists and exiles in southern France which, according to the media, has links with the Spanish police.

31. Rappaport has articulated the parallel: "Whereas lies are made possible by the freeing of signals from material significata, ultimate sacred postulates are made possible by the freeing of significata from material embodiment altogether" (1979:229).
32. Bateson has observed that a switch, when it is in either an on or off position as part of an electric circuit, does not exist from the point of view of the circuit—it is nothing but a gap between two conductors. "The switch is *not* except at the moments of its change of setting, and the concept 'switch' has thus a special relation to *time*" (1979:109; his emphasis). In the ritual system the reductive "not" is the conceptual equivalent to the switch.

EPILOGUE

1. Berango is a town in Vizcaya.

Bibliography

Agirreazkuenaga, J.
1974 "Etnografía de Busturia." *Anuario de Eusko-Folklore* 25:23–150.

Agud, M.
1980 *Elementos de cultura material en el País Vasco.* San Sebastián: L. Haranburu.

Aguirre, J. A. de
1943 *De Guernica a Nueva York pasando por Berlin.* Buenos Aires: Editorial Vasca Ekin.

Aguirre Franco, R.
1978 *Juegos y deportes vascos.* 2d ed. San Sebastián: Auñamendi.

Altuna, J.
1975 *Lehen euskal herria.* Bilbao: Ediciones Mensajero.

Altuna, J., and J. M. Apellániz
1978 *Las figuras rupestres paleolíticas de la cueva de Ekain.* Bilbao: Universidad de Deusto.

Amnesty International
1980 *Report of an Amnesty International Mission to Spain.* London: Amnesty International Publications.

Arana, S.
1965 *Obras completas.* Buenos Aires: Editorial Vasca Ekin.

Aranzadi, J.
1981 *Milenarismo vasco.* Madrid: Taurus.

Aresti, G.
1969 *Harri eta Herri.* 2d ed. Bilbao: Kriselu.

Aron, R.
1966 *Peace and War.* London: Weidenfeld and Nicholson.

Arpal, J.
1979 *La sociedad tradicional en el País Vasco*. Zarautz: Itxaropena.
1982 "Familia y territorio en el País Vasco: De la sociedad tradicional a la sociedad industrial." In *Familia y cambio social en España*, ed. R. Conde. Madrid: CIS.

Arrinda Albisu, A.
1965 *Religión prehistórica de los Vascos*. San Sebastián: Auñamendi.

Arrizabalo, J. M.
1979 *Baso-mutillak*. Tolosa: Auspoa.

Azcona, J.
1984 *Etnia y nacionalismo vasco*. Barcelona: Anthropos.

Azkue, R. M. de
1936–47 *Euskalerriaren Yakintza*. 4 vols. Madrid: Espasa-Calpe.
1969 *Diccionario Vasco-Español-Francés*. Vols. 1, 2. Bilbao: La Gran Enciclopedia Vasca.

Azurmendi, J.
1976 *Zer dugu Orixeren kontra?* Oñati: Jakin.
1977 *Zer dugu Orixeren alde?* Oñati: Jakin.
1979 *Arana Goiri-ren pentsamendu politikoa*. San Sebastián: Lur.
1980 "Bertsolaritzaren estudiorako." *Jakin* 14/15: 139–64.
1984 "Mitxelenaren bere lekutzerako." Introduction to *Idazlan Guztiak II*, by S. Mitxelena, pp. xvii–xcvi. Zarautz: EFA.

Baeschlin, A.
1930 *La arquitectura del caserío vasco*. Barcelona: Canosa.

Bähr, G.
1935 *Los nombres de parentesco en vascuence*. Bermeo: Gaubeka.

Bakhtin, M.
1984 *Problems of Dostoevsky's Poetics*. Minneapolis: University of Minnesota Press.

Barahona Arévalo, R.
1979 "The Making of Carlism in Vizcaya (1814–1833)." Ph.D. dissertation, Princeton University.

Barandiaran, J. M. de
1953 *El hombre prehistórico en el País Vasco*. Buenos Aires: Ekin.
1960–62 *El mundo en la mente popular vasca*. 4 vols. San Sebastián: Auñamendi.
1970 *Estelas funerarias del País Vasco*. San Sebastián: Txertoa.
1972 *Diccionario ilustrado de mitología vasca. Obras Completas*, vol. 1. Bilbao: La Gran Enciclopedia Vasca.
1978 "Exploración de la Cueva de Urtiaga." *Obras Completas*, vol. 12. Bilbao: La Gran Enciclopedia Vasca.

Barandiaran Irizar, L. de
1976 *José Miguel de Barandiaran. Patriarca de la cultura vasca.* San Sebastían: Caja de Ahorros Municipal.
Barriola, I. M.
1979 *La medicina popular en el País Vasco.* San Sebastián: Ediciones Vascas.
Barthes, R.
1971 *Sade, Fourier, Loyola.* Paris: Editions du Seuil.
Bateson, G.
1958 *Naven: A Survey of the Problems Suggested by a Composite Picture of the Culture of a New Guinea Tribe Drawn from Three Points of View.* 2d ed. Stanford: Stanford University Press.
1972 *Steps to an Ecology of Mind.* New York: Ballantine Books.
1979 *Mind and Nature: A Necessary Unity.* New York: E. P. Dutton.
Beidelman, T.
1986 *Moral Imagination in Kaguru Modes of Thought.* Bloomington: Indiana University Press.
Beltza
1976 *El nacionalismo vasco 1876–1936.* San Sebastián: Txertoa.
Benjamin, W.
1955 *Illuminations.* New York: Harcourt, Brace and World.
Bidart, P.
1977 *Le pouvoir politique à Baigorri.* Bayonne: Ipar.
Black, M.
1962 *Models and Metaphors: Studies in Language and Philosophy.* Ithaca: Cornell University Press.
Burke, K.
1945 *A Grammar of Motives.* New York: Prentice-Hall.
1966 *Language as Symbolic Action.* Berkeley: University of California Press.
Campbell, A., and B. Foster
1974 *The Mondragon Movement: Worker Ownership in Modern Industry.* Nottingham: Industrial Common Ownership Movement.
Campbell, J. K.
1964 *Honour, Family, and Patronage.* Oxford: Oxford University Press.
Camus, A.
1954 *The Rebel.* New York: Alfred A. Knopf.
Caro Baroja, J.
1943 *Los Pueblos del Norte de la Península Ibérica.* Madrid: Museo Etnológico.

1945 *Materiales para una historia de la lengua vasca en su relación con la latina*. Salamanca: Universidad de Salamanca.

1957 *Vasconiana*. Madrid: Minotauro.

1966a "Honour and Shame: A Historical Account of Several Conflicts." In *Honour and Shame*, ed. G. Peristiany. Chicago: University of Chicago Press.

1966b *Las brujas y su mundo*. Madrid: Alianza Editorial.

1971 *Los vascos*. Madrid: Istmo.

1974a *Introducción a la historia social y económica del Pueblo Vasco*. San Sebastián: Txertoa.

1974b *Ritos y mitos equívocos*. Madrid: Istmo.

1978 "Sobre los conceptos de 'casa', 'familia', y 'costumbre'." *Saioak* 2:2.

1984 *El laberinto vasco*. San Sebastián: Txertoa.

Carr, R.

1966 *Spain 1808–1939*. Oxford: Oxford University Press.

Castells Arteche, M.

1982 *Radiografía de un modelo represivo*. San Sebastián: Ediciones Vascas.

Cátedra, M.

1981 "Las vacas también son buenas para pensar." *Revista de Estudios Agro-Sociales* 116:221–54.

Christian, W. A.

1984 "Tapping and Defining New Power: The First Month of Visions at Ezkioga, July 1931." In *Cultural Dominance in the Mediterranean Area*, ed. A. Blok and H. Driessen. Nijmegen: Katholieke Universiteit.

Clark, R. P.

1984 *The Basque Insurgents: ETA, 1952–1980*. Madison: University of Wisconsin Press.

Clifford, J.

1986 "On Ethnographic Allegory." In *Writing Culture: The Poetics and Politics of Ethnography*, ed. J. Clifford and G. E. Marcus. Berkeley: University of California Press.

Comisión de Urbanismo

1978 *Deba: nora goaz?* Zarautz: Itxaropena.

Corcuera Atienza, J.

1979 *Orígenes, ideología y organización del nacionalismo vasco (1876–1904)*. Madrid: Siglo XXI.

Costa, J.

1902 *Derecho consuetudinario y economía popular de España*. 2 vols. Barcelona: Manuel Soler.

Crane, H.
1966 *The Complete Poems and Selected Letters and Prose of Hart Crane*. Edited with an introduction and notes by B. Weber. New York: Anchor Books.

Crawford Bamber, C. J.
1982 "La madre vasca y su contexto psicológico: Un estudio de la personalidad en la cultura." Ph.D. dissertation, Universidad de Barcelona.

De Quincey, T.
1890 "On Murder Considered as One of the Fine Arts." *Collected Writings*. Vol. 13. Edinburgh: Adam and Charles Black.

Dorronsoro, J.
1981 *Bertsotan: 1789–1936*. Bilbao: Ediciones Elexpuru.

Dougherty, J. W. D., and J. W. Fernandez
1982 "Afterword." *American Ethnologist* 9 (4).

Douglas, M.
1966 *Purity and Danger*. London: Routledge and Kegan Paul.

Douglass, W. A.
1969 *Death in Murelaga*. Seattle: University of Washington Press.
1971 "Rural Exodus in Two Spanish Basque Villages: A Cultural Explanation." *American Anthropologist* 73 (5):1100–1114.
1975 *Echalar and Murelaga: Opportunity and Rural Exodus in Two Spanish Basque Villages*. London: C. Hurst and Co.
1981 "The Stem Family Household of Northern Iberia." Manuscript.

Douglass, W. A., and J. Bilbao
1975 *Amerikanuak: Basques in the New World*. Reno: University of Nevada Press.

Douglass, W. A., and M. da Silva
1971 "Basque Nationalism." In *The Limits of Integration: Ethnicity and Nation in Modern Europe*, ed. O. Pi-Sunyer. Research Reports, no. 9, Department of Anthropology, University of Massachusetts, Amherst, October.

Drummond, L.
1981 "The Serpent's Children: Semiotics of Cultural Genesis in Arawak and Trobriand Myth." *American Ethnologist* 8 (3).

Durkheim, E.
1951 *Suicide: A Study in Sociology*. New York: Free Press.
1964 *The Division of Labor in Society*. New York: Free Press.

Duvert, M.
1976 "Contribution à l'étude de la stèle discoïdale basque." *Bulletin de Musée Basque* 71, 72 (3e. période nos. 49, 50).

Echegaray, B. de
1933 *La vecindad: Relaciones que engendra en el País Vasco.* San Sebastián: Eusko-Ikaskuntza.
Echeverria, J.
1980 *Sobre el juego.* Madrid: Taurus.
Egin
1982 *Euskadi 1977–1982.* San Sebastián: Orain.
Elorza, A.
1978 *Ideologías del nacionalismo vasco.* San Sebastián: L. Haranburu.
Erikson, E. H.
1958 *Young Man Luther.* New York: W. W. Norton and Co.
1966 "Ontogeny of Ritualization in Man." In *A Discussion of Ritualization of Behavior in Animals and Man,* ed. J. S. Huxley, series B, vol. 251. London: Royal Society.
Esnaola, J. de
1927 *Santa María de Itziar.* Vergara, Spain: El Santísimo Rosario.
Etxezarreta, M.
1977 *El caserío vasco.* Bilbao: Iker.
Euskaltzaindia
1978 *Euskararen liburu zuria.* Bilbao: Euskaltzaindia.
Evans-Pritchard, E. E.
1956 *Nuer Religion.* Oxford: Oxford University Press.
1961 *Anthropology and History.* Manchester: Manchester University Press.
1963 "The Divine Kingship of the Shilluk of the Nilotic Sudan." *Essays in Social Anthropology.* New York: Free Press of Glencoe.
Fanon, F.
1963 *The Wretched of the Earth.* New York: Grove Press.
Fernandez, J. W.
1965 "Symbolic Consensus in a Fang Reformative Cult." *American Anthropologist* 67:902–29.
1972 "Persuasions and Performances: Of the Beast in Every Body . . . and the Metaphors in Everyman." *Daedalus* 101 (1):39–60.
1974 "The Mission of Metaphor in Expressive Culture." *Current Anthropology* 15 (2):119–42.
1982 *Bwiti: An Ethnography of the Religious Imagination in Africa.* Princeton: Princeton University Press.
Fernández de Pinedo, E.
1974 *Crecimiento económico y transformaciones sociales del País Vasco, 1100–1850.* Madrid: Siglo XXI.

Filmore, C. J.
1975 *Santa Cruz Lectures on Deixis*. Bloomington: Indiana University Linguistics Club.
Fisher, R., and W. Ury
1981 *Getting to Yes: Negotiating Agreement without Giving In*. Boston: Houghton Mifflin.
Foucalt, M.
1977 *Discipline and Punish*. New York: Pantheon Books.
Frazer, J. G.
1963 *The Golden Bough: A Study in Magic and Religion*. New York: Macmillan.
Freeman, L. G., and J. González Echegaray
1981 "El Juyo: A 14,000-Year-Old Sanctuary from Northern Spain." *History of Religion* 21 (1):1–19.
Frege, G.
1948 "Sense and Reference." *The Philosophical Review* 62 (3): 209–30.
1977 *Logical Investigations*. New Haven: Yale University Press.
Freud, S.
1925 "Negation." *International Journal of Psycho-Analysis* 6:367.
Gale, R. M.
1967 "Indexical Signs, Egocentric Particulars, and Token-Reflexive Words." In *The Encyclopedia of Philosophy*, ed. P. Eluards, vol. 4, pp. 151–55. New York: Macmillan and Free Press.
García, Q.
1970 *Les coopératives industrielles de Mondragon*. Paris: Editions Ouvrières.
García de Cortázar, J. A.
1973 *La época medieval: Historia de España Alfaguara*. Madrid: Alianza Editorial.
García Fernández, J.
1974 *Organización del espacio y economía rural de la España Atlántica*. Madrid: Siglo XXI.
García Venero, M.
1945 *Historia del Nacionalismo Vasco 1793–1936*. Madrid: Editorial Nacional.
Garmendia, J. M.
1979 *Historia de ETA*. Zarautz: Itxaropena.
Garmendia, V.
1976 *La segunda guerra carlista*. Madrid: Siglo XXI.
1984 *La ideología carlista (1868–1876)*. Zarautz: Itxaropena.

Geach, P. T.
1965 "Assertion." *Philosophical Review* 74 (4):449–65.

Geertz, C.
1973 *The Interpretation of Cultures*. New York: Basic Books.
1976 "From the Native's Point of View." In *Meaning in Anthropology,* ed. K. H. Basso and H. A. Selby. Albuquerque: University of New Mexico Press.

Gennep, A. L. van
1960 *The Rites of Passage*. London: Routledge and Kegan Paul.

Genovés, S.
1986 *La violencia en el País Vasco y en sus relaciones con España*. Barcelona: Fontanella.

Giddens, A.
1971 *Capitalism and Modern Social Theory: An Analysis of the Writings of Marx, Durkheim and Max Weber.* Cambridge: Cambridge University Press.

Girard, R.
1977 *Violence and the Sacred*. Baltimore: Johns Hopkins University Press.

Goenaga, A.
1975 *Uts: La negatividad vasca*. Durango: Leopoldo Zugaza.

Goffman, E.
1961 *Asylums: Essays on the Social Situation of Mental Patients and Other Inmates*. New York: Anchor Books.

Goñi, J., and J. M. Rodríguez
1979 *Euskadi: La paz es posible*. Bilbao: Desclée de Brouwer.

Goodman, N.
1951 *The Structure of Appearance*. Cambridge: Harvard University Press.

Gorosabel, P. de
1971 *Diccionario histórico-geográfico descriptivo de los pueblos, valles, partidos, alcaldías y uniones de Guipúzcoa*. Bilbao: La Gran Enciclopedia Vasca.
1972 *Noticia de las cosas de Guipúzcoa*. 3d ed. Bilbao: La Gran Enciclopedia Vasca.

Gorroño, I.
1975 *Experiencia cooperativa en el País Vasco*. Durango: Leopoldo Zugaza.

Granja, J. L.
1985 "The Basque Nationalist Community during the Second Spanish Republic." In *Basque Politics: A Case Study in Ethnic Nationalism,* ed. W. A. Douglass. New York: Associated Faculty Press.

Greenwood, D.

1976a *Unrewarding Wealth: The Commercialization and Collapse of Agriculture in a Spanish Basque Town*. Cambridge: Cambridge University Press.

1976b "The Demise of Agriculture in Fuenterrabía." In *The Changing Faces of Spain*, ed. J. B. Aceves and W. A. Douglass. Cambridge: Schenkman.

Griaule, M.

1965 *Conversations with Ogotemmêli: An Introduction to Dogon Religious Ideas*. London: Oxford University Press.

Gurr, T. R.

1970 *Why Men Rebel*. Princeton: Princeton University Press.

Heiberg, M.

1981 "Basque Nationalism: Its Economic, Political and Cultural Determinants and Effects (with special reference to the village of Elgueta, Guipúzcoa)." Ph.D. diss., London School of Economics and Political Science, University of London.

1982 "Urban Politics and Rural Culture: Basque Nationalism." In *The Politics of Territorial Identity*, ed. S. Rokkan and Urbin. New York: Sage Publications.

Hill, C. A.

n.d. "Spatial Orientation: Cognition, Language, and Myth in Hausa Culture."

Hobsbawm, E. J.

1959 *Primitive Rebels*. New York: W. W. Norton and Co.

Hordago

1979 *Documentos*. 18 vols. San Sebastián: Lur.

Hornilla, T.

1981 *La ginecocracia vasca: Contribución a los estudios sobre el eusko-matriarcado*. Bilbao: Geu.

Huxley, J. S.

1966 *A Discussion of Ritualization of Behaviour in Animals and Man*. Organized by Sir Julian Huxley. Series B, vol. 251. London: Royal Society.

Iturriza y Zabala, J. R. de

1967 *Historia general de Vizcaya, y epítome de las encartaciones*. ed. Angel Rodríguez. Vol. 1. Bilbao: Fuentes para la Historia de Vizcaya.

Jackobs, S.

1979 "Community, Industrial Democracy, and the Cooperatives of Mondragon." B.A. thesis, Harvard University.

Jakin
1973 *Kooperatibak*. Arantzazu.
Jauregui, G.
1981 *Ideología y estrategia política de ETA*. Madrid: Siglo XXI.
Jenkins, B. M.
1975 *International Terrorism: A New Mode of Conflict*. Los Angeles: Crescent Publications.
Jones, E.
1967 *Papers on Psycho-Analysis*. Boston: Beacon Press.
Koiré, A.
1957 *From the Closed World to the Infinite Universe*. Baltimore: Johns Hopkins University Press.
Ladner, G. B.
1979 "Medieval and Modern Understandings of Symbolism—A Comparison." *Speculum* 54 (2).
Lafon, R.
1952 *Etudes Basques et Caucasiques*. Salamanca: Universidad de Salamanca.
1966 "La Particle *bait* en Basque: Ses emplois morphologiques et syntaxiques." *Bulletin de la Société de Linguistique de Paris* 61:217–48.
1972 "Basque." In *Current Trends in Linguistics*, ed. A. Sebeok. Vol. 9 of *Linguistics in Western Europe*. The Hague and Paris: Mouton.
Laing, R. D.
1966 "Ritualization and Abnormal Behaviour." In *A Discussion of Ritualization of Behaviour in Animals and Man*, ed. J. S. Huxley, series B, vol. 251. London: Royal Society.
Larramendi, M. de
1969 *Obras del padre Manuel de Larramendi*. Ed. J. I. Tellechea. San Sebastián: Sociedad Guipuzcoana de Ediciones y Publicaciones.
Larronde, C.
1972 *El nacionalismo vasco. Su origen y su ideología en la obra de Sabino Arana-Goiri*. San Sebastián: Txertoa.
Leach, E.
1966 "Ritualization in Man in Relation to Conceptual and Social Development." In *A Discussion of Ritualization of Behavior in Animals and Man*, ed. J. S. Huxley, series B, vol. 251. London: Royal Society.
1976 *Culture and Communication*. Cambridge: Cambridge University Press.

1977 *Custom, Law, and Terrorist Violence*. Edinburgh: Edinburgh University Press.

Lekuona, M. de

1923 "Creencias y ritos funerarios en Oyartzun." *Anuario de Eusko-Folklore* 3:76–87.

1935 *Literatura oral vasca*. San Sebastián: Colección Kardaberaz.

Letamendia, F. "Ortzi"

1979 *El no vasco a la reforma*. 2 vols. San Sebastián: Txertoa.

Lévi-Strauss, C.

1950 "Introduction a l'oeuvre de Marcel Mauss." In *Sociologie et antropologie*, by M. Mauss. Paris: PUF.

1963 *Structural Anthropology*. New York: Basic Books.

1966 *The Savage Mind*. Chicago: University of Chicago Press.

1975 *Tristes tropiques*. New York: Atheneum.

Lhande, P.

1926 *Dictionnaire Basque-Français et Français-Basque*. Paris: Gabriel Beauchesne.

Linz, J. J.

1966 "Within-Nation Differences and Comparisons: The Eight Spains." In *Comparing Nations: The Use of Quantitative Data in Cross-National Research*, ed. R. L. Merritt and S. Rokkan. New Haven: Yale University Press.

1986 *Conflicto en Euskadi*. Madrid: Espasa Calpe.

Lizardi, X.

1970 *Biotz-begietan*. 3d ed. Zarautz: Itxaropena.

Lizarralde, J. A. de

1926 *Semblanza religiosa de la provincia de Guipúzcoa—Ensayo iconográfico, legendario e histórico*. Vol. 1, *Andra Mari*. Bilbao: Imprenta C. Dochao de Uriguen.

Loizos, P.

1981 *The Heart Grown Bitter*. Cambridge: Cambridge University Press.

Lord, A. B.

1960 *The Singer of Tales*. Cambridge: Harvard University Press.

Loyola, I. de

1947 *Obras completas*. Vol. 1, *Autobiografía-diario espiritual*. Madrid: Biblioteca de Autores Cristianos.

Machiavelli, N.

1952 *The Prince*. New York: New American Library.

Mann, T.

1945 "Dostoevsky—in Moderation." Preface to *The Short Novels of Dostoevsky*. New York: Dial Press.

Marcuse, H.
1955 *Eros and Civilization*. Boston: Beacon Press.
Marx, K., and F. Engels
1955 *The Marx-Engels Reader*. Ed. R. C. Tucker. New York: W. W. Norton and Co.
Michelena. L.
1960 *Historia de la literatura vasca*. Madrid: Minotauro.
1973 *Apellidos vascos*. 3d ed. San Sebastián: Txertoa.
1976 *Fonética histórica vasca*. 2d ed. San Sebastián: Seminario Julio de Urquijo.
Mitxelena, S.
1949 *Arantzazu: Euskal-Sinismenaren Poema*. Aranzazu: Editorial Franciscana.
Montagu, A.
1976 *The Nature of Human Aggression*. Oxford: Oxford University Press.
Morán, G.
1982 *Los españoles que dejaron de serlo*. Barcelona: Planeta.
Morris, D.
1966 "The Rigidification of Behaviour." In *A Discussion of Ritualization of Behaviour in Animals and Man*, ed. J. S. Huxley, series B, vol. 251. London: Royal Society.
Múgica Berrondo, P.
1965 *Diccionario Castellano-Vasco*. Bilbao: El Mensajero del Corazón de Jesús.
Munn, N. D.
1971 "Visual Categories: An Approach to the Study of Representational Systems." In *Art and Aesthetics in Primitive Societies*, ed. C. F. Joplin. New York: E. P. Dutton and Co.
Needham, R.
1978 *Primordial Characters*. Charlottesville: University Press of Virginia.
Olaizola, M. "Uztapide"
1975 *Lengo egunak gogoan*. Tolosa: Auspoa.
1976 *Sasoia joan da gero*. Tolosa: Auspoa.
Ollman, B.
1971 *Alienation: Marx's Conception of Man in Capitalist Society*. Cambridge: Cambridge University Press.
Onaindia, A.
1964 *Gure bertsolariak*. Bilbao: Gráficas Bilbao.
Ong, W. J.
1962 *The Barbarian Within*. New York: Macmillan.

Ortega y Gasset, J.
1961 "The Pride of the Basques." *Atlantic Monthly* 207:113–16.
1972 *Meditations on Hunting*. New York: Charles Scribner's Sons.
Ortiz-Osés, A., and F. K. Mayr
1980 *El matriarcalismo vasco*. Bilbao: Publicationes de la Universidad de Deusto.
Osa, E.
1972 *Pedogogia eta Gizartea*. Donostia: Lur.
Otazu y Llana, A. de
1973 *El "igualitarismo" vasco: mito y realidad*. San Sebastián: Txertoa.
Oteiza, J.
1963 *Quousque tandem . . . ! Ensayo de interpretación estética del alma vasca*. Zarautz: Auñamendi.
1983 *Ejercicios espirituales en un túnel*. Donostia: Hordago.
Ott, S.
1981 *The Circle of Mountains: A Basque Sheepherding Community*. Oxford: Oxford University Press.
n.d. "*Indarra:* Some Reflections on a Basque Concept."
Paine, R.
1981 "When Saying Is Doing." In *Politically Speaking*, ed. R. Paine. Philadelphia: ISHI.
Peacock, J.
1975 *Consciousness and Change*. New York: John Wiley and Sons.
Peirce, C.
1885 "On the Algebra of Logic: A Contribution to the Philosophy of Notation." *American Journal of Mathematics* 8:181.
1955 *Philosophical Writings of Peirce*. Ed. J. Buchler. New York: Dover Publications.
Peristiany, J. G., ed.
1966 *Honour and Shame: The Values of Mediterranean Society*. Chicago: University of Chicago Press.
Rappaport, R. A.
1968 *Pigs for the Ancestors*. New Haven: Yale University Press.
1979 *Ecology, Meaning, and Religion*. Richmond: North Atlantic Books.
Redfield, J. M.
1975 *Nature and Culture in the Iliad: The Tragedy of Hector*. Chicago: University of Chicago Press.
Redfield, R.
1971 "Art and Icon." In *Anthropology and Art: Readings in Cross-*

Cultural Aesthetics, ed. C. M. Otten. New York: Natural History Press.

Redondo Barra, R.
1983 *Los vascos y el Rorschach*. Bilbao: Universidad del País Vasco.

Ricoeur, P.
1970 *Freud and Philosophy: An Essay on Interpretation*. New Haven: Yale University Press.
1971 "The Model of the Text: Meaningful Action Considered as a Text." *Social Research* 38:529–62.

Robertson Smith, W.
1901 *Lectures on the Religion of the Semites*. London: Adam and Charles Black.

Rosaldo, M. Z.
1980 *Knowledge and Passion: Ilongot Notions of Self and Social Life*. Cambridge: Cambridge University Press.

Rosaldo, R.
1986 "From the Door of His Tent: The Fieldworker and the Inquisitor." In *Writing Culture: The Poetics and Politics of Ethnography*, ed. J. Clifford and G. E. Marcus. Berkeley: University of California Press.

Russell, B.
1908 "Mathematical Logic as Based on the Theory of Types." *American Journal of Mathematics* 30:222–62.

Ryle, G.
1971 *Collected Papers*. Vol. 2. New York: Barnes and Noble.

Sands Redlick, A.
1979 "The Transnational Flow of Information as a Cause of Terrorism." In *Terrorism: Theory and Practice*, ed. Y. Alexander, D. Carlton, and P. Wilkinson. Boulder: Westview Press.

Sarasola, I.
1971 *Euskal literaturaren historia*. San Sebastián: Lur.

Sartre, J. P.
1971 Preface to *Le Procès de Burgos*, by Gisèle Halimi: Paris: Gallimard.

Savater, F.
1981 *La tarea del héroe (elementos para una ética trágica)*. Madrid: Taurus.

Scarry, E.
1985 *The Body in Pain*. New York: Oxford University Press.

Schuchardt, H.
1947 *Primitiae Linguae Vasconum*. Ed. A. Yrigaray. Salamanca: Colegio de la Universidad.

Servy, P.
1981 *Les coopératives de Mondragon*. Bayonne: Société Inter-Professions Service.
Silverstein, M.
1976 "Shifters, Linguistic Categories, and Cultural Description." In *Meaning in Anthropology*, ed. K. H. Basso and H. A. Selby. Albuquerque: University of New Mexico Press.
Solozábal, J. J.
1975 *El primer nacionalismo vasco*. Madrid: Túcar Ediciones.
Sperber, D.
1975 *Rethinking Symbolism*. Cambridge: Cambridge University Press.
Steiner, F.
1967 *Taboo*. Harmondsworth: Penguin Books.
Talde
1978 *Estudio socio-económico de Deba*. Mimeo.
Tambiah, S. J.
1968 "The Magical Power of Words." *Man* n.s. 3 (2):175–208.
Taylor, C.
1971 "Interpretation and the Sciences of Man." *Review of Metaphysics* 25 (97):3–51.
Tovar, A.
1980 *Mitología e ideología sobre la lengua vasca*. Madrid: Alianza Editorial.
Trevanian
1979 *Shibumi*. New York: Crown Publishers.
Turner, T. S.
1977. "Transformation, Hierarchy and Transcendence: A Reformulation of Van Gennep's Model of the Structure of *Rites de Passage*." In *Secular Ritual*, ed. S. F. More and B. G. Myerhoff. Assen, Netherlands: Van Gorcum.
Turner, V.
1969 *The Ritual Process: Structure and Anti-structure*. Chicago: Aldine.
1974 *Dramas, Fields, and Metaphors: Symbolic Action in Human Society*. Ithaca: Cornell University Press.
1982 *From Ritual to Theater: The Human Seriousness of Play*. New York: PAJ Publications.
Unamuno, M. de
1902 "Vizcaya: Aprovechamientos comunes; Lorra; Seguro mutuo para el ganado, etc." In *Derecho consuetudinario y economía popular de España*, ed. J. Costa, 2 vols. Barcelona: Manuel Soler.

1931 *Del sentimiento trágico de la vida*. 4th ed. Barcelona: Renacimiento.

Urkola, M.
1968 *Sekularrak apaiztu*. Vitoria: Gráficas ESET.

Urquijo, J. de
1923 "Cosas de antaño." *RIEV* 14:350–51.

Valle, T. del, J. M. Apalategi, B. Aretxaga et al.
1985 *Mujer vasca: Imagen y realidad*. Barcelona: Anthropos.

Verene, D. P.
1981 *Vico's Science of Imagination*. Ithaca: Cornell University Press.

Veyrin, P.
1931 "La dècoration des fourneaux a charbon de bois au Pais Basque." *Anuario de Eusko-Folklore* 11:115–21.

Vico, G.
1968 *The New Science of Giambattista Vico*. Rev. trans. of the 3d ed., T. G. Bergin and M. H. Fish. Ithaca: Cornell University Press.

Villasante, A.
1976 *Sintaxis de la oración compuesta*. Aránzazu: Editorial Franciscana.

Weber, M.
1949 *The Methodology of Social Sciences*. New York: Glencoe.
1968 *Economy and Society*. New York: Bedminster Press.

Wilkinson, P.
1979 "Social Scientific Theory and Civil Violence." In *Terrorism: Theory and Practice*, ed. Y. Alexander, D. Carlton, and P. Wilkinson. Boulder: Westview Press.

Winch, P.
1977 "Understanding a Primitive Society." In *Rationality*, ed. B. R. Wilson. Oxford: Basil Blackwell.

Wittgenstein, L.
1968 *Philosophical Investigations*. New York: Macmillan.
1971 "Remarks on Frazer's 'Golden Bough.'" *The Human World* 3:18–41.
1980 *Culture and Value*. Oxford: Basil Blackwell.
1983 *Lectures and Conversations on Aesthetics, Psychology and Religious Belief*. Berkeley: University of California Press.

Zabala, A.
1970 *Zubeltzu ta Sakiola bertsolariak*. Tolosa: Auspoa.

Zulaika. J.
1981 *Terranova: The Ethos and Luck of Deep-Sea Fishermen*. Philadelphia: ISHI.

1982 *Itziar: The Cultural Context of Basque Political Violence*. Ph.D. diss., Princeton University.

1984 "Iconic Imagery and Sacramental Symbolism in Basque Political Violence." In *Cultural Dominance in the Mediterranean Area*, ed. A. Blok and H. Driessen. Nijmegen: Katholieke Universiteit.

1985 *Bertsolariaren Jokoa eta Jolasa*. San Sebastián: Baroja.

1987a *Tratado Estético-Ritual Vasco*. San Sebastián: Baroja.

1987b "Terror, Totem, and Taboo: Reporting on a Report." Paper presented at a conference sponsored by the H. F. Guggenheim Foundation and the School of American Research, Santa Fe, New Mexico, October 10–16.

Index

The people of Itziar are called by their personal names in the community and in this book; hence they are indexed here by those names rather than by their surnames.